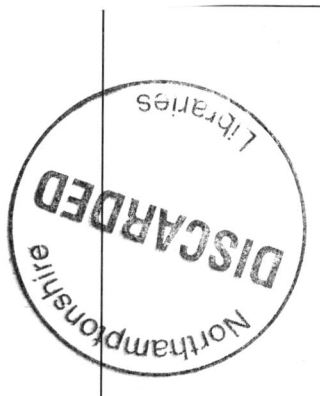

HEAD-DRESS BADGES
OF THE
BRITISH ARMY

HEAD-DRESS BADGES
OF THE
BRITISH ARMY

VOLUME ONE

UP TO THE END OF THE GREAT WAR

ARTHUR L. KIPLING

and

HUGH L. KING

FREDERICK MULLER LIMITED
LONDON

First published in Great Britain in 1973 by
Frederick Muller Ltd., 110 Fleet Street, London, EC4A 2AP
Second Revised Edition 1978

British Library Cataloguing in Publication Data

Kipling, Arthur Lawrence
  Head-dress badges of the British army.
  Vol. 1: Up to the end of the Great War—2nd
  revised ed.
  1. Great Britain.   Army—Medals, badges,
  decorations, etc
  2. Badges
  I. Title   II. King, Hugh Lionel
  355.1'4   UC535.67

  ISBN 0–584–10947–4

Book design by Laurence V. Archer

Printed by Clarke, Doble & Brendon Ltd., Plymouth and London
and bound by Webb, Son & Co Ltd, Ferndale, Glamorgan

ISBN 0 584 10947 4

TO
VIOLET AND PAMELA
FOR
THEIR PATIENCE AND UNDERSTANDING

Contents

Introduction

In the preparation of this work our object has been to describe and, where possible, illustrate the large variety of head-dress badges worn by the British Army from the period when they were taken first into use until just after the end of the Great War at which time many changes were made in the composition of the Armed Forces, particularly in the reduction of the number of Cavalry Regiments and the change in *rôle* of most of the Yeomanry.

Only head-dress badges are dealt with and no reference is made to other items of clothing or equipment on which regimental insignia is worn such as collars, waist-belts, band-pouches, shoulder-belts, sporrans, etc.

In covering such a long period it is inevitable that some errors will have occurred and the authors express their apologies for any that the reader may discover. This may be particularly the case with the earliest period where actual badges are not available and reliance has to be placed perforce in recorded details.

The first Dress Regulations were published in 1822 and others followed at irregular intervals. In these, certain regiments are cited as being authorised to wear special devices; all others to bear only the precedence number of the regiment. We have found, however, several examples of regiments wearing a badge of special design although not included in the published lists.

In the case of early badges, there is the additional possibility that an officer had one struck to his own design and actually wore it. A case in point is that of the 54th Foot and an example worn on the 'Waterloo' shako is illustrated. No similar badge has been discovered but there is no doubt that it is genuine as it was found on the field of Waterloo and now resides in the Dorset Regiment's museum.

On the other hand, the first helmet-plate of the 29th Foot – although authorised – was never worn due to the impending departure of the Regiment for India.

The dating of the period during which a badge was worn presents some difficulty for, although the official date of introduction of a new pattern head-dress is known, it does not follow that all regiments adopted it immediately or that all battalions of any one regiment adopted it at the same time. Those on service overseas probably would not take it into use until their return to the United Kingdom and, consequently, when regimental histories do record changes in dress, the date given often differs from the official one.

It is assumed generally that the cloth-helmet was worn from 1878. In fact, it was worn experimentally by some regiments in 1877 and, although universally adopted in 1878, it would appear that the new-pattern plate was worn mostly by officers: the rank-and-file in many instances merely transferred the badge worn on the last shako to the new helmet. An examination of photographs – some taken as late as 1881, which is three years after official adoption – show Colour parties in which the officers are wearing the helmet-plate but members of the escort have the old shako-plate on their helmets.

Dating the badges of Militia, Yeomanry and Volunteers presents many problems. Frequently head-dresses were worn of a pattern that had become obsolete in the Regular forces and, even when the head-dress was changed, the badge was transferred simply to the new pattern. Also, some continued to employ the Victorian crown long after the majority had adopted the Imperial crown. Dates given, therefore, must be regarded to a certain extent as approximate.

Where possible, the metals used in manufacture are specified but this cannot exclude the fact that specimens may be found in other metals or combinations thereof. These could be genuine badges worn by the regiment concerned but such specimens have not been seen by us.

A further complication arises in that some badges, especially those of the Arms and Services, have been struck by many different manufacturers with resultant variations in size, the length of scrolls, the style of lettering, etc. It is not possible to mention all of these in this work although, in those instances where the difference is considerable, more than one pattern is shown.

In describing the badge worn on the undress-cap we have referred normally to that head-dress as the forage-cap. This description is intended to cover other patterns such as the 'Brodrick', the field-service cap, and those described in Dress Regulations for wear on active-service and manœuvres.

Our gratitude and thanks are due to the many people who have helped in making this work possible and particularly to The Society for Army Historical Research and The Military Historical Society who kindly granted permission to consult the many articles on badges and head-dresses which have appeared in their journals, to the Controller of Her Majesty's Stationery Office for allowing us to quote from the Dress Regulations for the Army, and to the Chief Librarian of The Ministry of Defence Library (Central and Army) through whose kind offices we were able to study official lists and documents containing information not available elsewhere.

As we anticipated a number of errors occurred in the first printing of this work and we are most grateful to all those correspondents who took the trouble to write to us and give us the benefit of their knowledge.

We are grateful too to those who supplied additional information and photographs and we trust that this present edition will give a more accurate account of the badges worn on the head-dress up to the end of the Great War.

Acknowledgements

We are very grateful for the help and assistance given to us by the loan of badges, photographs, rubbings and sketches, descriptions of badges where a specimen was not available and much useful information as to the dates badges were taken into use.

In particular we must thank the following:

Army Museums Ogilby Trust
The Controller, Her Majesty's Stationery Office
The Military Historical Society
The National Army Museum
The Society for Army Historical Research
The Victoria and Albert Museum
Messrs. Wallis and Wallis of Lewes

———

Major P. E. Abbott R.A. (ret.)
Major J. F. Ainsworth, Regimental Headquarters, The Queen's Regiment (Royal Sussex Office)
C. G. Andrews Esq.
L. V. Archer Esq., F.C.C.A.
Major H. Barker M.B.E., Curator of Regimental Museum of Seaforth Highlanders, The Queen's Own Cameron Highlanders and Queen's Own Highlanders (Seaforth and Camerons)
R. H. Blethyn Esq.
Major G. A. N. Boyne J.P., Regimental Office, The Royal Irish Rangers (Armagh)
Major-General W. T. Campbell C.B.E., Colonel, The Royal Scots (The Royal Regiment)
W. Y. Carman Esq., F.S.A., F.R.HIST.S.
Major K. D. Clarke
Brigadier T. F. J. Collins C.B.E., D.L.
Colonel H. C. B. Cook O.B.E., Regimental Headquarters, The Staffordshire Regiment
Major-General F. W. J. Cowtan O.B.E., M.C.
F. W. Cranston Esq.
Lieutenant-Colonel D. C. E. Crew, Secretary, Royal Army Chaplains Department Association
Major W. G. Cripps, Regimental Secretary, The Royal Norfolk Regiment Association
Major N. P. Dawnay M.A.
The late W. J. Dear
Major A. J. Donald, Royal Marines
Major G. J. B. Egerton D.L., Regimental Headquarters, (Brecon Office) The Royal Regiment of Wales
Lieutenant-Colonel D. A. D. Eykyn D.S.O., D.L. Regimental Headquarters, The Royal Scots (The Royal Regiment)
Colonel J. M. Forbes J.P., D.L., Regimental Headquarters, The Green Howards
Lieutenant-Colonel J. E. E. Fry M.C., Regimental Secretary, Light Infantry Office (Cornwall)
Lieutenant-Colonel G. P. Gofton-Salmond O.B.E., Secretary, Sherwood Foresters Office, Worcestershire and Sherwood Foresters Regiment
K. W. S. Goodson Esq.

The late Major F. G. Harden

Colonel E. D. Harding D.S.O., Regimental Headquarters, The Gloucestershire Regiment

Lieutenant-Colonel P. St. C. Harrison D.S.O., O.B.E., Regimental Secretary, Regimental Headquarters, The King's Own Scottish Borderers

J. B. Hayward Esq.

The late Lieutenant-Colonel R. J. T. Hills

Lieutenant-Commander K. B. Hook R.N. (*ret.*)

D. Ivall Esq.

D. W. King Esq., O.B.E., F.L.A., Chief Librarian, Ministry of Defence (Central and Army)

Ernest J. Martin Esq.

Major J. G. Milligan, The Duke of Wellington's Regiment

Major J. H. Mott O.B.E., Regimental Headquarters, The York and Lancaster Regiment

Lieutenant-Colonel W. B. R. Neave-Hill, Historical Section, Ministry of Defence Library (Central and Army)

Bryn Owen Esq.

G. Archer Parfitt Esq.

J. B. Peters Esq.

K. D. Pickup Esq.

Lieutenant-Colonel R. M. Pratt, The Royal Northumberland Fusiliers

E. J. Priestley Esq., Assistant Keeper, (Military History) City of Liverpool Museums

Major F. J. Reed, Regimental Headquarters, The Queen's Regiment (Queen's Surrey Office)

Mrs. Douglas Ryan

Major T. P. Shaw M.B.E., The Lancashire Headquarters, The Royal Regiment of Fusiliers

Lieutenant-Colonel C. L. Speers, Regimental Headquarters, The Duke of Edinburgh's Royal Regiment (Berkshire and Wiltshire)

Major T. R. Stead, D.L., Regimental Secretary, Headquarters, The Royal Anglian Regiment (Essex)

Major J. M. A. Tamplin T.D.

Captain M. E. Taylor K.ST.J., F.S.A.SCOT.

Professor Charles Thomas M.A., F.S.A., HON.M.R.I.A.

Brigadier R. G. Thurburn C.B., C.B.E.

W. Turner Esq.

Lieutenant-Colonel A. C. M. Urwick, Regimental Secretary, Light Infantry Office, Taunton

H. Y. Usher Esq.

Lieutenant-Colonel D. V. W. Wakely M.C., Curator, Dorset Military Museum

Captain A. J. Wilson, Regimental Headquarters, The Royal Highland Fusiliers

A. E. Wright Esq.

T. Wylie Esq.

CHAPTER 1

Early Badges

The wearing of a device on the head-dress to indicate the body to which the wearer owes allegiance is as old as history itself.

Before the adoption of national uniforms there was little to distinguish friend from foe and, to overcome this problem, it became common practice for each side to wear some distinctive emblem such as a sprig of a particular plant or a piece of paper tucked in the hat. This small distinction gave the wearer at least some protection in the heat of battle but, if lost, brought dire results.

Although a general device served to unite the whole army, something better was needed to keep together the followers of a particular leader.

With the advent of armour which completely encased the wearer, some means of identification became essential. Heraldry had grown with the development of armour and gradually became a learned science administered by Kings of Arms under the supervision of Garter King of Arms. It certainly presented a sensible means of identification on the battle-field and the heraldic devices of noblemen were borne on their shields and surcoats, the trappings of their chargers, and on banners which could be displayed at any point where their followers were assembled. The latter, in many instances, wore on their dress some kind of badge derived from the arms of their overlord.

This was really the origin of each of the units comprising an army wearing individual insignia. From it has developed the custom of regiments having a badge which is special to themselves and which has been perpetuated in the granting of devices to be emblazoned on regimental Colours and incorporated into the modern cap-badge.

When Charles II came to the throne and the British Standing Army was formed, the various regiments comprising it were very much the property of the Colonels-commanding who were personally responsible for the clothing of their regiment. Each regiment and company had its own Colour and it was not unnatural that these tended to carry the armorial bearings of the Colonel or some device connected with his family. Those regiments which had the Sovereign as their Colonel bore some of the Royal badges on their Colours; a practice which has continued to the present day in the Company badges borne in rotation on the regimental Colours of the Foot Guards.

The basic Infantry head-dress of the eighteenth century—the tricorne hat—did not carry a regimental badge, each regiment being distinguished by the colour of its facings and the pattern of its lace.

A trend towards a more individual method of identification was being developed however and, about 1767, in place of the plain pewter buttons previously worn, distinctive

regimental buttons engraved with the regiment's number in order of precedence made their appearance.

The introduction of Light Troops to certain cavalry regiments in 1756 necessitated a new head-dress for the men engaged in these duties and the first Light Dragoon helmet made its appearance. It consisted of a black leather skull with a metal crest and, in front, the Royal Cypher and crown together with the number of the regiment.

The Light Troop of the *1st (Royal) Dragoons* wore this pattern from 1756 to 1763, when it was disbanded as complete regiments of Light Dragoons had now been raised. The black skull had a white-metal crest and a front-plate of black-enamel with brass edging: on this the Royal Cypher and crown with the numeral *1* on the left of the cypher and the letter *D* on the right, all in yellow enamel (Fig. 1).

The *21st Light Dragoons* or *Royal Windsor Foresters*, raised in 1759 and disbanded in 1763, departed from the authorised pattern. They wore on the front of their helmets the Royal Cypher and crown but on the left of the cypher the letter *R* and on the right the letter *F:* below the cypher a scroll inscribed *Hic et Ubique* (Fig. 2).

Regiments of Light Dragoons were raised in 1759 and were ordered to wear the helmet: the device on this to be the crown, Royal Cypher, the number of the regiment and the letters *LD*.

During the American War of Independence, Light Troops adopted a leather cap with a fur crest and a pleated turban round the base which could be let down to protect the neck. Sometimes a plume was worn, rising from the turban on the left of the helmet, and there was generally a horizontal metal band above the peak on which the title of the regiment was inscribed. This helmet was taken into use by some Light Dragoon regiments for wear in Great Britain as early as 1780 and is often referred to as the 'Tarleton' after Sir

Banastre Tarleton who was depicted wearing such a head-dress in a portrait painted by Sir Joshua Reynolds in 1782. The badge on the side is the Royal Cypher within the Garter surmounted by a crown (Fig. 3).

It was not long before regiments began placing their own individual designs on the helmet in place of the authorised pattern—although mostly without any authority for doing so.

In the Summer 1941 issue of the Journal of the Society for Army Historical Research, the late Lionel Buckell contributed an illustrated article on these metal badges —possibly the earliest worn by a distinctive branch of the Service. The Society has kindly granted permission to reproduce the following details from it:

3

7th (Queen's Own) Light Dragoons
Within a circle surmounted by a crown a double *CR* cypher. $3\frac{3}{4}'' \times 2''$. Worn prior to 1803.

8th (King's Royal Irish) Light Dragoons
A crowned harp. Worn c. 1796.

9th Light Dragoons
A heraldic rose, thistle and shamrock surmounted by a crown and, at the base, a scroll which twines round the stalks and is inscribed with the Garter motto. Size $6'' \times 5\frac{5}{8}''$. Worn c. 1807.

10th (Prince of Wales's) Light Dragoons
Several patterns of the Prince of Wales's plumes, coronet and motto worn on both the front of the early type of helmet c. 1760 and the side of the later pattern c. 1800. The latter size $4\frac{1}{2}'' \times 4''$.

12th (or Prince of Wales's) Light Dragoons
The Prince of Wales's plumes, coronet and motto. Worn c. 1794.

13th Light Dragoons
Within a laurel wreath surmounted by a crown the Roman numerals *xiii* above the letters *LD* in script form. Below, a scroll inscribed *Viret in Aeternum*. Size $2'' \times 2\frac{1}{4}''$. Worn c. 1800.

14th (or Duchess of York's Own) Light Dragoons
(1) A strap inscribed *Duchess of York's Own* and surmounted by a crown. In the centre, the Prussian Eagle which was authorised as a special badge for the 14th Light Dragoons in 1798. Size $4\frac{3}{8}'' \times 2\frac{3}{8}''$. Worn c. 1799.
(2) On a star of eight points a strap inscribed *Duchess of York's Own*. In the centre the Prussian Eagle. Size $3\frac{7}{8}'' \times 2\frac{5}{8}''$. Worn c. 1801.

15th (or King's) Light Dragoons

The Garter proper surmounted by the Royal Crest. In the centre the Royal Cypher *GR*. A scroll extends from both sides of the base of the Garter and is inscribed *Emsdorf 16th July, 1760*. Size $4\frac{3}{4}'' \times 5''$. Worn c. 1800.

17th Light Dragoons

Crossed bones above the skull with scroll below inscribed *or Glory*. Worn from the raising of the regiment in 1759. This arrangement of the skull and bones appears to have been worn on all items of dress and equipment prior to about 1821.

18th Light Dragoons

On a star of eight points the Garter proper and within it the Royal Cypher *GR*. Size $4\frac{3}{4}'' \times 4''$. Worn c. 1804.

19th Light Dragoons

The Garter proper surmounted by a crown. Within this an Elephant superscribed *Assaye*. Size $4\frac{7}{8}'' \times 2\frac{11}{16}''$. Worn in 1807 on return to England.

20th Light Dragoons

An alligator with *XXLD* above in two lines. The trumpeters had a special plate with the device of a trumpet replacing the alligator. The farriers also had a special plate of a horseshoe within which crossed hammer and pincers with *XXLD* above in two lines. Size $4\frac{1}{2}'' \times 4\frac{7}{8}''$. Worn in Jamaica, c. 1797. On return to England, in 1802, the badge was altered to the Garter proper surmounted by the Royal Crest, within this the Royal Cypher *GR*. Size $4\frac{1}{2}'' \times 2\frac{1}{8}''$.

21st Light Dragoons

(1) An eight-pointed star; on this a strap inscribed *Dieu et mon droit* with the Royal Arms in the centre. Size $3\frac{5}{8}'' \times 3\frac{1}{4}''$. Worn c. 1799.

(2) As above but with the Garter proper and with the new Royal Arms in the centre, following the Act of Union in 1802. In silver, centre pierced on a ground of blue enamel. Size $3\frac{5}{8}'' \times 3\frac{1}{2}''$. Worn c. 1804.

25th (later 22nd) Light Dragoons

A strung bugle with, above, the title of the regiment set out in three lines as follows: *L* in the top line, *XXV* in the centre line and *D* in the bottom line. All on a triangular-shaped plate. Size $4\frac{1}{2}'' \times 5\frac{1}{4}''$. Worn c. 1800.

26th (later 23rd) Light Dragoons

The Sphinx with cuneiform characters on the plinth. Worn on the side of the leather helmet, c. 1802.

29th (later 25th) Light Dragoons

The union wreath of Roses, Thistles and Shamrocks surmounted by a crown. Below, a scroll inscribed *Leswarree*. Size $3\frac{3}{8}'' \times 3''$. Worn c. 1807.

4

As far as the Infantry of the Line is concerned we can trace the practice of wearing a distinctive head-dress badge from the Royal Warrants published on the 1st July 1751 and the 19th October 1768. Here, for the first time in official documents, was published the authorised individual distinctions which regiments could bear and at the same time it did away with the placing of private arms on Colours and appointments.

Although the infantry was destined to wear the tricorne hat for the rest of the century, the grenadier cap afforded an opportunity for displaying a distinctive badge, although only to a very few regiments. Nevertheless those without a specially authorised badge could place on their caps their regimental number.

The Warrants stated that the caps of grenadiers were to be of black bear-skin and on the front the King's crest of silver-plated metal on a black ground with the motto *Nec aspera terrent*; a grenade on the back part of the cap with the number of the regiment on it.

A similar instruction was given for drummers and fifers but, in their case, the badge was to be the King's crest of silver-plated metal on a black ground with trophies of Colours and drums; on the back part the number of the regiment and also the badge, if entitled to any, as ordered for grenadiers.

We can take this Warrant as the starting point from which individual regiments could be identified by their head-dress badge for, although wearing a device of a general pattern, it was differentiated either by the regimental number or the special authorised badge.

The actual wording of the Royal Warrant which gave authority for the wearing of special badges by certain regiments is:

First or Royal Regiment: The King's Cypher within the circle of St. Andrew and crown over it.

IId or Queen's Royal Regiment: The Queen's Cypher within the Garter and crown over it.

IIId or Buffs: The Dragon.

IVth or The King's Own Royal Regiment: The King's Cypher within the Garter and crown over it.

Vth: St. George killing the Dragon.

VIth: The Antelope.

VIIth or Royal Fuzileers: The Rose within the Garter and crown over it.

VIIIth or King's Regiment: The White Horse within the Garter and crown over it.

XVIIIth or Royal Irish: The Harp and the crown over it.

XXIst or Royal North British Fuzileers: The Thistle within the circle of St. Andrew and crown over it.

XXIIId or Royal Welch Fuzileers: The Device of the Prince of Wales, viz. Three Feathers issuing out of the Prince's Coronet.

XXVIIth or Inniskilling Regiment: A Castle with Three Turrets St. George's Colours flying, and the name *Inniskilling* over it.

XLIst or Invalids: The Rose and Thistle within the Garter and crown over it.

XLIId or Royal Highlanders: St. Andrew with the motto *Nemo me impune lacessit*.

LXth or Royal Americans: The King's Cypher within the Garter and crown over it.

Although this Warrant authorised the practice of wearing distinctive Grenadier caps, they were being worn long before this date and not only by the Regular forces.

As early as 1702, officers of the grenadier company of the *Honourable Artillery Company* wore a cap made of leather and crimson velvet embroidered with a silver portcullis and the Company's crest above (Fig. 4). On the 'little flap' was the cypher of Queen Anne; On the back of the cap, an embroidered grenade.

5

In 1714 they wore a cap of leather and tawny-red velvet which bore the full arms of the Company in stamped metal and embroidery; the earliest known example of the use of a metal badge on military uniform. On the flap is the cypher of King George I and on the turn-up at the back, an embroidered grenade.

Later patterns followed the instructions laid down in the Royal Warrants and Fig. 5 depicts an officer's grenadier cap of the 65th Foot, c. 1760.

The front is of white cloth elaborately embroidered and decorated with sequins. The central circular patch is of crimson velvet bearing *GR* in silver and encircled by a wreath of laurels with silver leaves, gold stalks and gold berries. Above, is a gold crown with a crimson velvet cap and a circlet decorated with silver pearls, three red and two green jewels. The scroll-work at the sides is all in gold.

The 'little flap' is of crimson velvet with a silver 'White Horse' galloping over a yellow ground, the top of which is edged with green. Around the top and sides of the flap is a band of silver bearing the motto *Nec aspera terrent* in black letters.

The back is of scarlet cloth with two silver cords dividing it into three vertical triangular sections each of which is ornamented with laurel sprays of silver leaves, gold stems and gold berries. The turn-up at the base is of white cloth edged at the top with silver and embroidered at the centre with a gold grenade having flames in five colours:

Gold, light-blue, silver, black, red; gold in the middle; then repeating the colours for the other side of the flame.

On the left of the grenade is the numeral *6* and on the right, the numeral *5*; laurel-leaves and swords on either side. The *6*, *5*, laurel-leaves and sword-blades are in silver; the sword-hilts, stems and berries of the laurel are in gold.

The cap is edged with silver cord and has a silver tassel at the top: its overall height without the tassel is 11 inches.

As an example of a regiment authorised to wear a special badge, the head-dress of the 3rd Foot, c. 1760, is depicted. The front bears the White Horse of Hanover surmounted by the motto *Nec aspera terrent* above which is a circlet inscribed *Veteri frondescit honore* with the Dragon in the centre and a crown above the circlet; a rose on either side (Fig. 6). In the centre of the 'little flap' at the back is the roman numeral *III* with crossed muskets and swords on either side (Fig. 7).

The later pattern of the Infantry Grenadier fur cap had a metal plate on the front consisting of the Royal Crest on an ornamental base, with the initials *G* and *R* on either side and above this a scroll inscribed *Nec aspera terrent*. The pattern worn 1770–85 is illustrated (Figs. 7A and 7B).

During the American War of Independence it was considered more convenient to wear the sword-belt over the right shoulder instead of round the waist. At first it was worn so with the original waist-belt clasp, but this was soon replaced by a specially designed plate. The shoulder-belt plates, as they came to be designated, afforded regiments the opportunity to display their special badges and battle honours as well as the regimental number.

Early plates were mostly oval in shape and the majority did not display much more than the regimental number, but later they became oblong and much more decorative. With the granting of further battle-honours, larger plates were introduced.

The shoulder-belt plate was abolished in 1855 with the exception of Scottish regiments whose officers continued to wear them on full-dress uniforms.

Having worn the tricorne hat for the whole of the eighteenth century the infantry was

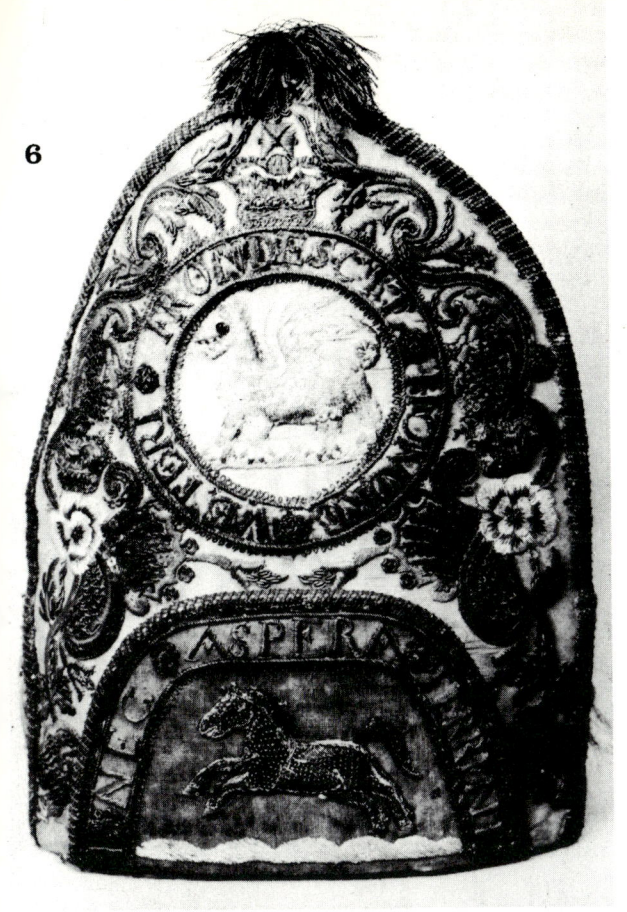

6

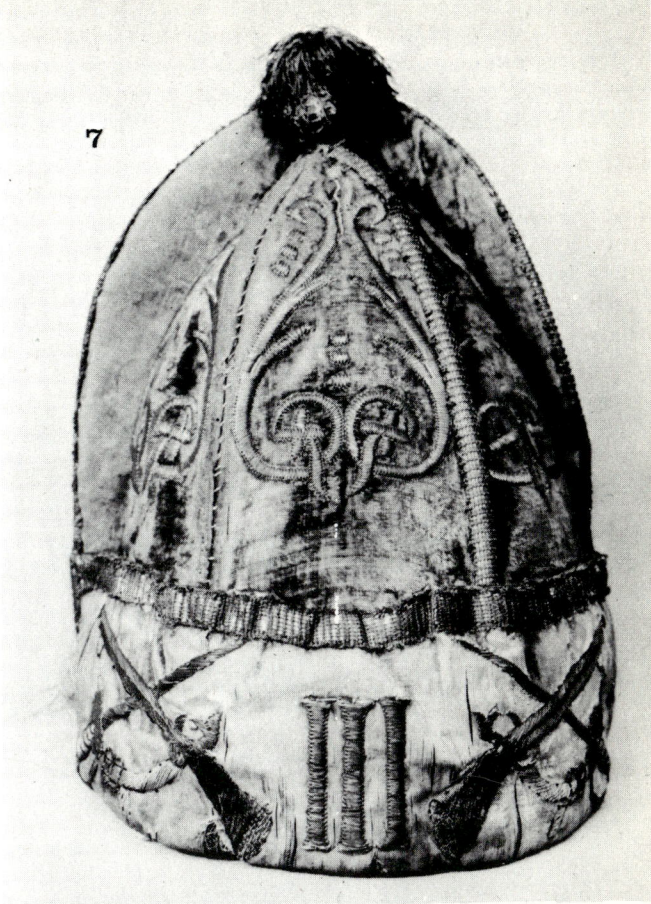

7

7A

7B

destined to wear, for the first seventy-eight years of the next, a new form of head-dress called the shako: a word of Hungarian origin which simply means a peaked hat.

It derives from the Magyar *csakós süveg* which was the tall cylindrical cap, commonly worn by the Hungarian Magyars, to which a *csak* or 'peak' had been added. In its latter form it appears to have been adopted first by the Hungarian *Grenz Infanterie* (Light troops) c. 1796, and by the Hungarian Hussar regiments shortly after. The practical advantages of this type of head-dress, which protected the eyes from the sun or bad weather, were apparent and it was adopted speedily by most European countries.

The first British shako was authorised by a General Order dated 24th February 1800 and, because of its shape, was dubbed the 'Stovepipe' shako. It was made of lacquered material with a plain leather peak and was eight inches high. At the top-front was a cockade in the centre of which was a regimental button. Behind the cockade was fitted a short straight plume which was white for grenadier companies, dark-green for light companies and white-over-red for battalion companies.

On the front was a large plate, $6\frac{1}{4}'' \times 4''$, die-struck in one piece. For officers it was in copper-gilt with shanks at the back for fastening it to the shako. For other ranks it was of brass with small holes in the corners for securing by thin brass wire.

The design of the plate consisted of the Royal Cypher *GR* surrounded by the Garter and surmounted by a crown. On either side were trophies of flags, weapons and trumpets and, below, the crowned Lion of England.

Regiments which had been awarded special badges were allowed to place these in the centre instead of the Royal Cypher and those without, to have the number of their regiment on each side of the Lion. In practice, however, some regiments placed it across the top or substituted it for the Lion, while others do not appear to have added it at all.

It must be remembered that this shako was worn not only by the Regular Army but also by the Militia, Local Militia and Volunteers as well as the *King's German Legion* and certain other Corps in British pay—so a wide variety of plates are in existence. Some examples are:

General pattern
In the centre, the Royal Cypher within the Garter; trophies of flags, arms and musical instruments either side. Above the Garter the crown and below it the Lion of England (Fig. 8).

A Grenadier Company
As the general pattern but with the crown displaced by a fused grenade (Fig. 9).

Coldstream Guards
The Garter with the Garter Star in the centre and surmounted by a crown. At either side of the Garter a pair of Colours with the fore-part of a lion below left and unicorn right. Beneath the Garter a tri-part scroll inscribed *Dieu et mon droit* and below this the Lion of England standing on a heraldic wreath.

1st Foot
In place of the Garter and Royal Cypher a strap inscribed *Nemo me impune lacessit* with a thistle with two leaves in the centre.

1st Royal Garrison Battalion
As the general pattern but with a scroll above the crown inscribed *First Royal Garrison Battalion* (Fig. 10).

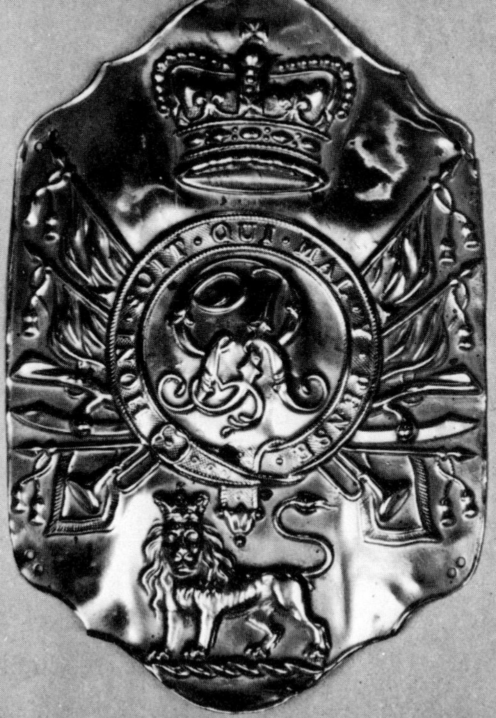
HONI·SOIT·QUI·MAL·Y·PENSE

8

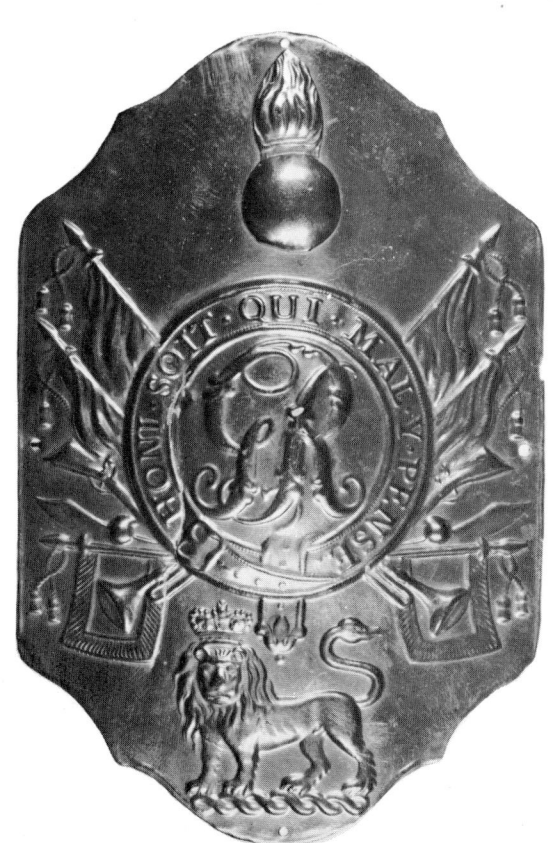

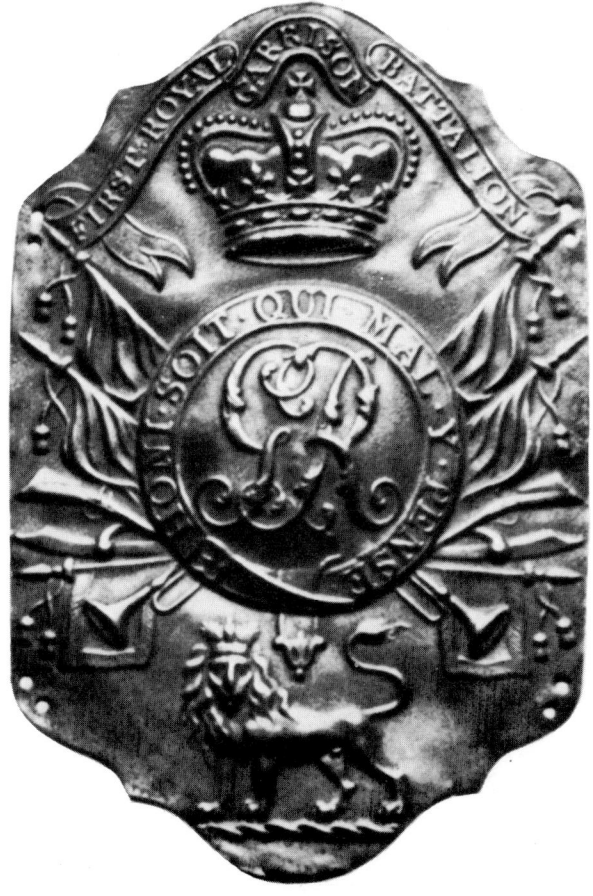

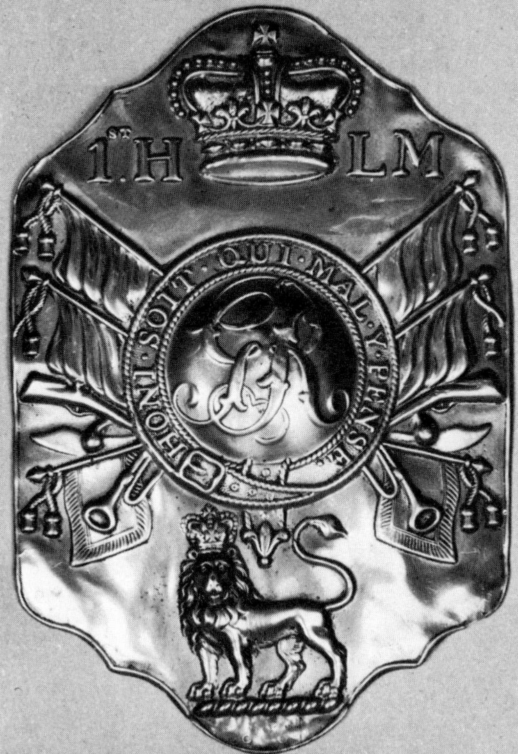
1ST H
LM
HONI·SOIT·QUI·MAL·Y·PENSE

11

HONI·SOIT·QUI·MAL·Y·PENSE

9

FIRST ROYAL GARRISON BATTALION
HONI·SOIT·QUI·MAL·Y·PENSE

10

1st Hampshire Local Militia
As the general pattern but with the addition at the top of the plate of *1st HLM* (Fig. 11).

Because lacquered material was found to be unsuitable the shako was made of felt from 1806 to 1812 when it was superseded by another form.

The new pattern, ordered by Circular Letter of the 18th March 1812, is often referred to as the 'Waterloo' shako simply because it was worn during that battle although it had already been taken into use during the concluding stages of the Peninsular War.

It, too, was made of black felt with a lacquered-peak and a false front which gave an illusion of height; the front being 8¼" high while the back was only 6¾" high. The plume and cockade were now worn on the left side; at the request, it is believed, of the Duke of Wellington so that men wearing this type of shako should not be confused with the French who wore their shako-plumes at the front. In the centre of the cockade was a regimental button except for light companies, which had a silver bugle; and grenadier companies, a gilt grenade. Across the front was a plaited cord with two tassels hanging down on the right side; all in gold and crimson for officers, white worsted for all other-ranks except those of light infantry regiments and companies who had dark-green.

For this shako an entirely different plate was devised in the shape of a shield, about 5½" deep and 3¾" wide, surmounted by a crown; the whole in gilt for officers and brass for other-ranks. On the plate was a large Royal Cypher GR, intertwined and reversed, with the regimental number below; but those regiments having special badges displayed a smaller cypher with their badge and description below.

Like the previous shako it was worn by the Militia, but the *King's German Legion* and the *Royal Regiment of Artillery* had their own plates.

The 1st, 2nd and 3rd Foot Guards had special plates and, of the Infantry of the Line, the 1st, 2nd, 3rd, 4th, 5th, 6th, 7th, 8th, 9th, 21st, 23rd, 27th, 54th, 76th, 81st, 82nd, 87th and the 94th Regiments of Foot are known to have had their own regimental plates. Some examples of this pattern are:

OFFICERS
1st Foot
The collar and badge of the Order of the Thistle with, in the centre, the Royal Cypher: a Union wreath of roses, thistles and shamrocks beneath the collar on either side of the star bearing St. Andrew and Cross. Below this, a laurel wreath enclosing the Sphinx superscribed *Egypt*. A tri-part scroll at the base inscribed *The Royal Scots* (Fig. 12).

5th Foot
Above the cypher a scroll inscribed *Quo fata vocant*. Below the cypher, St. George and the Dragon above the Roman numeral *V*.

8th Foot
Below the cypher, the White Horse of Hanover above the numeral *8*.

54th Foot
Beneath the cypher the Sphinx superscribed *Egypt*. Below this the numerals *54* (Fig. 13).

62nd Foot
Beneath the cypher the Roman numerals *LXII* (Fig. 14).

12

13

14A

14

76th Foot
Above the cypher the battle honour *Hindoostan*. Below the cypher an Elephant and beneath this the numerals *76*.

81st Foot
A gilt strap occupying the whole of the plate inscribed in silver *Maida, Corunna;* the honours being divided below the crown by a silver quatrefoil. Within the strap in gilt a small Royal Cypher above the numerals *81* (Fig. 14A).

This plate was worn by the 2nd Battalion, 81st Foot raised in October 1803 and disbanded 24th March 1816. The honour *Corunna* was not granted to the regiment as a whole until 18th July 1816, by which date the 'Waterloo' shako was obsolete.

Leeds Local Militia
Below the cypher a Rose and beneath this a scroll inscribed *Leeds Local Militia* (Fig. 15).

King's German Legion Artillery
A shield bearing the Arms of the Board of Ordnance viz. three cannon in pale surmounted by three cannon balls. This device occupies the whole of the plate.

OTHER RANKS
1st Regiment of Foot Guards
In place of the Royal Cypher, an eight-pointed star on which the Garter with, in the centre, the Royal Cypher reversed and intertwined (Fig. 16).

4th Foot
The Lion of England within the Garter. The Royal Cypher beneath, nearly surrounded by a scroll inscribed *The King's Own Infantry*.

5th Foot
Beneath the cypher the numeral *5* (Fig. 17).

23rd Foot
Below the cypher the Prince of Wales's plumes, coronet and motto and the Sphinx superscribed *Egypt* side by side with the Roman numerals *XXIII* beneath (Fig. 18).

27th Foot
Beneath the cypher the Castle of Inniskilling with St. George's flag flying to the left from the central turret. Beneath this a scroll inscribed *Enniskillen* with the numerals *27* at the base (Fig. 19).

67th Foot
Beneath the cypher the numerals *67* (Fig. 20).

2nd King's German Legion
Below the cypher an oval strap inscribed *King's German Legion* with the numeral *2* in the centre.

15

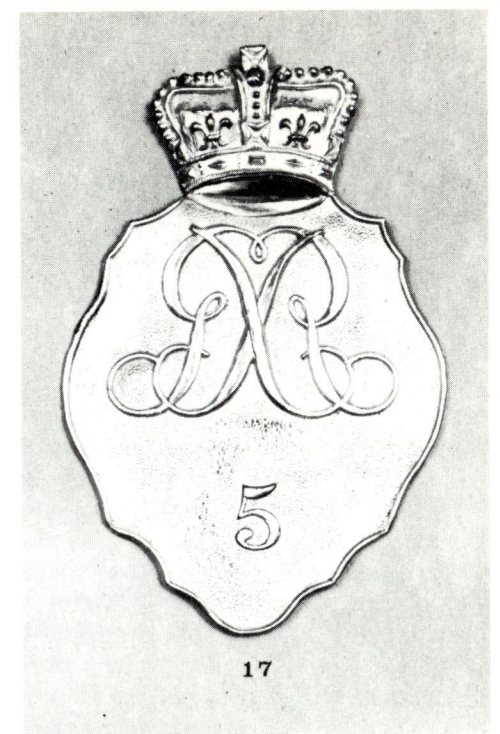

17

16

18

19

General pattern

A large Royal Cypher only (Fig. 21).

On the 28th December 1814, a further General Order was published to the effect that Rifle and Light Infantry Corps and companies would wear on the shako a bugle-horn with the number of the regiment instead of the plate worn by the rest of the Infantry of the Line.

20

21

CHAPTER 2

The Regency Shako:
1816 to 1829

Following the defeat of Napoleon at Waterloo, the Allies occupied France for three years and during that period the British Army wore the most extravagant dress it had ever known as it vied with the gorgeous uniforms then in vogue on the Continent. A new shako, generally referred to as the 'Regency' shako, was authorised by a General Order dated 10th August 1815. It was bell-topped, made of black felt, with a height of about $7\frac{1}{2}''$ in the front and a polished leather peak.

For officers it was ornamented with a narrow band of gold or silver lace at the base and a wider band at the top, in the centre of which was a black Hanoverian cockade. On the cockade was a regimental button or, in the case of rifle regiments, a bugle. An upright plume, $12''$ in height, was secured behind the cockade; the colours being the same as for the previous shako.

A circle of lace with a central crimson line was on the front of the shako and on this the plate was mounted. It was usually circular but occasionally oval in shape and carried the designation of the regiment; this was surmounted by a crown.

A feature of this shako was the gilt- or silver-plated chin-scales made in two separate pieces and joined with black tape which could be tied under the chin or looped up to the cockade.

Officers of Light companies and Light Infantry Regiments wore a silver bugle with the regimental number within the strings instead of the circular plate.

In most instances only the regimental number appeared on the plate but some regiments had special devices. Usually the plate was of gilt and varied in diameter from $2\frac{1}{4}''$ to $2\frac{1}{2}''$ but, where a regiment wore silver lace, the plate was generally of silver.

Some variations from the general pattern are:

3rd Regiment of Foot Guards
The Star of the Order of the Thistle in silver with a green enamel ground to the motto and centre.
The shako was discontinued and the bearskin worn from 1831.

2nd Foot
In the centre, a silver Paschal Lamb and Sphinx and above this two scrolls, one inscribed *Peninsula* and the other with the regimental motto, *Pristinae Virtutis Memor*. At the base, the title *The Queen's Royals*.

3rd Foot

Within a wreath a gilt Dragon above the numeral *3*. On scales above the plate reaching to the plume socket the following battle honours: *Peninsula, Douro, Talavera, Albuhera, Pyrenees, Nive, Nivelle.*

4th Foot

The Lion of England above the Roman numerals *IV*. It is believed that battle-honours were carried on narrow plates placed on a scaled-loop below the cockade. In 1819, the design was changed to an all-gilt badge consisting of a 2½″ strap, inscribed *The King's Own Regiment,* with the Lion and the Roman numerals *IV* in the centre. The whole ensigned with the crown.

8th Foot

The White Horse of Hanover above a Sphinx resting on a tablet inscribed *Egypt* and below this the Roman numerals *VIII.*

9th Foot

The figure of Britannia seated, bareheaded and holding a spear in her left hand: an oval shield bearing the Great Union rests against her hip and she is holding an olive branch in her right hand. Above, a scroll inscribed *Peninsula* and below, the Roman numerals *IX.* All in silver. (Fig. 22).

20th Foot

Within a laurel chaplet the Roman numerals *XX*. Above this, a scroll inscribed *Minden Maida* and below, a similar scroll inscribed *Peninsula*. All in silver.

26th Foot

On a burnished gilt plate, mounted in silver, a thistle with two leaves with below, the Sphinx superscribed *Egypt*. Below this the numerals *26* with at the base a scroll inscribed *Cameronians.*

28th Foot

In the centre, the Royal Crest above the numerals *28* with a spray of laurels on the left and palm on the right, all within a circlet with a continuous rope border and inscribed *Egypt, Waterloo, Barossa, Peninsula*. Size 2½″ × 3½″ with gilt burnished plate and crown. All mounts silver with black cloth behind centre (Fig. 23).

30th Foot

On a gilt burnished disc surmounted by a crown a circlet inscribed *Peninsula* at top and *Waterloo* at base. In the centre the Roman numerals *XXX*. Below the circlet two sprays of laurel. Beneath the disc, on the rosette the Sphinx superscribed *Egypt*. All in silver (Fig. 23A).

32nd Foot

In the centre, the numerals *32* in raised silver over two laurel sprays. Above, a scroll inscribed *Peninsula*. Below, a similar scroll inscribed *Waterloo*.

34th Foot

In the centre, the numerals *34* surrounded by a complete laurel wreath, all within a strap inscribed *Vittoria, Peninsula, Albuera*. All in silver (Fig. 24).

22

23

23A

24

38th Foot
Within a wreath of palm the Roman numerals *XXXVIII*. Above, a scroll inscribed *Peninsula*, below, the Stafford Knot. Above the plate scales bearing scrolls inscribed *Monte Video*, *Salamanca*, *St. Sebastian*. All in silver (Fig. 24A).

39th Foot
On a gilt plate, mounted in silver the numerals *39* within a laurel-wreath. Above, a scroll inscribed *Gibraltar*.

55th Foot
Within a gilt laurel wreath the numerals *55* in silver.

65th Foot
Within a laurel wreath the numerals *65*.

72nd Foot
A solid silver oval surmounted by a silver-gilt crown. In the centre all in gilt the numerals *72* with a scroll inscribed *Cape of* above and one inscribed *Good Hope* below.
In 1823, the regiment ceased to wear the shako on reverting to Highland garb.

76th Foot
In silver, a laurel wreath enclosing the numerals *76* and above this an Elephant supporting a castle on its back. On gilt scales above the plate two silver scrolls inscribed *Hindoostan*, *Peninsula*.

25

25D

80th Foot
Within a laurel wreath the numerals *80* and below this the Stafford Knot. Between the top join of the wreath, the Sphinx resting on a tablet inscribed *Egypt*. Original issue was oval but soon replaced. (Fig. 25).

83rd Foot
Within a laurel wreath the numerals *83*.

86th Foot
Within a laurel wreath the numerals *86*. All in silver.

91st Foot
In the centre, the Roman numerals *XCI* with a scroll above inscribed *Peninsula* and one below inscribed *Argyleshire*. All in silver (Fig. 25D).

96th Foot
A round silver plate $2\frac{1}{2}''$ diameter with a gilt crown above. At the top of the plate below the crown a scroll inscribed *Peninsula* and at the bottom of the plate a similar scroll inscribed *Queen's Own*. In the centre the numerals *96* surmounted by the Sphinx carrying a flag and resting on a tablet inscribed *Egypt*. Laurel sprays either side, the ends of which protrude below the bottom of the silver plate. All mounts in gilt.

The men's shako was similar in design to that of the officers, but made of inferior material. The plume was of worsted and only half the height of the officers'.

25A   25B   25C

Their badge was made of brass and consisted of a small circular convex plate 2″ in diameter surmounted by a crown. In the centre of the plate was the number of the regiment. These badges were identical except for the number and those of the 2nd, 19th and 37th Foot are shown (Figs. 25A, 25B and 25C).

In 1822, the officers' pattern shako was increased by one inch in height, the circle of lace on the front was discarded and, in place of the circular plate and crown device, the badge now consisted of an ornamental star usually silver but occasionally gilt and which, in addition to the regiment's number and special insignia, now carried the many battle-honours which had been awarded the previous year.

No alteration was made to the men's shako at this date and they continued to wear the circular plate and crown with the regimental number on it.

The back-badge of the *Gloucestershire Regiment* made its first appearance at this time. The first pattern was a plate 1¾″ square on which was the Sphinx with the numerals *28* below.

It has not been possible to trace all the devices worn by officers on this pattern shako but it is known that, in many instances, the star was transferred to the centre of the large 'star and crown' plate that was worn on the succeeding bell-topped shako. Where the star had been surmounted by a crown this was omitted as it was unnecessary, the large one on the back-plate taking its place.

It is therefore fairly safe to assume that, in most cases, the star described as being worn on the bell-topped shako is the same as that worn on the last Regency shako—with possibly the addition of further battle honours when these had been awarded subsequently.

5th Foot

A silver star surmounted by a crown. On this a strap inscribed *Quo fata vocant* and, in the centre, St. George killing the Dragon above the Roman numeral *V*. The strap surrounded by a laurel wreath; on the left, scrolls inscribed: *Corunna, Vimiera, Toulouse, Nivelle, Vittoria, Salamanca*; on the right, *Badajoz, Ciudad Rodrigo, Roleia, Busaco, Orthes, Peninsula*.

8th Foot

A gilt star, on this the Garter proper surmounted by a crown. Within the Garter the White Horse of Hanover. Above, a scroll inscribed *King's*. Above the crown, the Sphinx superscribed *Egypt* and two scrolls inscribed *Martinique* and *Niagara*.

11th Foot

On a facetted silver star a gilt pierced strap inscribed *North Devonshire* with a green enamel backing and surmounted by a crown. In the centre the Roman numerals *XI* in gilt on a mother-of-pearl backing.

12th Foot

A star. On this a laurel wreath surrounding an oval inscribed *Minden, Gibraltar, Seringapatam* and surmounted by a crown. Within the oval the Roman numerals *XII* (Fig. 35).

13th Foot

A bugle-horn with strings with the numerals *13* in the centre and surmounted by the Sphinx.

14th Foot

A small silver star. On this a gilt strap inscribed *Corunna, Waterloo* and surmounted by a crown In the centre the White Horse of Hanover with the Roman numerals *XIV* below.

15th Foot

A silver hand-cut star on a dull gilt background. On this the Garter proper surmounted by a crown and within the Garter the Roman numerals *XV*. A laurel wreath surrounds the Garter and below the wreath two scrolls inscribed *Martinique* and *Guadaloupe*. All mounts in gilt; black material beneath. Size $4'' \times 3\frac{3}{16}''$ (Fig. 36).

17th Foot

A silver star. On this an oval with a rope border inscribed *Leicestershire Regiment* surmounted by a crown. In the centre the Roman numerals *XVII*. A laurel wreath surrounds the oval (Fig. 37).

Replaced, 13th October, 1825, by a diamond-cut silver star on which in dead gilt a Tiger with a scroll inscribed *Hindoostan* above and the Roman numerals *XVII* in dead matt gilt below (Fig. 38).

19th Foot

A silver star. On this a gilt pierced strap inscribed *1st North York Regt* and surmounted by a crown. In the centre the Roman numerals *XIX*. A green enamel background to the centre and strap and the star on a burnished gilt backplate. Size $3\frac{1}{2}'' \times 2\frac{7}{8}''$ (Fig. 39).

20th Foot

A silver star. On this a gilt laurel wreath within which is a strap inscribed *East Devonshire*. The centre voided to show *XX* on a silver background.

22nd Foot

A silver star on a gilt back-plate. On this in gilt a rope circle surmounted by a crown and within this a wreath of oak with the numerals *22* in the centre.

24th Foot

A silver star. On this a gilt wreath surmounted by a crown with red velvet in the cap. Two gilt pierced scrolls on the wreath: left, *Pyrenees*; right, *Orthes*. Within the wreath a pierced circlet inscribed *Talavera, Fuentes d'Onor, Peninsula*. Within this a pierced strap inscribed *Warwickshire* with in the centre the numerals *24*. All pierced scrolls and the numerals in gilt with a backing of black velvet.

25th Foot

In the centre of a silver star a Garter and a strap side by side. The Garter inscribed with the Garter motto and the Royal Cypher in the centre. The strap inscribed *In veritate religionis confides* with the White Horse of Hanover in the centre. Above the Garter and strap the Sphinx superscribed *Egypt* and below the Roman numerals *XXV*. On the four diagonal rays of the star the battle honours *Egmont-op-Zee, Martinique, Namur, Minden*. At the base a scroll inscribed *The King's Own Borderers*. The whole design surmounted by a crown.

  There are several variations of this design.
  (a) The Castle of Edinburgh substituted for the Royal Cypher and the motto *In veritate religionis confides* transferred to take the place of the Garter motto. On the strap the motto *Nec aspera terrent* with the White Horse in the centre.
  (b) The Sphinx below the numerals *XXV*.
  (c) The addition of a wreath of thistles.
  (d) The Royal Crest in place of the crown.

27th Foot

A silver star. On this a gilt strap inscribed *Enniskillen* and surmounted by a crown. Below the strap the Sphinx superscribed *Egypt*. In the centre, on a blue enamel background, the Castle of Inniskilling, standing on a green mound, with St. George's flag flying from the centre turret.

29th Foot

An eight-pointed silver star. On this a solid gilt Garter with the motto in raised burnished letters and surmounted by a crown. In the centre a gilt lion on a blue enamel ground.

30th Foot

A silver diamond cut star of eight points. On this a gilt laurel-wreath surmounted by a crown. Within the wreath a gilt strap inscribed *Spectamur agendo* with, in the centre on a silver ground, the Roman numerals *XXX* in gilt. Between the wreath and the strap are four scrolls: (left) *Peninsula*; (top) *Salamanca*; (right) *Badajoz*; (bottom) *Waterloo*. On the lowest ray of the star a gilt Sphinx superscribed *Egypt* (Fig. 39A).

35

37

36

38

39　　　　　　　　　　　**39A**

32nd Foot

A silver star. In the centre, a pierced circlet with rope edging inscribed *Cornwall Regt* and within this the numerals *32*. Above the circlet, a scroll inscribed *Peninsula* and surmounted by a crown. Below the circlet, a scroll inscribed *Waterloo* and below this a wreath of laurel. All in gilt with a black enamel backing to the circlet. Size $3\frac{3}{8}''$ high (Fig. 40).

33rd Foot

A silver star. On this a strap inscribed *1st York West Riding*, surmounted by a crown, and with the numerals *33* in the centre. A scroll inscribed *Seringapatam* above and another inscribed *Waterloo* below. All mounts in gilt.

35th Foot

A silver star of twelve points. On this a gilt laurel wreath with a scroll inscribed *Maida* at the base and surmounted by a crown. In the centre the Roman numerals *XXXV*. Red enamel backing to centre and crown.

36th Foot

A silver star. On this a continuous scroll inscribed *Nivelle, Salamanca, Toulouse, Peninsula*, with a further scroll above inscribed *Vimiera*, and above this a crown. In the centre between two sprays of laurel the numerals *36* above a tablet inscribed *Firm*.

38th Foot

A silver star. On this a laurel wreath surmounted by a crown. On the wreath, four scrolls inscribed *Monte Video, Salamanca, St. Sebastian, Peninsula*. Within the wreath a circlet inscribed *1st Staffordshire* and in the centre the Roman numerals *XXXVIII*. Below the wreath the Stafford Knot.

43rd Foot

A silver star. On this a circlet inscribed *Peninsula* at top and with laurel sprays at the bottom. In the centre a strung bugle with the numerals *43* within the strings.

44th Foot

A silver star. On this a gilt strap inscribed *East Essex* and with the numerals *44* in the centre. The strap surrounded by a laurel wreath.

46th Foot

On a hand-cut silver star within two sprays of laurel a crowned strap inscribed *South Devon Regt*. Below the strap a scroll inscribed *Dominica*. All mounts in gilt.

47th Foot

(1) A silver star. On this a gilt strap inscribed *Lancashire* with the Roman numerals *XLVII* in the centre. The strap surrounded by scrolls inscribed *Vittoria, St. Sebastian, Peninsula* within a wreath. The whole surmounted by the Royal Crest.

(2) A silver star. On this a gilt strap inscribed *Tarifa, Vittoria, St. Sebastian, Peninsula.* Within the strap on a royal blue enamel ground the numerals *47* surmounted by the Royal Crest in silver with gilt laurel sprays on either side (Fig. 40A).

58th Foot

A silver star. On this a laurel wreath surmounted by a crown. The whole of the centre within the wreath voided. In the centre of this the Roman numerals *LVIII* surrounded by a circlet with rope edges inscribed *Salamanca, Peninsula* which is also surrounded by a further rope circlet with extensions inscribed *Gibraltar, Nivelle, Orthes, Pyrenees, Maida, Vittoria* (Fig. 41).

62nd Foot

On an eight-pointed gilt star a laurel spray from the ends of which a scroll inscribed *Peninsula* and surmounted by a crown. In the centre in silver ornamental characters the numerals *62*. Red velvet underneath the crown (Fig. 41A).

63rd Foot

A silver star. On this a gilt Garter with the Garter motto and surmounted by a crown. The numerals *63* in the centre.

42

64th Foot

A silver star. On this a laurel wreath with the numerals *64* in the centre. Above the wreath a scroll inscribed *St. Lucia* and below the wreath a scroll inscribed *Surinam*. Below this the Stafford Knot.

65th Foot

A silver star. On this a gilt strap inscribed *India, Arabia* and surmounted by a crown. Within this a Tiger standing on a wreathed bar above the numerals *65*. Size $3\frac{1}{2}'' \times 2\frac{3}{4}''$.

69th Foot

A silver star of eight points. On this a gilt laurel wreath surmounted by a crown with red enamel in the cushion. In the centre, gilt numerals *69* on a mother-of-pearl base. At the top of the shako a green cord boss with a gilt regimental button in the centre. Between the top of the star and the boss, an ornamented gilt bar on which are four silver scrolls inscribed *Waterloo, Bourbon, India, Java* (Fig. 42).

80th Foot

A silver star. On this a laurel wreath with the numerals *80* in the centre. Above the wreath the Sphinx superscribed *Egypt*. Below the wreath the Stafford Knot.

82nd Foot

A silver star on a gilt ground. On the principal rays the following battle honours are inscribed: *Vimiera, Pyrenees, Orthes, Niagara, Nivelle, Vittoria, Roleia, Peninsula*. In the centre, a silver circle enclosing the Prince of Wales's plumes, coronet and motto on a blue enamel ground. Below the circle the numerals *82*. Size $3\frac{1}{4}'' \times 2\frac{3}{4}''$. (Fig. 43).

84th Foot

(1) A silver star. On this a gilt laurel wreath surmounted by a coronet. Within the wreath a strap inscribed *York and Lancaster* in gilt lettering with a blue enamel background. In the centre a silver Rose above the numerals *84* with a red enamel background. Below the wreath a silver scroll inscribed *Nive*.

(2) A silver star. On this a small gilt laurel wreath surmounted by a large gilt coronet. Within the wreath a strap inscribed *York and Lancaster* in gilt lettering with a blue enamel background. In the centre the numerals *84* in gilt on a red enamel ground. Below the wreath a silver scroll inscribed *India*. Also there are three separate pieces affixed to the shako—above the star a silver scroll inscribed *Peninsula*, above this a silver Rose; below the star a silver scroll with sprigs of laurel at both ends and inscribed *Nive*.

85th Foot

A silver star. On this a gilt strap inscribed *Aucto splendore resurgo* surmounted by a crown. In the centre the numerals *85*.

43

44

45

46

87th Foot

A silver star. On this a silver strap with green enamel background inscribed in gilt letters *Prince's Own Irish*. In the centre the Prince of Wales's plumes, coronet and motto in silver with *Ich Dien* in gilt letters. Below this a silver scroll with gilt letters inscribed *Barrosa, Tarifa*. Below this the Irish Harp in gilt and below this a further scroll inscribed *Peninsula*. At the base a gilt Eagle standing on a tablet inscribed *8* commemorating the capture of a French 'Eagle' at Barrosa

88th Foot

A silver star of twelve points. On the major rays the following battle honours are inscribed: *C. Rodrigo, Toulouse, Orthes, Badajoz, Talavera, Egypt, Salamanca, Nivelle, Busaco, Vittoria, Fuentes d'Onor*. On the star a circlet inscribed (top) *Peninsula* and (bottom) *Connaught Rangers* and surmounted by a crown. In the centre the numerals *88*.

94th Foot

A silver star. In the centre the numerals *94* in gilt on a silver ground within a gilt Union wreath of roses, thistles and shamrocks. Surmounted by a small gilt crown.

96th Foot

A silver star with gilt metal edging. On this a gilt Garter proper. In the centre the numerals *96* in silver on a frosted gilt ground.

98th Foot

A silver star. On this a laurel wreath surmounted by a crown and enclosing the numerals *98* on a silver background (Fig. 44).

5th Royal Veteran Battalion

A silver star of twelve points. On this a gilt laurel wreath surmounted by a crown. Within the wreath an ornamental figure *5* above the letters *RVB* on a blue enamel background (Fig. 45).

Royal Staff Corps

On a silver star of eight points a gilt laurel wreath surmounted by a crown. Within this a strap inscribed *Royal Staff Corps* on a blue enamel background. In the centre the Royal Cypher reversed and intertwined on a red enamel background. Size $3\frac{1}{4}'' \times 2\frac{3}{4}''$ (Fig. 46).

By Horse Guards Circular Letter dated 10th February 1826, Fusilier Regiments were authorised to wear shakos instead of bearskin caps in certain stations abroad. Special devices were worn on these shakos, which were also worn by the Guards.

OFFICERS
Scots Fusilier Guards

On a diamond-cut silver star a gilt crown with, below, a gilt shield on which the Star of St. Andrew in silver. The shield is surrounded by a wreath of laurel on the left and oak on the right. Approx. 4″ diameter.

87th Foot

On a diamond-cut silver star a gilt crown with, below, a gilt shield on which a gilt fused grenade with a silver Eagle on the ball. The Eagle is standing on the head of a pike with a tablet inscribed *8*. The shield is surrounded by a wreath of laurel on the left and oak on the right. Approx. 4″ diameter.

OTHER RANKS
Coldstream Guards

On a star a crown with shield below on which the Star of the Order of the Garter surrounded by a wreath of laurel and oak. All in brass.

47

CHAPTER 3

The Bell-Topped Shako:
1829 to 1844

A new shako was introduced in 1829. It was authorised by Horse Guards Circular Memorandum for the Infantry of the Line on the 22nd December 1828, and for the Foot Guards on the 18th February 1829. This pattern is known as the bell-topped shako as it was very much wider at the top than at the bottom.

The officers' pattern was made of black beaver with a leather top and a leather peak. The ornamental lace and Hanoverian cockade disappeared, but the high feather-plume was retained for two years, to be replaced by a red-and-white hackle-plume of the same height. However, in the following year, this was reduced in size to eight inches and changed to all-white in colour. In 1835, a further change was made and a ball-tuft substituted for the plume. This was white for the Infantry but Light Infantry had dark-green and Rifles, black.

For this new shako, the badge was a universal large gilt star surmounted by a crown and superimposed on the star was the smaller silver star worn on the previous shako.

There were a number of variations. When the previous shako-badge had been surmounted by a crown, this was usually omitted. In some cases, the star had additional battle honours and the 5th, 27th, 66th and 84th bore a Maltese cross instead of the star.

The same shako was also worn by the Royal Marines and the Militia.

The other-ranks' shako was similar in design to that of the officers but made of felt and with a shorter plume. The latter was changed to a ball-tuft in 1835 when adopted for the officers' shako.

Other ranks also had the universal star-and-crown plate but made of brass and bearing a circle with the regimental number. That of the 99th Foot is shown (Fig. 47).

There were the same variations as before: battalion companies had the number only, grenadier companies a smaller number with a fused grenade above and light companies a smaller number with a strung bugle-horn above.

A further change was made by Horse Guards Circular Letter of the 22nd February 1839. The large star-and-crown plate was removed and replaced by a circular plate surmounted by a crown placed high on the top-front of the shako. A large regimental number was placed in the centre of the circle with the usual differences for the grenadier and light companies.

48

1st Foot

On the universal plate: A silver cut star with gilt rays, the centre pierced showing a gilt burnished backing. On the rays, battle-honours are inscribed as follows: *Maheidpore, Nagpore, Busaco, St. Lucia, Salamanca, Peninsula, Waterloo, St. Sebastian, Niagara, Nive, Vittoria, Egmont-op-Zee, Ava*. On the star, the Collar of the Order of the Thistle with pendant of St. Andrew and Cross and, in the centre of the collar, the Royal Cypher reversed and intertwined. Above the collar the Sphinx superscribed *Egypt* resting on a scroll inscribed *Royal Regiment* (Fig. 48).

2nd Foot

(1) On the universal plate: A silver star with battle-honours on the rays: (left) *Salamanca, Pyrenees, Toulouse*; (right) *Vittoria, Nivelle, Peninsula*. On the star, a pierced strap inscribed *Pristinae virtutis memor* and within this a silver Paschal Lamb above the numeral *2*. Above the strap, the Sphinx superscribed *Egypt* within a laurel wreath (Fig. 49).

49

50ᴬ

50

(2) On the universal plate: A silver star and on this a laurel wreath with battle-honour scrolls intertwined in the wreath: (left) *Corunna, Vittoria, Nivelle, Peninsula*; (right) *Vimiera, Salamanca, Pyrenees, Toulouse*. Within the wreath, a strap inscribed *Pristinae virtutis memor* surmounted by the Sphinx superscribed *Egypt*. Within the strap a Paschal Lamb above the numeral *2* (Fig. 50).

3rd Foot
On the universal plate: A laurel wreath. On the left spray, scrolls inscribed *Talavera, Nivelle*. On the right spray, *Albuhera, Nive*. At the top of the spray *Douro, Pyrenees*, and at the foot *Peninsula*. Within the wreath the Dragon above the numeral *3*. All in gilt.

4th Foot
On the universal plate: The same design as on the previous shako.

5th Foot
On the universal plate: Superimposed on a Maltese Cross a silver star. In the centre a strap inscribed *Quo fata vocant* surmounted by a crown. Within this St. George killing the Dragon. The whole within a laurel-wreath bearing scrolls inscribed with battle-honours. On the left *Corunna, Vimiera, Toulouse, Nivelle, Vittoria, Salamanca*. On the right, *Badajoz, Ciudad Rodrigo, Roleia, Busaco, Orthes, Peninsula*. Below the wreath the Roman numeral *V* (Fig. 50A).

6th Foot

(1) On the universal plate: A silver star on which a laurel wreath and within this an Antelope on a plinth inscribed *Warwickshire*. Above the wreath, scrolls inscribed *Nivelle, Niagara, Orthes, Peninsula, Pyrenees* and below, scrolls inscribed *Vittoria, Corunna, Roleia, Vimiera*.

(2) On the universal plate: A silver Maltese cross, the edges of the cross inscribed with the following battle-honours: *Vimiera, Roleia, Orthes, Vittoria, Nivelle, Pyrenees, Corunna, Niagara, Peninsula*. On this a gilt laurel-wreath and in the centre an Antelope standing on a wreathed bar with the Roman numerals *VI* below in silver.

7th Foot

On the universal plate: A fused grenade with, on the ball, the Garter surmounted by a crown. In the centre, a Rose within a wreath. Silver crown and flames, remainder gilt.

8th Foot

(1) On the universal plate: A silver star on which a wreath and within it a circlet inscribed *Nec aspera terrent*. In the centre, the White Horse of Hanover above the Roman numerals *VIII*. Above the circlet a scroll inscribed *King's* and above this the Sphinx superscribed *Egypt*.

(2) An eight-pointed star, the topmost point displaced by a Victorian crown. On the star, the Garter surmounted by a tablet inscribed *King's*. In the centre the White Horse on ground and below this the Roman numerals *VIII* (Fig. 50A).

9th Foot

On the universal plate: A diamond-cut silver star on which a gilt laurel-wreath entwined with eight battle-honours on green enamel: *Roleia, Busaco, Vittoria, Nive, St. Sebastian, Salamanca, Vimiera, Peninsula*. In the centre, the figure of Britannia bareheaded, with trident, Union shield and Lion facing front with a black-enamel backing. The trident is passed under the left shoulder and the right hand is not visible. Below Britannia the Roman numerals *IX* (Fig. 51).

10th Foot

On the universal plate a silver star. On this a gilt circlet inscribed (top) *Egypt*, (bottom) *Peninsula*. In the centre a gilt Roman numeral *X* on a silver ground (Fig. 51A).

11th Foot

On the universal plate a diamond-cut silver star. On this a gilt laurel-wreath with scrolls inscribed (left) *Toulouse* and (right) *Peninsula*. Within the wreath a circlet inscribed *Salamanca, Pyrenees* and in the centre the Roman numerals *XI*. Above the circlet a three-part scroll inscribed *Nive, Nivelle, Orthes*.

12th Foot

On the universal plate: The same design as worn on the previous shako but without the crown (Fig. 52).

The Light Company had a large bugle with strings on the star, with the Roman numerals *XII* within the strings (Fig. 53).

50A

13th Foot

On the universal plate: In silver, a strung bugle and the numerals *13* within the strings. Scrolls above inscribed *Ava Martinique* and above these the Sphinx superscribed *Egypt* with laurel-sprays either side (Fig. 54).

54

14th Foot

On the universal plate: A silver star on which a gilt strap inscribed *Corunna, Waterloo, Java* and surmounted by a laurel-wreath. In the centre the White Horse of Hanover with the Roman numerals *XIV* below.

15th Foot

On the universal plate a diamond-cut silver star. On this a Maltese cross with on the top edge *Martinique* and on the bottom edge *Guadaloupe* facing inwards. Gilt lions between each arm of the cross. In the centre of the cross the Roman numerals *XV* (Fig. 55.)

16th Foot

On the universal plate: A silver star and on this in gilt a Maltese cross surmounted by a crown. On the cross a laurel-wreath within which a circlet inscribed *Bedfordshire*. In the centre the numerals *16*.

17th Foot

On the universal plate a diamond-cut silver star. On this the Tiger with a scroll above inscribed *Hindoostan*. Below the Tiger the Roman numerals *XVII* (Fig. 56).

18th Foot

On the universal plate: A large silver Maid of Erin Harp.

19th Foot

On the universal plate: A silver star on which a laurel-wreath surrounding a strap inscribed *1st North York Regt*. In the centre the Roman numerals *XIX* (Fig. 56A).

21st Foot

On the universal plate: A fused grenade with, on the ball, the numerals *21* below which the letters *RNBF* (Fig. 57).

22nd Foot

On the universal plate: A silver star, on this a gilt oak-wreath with the numerals *22* in the centre on a blue enamel ground.

51

51A

52

53

55

56A

56

57

27th Foot

On the universal plate: A silver Maltese cross with the Sphinx superscribed *Egypt* above. On the border of the arms of the cross the following battle-honours are inscribed: (top) *Peninsula*; (bottom) *Waterloo*; (left) *Maida, Salamanca, Badajoz, Nive*; (right) *Orthes, Vittoria, Pyrenees, Toulouse*. In the centre of the cross, the Castle of Inniskilling with St. George's flag flying from the central turret. Below, a scroll inscribed *Enniskillen* (Fig. 58).

29th Foot

On the universal plate a silver star on which the Garter proper. In the centre the Lion (Fig. 59).

31st Foot

On the universal plate: A gilt unbroken wreath of oak on which six silver scrolls inscribed with battle-honours: (left) *Pyrenees, Albuhera, Nive*; (right) *Talavera, Vittoria, Nivelle*. Within this a silver laurel-wreath with, across the top, a scroll inscribed *Peninsula*. In the centre the Roman numerals *XXXI* in silver (Fig. 60).

58   59

32nd Foot

On the universal plate: A silver star with, on the main rays, the following battle-honours: *Peninsula, Waterloo, Salamanca, Nivelle, Nive.* On the star a strap inscribed *Cornwall* surmounted by a crown and surrounded by a laurel-wreath. In the centre the numerals *32.* All in gilt.
In 1830, the star was altered to take eight battle-honours instead of five. The three additional honours were *Orthes, Vimiera, Roleia.*

33rd Foot

On the universal plate: The same design as on the previous shako but without the crown.

34th Foot

On the universal plate: A silver diamond-cut star on which a Maltese cross superimposed on a laurel-wreath with lions between the arms of the cross. On the arms of the cross the following battle-honours: (top) *Peninsula*; (left) *Pyrenees*; (right) *Vittoria, Orthes*; (bottom) *Nivelle, Albuera.* In the centre a circlet inscribed *Cumberland* and within this the numerals *34.*

36th Foot

On the universal plate: A silver star, on this a gilt wreath with battle-honour scrolls entwined. Top, *Nive*; left, *Vimiera, Toulouse, Salamanca, Nivelle*; right, *Roleia, Pyrenees, Peninsula, Corunna.* Within this a gilt strap inscribed *Or Herefordshire.* On a silver centre, gilt numerals *36* above a scroll inscribed *Firm.*

38th Foot

On the universal plate: A silver star on which a continuous laurel-wreath with intertwined battle-honour scrolls. At the top of the wreath *Nive* and *Ava.* On each side of these, reading vertically, *Vimiera* and *Roleia* and, on the right, *Badajoz* and *St. Sebastian.* Bottom left *Salamanca* above *Vittoria* and right *Peninsula* above *Corunna.* Within the wreath a strap inscribed *1st Staffordshire* enclosing the Roman numerals *XXXVIII.* Below the wreath the Stafford Knot (Fig. 61).

61

43rd Foot

On the universal plate: A silver scroll with down-pointed ends inscribed *Peninsula* with below, a silver strung bugle-horn with the numerals *43* in the strings.

62   62ᴬ

44th Foot

On the universal plate an eight-pointed diamond-cut silver star. On this a gilt laurel-wreath with at the top of the wreath the Sphinx superscribed *Egypt*. Within this, an ornamental continuous scroll inscribed *Bladensburg, Badajoz, Ava, Salamanca* and within this a circlet inscribed *Peninsula, Waterloo*. The scroll and circlet pierced to show a silver background to the lettering. In the centre the numerals *44* in silver on a raised dome (Fig. 62).

45th Foot

On the universal plate: A silver star 2½″ diameter with sixteen principal points. On fourteen of these the following battle-honours are inscribed: *Roleia, Talavera, Busaco, Ava, C. Rodrigo, Nivelle, Vittoria, Salamanca, Pyrenees, Orthes, Badajoz, Fuentes d'Onor, Vimiera, Toulouse.* In the centre a circlet inscribed *Nottinghamshire Regt* and within this the numerals *45* on a black-enamel domed centre (Fig. 64).

46th Foot

On the universal plate: A silver star on which a wreath of laurel (left) and palm (right) and within this a strap inscribed *South Devon* with the numerals *46* in the centre. On the base of the wreath a scroll inscribed *Dominica* (Fig. 63).

47th Foot
On the universal plate: A silver star of eight points on which a gilt strap pierced to show a blue-enamel background and inscribed *Tarifa, Vittoria, St. Sebastian, Peninsula*. In the centre the numerals *47* surmounted by the Royal Crest and surrounded by a laurel-wreath all on a blue-enamel ground. Above the strap a gilt scroll inscribed *Ava* (Fig. 62A).

51st Foot
On the universal plate: A silver bugle without strings and with the numerals *51* within the curl of the bugle.

52nd Foot
On the universal plate: A large strung bugle-horn with the numerals *52* in the strings. All gilt.

53rd Foot
On the universal plate: A diamond-cut silver star on which a gilt Maltese cross; in the centre of this a circlet inscribed *Shropshire Regiment* with the numerals *53* in the centre. On the arms of the cross the following battle-honours are inscribed: *Peninsula, Nieuport, St. Lucia/Nivelle, Tournay, Pyrenees, /Salamanca, Toulouse, /Talavera, Vittoria.*

55th Foot
On the universal plate: A silver burnished star on which a laurel-wreath and within this a strap inscribed *Westmoreland*, the background pierced to show a blue-enamel ground. The Roman numerals *LV* in the centre, pierced to show an orange-enamel ground.

56th Foot
On the universal plate: A star with the left-centre ray inscribed *Moro* and the right-centre ray *Gibraltar*. On the star a complete wreath of laurel enclosing the Castle and Key of Gibraltar. On the bottom-centre ray of the star an oval inscribed *LVI* (Fig. 65).

60th Foot
The universal plate in bronze. On this a laurel-wreath with a scroll at the top inscribed *Peninsula* and one at the foot inscribed *Celer et Audax*. Within the wreath the Cross of the Order of the Bath. On the arms of the cross the following battle-honours: (top) *Martinique, Toulouse, Nive*; (left) *Fuentes d'Onor, Ciudad Rodrigo, Albuhera, Badajoz*; (right) *Talavera, Vimiera, Roleia, Orthes*; (bottom) *Nivelle, Vittoria, Pyrenees, Salamanca*. In the centre of the cross a circlet inscribed *Duke of York's Own Rifle Corps* and in the centre of this a strung bugle with the numerals *60* in the strings. In December 1830, the title was changed to *The King's Royal Rifle Corps*. This badge was worn without the universal star-and-crown plate from 1831 to 1835 but with a small crown on the cockade.

61st Foot
On the universal plate: A laurel-wreath surmounted by the Sphinx. Within this, battle-honour scrolls: (top) *Egypt*; (left) *Nivelle, Toulouse*; (right) *Talavera, Peninsula*; (bottom) *Salamanca*. Within these a circlet inscribed *South Gloucestershire* and in the centre the Roman numerals *LXI*.

63

64   65

52

63rd Foot

On the universal plate: A silver Maltese cross 3½″ square with a dead silver edge and balls on the points of the arms. On the edge of the top arm *Martinique* and on the bottom edge *Guadaloupe*. Gilt lions between each arm. On the cross a laurel-wreath. Within this a strap inscribed *West Suffolk Regiment* and in the centre the numerals *63* on a green-enamel ground.

64th Foot

On the universal plate: The same design as on the previous shako.

65th Foot

On the universal plate: A diamond-cut silver star 3½″ × 3½″. In the centre of this a gilt Tiger standing on ground. Above, a silver scroll inscribed *India*. Below, a similar scroll inscribed *Arabia*. Below this the numerals *65*.

66th Foot

On the universal plate: A Maltese cross with, on the four edges of the arms of the cross, the following battle-honours: (top) *Talavera*; (left) *Vittoria*; (right) *Albuhera*; (bottom) *Nivelle*. In the centre of the cross, a circlet inscribed *Orthes, Douro, Pyrenees, Nive*. In the centre, the numerals *66* within a wreath of laurel and, below this but inside the circlet, the battle-honour *Peninsula* (Fig. 66).

67th Foot

On the universal plate: A complete circlet inscribed at top *India* and at the foot *Barrosa*. Within this a Tiger with the numerals *67* below, the whole surrounded by a laurel-wreath. Across the base of the wreath a scroll inscribed *Peninsula*.

70th Foot

On the universal plate a diamond-cut silver star. On this a laurel-wreath and within it the numerals *70*. Below the wreath a scroll inscribed *Surrey* (Fig. 67).

74th Foot

On the universal plate: A diamond-shaped star on which an Elephant. Surrounding this, thirteen scrolls inscribed with battle-honours as follows: *Fuentes d'Onor, Badajoz, Orthes, Salamanca, Seringapatam, Assaye, Toulouse, Ciudad Rodrigo, Pyrenees, Vittoria, Peninsula, Nivelle, Busaco*. The whole within a laurel-wreath (Fig. 68).

76th Foot

On the universal plate: A star, on which a laurel-wreath surmounted by an Elephant on a scroll inscribed *Hindoostan*. Below the Elephant a scroll inscribed *Peninsula*. In the centre the numerals *76*.

77th Foot

On the universal plate: A circlet inscribed with the following battle-honours: *Seringapatam, Badajoz, Ciudad Rodrigo*, with a mural crown between each honour. Within this the Prince of Wales's plumes, coronet and motto above the numerals *77* surrounded by a laurel-wreath bearing a scroll inscribed *Peninsula* at the foot (Fig. 69).

79th Foot

On the officers' feathered bonnet (1827 to 1849), a diamond-cut silver star with, on the rays, the following battle-honours: *Pyrenees, Fuentes d'Onor, Salamanca, Peninsula, Toulouse, Waterloo, Nivelle, Nive, Egmont-op-Zee.* In the centre of the star, a circlet inscribed *Nemo me impune lacessit* and in the centre of this a St. Andrew's Cross with the Sphinx superscribed *Egypt* superimposed; the star and cross in silver, remainder gilt. Green cloth behind the Sphinx and battle-honours. Arising from the top of the star a large thistle flanked by two smaller thistles with leaves.

80th Foot

On the universal plate a silver star. On this a laurel-wreath with the numerals *80* in the centre. Above the wreath the Sphinx superscribed *Egypt* and below, the Stafford Knot. *Light Company:* On the universal plate a strung bugle-horn with the numerals *80* within the strings.

81st Foot

On the universal plate: A strap inscribed *Loyal Lincoln Volunteers* with the Roman numerals *LXXXI* in the centre. Silver scrolls inscribed with the following battle-honours: *Maida, Corunna, Peninsula.* A wreath of silver either side.

82nd Foot

On the universal plate: A silver star on which the Prince of Wales's plumes, coronet and motto within a circlet inscribed *The Prince of Wales's Volunteers* with the numerals *82* below the circlet. On the star the following battle-honours are inscribed: *Peninsula, Roleia, Vittoria, Nivelle, Niagara, Orthes, Pyrenees, Vimiera.* The circlet in gilt, remainder in silver.

83rd Foot

On the universal plate the numerals *83* in the centre and surrounded by a laurel-wreath. Radiating outwards from the centre the following battle-honours: *Ciudad Rodrigo, Busaco, Vittoria, Badajoz, Orthes, Nivelle, Talavera, Fuentes d'Onor, Toulouse, Salamanca, Peninsula.* All gilt (Fig. 70).

84th Foot

On the universal plate a silver Maltese cross. On the borders of the cross, battle-honours are inscribed: (left) *India*; (top) *Peninsula*; (right) *Nive.* In the centre of the cross a gilt-and-silver rose with, in its centre, the numerals *84* in silver.

85th Foot

On the universal plate: The same device as worn on the previous shako, but with a bugle-horn substituted for the crown.

86th Foot

(1) On the universal plate: A silver cut star with gilt labels on centre points: (left) *India*, (right) *Bourbon.* On the star a laurel-wreath with the Sphinx superscribed *Egypt* above and the numerals *86* below. Within the wreath a strap inscribed *Royal County Down* with, in the centre, the Harp and Crown. Blue-enamel behind the strap and centre. All in gilt except the star (Fig. 71).

(2) On the universal plate: A silver cut star with gilt labels on centre points: (left) *India*, (right) *Bourbon.* On the star a laurel-wreath surrounding a strap inscribed *Royal County Down.* Blue-enamel centre on which the Sphinx superscribed *Egypt* and the numerals *86.*

70

71

87th Foot

On the bearskin cap a large fused grenade. Occupying the whole of the ball an Eagle resting on a plinth inscribed *8*. All in gilt.

88th Foot

On the universal plate a silver star with twelve points. On these battle-honours are inscribed as follows: *Peninsula, C. Rodrigo, Badajoz, Vittoria, Busaco, Fuentes d'Onor, Salamanca, Nivelle, Orthes, Talavera, Toulouse, Egypt.* In the centre a wreath of laurel (left) and palm (right). Within this the Irish Harp above the numerals *88*. Below the wreath, the Sphinx on a tablet inscribed *Egypt*.

89th Foot

On the universal plate: A wreath of laurel (left) and palm (right); within this a strap inscribed *Regiment* and in the centre the numerals *89*. On the left-centre ray of the star *Java* and on the right, *Ava*. Below the crown a scroll inscribed *Niagara*. Across the lower point of the star the Sphinx superscribed *Egypt*.

91st Foot

On the universal plate. St. Andrew's Cross, superimposed a laurel-wreath. On the wreath two scrolls, left inscribed *Nive*, right inscribed *Orthes*. Within the wreath a four-part scroll inscribed *Pyrenees, Nivelle, Toulouse, Peninsula*. Within this a strap inscribed *Argyllshire* and in the centre the Roman numerals *XCI*. Below the wreath a three-part scroll inscribed *Corunna, Roleia, Vimiera*.

93rd Foot

Officers' feathered bonnet, 1837–1845. Within a wreath of thistles a circlet inscribed *Sutherland Highlanders* and surmounted by a crown. In the centre the numerals *93*. Below the wreath a scroll inscribed *Cape of Good Hope*. Frosted silver disc (Fig. 71A).

94th Foot

On the universal plate: The same design as on the previous shako but without the crown and the wreath extended to meet at the top.

98th Foot

On the universal plate: A silver star on which a complete laurel-wreath enclosing the numerals *98* on a domed background (Fig. 72).

1st Bengal European Regiment (Light Infantry) (later 101st Foot)

   (1) On the universal plate: A strap inscribed *Plassey, Buxar, Guzerat, Deig, Bhurtpore, Affghanistan, Ghuznee*. Within the strap a Maltese cross. On this a wreath of oak enclosing a strap inscribed *Bengal European Regt*. In the centre the numeral *1*.

   (2) On the universal plate: A laurel-wreath within which a bugle with the numeral *1* in the curl. The wreath and *1* in silver, bugle in gilt (Fig. 73).

74

75

1st Bombay European Regiment (later 103rd Foot)
On the universal plate: A diamond-cut silver star on which a Maltese cross. On the edges of the cross, battle-honours are inscribed as follows: (left) *Kirkee*; (right) *Beni Boo Ali*; (bottom) *Seringapatam*; the top edge is blank. On the cross a laurel-wreath and within this a strap inscribed *Bombay European Regt.* Within this a lion rampant guardant holding a crown and standing on a heraldic wreath.

2nd (Bengal European) Fusiliers (later 104th Foot)
A large fused Grenade in gilt, 5½″ high by 4¼″ wide. On this, in silver, a laurel-wreath with a scroll inscribed *Punjab* intertwined in the base of the wreath. Within this a strap inscribed *European Bengal* and surmounted by a Victorian crown. In the centre within a scroll inscribed *Fusiliers* the numeral *2*.

The Rifle Brigade
The universal plate in bronze. On this a laurel-wreath with a bar inscribed *Waterloo* joining the top ends of the wreath and a scroll inscribed *Peninsula* just above the bottom join of the wreath. Within the wreath, a cross similar to that of the Order of the Bath with battle-honours on the arms of the cross as follows: (top) *Ciudad Rodrigo, Copenhagen, Corunna, Busaco*; (left) *Monte Video, Barossa, Roleia, Orthes*; (right) *Fuentes d'Onor, Badajoz, Vimiera, Nivelle*; (bottom) *Salamanca, Toulouse, Vittoria, Nive*. In the centre of the cross a circlet inscribed *Rifle Brigade* and within this a bugle with strings surmounted by a crown (Fig. 74).

Royal Jersey Militia
On the universal plate: A silver laurel wreath within which a strap inscribed *Royal Jersey Regt* and surmounted by the numeral *1*. In the centre three lions-leopardé in pale (Fig. 75).

OTHER RANKS
Royal Alderney Militia
On the universal plate: A lion rampant regardant holding a sprig of laurel in his paws and standing on a tri-part scroll inscribed *Royal Alderney Militia*. All in brass. (Fig. 76).

Royal Jersey Militia
On the universal plate three lions-leopardé in pale. Below, a tri-part scroll inscribed *Royal Jersey Militia*. All in brass. (Fig. 77).

76   77

78

CHAPTER 4

The Albert Shako:
1844 to 1855

The next in the series of shakos worn by the infantry was authorised by Horse Guards Circular Memorandum of 4th December 1843, and is usually referred to as the 'Albert' shako being named after the Prince Consort. It was worn at the battles of the Alma and Inkerman but was found most unsuitable for wear in an engagement and, for the remainder of hostilities, the forage cap was worn invariably by troops in action.

The officers' pattern was made of black beaver mounted on felt $6\frac{3}{4}''$ high and had, round the base, a narrow leather band with a small buckle; a leather peak, $2\frac{3}{8}''$ deep, and a small peak at the back $1\frac{1}{4}''$ deep. The gilt chin-chain was of a ribbed pattern and secured by gilt rose-pattern side-ornaments.

The plate was usually a gilt star of eight points, the topmost being displaced by a crown, but the 43rd had a ten-pointed star and the 27th, 45th and 88th had stars of twelve points. The size was $4\frac{1}{2}''$ wide by $5\frac{3}{8}''$ deep and on the star was a wreath of half-laurel (left) and half-palm (right). Within this was a strap inscribed with the regimental title, or sometimes with the regimental motto, and in the centre the number giving the seniority of the regiment. On the major rays of the star battle-honours were inscribed and, occasionally, on scrolls on the wreath. Grenadier companies, Light companies and Light Infantry regiments were distinguished by the inclusion of a fused grenade or bugle-horn in the centre of the design.

The shako was ornamented with a large worsted ball-tuft, $2\frac{1}{2}''$ diameter, in a gilt-metal holder of a plain ball pattern. From 1844 to 1846 it was all white in colour but, for the remainder of the period in which it was worn, it was two-thirds white and one-third red with the white uppermost.

The other-ranks' shako was the same shape as the officers' but made of stout felt with plain-cut lacquered peaks, front and back. A leather chin-strap with buckle and brass rose side-ornaments.

The badge was worn high on the front of the shako and consisted of a round brass plate $3''$ in diameter, ribbed horizontally and edged with a raised wreath of oak (left) and laurel (right), the whole surmounted by a crown. The regimental number in the centre was in raised burnished numerals. Battalion companies had the numeral only, but Grenadier companies had a smaller number with a fused grenade above and light companies a smaller number surmounted by a stringed bugle.

These badges were identical except for the number and those of the 8th, 14th, 15th and 47th Foot are shown in Figs. 26, 27, 28 and 29.

The badges of the 69th Foot are also shown to illustrate the three different types (Figs. 30, 31 and 32).

The Militia had plates of similar pattern. Those of the Royal Jersey Militia had their own special devices.

(1) The Arms of Jersey: three lions leopardé in pale. Below a tri-part scroll inscribed *Royal Jersey Militia* (Fig. 33).

(2) Three cannons in pale. Below a tri-part scroll inscribed *Royal Jersey Militia* (Fig. 34).

1st Foot

1st Battalion: On the standard star-and-crown plate a laurel-wreath with a scroll inscribed *Peninsula* across the bottom join. Within this, a circlet inscribed *Royal Regiment* and in the centre the numeral *1*. On the lowest point of the star the Sphinx superscribed *Egypt*. On the rays of the star, some partly hidden, are the following battle-honours: *Salamanca, Niagara, St. Sebastian, Waterloo, Maheidpore, Nagpore, Nive, Corunna, Saint Lucia, Busaco, Egmont-op-Zee, Ava, Vittoria*. All gilt (Fig. 78).

2nd Battalion: On the standard star-and-crown plate a thistle-wreath with a scroll inscribed *Waterloo* across the bottom join. Within this a circlet inscribed *The Royal Regiment* and in the centre the numeral *1*. Above the wreath the Sphinx superscribed *Egypt* and above this a scroll inscribed *Peninsula*. On the lowest point of the star, St. Andrew's badge. On the rays of the star, some partly hidden, are the following battle-honours: *Salamanca, Niagara, St. Sebastian, Nive, Maheidpore, Nagpore, Corunna, Saint Lucia, Busaco, Egmont-op-Zee, Ava, Vittoria* All gilt.

2nd Foot

On the standard star-and-crown plate a wreath of laurel (left) and palm (right) on which are battle-honours *Ghuznee* (left) and *Khelat* (right). Below are further scrolls inscribed: (left) *Vimiera, Corunna, Vittoria*; (right) *Salamanca, Pyrenees, Nivelle*; (at base) *Toulouse* vertically. In the centre of the wreath, a circlet inscribed *Pristinae virtutis memor* with the numeral *2* in the centre. Below, a scroll inscribed *Afghanistan* and below this the Paschal Lamb. Above the wreath, a further scroll inscribed *Peninsula* and above this the Sphinx superscribed *Egypt*.

3rd Foot

Grenadier company: On the standard star-and-crown plate a wreath of laurel (left) and palm (right). Within this a strap inscribed *Veteri frondescit honore* with, in the centre, a fused grenade with the Dragon on the ball. Above the wreath a scroll inscribed *Peninsula*. On the main rays of the star the following battle honours are inscribed: *Douro, Albuhera, Nivelle, Punniar, Nive, Pyrenees, Talavera* (Fig. 79).

4th Foot

On the standard star-and-crown plate a large strap with rope edges inscribed *The King's Own Regiment*. In the centre, on a background of green-velvet, the Lion. Below this the Roman numerals *IV*. All gilt. (Fig. 80.)

(Worn by the Light company, hence the green-velvet backing to the centre.)

26   27   28

30   31   32

29   33   34

80

79

6th Foot

On the standard star-and-crown plate a wreath of laurel (left) and oak (right). On this three battle-honour scrolls: across top *Peninsula*; bottom left *Nivelle*; bottom right *Pyrenees*. In the centre of the wreath a strap inscribed *Royal Warwickshire Regt* with the numeral *6* in the centre. Below the wreath the Antelope, ducally chained and gorged, completely enclosed by the Garter and surmounted by a crown. On the main rays of the star the following battle-honours are inscribed: *Vimiera, Orthes, Corunna, Niagara, Vittoria, Roleia.* (Fig. 81.)

7th Foot

A fused grenade. On the ball the Garter surmounted by a Victorian crown. In the centre the Rose. Below the Garter the White Horse of Hanover. Officers' pattern: Background to the Garter blue enamel, the White Horse in silver, remainder gilt. (Fig. 81A.)

8th Foot

An eight-pointed star, the topmost point displaced by a Victorian crown. On the star the Garter surmounted by a scroll inscribed *Kings* in Old English characters. In the centre the White Horse on ground with the Roman numerals *VIII* below. Above the Horse a scroll inscribed *Nec aspera terrent* in Old English characters. On the lowest point of the star the Sphinx superscribed *Egypt* (Fig. 81B).

81ᴬ

81ᴮ

9th Foot

On the standard star-and-crown plate a laurel-wreath with battle-honour scrolls intertwined in the wreath: (across the top) *Roleia*; (left) *Vimiera, Salamanca, St. Sebastian*; (right) *Busaco, Vittoria, Nive*; (across the bottom) *Peninsula*, and *Cabool, 1842* in two scrolls below. In the centre, Britannia with the Lion beside her, the shield of the Great Union resting against her left hip with, underneath, the Roman numerals *IX* (Fig. 82).

82

10th Foot

A silver star surmounted by a crown. On this a wreath of laurel (left) and palm (right). In the centre a strap inscribed *North Lincoln Regt* and within this the Roman numeral *X*. Below, a scroll inscribed *Peninsula* and on the bottom ray of the star the Sphinx superscribed *Egypt*.

12th Foot

Battalion companies: On the standard star-and-crown plate a wreath of laurel (left) and palm (right) within which a strap inscribed *East Suffolk* with the numerals *12* in the centre. On the bottom ray of the star the Castle of Gibraltar. On the main rays of the star the following battle honours are inscribed *Minden, Seringapatam, Gibraltar, India* (Fig. 83).

Grenadier company: In the centre a fused grenade with, on the ball, a strap inscribed *Regiment* with the numerals *12* in the centre. Other details as the battalion companies. (Fig. 84.)

Light company: In the centre a bugle with the numerals *12* in the curl. Other details as the battalion companies. (Fig. 85.)

13th Foot

On the standard star-and-crown plate a wreath of laurel (left) and palm (right) within which a bugle-horn with the numerals *XIII* in the curl and surmounted by a mural crown with a scroll inscribed *Jellalabad* above. Below the bugle a scroll inscribed *Cabool 1842* and below this the Sphinx superscribed *Egypt*. On the rays of the star the following battle-honours are inscribed: *Ava, Afghanistan, Ghuznee, Martinique*. All in gilt.

14th Foot

On the standard star-and-crown plate a laurel-wreath. Within this a strap inscribed *Buckinghamshire* with the Roman numerals *XIV* in the centre. Below, the Royal Tiger. Above, the White Horse of Hanover standing on a tri-part scroll inscribed *Nec aspera terrent*.

17th Foot

On the standard star-and-crown plate a complete laurel-wreath. Within this a circlet inscribed *Leicestershire* with the Royal Tiger above the numerals *17* in the centre. Across the bottom of the wreath a scroll inscribed *Hindoostan*. On the left-centre ray of the star the battle-honour *Affghanistan*, on the bottom ray *Khelat* and on the right-centre ray *Ghuznee* (Fig. 86).

83   84

85   86

19th Foot

Battalion companies: On the standard star and crown plate a laurel-wreath within which a strap inscribed *1st North York Regt*. In the centre the Roman numerals *XIX* (Fig. 86A).

Grenadier company: In the centre a fused grenade with, on the ball, the Roman numerals *XIX*. Other details as battalion companies (Fig. 86B).

Light company: In the centre a bugle with the Roman numerals *XIX* in the curl and the wreath half oak and half palm. Other details as battalion companies (Fig. 86C).

86A   86B   86C

20th Foot

On the standard star-and-crown plate a complete laurel-wreath on which scrolls: (left) *Toulouse*, (bottom) *Peninsula*, and (right) *Maida*. A further scroll inscribed *Minden* immediately above. Within the wreath, a circlet inscribed *East Devonshire* with the Roman numerals *XX* in the centre. On the main rays of the star the following battle-honours are inscribed: *Orthes, Vittoria, Pyrenees, Egmont-op-Zee, Corunna, Vimiera,* and on the bottom ray of the star the Sphinx superscribed *Egypt* (Fig. 87).

   Light company: Within the wreath which is not closed a bugle with the Roman numerals *XX* in the curl. Other details as battalion companies (Fig. 87D).

21st Foot

A fused grenade. On the ball the Royal Arms. Officers' in gilt (Fig. 87A).

22nd Foot

On the standard star-and-crown plate a wreath of oak within which a circlet inscribed *Cheshire Regiment*, with in the centre the numerals *22*. On the left main ray of the star is inscribed *Meanee*, on the right *Hyderabad*, and on the bottom *Scinde*. All gilt.

23rd Foot

Officers: A gilt fused grenade with the Prince of Wales's plumes, coronet and motto in silver on the ball (Fig. 87B). Non-Commissioned Officers: A brass fused grenade with the Prince of Wales's plumes, coronet and motto in white metal on the ball. (Fig. 87C.)

24th Foot

On the standard star-and-crown plate a complete laurel-wreath. Within this a circlet inscribed *2nd Warwickshire* with, in the centre, the Roman numerals *XXIV*. Below the wreath, two small scrolls inscribed *Cape of Good Hope* and *Peninsula*. On the main rays of the star the following battle-honours are inscribed: *Talavera, Fuentes d'Onor, Pyrenees, Orthes, Nivelle, Salamanca, Vittoria.*

26th Foot

On the standard star-and-crown plate a white enamel mullet with the numerals *26* in the centre.

87

87D

88

89

27th Foot (Light Company)

A star of twelve points, the topmost displaced by a crown. On this a wreath of laurel (left) and palm (right) within which a strap inscribed *Inniskilling*. In the centre, a strung bugle-horn with the numerals *27* inside the strings. Across the bottom of the wreath a scroll inscribed *Nec aspera terrent* in Old English characters. Below this the White Horse of Hanover. Above the strap, the Sphinx superscribed *Egypt* and above this the Castle of Inniskilling with St. George's flag flying from the central turret. On the main rays of the star the following battle honours are inscribed: *St. Lucia, Toulouse, Vittoria, Waterloo, Nivelle, Salamanca, Maida, Pyrenees, Badajoz, Orthes*. All in gilt. (Fig. 88.)

28th Foot

On the standard star-and-crown plate a wreath of laurel (left) and palm (right) on which are scrolls inscribed *Barossa* (left), *Pyrenees* (right) and *Waterloo* across the bottom join of the wreath. Within the wreath a strap inscribed *North Gloucestershire* and in the centre the numerals *28*. On the main rays of the star the following battle-honours are inscribed: *Corunna, Albuhera, Vittoria, Peninsula, Nivelle, Nive, Orthes*. All in gilt. (Fig 89.)

29th Foot

On the standard star-and-crown plate a laurel wreath. Within this the Garter proper and in the centre the Lion from the Royal Crest.

30th Foot

On the standard star-and-crown plate a complete laurel wreath. Within this a strap inscribed *Spectamur agendo*. In the centre the Roman numerals *XXX*. Below the wreath the Sphinx superscribed *Egypt*. On the main rays of the star the following battle-honours are inscribed: (left) *Badajoz, Salamanca*; (right) *Waterloo, Peninsula* (Fig. 90).

90

32nd Foot

On the standard star and crown plate a wreath of laurel, within this a circlet inscribed *Cornwall Regt.* with the numerals *32* in the centre. Above the circlet a scroll inscribed *Peninsula* and below the circlet a scroll inscribed *Waterloo*. On the main rays of the star the following battle-honours are inscribed: *Roleia, Vimiera, Corunna, Salamanca, Pyrenees, Nivelle, Orthes, Nive*.

33rd Foot

On the standard star-and-crown plate a strap
inscribed *1st Yorkshire West Riding Regiment*,
within which a laurel-wreath and in the centre the numerals *33* in ornamental characters. Below the strap, two scrolls side by side inscribed (left) *Seringapatam,* (right) *Waterloo* (Fig. 91).

34th Foot

On the standard star-and-crown plate a complete laurel-wreath with, across the bottom, a scroll inscribed *Arroyo dos Molinos*. Within the wreath a circlet inscribed *Cumberland Regt* and in the centre the numerals *34*. On the main rays of the star the following battle-honours are inscribed: *Albuhera, Vittoria, Nivelle, Peninsula, Pyrenees, Nive, Orthes*. All in gilt. (Fig. 92.)

35th Foot

On the standard star-and-crown plate a wreath of laurel (left) and palm (right). Within this the Garter proper and in the centre the numerals *35*.

91   92   93

38th Foot

On the standard star-and-crown plate a wreath of laurel (left) and palm (right). On the wreath, battle-honour scrolls are inscribed as follows: (left) *Monte Video, Roleia*; (right) *Vimiera, Ava*. Across the bottom join of the wreath, a further scroll inscribed *Peninsula* and below this the Stafford Knot. Within the wreath, a strap inscribed *1st Staffordshire* and in the centre the numerals *38*. On the main rays of the star the following battle-honours are inscribed: *Corunna, Busaco, Badajoz, Nive, St. Sebastian, Vittoria, Salamanca* (Fig. 93).

   Grenadier company: A fused grenade above the strap and *Regiment* substituted for *1st Staffordshire*.

   Light company: The strap omitted. In the centre a bugle-horn with the numerals *38* within the strings.

40th Foot

On the standard star-and-crown plate a wreath of laurel (left) on which scrolls inscribed: *Candahar, Ghuznee* and palm (right) on which scrolls inscribed: *Cabool, Maharajpore*. Within the wreath a strap inscribed *2nd Somersetshire* with the numerals *40* in the centre. Radiating outwards from the wreath scrolls inscribed: *Egypt, Peninsula, Toulouse, Orthes, Nive, Pyrenees, Vittoria, Waterloo, Salamanca, Badajoz, Talavera, Vimiera, Roleia, Monte Video*. All in gilt.

41st Foot

On the standard star-and-crown plate a wreath of laurel (left) and palm (right). Within the wreath a strap inscribed *Gwell Augua Neu Chwllydd* with, in the centre, the Prince of Wales's plumes, coronet and motto. Below the wreath, the Roman numerals *XLI*. On the main rays of the star the following battle honours are inscribed: *Ava, Queenstown, Niagara, Ghuznee, Detroit, Miami, Candahar, Cabool*.

42nd Foot

Officers' feathered bonnet: The Sphinx superscribed *Egypt* in silver. Other Ranks: The Sphinx superscribed *Egypt* surmounted by St. Andrew with the numerals *42* below. All within a thistle-wreath with a scroll inscribed *Waterloo* at head and a further scroll inscribed *Peninsula* at base.

Grenadier company: St. Andrew replaced by a grenade.

43rd Foot

A ten-pointed star with the topmost point displaced by a crown. On the star a wreath of laurel (left) and palm (right) with a scroll inscribed *Nive* across the bottom join and a further scroll inscribed *Peninsula* below this. Within the wreath a large bugle-horn and within this a circlet inscribed *Monmouthshire* with the numerals *43* in the centre. On the main rays of the star the following battle honours are inscribed: *Corunna, F. d'Onoro, Toulouse. Vittoria, Badajoz, Nivelle, Salamanca, C. Rodrigo, Busaco* (Fig. 94).

45th Foot

A twelve-pointed star with the topmost point displaced by a crown. On this a wreath of laurel (left) and palm (right) with battle-honour scrolls on the wreath: (left) *Roleia, Vimiera*; (right) *Pyrenees, Ava*. Within the wreath a strap inscribed *1st Nottinghamshire Regt* and in the centre the numerals *45*. On the main rays of the star the following battle honours are inscribed: *Fuentes d'Onoro, Toulouse, Vittoria, Busaco, Nivelle, Peninsula, Orthes, Badajoz, Ciudad Rodrigo, Talavera, Salamanca* (Fig. 95).

46th Foot

On the standard star and crown plate a wreath of laurel (left), palm (right). Within this a strap inscribed *South Devon* with, in the centre, the numerals *46*. Below the strap a scroll inscribed *Dominica*. All gilt.

Grenadier company: As above but with a fused grenade in the centre. On the ball of the grenade a strap inscribed *South Devon* with in the centre the numerals *46*. On the base of the wreath a scroll inscribed *Dominica*.

Light company: As above but with a bugle-horn in the centre with the numerals *46* in the curl. On the base of the wreath a scroll inscribed *Dominica*. No name of regiment.

47th Foot

On the standard star-and-crown plate a wreath of laurel (left) and palm (right) within which a strap, inscribed *Lancashire*, and surmounted by the Royal Crest. In the centre the numerals *47*. Below the strap a scroll inscribed *Peninsula* and below this a Rose. On the main rays of the star the following battle-honours are inscribed: *Tarifa, Vittoria, St. Sebastian, Ava*.

48th Foot

A gilt star. On this a strap, inscribed *Northamptonshire* with, in the centre, the Roman numerals *XLVIII*, surrounded by a wreath of laurel (left) and palm (right). On the principal rays of the star the following battle-honours are inscribed: *Peninsula, Talavera, Albuhera, Badajoz, Salamanca, Vittoria, Pyrenees, Nivelle, Orthes, Toulouse, Douro*.

50th Foot

On the standard star-and-crown plate a complete laurel wreath with, on the left, two scrolls inscribed *Moodkee, Ferozeshah*, and, on the right, two scrolls inscribed *Aliwal, Sobraon*. At the foot of the wreath a further scroll inscribed *Peninsula*. Within the wreath a circlet inscribed *The Queen's Own* with the numerals *50* in the centre. Above the wreath a scroll inscribed *Royal West Kent* and below the wreath the Sphinx superscribed *Egypt*. On the main rays of the star the following battle honours are inscribed: *Vimiera, Corunna, Almaraz, Nive, Vittoria, Pyrenees, Orthes*. All gilt except *Royal West Kent* which is in silver (Fig. 96).

96

51st Foot

On the standard star-and-crown plate a wreath of laurel (left) and palm (right) with a scroll inscribed *Peninsula* across the bottom join of the wreath. Within the wreath a bugle-horn with the numerals *51* in the curl. On the main rays of the star the following battle honours are inscribed: *Minden, Pyrenees, Nivelle, Orthes, Waterloo, Vittoria, Salamanca, Corunna*. All in gilt. (Fig. 97.)

52nd Foot

On the standard star-and-crown plate a bugle with a bow of ribbon at the top of the strings and surmounted by a crown. The numerals *52* within the strings.

53rd Foot

On the standard star-and-crown plate within a laurel-wreath a circlet inscribed *Shropshire Regiment* with the numerals *53* in the centre. Below the crown a scroll inscribed *Peninsula*. On the main rays of the star the following battle-honours are inscribed: *Nieuport, St. Lucia, Nivelle, Tournay, Pyrenees, Salamanca, Toulouse, Talavera, Vittoria*.

97   98A

54th Foot

On the standard star-and-crown plate a laurel-wreath. Across the top a scroll inscribed *Marabout* and across the foot a scroll inscribed *Ava*. Within the wreath a strap with a rope edge inscribed *West Norfolk* and in the centre the numerals *54*. Below the bottom scroll the Sphinx superscribed *Egypt* (Fig. 98).

55th Foot

On the standard star-and-crown plate a wreath of laurel (left) and palm (right) on which is a scroll inscribed *China* across the bottom join of the wreath. Below this a China Dragon. Within the wreath a strap inscribed *Westmoreland* and, in the centre, the numerals *55*. All in gilt (Fig. 98A).

58th Foot

On the standard star-and-crown plate a laurel-wreath on which are battle-honour scrolls as follows: (across the top) *Maida, Orthes*; (left) *Vittoria, Salamanca*; (right) *Nivelle, Pyrenees*. Within the wreath a strap inscribed *Rutlandshire* with the numerals *58* in the centre. Above the strap the Castle and Key with a scroll below inscribed *Gibraltar*. Below the strap the Sphinx superscribed *Egypt*, below this a tri-part scroll inscribed *Montis Insignia Calpe* and at the base a scroll inscribed *Peninsula* (Fig. 99).

99

98

100

62nd Foot

On the standard star-and-crown plate a complete laurel-wreath. Within this a strap inscribed *Wiltshire* and in the centre the numerals *62*. On the four corner rays of the star the battle-honours: *Peninsula, Ferozeshah, Sobraon, Nive*. All in gilt. (Fig. 100.)

63rd Foot

On the standard star-and-crown plate a wreath of laurel (left) and palm (right) within which a strap inscribed *West Suffolk* and in the centre the numerals *63*. On the right horizontal ray of the star *Egmont-op-Zee*, on the left horizontal ray *Martinique* and on the lower vertical ray *Guadaloupe*. All in gilt.

Light company: A bugle with the numerals *63* in the strings surrounded by a wreath of laurel and palm.

Grenadier company: Within a wreath of laurel and palm a strap inscribed *West Suffolk* with the numerals *63* in the centre and grenade flames arising from the top.
Both on same star as Battalion officers above.

64th Foot *Grenadier company*

On the standard star-and-crown plate a wreath of laurel (left) and palm (right). Within this, a strap inscribed *Regiment* with grenade-flames arising from the top of the strap. In the centre the numerals *64*. Below the wreath the Stafford Knot. On left horizontal ray *St. Lucia*, on right horizontal ray *Surinam* (Fig. 101).

65th Foot

OFFICERS: On the standard star-and-crown plate a laurel-wreath. Within this a circlet inscribed *2D York North Riding* in silver and in the centre silver numerals *65*. On the centre-left point of the star the honour *India* in silver and on the right the honour *Arabia*. Across the lowest point of the star a silver Tiger.

OTHER RANKS

Battalion companies: On the standard star-and-crown plate a wreath of laurel (left) and palm (right). Within this a strap inscribed *2nd York North Riding* and in the centre the numerals *65*. Above the wreath a white-metal scroll inscribed *Arabia* and across the bottom of the wreath a similar scroll inscribed *India*. Below this a Tiger in white-metal.

Grenadier company: In place of the numerals *65* a fused grenade with *65* on the ball.

Light company: In place of the numerals *65* a bugle with *65* in the curl.

68th Foot

On the standard star-and-crown plate a wreath of laurel (left) and palm (right). Within this a bugle with the numerals *68* in the curl. On the main rays of the star the following battle honours are inscribed: (left) *Salamanca, Vittoria, Pyrenees*; (right) *Nivelle, Orthes, Peninsula* (Fig. 102).

73rd Foot

(1) On the standard star-and-crown plate a wreath of thistles (left) and laurel (right). Within this a circlet inscribed (top) *Mangalore*, (bottom) *Seringapatam*. In the centre the numerals *73*. Below the circlet a scroll inscribed *Waterloo*.

(2) On the standard star-and-crown plate a wreath of thistles (left) and laurel (right). Within this a strap inscribed *Regiment*. In the centre the numerals *73*. Below the wreath a scroll inscribed *Waterloo*.

76th Foot

On the standard star-and-crown plate a strap inscribed *Regiment* with the numerals *76* in the centre and surrounded by a wreath of laurel (left) and palm (right). Above the strap an Elephant. On the rays of the star the following battle-honours are inscribed: *Hindoostan, Peninsula, Nive.*

79th Foot

Officers' feathered bonnet: Star of the Order of the Thistle in gilt and silver surmounted by a gilt hackle socket of a thistle surrounded by a wreath. Other Ranks: St. Andrew within a wreath of thistles.

80th Foot

On the standard star-and-crown plate a wreath of laurel (left) and palm (right). Within this a strap inscribed *Stafford Volunteers* and, in the centre, the numerals *80*. Above the strap the Sphinx superscribed *Egypt*. Below the Stafford Knot (Fig. 103).

81st Foot

On the standard star-and-crown plate a wreath of laurel. Within this a strap inscribed *Loyal Lincoln Volunteers* with, in the centre, the Roman numerals *LXXXI*. On the wreath battle-honour scrolls (left) *Maida*, (right) *Corunna*. Below the wreath a further scroll inscribed *Peninsula* (Fig. 103A).

103   103A

82nd Foot

On the standard star-and-crown plate a wreath of laurel (left) and palm (right). Within this a strap inscribed *The Prince of Wales's Volunteers* with the numerals *82* in the centre. Across the bottom of the wreath a scroll inscribed *Peninsula*, and, above the strap, the Prince of Wales's plumes, coronet and motto. On the main rays of the star the following battle-honours are inscribed: *Roleia, Vimiera, Niagara, Pyrenees, Nivelle, Orthes* (Fig. 104).

84th Foot

Battalion companies: On the standard star-and-crown plate a wreath of laurel (left) and palm (right). Within this a strap inscribed *York & Lancaster* with the numerals *84* in the centre. Across the bottom of the wreath a scroll inscribed *Peninsula*. On the left-centre ray of the star *Nive* and, on the right, *India*. On the bottom point of the star a silver Rose.

Grenadier company: In the centre of the plate a fused grenade with *York & Lancaster* inscribed in a circlet on the ball and the numerals *84* in the centre.

Light company: In the centre of the plate a bugle inscribed *York & Lancaster* with the numerals *84* in the curl.

85th Foot

On the standard star-and-crown plate a wreath of laurel (left) and palm (right). Within this a bugle with the numerals *85* in the curl. On the four corner rays of the star the following battle honours are inscribed: *Fuentes d'Onor* (top left), *Peninsula* (bottom left), *Nive* (top right), *Bladensburg* (bottom right).

88th Foot

A twelve-pointed star with the topmost point displaced by a crown. On this a wreath of laurel (left) and palm (right), within which an oval inscribed *Connaught Rangers* with the numerals *88* in the centre. Above the wreath the Sphinx superscribed *Egypt*. Below, a scroll inscribed *Quis Separabit* with the Irish Harp below this. On the main rays of the star the following battle honours are inscribed: *Fuentes d'Onoro, Toulouse, Vittoria, Busaco, Nivelle, Peninsula, Salamanca, Talavera, Ciudad Rodrigo, Badajoz, Orthes* (Fig. 105).

89th Foot

On the standard star-and-crown plate a wreath of laurel (left) and palm (right). Within this a strap inscribed *Regiment* with the numerals *89* in the centre. Above the wreath a scroll inscribed *Niagara* and, below, the Sphinx superscribed *Egypt*. On the left-centre ray of the star *Java* and, on the right-centre ray, *Ava* (Fig. 106).

90th Foot

On the standard star-and-crown plate a wreath of laurel (left) and palm (right). Within this a bugle with the numerals *90* in the curl and surmounted by the Sphinx superscribed *Egypt*. On the left-centre ray of the star *Mandora*, on the right, *Martinique* and, on the bottom point, *Guadaloupe* (Fig. 107).

104

105

106

93rd Foot

Officers' feathered bonnet: Within a wreath of thistles a circlet inscribed *Sutherland Highlanders* and surmounted by a crown. In the centre the numerals *93*. Below the wreath a scroll inscribed *Cape of Good Hope*. The circlet in silver remainder gilt (Fig. 107A). Other Ranks: As officers but all in brass.

Flank companies: Grenade or bugle below.

95th Foot

On the standard star and crown plate a voided Garter with a Garter-blue backing. A ribbed silver centre with gilt numerals *95* superimposed (Fig. 107B).

98th Foot

On the standard star-and-crown plate a wreath of laurel (left) and palm (right). Within this a strap inscribed *Regiment* with the numerals *98* in the centre. Across the bottom join of the wreath a scroll inscribed *China* and below this the China Dragon (Fig. 108).

99th Foot

On the standard star-and-crown plate a wreath of laurel (left) and palm (right). Within this a strap inscribed *Lanarkshire* with the numerals *99* in the centre.

1st Madras (European) Fusiliers (later 102nd Foot)

A star of twelve points, the topmost point displaced by a Victorian crown having on the main rays the following battle-honours; (right) *Condore, Sholinghur, Pondicherry, Ternate*; (left) *Plassey, Wandewash, Nundy Droog, Amboyna*. In the centre of the star, a strap inscribed *Spectamur Agendo* with a Tiger in the centre. Above the strap a scroll inscribed *Arcot* and below the strap three scrolls inscribed *Banda, Mahidpore, Ava* (Fig. 109).

107A   107B

Rifle Brigade

A bugle-horn in blackened yellow-brass. Size 3½" wide (Fig. 110).

Above the bugle-horn at the base of the tufted ball plume a small Victorian crown in blackened metal mounted on a black cord boss.

108

110

109

CHAPTER 5

The French-Pattern Shako:
1855 to 1861

The Crimean War found the British and French as allies and gave the opportunity of com-paring dress. The superiority of the French head-dress was most noticeable when compared with the tall and clumsy 'Albert' shako (which, as previously mentioned, was discarded in favour of the forage cap for the greater part of the campaign), so a new head-dress based on the French pattern, was taken into use at the end of the war. It was authorised by Horse Guards Circular Memorandum dated 16th January 1855.

Dress Regulations of 1st April 1855 stated that the shako was to be of black felt, $5\frac{1}{4}''$ deep in front and $7\frac{1}{8}''$ deep behind, with a patent-leather sunk top turned over at the edge to a breadth of $\frac{3}{8}''$ and stitched; a band of similar material double-stitched $\frac{5}{8}''$ wide at the bottom. The front peak of patent leather was $2\frac{3}{8}''$ wide and a narrower back peak $1\frac{3}{8}''$ wide. It had a leather chin-strap, with a buckle on the right side, secured inside to the top of the cap.

A worsted ball-tuft, $2''$ in diameter and of the same colours as for the previous shako, was carried in a gilt socket and a bronze gorgon's-head at the back acted as a ventilator.

The shako-plate was of gilt in the form of an eight-pointed star surmounted by a crown, the whole measuring $3\frac{5}{8}''$ in extreme diameter and $4\frac{1}{8}''$ in depth. On the centre of the star, the Garter with pierced motto *Honi soit qui mal y pense* on a burnished gilt background and, in the centre, the regimental number in burnished gilt backed by a piece of black leather.

The Royal Marines and the Militia also wore this pattern shako.

The other-ranks' shako was similar to that of the officers, but made of stout felt, napped surface, the leather parts lacquered and the front- and back-peaks without binding. For ventilation, circular black-metal discs with seven holes were on each side; the ball tufts were the same as for the officers. The shako-plate was of the same size and design as the officers' but the background to the regimental number was painted black on horizontal ribs.

Although the regulation-pattern plate was as described above there were departures from it; some possibly by different manufacturers; others maybe because certain regiments had plates made to their own specification.

Specimens are found with the Garter solid instead of pierced, and the size of the Garter varies as does the shape of the star but for this pattern shako-plate the overall size is consistent.

Although, as was to be expected, Royal regiments had a backing of red velvet instead of black leather this was not confined to them.

The practice of incorporating special regimental devices in the badge was not nearly so prevalent with this pattern shako, the majority of regiments contenting themselves with just the regimental number.

111   112

A close examination of the illustrations of the badge will show some of the slight differences in design mentioned above. Both officers' and other-ranks' plates are included.

1st Foot
On the star, the Collar of the Order of the Thistle with St. Andrew and Cross pendant. In the centre, the letters *RR*, reversed and intertwined, with the numeral *1* below. Above the Collar a scroll inscribed *Royal Regiment* (Fig. 111).

3rd Foot
Officers: On the star within a pierced Garter the Dragon above the numeral *3* (Fig. 112).
Other Ranks: Within a pierced Garter the numeral *3* with a black-painted ribbed background (Fig. 113).

5th Foot
On the star within a pierced Garter the numeral *5* on a red velvet background (Fig. 114).

8th Foot
On the star a solid large-size Garter above which a tablet inscribed *King's*. Within the Garter a silver White Horse on a gilt ground with the Roman numerals *VIII* beneath on a red velvet background (Fig. 115).

113   114   115

116

14th Foot

Other Ranks: On the star within a solid Garter the numerals *14* with a black-painted ribbed background (Fig. 116).

18th Foot

In place of the Garter a circlet inscribed *Namurcensis praemium virtutis*. In the centre the Harp and Crown within a wreath of shamrocks (Fig. 116A).

27th Foot

On the star within a pierced Garter the Castle of Inniskilling in silver on a black-leather background. The numerals *27* are in silver above the Garter (Fig. 117).

28th Foot

On the star within a pierced Garter the numerals *28* (Fig. 118).

30th Foot

On the star within a pierced Garter the numerals *30* (Fig. 119).

33rd Foot

On the star within a pierced Garter the numerals *33* (Fig. 120).

120

38th Foot

Officers: On the star within a pierced Garter the numerals *38* with the Stafford Knot above. *Other Ranks*: On the star within a pierced Garter the numerals *38* with the Stafford Knot below.

48th Foot

On the star within a pierced Garter the numerals *48* (Fig. 121).

50th Foot

On the star within a pierced Garter the numerals *50* (Fig. 122).

117

119

118

121

122

124

123

123A

125

126

127

128

55th Foot
On the star within a pierced Garter the numerals *55* (Fig. 123).

60th Foot
On a round black corded boss a small blackened-brass Victorian crown with below a $3\frac{1}{2}''$ high plate consisting of a Maltese Cross with lions between the limbs. On the four arms of the cross the following battle-honours are inscribed. Top: *Orthes, Nive, Pyrenees, Vittoria, Nivelle.* Left: *Fuentes d'Onor, Ciudad Rodrigo, Albuhera, Badajoz.* Right: *Martinique, Talavera, Vimiera, Roleia.* Bottom: *Delhi, Punjaub, Mooltan, Goojerat.* A continuous scroll linking the top left and top right arms of the cross inscribed *Salamanca, Peninsula, Toulouse.* A similar scroll linking bottom left, bottom and bottom right arms of the Cross inscribed *Celer et audax.* In the centre of the Cross a circlet inscribed *The King's Royal Rifle Corps* and within this a strung bugle with the numerals *60* within the strings. In blackened-brass (Fig. 123A).

63rd Foot
On the star within a pierced Garter the numerals *63* (Fig. 124).

68th Foot
On the star, within a pierced Garter, a bugle-horn surmounted by the numerals *68* (Fig. 125).

82nd Foot
On the star within a pierced Garter the numerals *82* (Fig. 126).

89th Foot
On the star within a pierced Garter the numerals *89* (Fig. 127).

98th Foot
On the star within a pierced Garter the numerals *98* (Fig. 128).

Rifle Brigade
A bugle-horn in blackened-yellow-brass. Size $3\frac{1}{2}''$ wide. The same as worn on the Albert Shako (Fig. 110).

CHAPTER 6

The Quilted Shako:
1861 to 1869

The next pattern shako witnessed a complete departure from those worn previously. It consisted of dark blue cloth mounted on cork, ribbed from top to bottom, and is usually referred to as the 'Quilted' shako.

It was not so tall as the last, the height in front being 4″, the back 6¾″, and the flat top 5½″ by 6″. At the top of the back was a small gorgon's-head for ventilation. There was no back peak but the bottom edge was pointed. Round the base was a leather band, ⅝″ wide and double-stitched, with an oval metal buckle at the back. A chin-strap, ½″ wide of patent-leather, had a buckle for adjustment on the right side.

For the first time the shako showed the officer's rank; Colonels and Lieutenant-Colonels having two rows of regimental lace ¼″ apart around the top, and Majors one row.

The badge was a plain gilt eight-pointed star, the topmost point displaced by a crown. On the star was the Garter but the motto was not pierced as in the previous pattern; in the centre, the regimental number in stencilled figures. The size of the badge was 3¼″ deep by 2¾″ wide. The shako carried a ball-tuft of 1¾″ diameter of the same colours as for the previous shako.

Other-ranks wore a similar pattern to that of the officers but of lacquered leather ventilated by a black-metal disc high on each side. It carried a brass plate, of the same design as the officers', with stencilled numerals.

Apart from size, the main difference between the plate for this shako and its predecessor, should be that the Garter was not pierced. This was the Regulation—but many badges exist in the stipulated size with a pierced Garter! Some officers' badges have a fine wire mesh behind the centre and Garter which probably afforded additional ventilation.

Some Light Infantry and Rifle regiments did not wear the standard plate. The 60th Kings Royal Rifles Corps and the Rifle Brigade both wore a bronze bugle-horn and the 71st had a bugle-horn with the number of the regiment in the curl.

1st Foot
On the star, the Collar of the Order of the Thistle with St. Andrew and Cross pendant. In the centre the Royal Cypher *VR* with the numeral *1* below. Above the collar a scroll inscribed *Royal Regiment.* All gilt, centre and collar pierced, on ground of blue enamel (Fig. 129).

8th Foot

On the star within the Garter the White Horse on ground with the numeral *8* below. Above the Garter a scroll inscribed *Kings* (Fig. 129A).

9th Foot

On the star within the Garter the figure of Britannia seated holding an olive branch in her right hand and a trident in her left hand. The Union shield rests beside her and the Lion lying down. Below, the Roman numerals *IX* (Fig. 130).

13th Foot

Officers: On the star within the Garter a strung bugle-horn with the numerals *13* within the strings. Above this is a mural crown, over which a scroll inscribed *Jellalabad* (Fig. 131).
Other Ranks: On the star within a non-voided Garter the numerals *13*. Struck in one piece with cut-out figures (Fig. 132).

14th Foot

On the star within the Garter the White Horse on ground with a scroll above inscribed *Nec aspera terrent* and the numerals *14* below (Fig. 133).

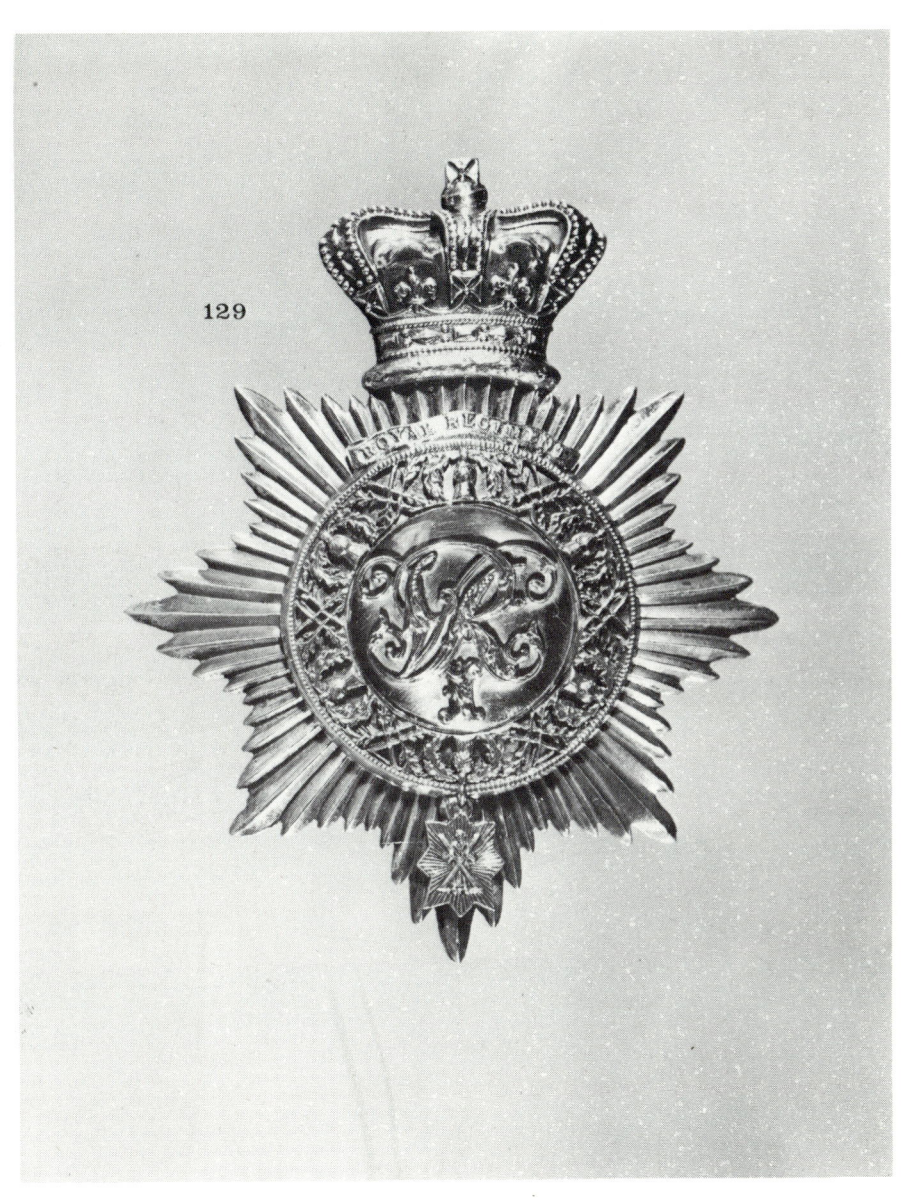

130

131

132

133

134

135

137

136

23rd Foot
On the star a voided Garter with wire mesh behind the centre and Garter. In the centre the numerals *23* (Fig. 134).

27th Foot
On the star within the Garter in silver the Castle of Inniskilling with St. George's flag flying from the centre turret. Below the Garter the numerals *27* in gilt (Fig. 135).

28th Foot
On the star within the Garter the numerals *28* (Fig. 136).

37th Foot
On the star within the Garter the numerals *37* (Fig. 137).

138   139

140   141   143

39th Foot
On the star within the Garter the numerals *39* (Fig. 138).

40th Foot
On the star within the Garter the numerals *40* (Fig. 139).

43rd Foot
On the star within the Garter a strung bugle-horn with the numerals *43* within the strings (Fig. 140).

44th Foot

On the star within the Garter the numerals *44* (Fig. 141).

45th Foot

On the star within the Garter the numerals *45* (Fig. 142).

142

48th Foot

On the star within the Garter the numerals *48* (Fig. 143).

52nd Foot

On the star within the Garter a strung bugle-horn with the numerals *52* within the strings (Fig. 144).

54th Foot

On the star within the Garter the numerals *54* (Fig. 145).

64th Foot

On the star a voided Garter with wire mesh behind the centre and Garter. In the centre the numerals *64* (Fig. 146).

65th Foot

On the star within the Garter a Tiger above the numerals *65*. A scroll above the Garter inscribed *India* and one below inscribed *Arabia* (Fig. 147).

83rd Foot

Other Ranks: On the star within a non-voided Garter the numerals *83*. Struck in one piece with cut-out figures (Fig. 148).

108th Foot

On the star a laurel-wreath within which a strap inscribed *Madras Infantry* with the numerals *108* in the centre. Across the base of the wreath a scroll inscribed *Central India* (Fig. 149).

109th Foot

On the star a laurel-wreath within which a strap inscribed *Bombay Infantry* with the numerals *109* in the centre. After 1863 across the bottom of the wreath a scroll inscribed *Central India*.

Rifle Brigade

A bugle-horn in blackened-yellow-brass size $3\frac{1}{2}''$ wide. The same as worn on the Albert and French Shakos (Fig. 110).

144

145

147

146

148

149

CHAPTER 7

The Last Shako:
1869 to 1878

The last shako was authorised by General Order 65 of June 1869, and was worn by all Infantry Regiments until 1878 and by Depot Companies until 1881. It was also worn by Departmental Corps, the Militia, many of the Volunteer Rifle Corps and the Royal Marines. It was not worn by Fusilier, Rifle, or the majority of Highland, Regiments.

Like the previous shako, it was of dark blue cloth mounted on cork and was very similar in size, being 4″ high in front and $6\frac{1}{2}$″ at the back. Round the top were two lines of gold braid $\frac{1}{4}$″ wide and $\frac{1}{4}$″ apart but Colonels and Lieutenant-Colonels had two lines $\frac{1}{2}$″ wide of special-pattern lace instead of the braid. Round the bottom was another line of gold braid, one line up each side slanting forward from the side-ornaments and one line up the back.

It had a patent-leather peak and for side ornaments small gilt roses, the right-hand one having a small brass hook for adjusting the chin-chain which was lined with black velvet. At the top-back of the shako was a gilt lion's-head with a hook from its mouth for securing the chin-chain when not in use.

For this shako, the star device was dispensed with, and the new design consisted of a gilt laurel-wreath surmounted by a crown enclosing the Garter, inscribed with the motto *Honi soit qui mal y pense*, within which was the regimental number in cut-out or stencil form. The plate measured 3″ wide and $3\frac{1}{4}$″ high.

Those for non-commissioned officers were gilt but of the same design as for the rank-and-file whose plates were made of gilding-metal. In every instance, including the Light Infantry Regiments, the regimental number was cut-out or stencilled within the Garter.

The officers' plates were affixed to the shako by two small copper shanks which pierced the wall of the head-dress. These were positioned on the reverse of the laurel-wreath, horizontally, just below the half-way line. The other-ranks' badge was struck in one piece and, in this case, the two shanks were positioned horizontally on the reverse of the Garter at the half-way line. These were more robust than those on the officers' plates, and the plate itself was made of a heavier-gauge metal.

Black-velvet backing was usually worn in the centre of the officers' plates but there were exceptions. Some Royal Regiments had crimson; the 1st Bn. Royal Scots also had crimson and the 2nd Bn., green.

An illustration showing the standard design is shown in Fig. 168 but as usual there were variations in the officers' patterns and these are shown below.

1st Foot

In place of the Garter, the Collar of the Order of the Thistle, with an ornamental figure *1* immediately below the Royal Cypher. A small scroll inscribed *Royal Regiment* appears just below the crown. All in gilt (Fig. 150).

2nd Foot

In the centre the Paschal Lamb with the numeral *2* below. All in gilt. Also found all in silver (Fig. 151).

3rd Foot

In the centre the Dragon with the numeral *3* below. All in gilt. Also found all in silver.

4th Foot

In the centre the Lion of England with the numeral *4* below. All in gilt.

6th Foot

In the centre the Antelope with the numeral *6* below. All in silver.

8th Foot

In the centre the White Horse of Hanover on Ground in silver with the Roman numerals *VIII* below in gilt (Fig. 151A).

9th Foot

In the centre the figure of Britannia seated with trident and shield depicting the Great Union, the Lion of England lying down beside her, and with the Roman numerals *IX* below. All in silver (Fig. 152).

10th Foot

On the bottom join of the wreath the Sphinx superscribed *Egypt*. In silver.

152

12th Foot

In the centre, the Castle and Key of Gibraltar with a scroll inscribed *Montis Insignia Calpe* below, and a scroll inscribed *Gibraltar* above. All in silver (Fig. 153).

13th Foot

In the centre, a bugle-horn with the numerals *13* within the strings and surmounted by a mural crown superscribed *Jellalabad*. All in silver. Also found all in gilt (Fig. 154).

14th Foot

In the centre the White Horse of Hanover with a scroll above inscribed *Nec aspera terrent* and the numerals *14* below. All in silver (Fig. 155).

151ᴬ

153

17th Foot
    (1) On the bottom join of the wreath the Royal Tiger. All in gilt (Fig. 156).
    (2) In the centre the Royal Tiger above the numerals *17*. All in silver (Fig. 157).

18th Foot
In place of the Garter, a circlet inscribed *Virtutis Namurcensis Praemium* and in the centre a crowned Harp within a wreath of shamrocks. All in gilt (Fig. 158).

20th Foot
On the bottom join of the wreath the Sphinx superscribed *Egypt*. In silver (Fig. 159).

24th Foot
On the bottom join of the wreath the Sphinx superscribed *Egypt*. In gilt (Fig. 160).

25th Foot
In the centre, the Castle of Edinburgh and the numerals *25* below. On the bottom join of the wreath a scroll inscribed *Nisi Dominus Frustra*. All in silver.

26th Foot
On the bottom join of the wreath the Sphinx superscribed *Egypt*. In gilt.

27th Foot
In the centre, the Castle of Inniskilling in silver. At the bottom join of the wreath the numerals *27* in gilt (Fig. 161).

28th Foot
On the bottom join of the wreath the Sphinx superscribed *Egypt* in silver. Also in gilt (Fig. 162).
A small gilt Sphinx was worn on the back of the shako.

38th Foot
On the bottom join of the wreath the Stafford Knot in silver.

39th Foot
In the centre the Castle and Key of Gibraltar with a scroll inscribed *Gibraltar* above and a similar scroll inscribed *Montis Insignia Calpe* below. On the bottom join of the wreath a scroll inscribed *Primus in Indis*. The centre in silver and the bottom scroll in gilt (Fig. 163).

41st Foot
In the centre the Prince of Wales's plumes, coronet and motto with the numerals *41* below. All in silver.

47th Foot
On the bottom join of the wreath a Rose in gilt (Fig. 164).

51st Foot
On the bottom join of the wreath the Sphinx superscribed *Egypt*. In silver.

54th Foot
  (1) On the bottom join of the wreath the Sphinx superscribed *Egypt*. In silver. Also in gilt (Fig. 165).
  (2) As above but with a much larger Sphinx and tablet (Fig. 166).
  (3) As (2) but the Sphinx superscribed *Marabout* (Fig. 167).

55th Foot
On the bottom join of the wreath the China Dragon in silver.

150
151
154

155
156
157

158
159
160

60th Foot

Astrakhan busby, 1873–78. A cross based on that of the Order of the Bath with lions between the limbs. On the arms of the cross the following battle-honours are inscribed. Top: *Roleia, Vimiera, Martinique, Talavera, Albuhera.* Left: *Badajoz, Vittoria, Fuentes d'Onor, Salamanca, Pyrenees.* Right: *Nivelle, Nive, Ciudad Rodrigo, Toulouse, Orthes.* Bottom: *Delhi, Punjaub, Mooltan, Goojerat, Taku Forts, Pekin.* Above the Cross a scroll inscribed *Peninsula.* Below the Cross a scroll inscribed *Celer et audax.* In the centre of the Cross a circlet inscribed *The King's Royal Rifle Corps.*, with in the centre a bugle-horn with strings and the numerals *60* within the strings. In blackened-brass (Fig. 167A).

61st Foot

On the bottom join of the wreath the Sphinx superscribed *Egypt.* In silver.

68th Foot

In the centre a bugle-horn with the numerals *68* in the curl.

64th Foot

On the bottom join of the wreath the Prince of Wales's plumes, coronet and motto in silver.

65th Foot

The crown replaced by a coronet. In the centre a Tiger above a chevron inscribed *India-Arabia.* Below the numerals *65.* All in silver.

76th Foot

The numerals *76* in the centre. This example shows the standard design (Fig. 168).

171   172   173

162

163

164

165

167A

166

168

169

170

77th Foot
    (1) In the centre the Prince of Wales's plumes, coronet and motto with the numerals *77* below in silver (Fig. 169).
    (2) Similar to above but the numerals in a different form (Fig. 170).

80th Foot
In the centre the Roman numerals *LXXX*.

82nd Foot
In the centre the Prince of Wales's plumes, coronet and motto with the numerals *82* below. In silver (Fig. 171).

84th Foot
On the bottom join of the wreath a Rose. In silver. Also found in gilt and silver (Fig. 172).

86th Foot
In the centre a crowned Harp. The Garter replaced by a strap inscribed *Quis Separabit*. In gilt (Fig. 173).

174

88th Foot

In place of the Garter a circlet inscribed *Connaught Rangers*. In the centre a Harp with the numerals *88* below. On the bottom join of the wreath a scroll inscribed *Quis Separabit*. All in silver (Fig. 174).

94th Foot

On the bottom join of the wreath an Elephant. In silver.

96th Foot

On the bottom join of the wreath the Sphinx superscribed *Egypt*. In gilt.

97th Foot

On the bottom join of the wreath a scroll inscribed *Quo fas et gloria ducunt*. In gilt.

98th Foot

On the bottom join of the wreath the China Dragon. In silver.

100th Foot

In place of the Garter a circlet inscribed *Prince of Wales's Royal Canadian Regiment*. In the centre the Prince of Wales's plumes, coronet and motto and below this the numerals *100* (Fig. 175).

175   176

105th Foot

In place of the Garter a second wreath of half-laurel, half-palm. On this, a bugle-horn inscribed *Madras Light Infty* with the numerals *105* in the curl. Below a scroll inscribed *Cede Nullis* (Fig. 176).

107th Foot

A small Maltese cross on which a laurel-wreath. Within this a strap inscribed *Bengal Infantry*. In a voided centre the numerals *107*. All in silver (Fig. 177).

108th Foot

Within the laurel-wreath a second smaller laurel-wreath surrounding a strap inscribed *Madras Infantry*. In a voided centre the numerals *108*. On the bottom join of the wreath a scroll inscribed *Central India*.

109th Foot

Within the laurel-wreath a second smaller laurel-wreath surrounding a strap inscribed *Bombay Infantry*. In a voided centre the numerals *109*. On the bottom join of the wreath a scroll inscribed *Central India*.

Light Infantry Regiments

The 13th had a special design (Fig. 153) but the 32nd, 43rd, 51st, 52nd, 85th, 90th and 106th all wore a plate depicting a strung bugle and the regimental number within the Garter.

There is in existence, however, a plate of the 85th Light Infantry which is of the standard pattern with cut-out numerals *85* and without the bugle-horn.

Highland Regiments

71st: A bugle-horn with the numerals *71* in the curl.
74th: The Cross of St. Andrew on a star of four-points on which a circlet inscribed *Highlanders* with the numerals *74* in the centre (Fig. 178).
91st: The Cross of St. Andrew on a star of four-points on which a strap inscribed *Argyllshire Highlanders* with the numerals *91* in the centre.
   (1) Silver numerals on a gilt plate (Fig. 178A).
   (2) Gilt numerals on wire mesh (Fig. 178B).
Other ranks was similar but all brass.

Rank-and-File Plates

All the plates of the rank-and-file were of gilding-metal and in every instance, including the Light Infantry Regiments, the regimental number was cut-out or stencilled within the Garter.

Two examples are shown: the 1st Foot (Fig. 179) and the 64th Foot (Fig. 180).

Army Service Corps

Officers: In the centre the letters *ASC* entwined. All in gilt (Fig. 181).
Other Ranks: In the centre the letters *ASC* entwined but differing slightly from the officers' pattern. All in gilding-metal (Fig. 182).

178

178A

178B

Army Medical Department
In place of the Garter a rope circle in the centre of which a Red Cross in red enamel. All in gilt (Fig. 183).

Army Hospital Corps
Similar to the officers' of the Army Medical Department but in gilding-metal and with the Red Cross in red cloth.

Royal Staff Corps
In the centre the Royal Cypher *VR*. All in gilt.

177   179   180

181   182   183

CHAPTER 8

The Cloth Helmet:
1878 to 1881

No doubt the outcome of the Franco-Prussian War of 1870 to 1871 influenced the Dress Authorities to model the full-dress head-dress of the Infantry on the lines of the German helmet rather than the French shako, on which it had been based hitherto.

The first mention of the new pattern is in General Order 35 of 1st June 1877, which laid down that officers serving overseas in the Mediterranean, West Indies, Bermuda, Cape of Good Hope, St. Helena, Mauritius, Dominion of Canada and West African Settlements would wear a helmet covered in white cloth and worn without a puggaree. These were to be ornamented on the front with crowned star plates, 5″ in height and 4¼″ wide, with the number of the regiment in the centre within a Garter inscribed *Honi soit qui mal y pense* surrounded by a laurel-wreath.

Officers of regiments authorised to wear a special device on their shako-plates were to continue the same devices on their helmet-plates.

In accordance with this Order, the universal star-and-crown helmet-plate was adopted by all infantry regiments, including Highland regiments, in the stations named. It did not, however, include Fusilier or Rifle regiments.

In 1878, by authority of General Order No. 40 of 1st May, this helmet became the full-dress wear for home, but covered in blue cloth instead of white and with green cloth for Light Infantry and Rifle regiments.

As regards the helmet itself, it was made of cork, covered with blue (or dark-green for Light Infantry) cloth, peaks front and back, the front peak bound with metal and the back peak with patent-leather. A curb-chain chin-strap was lined with patent-leather and backed with black velvet. There were rose fastenings at the sides and a convex bar down the centre of the back and to the bottom of the back peak. At the top of the helmet was a spike mounted on a cross-piece base.

Some of the designs on officers' plates were as follows (only the design of the centre or additions to the standard pattern are given):

1st Foot
The Garter omitted. Within the laurel-wreath the Collar of the Order of the Thistle with St. Andrew and Cross in the centre. A scroll above inscribed *The Royal Scots* and a scroll below inscribed *Nemo me impune lacessit*. All gilt except St. Andrew which is in silver. A blue-enamel ground to St. Andrew and the Collar of the Order of the Thistle (Fig. 184).

4th Foot

On a black-velvet ground the Lion of England above the Roman numerals *IV*. The laurel-wreath in gilt for the 1st Battalion and in silver for the 2nd Battalion.

6th Foot

The Antelope ducally gorged and chained standing on ground above the Roman numerals *VI* (Fig. 185).

8th Foot

On a red-velvet ground the White Horse of Hanover in silver standing on a gilt mound. Below this the Roman numerals *VIII* in gilt (Fig. 186).

10th Foot

The Sphinx superscribed *Egypt*. Below this the numerals *10* (Fig. 187).

11th Foot

On a black velvet ground the numerals *11* in gilt.

12th Foot

On a red-velvet ground the Castle and Key in silver. Above the Garter a silver scroll inscribed *Gibralter* and below the Garter a silver scroll inscribed *Montis Insignia Calpe* (Fig. 188).

13th Foot

(1) On a black-velvet ground a bugle-horn surmounted by a mural crown and above this a scroll inscribed *Jellalabad*. Within the strings of the bugle the Roman numerals *XIII*. All in silver.

(2) As above but with the numerals *13* in gilt.

14th Foot

The White Horse of Hanover with a scroll above inscribed *Nec aspera terrent*. Below the Horse the numerals *14* (Fig. 189).

17th Foot

The Royal Tiger above the numerals *17*. All in silver.

19th Foot

On a black-leather ground a gilt Rose beneath which the Roman numerals *XIX*. Across the base of the wreath a gilt scroll inscribed *The Princess of Wales's Own* (Fig. 190).

20th Foot

On a black-velvet ground the numerals *20* in gilt. Below the Garter the Sphinx superscribed *Egypt* (Fig. 191).

24th Foot

On a black-velvet ground the Sphinx superscribed *Egypt*. Below this the Roman numerals *XXIV*.

186

190

188

193

194

202

198

203

26th Foot

On a black-velvet ground a mullet. At the top join of the wreath the numerals *26*. Below the Garter a scroll inscribed *Cameronians*. In gilt.

27th Foot

On a red-velvet ground in silver the Castle of Inniskilling with St. George's flag flying from the centre turret.
Below, the numerals *27* (Fig. 192).

29th Foot

In the centre the numerals *29*. This pattern was never taken into general use as the 29th were due to go to India and officers joining were ordered to obtain a shako for the sake of uniformity. (*Firm*, The Magazine of the Worcestershire Regiment, October, 1947.)

30th Foot

On a black-velvet ground the numerals *30*. On the base of the wreath the Sphinx superscribed *Egypt*. In gilt.

32nd Foot

A strung bugle-horn with the Roman numerals *XXXII* within the strings on a green-velvet ground, all within the Garter in gilt superimposed on a silver star 2·54″ high by 2·34″ wide. The rays of the star have beaded edges. All within the standard gilt laurel-wreath.

33rd Foot

On a black-velvet ground a circlet inscribed with the motto of the Duke of Wellington, *Virtutis fortuna comes* and within this his crest viz.: Out of a ducal coronet a demi-lion rampant holding a forked pennon flowing to the sinister one third per pale from the staff charged with the Cross of St. George. At the junction of the laurel-wreath the numerals *33*. All in silver.

34th Foot

   (1) On a black-velvet ground a silver laurel-wreath and within this the numerals *34*.
   (2) On a centre of red-and-white enamel, in gilt, the numerals *34*. Below the Garter a silver scroll inscribed *Arroyo dos Molinos*.

36th Foot

On a green-cloth ground the numerals *36*. Below the Garter a scroll inscribed *Firm* in silver.

38th Foot

The numerals *38* in gilt in the centre. Below the Garter the Stafford Knot in silver.

40th Foot

On a black-velvet ground the numerals *40* in gilt. Below the Garter the Sphinx superscribed *Egypt* in silver.

41st Foot

On a red-velvet ground in silver the Prince of Wales's plumes, coronet and motto. Below this in silver the numerals *41* (Fig. 193).

44th Foot

On a black-velvet ground the Sphinx superscribed *Egypt*. Below this the numerals *44*.

184   185   187

189   191   192   195

45th Foot

On a red-velvet ground the numerals *45* in gilt. Beneath the Garter, in silver, a scroll inscribed *Sherwood Foresters* (Fig. 194).

46th Foot

On a black-velvet ground the numerals *46* in gilt.

48th Foot

On a black-velvet ground the numerals *48* in gilt (Fig. 195).

50th Foot

The White Horse of Kent. A silver scroll above inscribed *Queen's Own* and on the base a silver Sphinx superscribed *Egypt*.

51st Foot

A silver bugle-horn with the numerals *51* in the curl and a silver rose at juncture of points of the laurel-wreath.

53rd Foot

(1) The numerals *53* in the centre. Below the Garter a scroll inscribed *The Shropshire Regiment*.

(2) As above but without the scroll (Fig. 196).

55th Foot
The numerals *55* in the centre. Below the Garter in silver the China Dragon.

57th Foot
On a black-velvet ground the numerals *57*.

60th Foot
A Maltese Cross with lions between the limbs. On the four arms of the cross the following battle-honours are inscribed. Top: *Roleia, Vimiera, Martinique, Talavera, Albuhera*. Left: *Badajoz, Vittoria, Fuentes d'Onor, Salamanca, Pyrenees*. Right: *Nivelle, Nive, Ciudad Rodrigo, Toulouse, Orthes*. Bottom: *Delhi, Punjaub, Mooltan, Goojerat, Taku Forts, Pekin*. Above the cross a scroll inscribed *Peninsula* and surmounted by a Victorian crown. Below the cross a scroll inscribed *Celer et audax*. In the centre of the cross a circlet inscribed *The King's Royal Rifle Corps* and within this on a red cloth ground a strung bugle-horn with the numerals *60* within the strings. In blackened-white-metal (Fig. 196A).
Note: The same badge was worn from 1881–83 but without the numerals *60*.

63rd Foot
On a black-velvet ground the numerals *63* in gilt.

64th Foot
On a black-velvet ground the numerals *64* in gilt (Fig. 197).

65th Foot
The Royal Tiger above a chevron inscribed *India-Arabia*. Below, the numerals *65*. All in silver.

66th Foot
On a black-velvet ground the numerals *66* in gilt.

67th Foot
On a black-velvet ground in silver the Royal Tiger above the numerals *67* (Fig. 198).

71st Foot
On a black-velvet ground a bugle-horn with the numerals *71* in the curl.

76th Foot
On a black-velvet ground an elephant with howdah above the numerals *76*. All in silver.

79th Foot
A thistle, with two leaves, surmounted by a crown. On the base of the wreath the numerals *79*.

80th Foot
On a black-velvet ground the numerals *80* in gilt.

82nd Foot
The Prince of Wales's plumes, coronet and motto. **Below this the numerals *82*** (Fig. 199).

83rd Foot
On a black-velvet ground the Irish Harp surmounted by a Victorian crown in silver. Below the Garter a silver scroll inscribed *Quis Separabit*.

84th Foot
A silver Rose in the centre. On the base of the Garter in silver the numerals *84*.

85th Foot
A strung bugle with the numerals *85* within the strings.

88th Foot
The Irish Harp above the numerals *88*. Below the Garter a scroll inscribed *Quis Separabit*.

89th Foot
The Garter omitted. In the centre a circlet inscribed *Princess Victoria's Regiment* and within this the Sphinx superscribed *Egypt* above the numerals *89*. Above the circlet, two scrolls inscribed *Java, Ava* and below the circlet two scrolls inscribed *Niagara, Sevastopol*. All in gilt (Fig. 200).

94th Foot
On a black-velvet ground the numerals *94* in gilt. Beneath the Garter a silver Elephant.

96th Foot
The Sphinx superscribed *Egypt*. Below this the numerals *96* (Fig. 201).

97th Foot
On a black-velvet ground the numerals *97* in gilt. On the base of the wreath a scroll inscribed *Quo fas et gloria ducunt*.

98th Foot
On a red-velvet ground the Prince of Wales's plumes, coronet and motto. Below this the Roman numerals *XCVIII*. Across the base of the Garter the China Dragon. All in silver (Fig. 202).

105th Foot
The Garter omitted. Within the laurel-wreath a second wreath of laurel (left) and palm (right) with, across the base of the wreath, a scroll inscribed *Cede Nullis*. In the centre, and extending into the wreath on either side, a bugle-horn inscribed *Madras Light Infty*. Within the curl of the bugle the numerals *105* on a red-velvet ground. All in gilt (Fig. 203).

108th Foot
The Garter omitted. Within the laurel-wreath a second wreath of laurel with, across the base of the wreath a scroll inscribed *Central India*. Within the wreath a strap inscribed *Madras Infantry* and in the centre the numerals *108*.

109th Foot
On a black-velvet ground the numerals *109* in gilt.

The other-ranks' helmet-plate was of gilding-metal with a voided centre. In this was a detachable circular plate, bearing the number of the regiment, which fitted into the Garter belt and had a tag at the base for this purpose. In some instances a plate of special design, instead of the regimental number, was worn.

Judging from photographs of this period it would appear that some regiments did not adopt the new plate for their helmets but transferred to it the plate worn on the last shako. Groups taken as late as 1881 show officers with the new plate but non-commissioned officers wearing the previous badge.

As representative of this pattern eight examples are shown:

13th Foot
The numerals *13* in the centre (Fig. 204).

49th Foot
The back-plate and the inset with the numerals *49* are shown separately to illustrate the method of fixing (Figs. 205 and 206).

65th Foot
In place of the number the United Red-and-White Rose in white-metal and gilding-metal (Fig. 207).

67th Foot
The numerals *67* in the centre (Fig. 208).

75th Foot
The numerals *75* in the centre (Fig. 209).

80th Foot
The numerals *80* in the centre (Fig. 210).

97th Foot
The numerals *97* in the centre (Fig. 211).

99th Foot
The numerals *99* in the centre (Fig. 212).
Note that the tag at the base of the inset-plate prevents this being confused with the 66th Foot.

60th The King's Royal Rifle Corps
In 1878 the busby was superseded by a helmet made of black felt with bronze binding, spike, chain and plate. The design for this was:

A Maltese cross with a lion between each division. On the arms of the cross the following battle-honours are inscribed: (top) *Roleia, Vimiera, Martinique, Talavera, Albuhera*; (left) *Badajoz, Vittoria, Fuentes d'Onor, Salamanca, Pyrenees*; (right) *Nivelle, Nive, Ciudad Rodrigo, Toulouse, Orthes*; (bottom) *Delhi, Punjaub, Mooltan, Goojerat, Taku Forts, Pekin*. In the centre of the cross a circlet inscribed *The King's Royal Rifle Corps* and within this a strung-bugle with the numerals *60* within the strings. Above the cross a scroll inscribed *Peninsula* surmounted by a Victorian crown. Below the cross a scroll inscribed *Celer et Audax*. In bronze with scarlet-cloth backing to the centre.

The Rifle Brigade also had their own special pattern plate.

The Rifle Brigade

A white-metal star 5″ deep. The star having eight points and on the star a laurel-wreath with scrolls inscribed: (left) *Peninsula, Alma, Inkerman*; (right) *Sevastopol, Lucknow, Ashantee*, and across the base of the wreath a scroll inscribed *The Prince Consort's Own*. Within the wreath, a cross similar to that of the Order of the Bath with, on the arms, the following battle-honours: (top) *Ciudad Rodrigo, Copenhagen, Corunna, Busaco*; (left) *Monte Video, Barossa, Roleia, Orthes*; (right) *Fuentes d'Onor, Badajoz, Vimiera, Nivelle*; (bottom) *Salamanca, Toulouse, Vittoria, Nive*. In the centre of the cross a circlet inscribed *Rifle Brigade*. Within this a bugle with strings surmounted by a crown. Above the cross a tablet inscribed *Waterloo* surmounted by a Guelphic crown. (Fig. 213.)

213   213A

204

205

206

207

208

209

210

211

212

CHAPTER 9

The Cloth Helmet:
Officers' Badges of 1881 to 1914

The main feature of the Cardwell reforms of 1881 was the disappearance of the old regimental numbers, which were replaced by territorial titles.

Regiments, therefore, required new devices on their helmet plates and, as the Militia and Volunteers had now become integral parts of the regiment, the opportunity was taken in some instances to incorporate their special devices in the new designs. (Collar badges were also introduced at this time but they are outside the scope of the present work.)

The helmet plate, in gilt or gilding-metal, was an eight-pointed star surmounted by the crown; on the star a laurel-wreath; within the wreath the Garter inscribed with the Garter motto. Within the Garter, the badge approved for the regiment in gilt, silver or a combination of both. On the bottom of the wreath a silver scroll with the designation of the regiment.

With the kind permission of Her Majesty's Stationery Office, we reproduce the full description of these badges as they appeared in the 1883 Dress Regulations which were the first to be published after the reorganisation.

A note is made where an alteration was notified in a later Dress Regulations. Also all plates were altered following the death of Queen Victoria: the Victorian crown, wherever it appeared, being replaced in 1902 by the Imperial crown. When the only difference in the plate was in the design of the crown, we have not thought it necessary to show both types.

For the sake of completeness, we have included in this chapter the badges worn on other head-dress by the Highland regiments, the Highland Light Infantry and the Rifle regiments. The grenade worn by Fusilier regiments is described in Chapter 18.

The Royal Scots (Lothian Regiment)

The Garter and universal wreath are omitted. The Star of the Order of the Thistle in gilt metal. On the Star, a silver Thistle within a silver circle pierced with the motto *Nemo me impune lacessit* all on a convex ground of green enamel. On the universal scroll *The Lothian Regt* (Fig. 213A).

In 1891, the title on the universal scroll was altered to read *The Royal Scots* and, in 1904, the regiment ceased to wear the helmet.

214

216

215

217

218

219

220

221

The Queen's (Royal West Surrey Regiment)

On a scarlet-velvet ground the Paschal Lamb in silver. On the universal scroll *The Royal West Surrey Regiment* (Fig. 214).

In 1911, an additional scroll was placed above the Garter inscribed *The Queen's* (Fig. 215).

The Buffs (East Kent Regiment)

On a black-velvet ground the Dragon in silver. On the universal scroll *The East Kent Regiment.*

In 1900, an additional scroll was placed above the Garter inscribed *The Buffs* (Fig. 216).

The King's Own (Royal Lancaster Regiment)

In silver, on a scarlet-velvet ground, the Lion of England. On the universal scroll *Royal Lancaster Regt.*

In 1900, the ground in the centre was changed to crimson and, in 1911, the title on the universal scroll was altered to *The Royal Lancaster Regiment* and an additional scroll was placed above the Garter inscribed *The King's Own* (Fig. 217).

The Royal Warwickshire Regiment

On a black-velvet ground the Antelope in silver with gilt collar and chain. On the universal scroll *The Royal Warwickshire Regiment* (Fig. 218).

Another version shows the Antelope with one fore-foot raised (Fig. 219).

The King's (Liverpool Regiment)

In silver, on a crimson-velvet ground, the White Horse with scroll above inscribed, in old English capitals, *Nec aspera terrent.* On the universal scroll *The Liverpool Regiment* (Fig. 220).

In 1911, an additional scroll was placed above the Garter inscribed *The King's* (Fig. 221).

The Norfolk Regiment

The figure of Britannia, in silver, on a black-velvet ground. On the universal scroll *The Norfolk Regiment* (Fig. 222).

A later version shows Britannia with hand raised (Fig. 223).

The Lincolnshire Regiment

In silver, on a black-velvet ground, the Sphinx over *Egypt.* On the universal scroll *The Lincolnshire Regt* (Fig. 224). A later version has the spelling *Regiment.*

The Devonshire Regiment

The Castle of Exeter, with scroll inscribed *Semper Fidelis* in silver on a black-velvet ground. On the universal scroll *The Devonshire Regiment* (Fig. 225). A later version has the spelling *Regt.*

The Suffolk Regiment

In silver, on a black-velvet ground, the Castle and Key with scroll above inscribed *Gibraltar,* and scroll below inscribed *Montis Insignia Calpe.* On the universal scroll *The Suffolk Regiment* (Fig. 226).

In 1900, in accordance with War Office Instruction of 30th January, the Castle and Key were redesigned (Fig. 227).

222

224

223

225

226

227

228

229

The Prince Albert's (Somerset Light Infantry)
In silver, on a black-velvet ground, a bugle with strings surmounted by a mural crown with scroll above inscribed *Jellalabad*; the Sphinx over *Egypt* within the strings of the bugle. On the universal scroll *Somerset Light Infantry* (Fig. 228). Before 1912 *Somersetshire*. In 1912 the title on the universal scroll was altered to read *Somerset Light Infantry*.

The Prince of Wales's Own (West Yorkshire Regiment)
In silver, on a black-velvet ground, the White Horse with motto *Nec aspera terrent* on a scroll above. On the universal scroll *The West Yorkshire Regiment* (Fig. 229).
In 1904, the ground in the centre was changed to red-velvet and, in 1911, to scarlet-velvet.

The East Yorkshire Regiment
In gilt metal, on a ground of black-enamel, a laurel-wreath on an eight-pointed star. Within the wreath the White Rose in silver. On the universal scroll *The East Yorkshire Regt* (Fig. 230).
In 1894, the title on the universal scroll was altered to *The East Yorkshire Regiment*.

The Bedfordshire Regiment
In silver, on a raised ground of blue-enamel, an eight-pointed star; on the star, in gilt metal, a Maltese cross. Within a gilt circle on the cross, a Hart, in silver, crossing a ford. On the universal scroll *The Bedfordshire Regiment*. A later version has the spelling *Regt*.
In 1900, the ground in the centre was changed to black-velvet. (Fig. 231.)

The Leicestershire Regiment
On a black-velvet ground, the Royal Tiger in silver, with silver scroll above inscribed *Hindoostan*. On the universal scroll *Leicestershire Regiment*.
In 1904, the title on the scroll was altered to *The Leicestershire Regiment* (Fig. 232).

The Royal Irish Regiment
In silver, on a scarlet ground, the Harp and Crown within a wreath of shamrock. On the universal scroll *The Royal Irish* (Fig. 233).
In 1904, the title on the scroll was altered to *The Royal Irish Regiment*.
The first striking of the plate with the Imperial crown had a different arrangement of the shamrock-wreath to the later pattern (Fig. 234).

The Princess of Wales's Own (Yorkshire Regiment)
On a black-velvet ground, the Cypher of H.R.H. the Princess of Wales combined with a cross and surmounted by the Coronet of the Princess. On the centre of the cross, the figures *1875*. The Cypher and Coronet in gilt metal; the cross in silver. On the universal scroll *The Yorkshire Regiment* (Fig. 235).
In 1904, the title on the scroll was altered to read *The Princess of Wales's Own Yorkshire Regiment*.
In 1911, following the accession of the Princess of Wales as Queen Alexandra, the description of the badge was altered to read as follows: on a ground of black-velvet, the Cypher of H.M. Queen Alexandra as Princess of Wales combined with the Dannebrog and surmounted by the Coronet of the Princess, in silver. On the centre of the cross the figures *1875* and the word *Alexandra*. On the universal scroll *The Yorkshire Regt. Princess of Wales*. The White Rose in the centre of the scroll (Fig. 236).

230

232

231

233

235

234

236

237

The Cheshire Regiment

In silver, on a black-velvet ground, an eight-pointed star. Within a gilt circle on the star, the Prince of Wales's Plume on a burnished silver ground. On the universal scroll *The Cheshire Regiment*.

In 1900, the Prince of Wales's Plume to be in silver and the Coronet in gilt (Fig. 237).

The South Wales Borderers

In silver, on a black-velvet ground, the Welsh Dragon within a laurel-wreath. On the universal scroll *The South Wales Borderers* (Fig. 238).

The King's Own Borderers

In silver, on a black-velvet ground, the Castle of Edinburgh. On the universal scroll *The King's Own Borderers*.

In 1891, following the change of title, the new design was as follows: In silver, a thistle wreath; within the wreath a circle pierced with the designation *King's Own Scottish Borderers*. Above the circle, a scroll surmounted by the Royal Crest and pierced with the motto *In veritate religionis confido*. Over the circle, the Cross of St. Andrew in burnished silver. On the cross the Castle of Edinburgh. On the wreath, at the bottom of the circle, a scroll with the motto in relief, *Nisi Dominus frustra*. In 1904, the regiment ceased to wear the helmet but continued to wear the above badge on the Kilmarnock bonnet (Fig. 239).

The Cameronians (Scottish Rifles)

A thistle-wreath surmounted by a crown. On the leaves of the wreath the battles of the regiment. Within the wreath a mullet, and, below the mullet, a bugle with strings. On a tablet to the right of the wreath, the Dragon of China; on a tablet to the left, the Sphinx. On the bottom of the wreath a scroll inscribed *The Scottish Rifles* (Fig. 240).

The regiment ceased to wear the helmet in 1892 and adopted the shako. The badge for this was a bugle and strings in bronze; above the bugle a mullet on a black-corded boss. On the puggaree, in silver, a mullet with a scroll below inscribed *The Cameronians*.

The Gloucestershire Regiment

In silver, on a black-velvet ground, the Sphinx over *Egypt*. On the universal scroll *The Gloucestershire Regiment* (Fig. 241).

Badge for back of helmet: In dead gilt metal the Sphinx over *Egypt* within a laurel-wreath.

The Worcestershire Regiment

On a black-velvet ground, a silver eight-pointed star. In gilt metal, within a silver circle on the star, a Castle on a raised ground of blue-enamel. On the star, at the bottom, a scroll in gilt metal inscribed *Firm*. On the universal scroll in gilt letters *The Worcestershire Regiment*. Worn from 1881 to 1885. In 1885, the star was altered to a more delicate design with only one point at the top. Worn until 1890.

The design was changed in 1891 to: On a black-velvet ground, a silver eight-pointed star. On the star, in gilt metal, the Garter with motto. Within the Garter, the Lion in silver on a black-velvet ground. Below the Garter, a scroll in gilt inscribed *Firm*. From 1894 the universal scroll was in silver (Fig. 242).

238

239

240

241

242

243

244

245

246

The East Lancashire Regiment

In silver, on a black-velvet ground the Sphinx over *Egypt*. On the universal scroll *The East Lancashire Regiment* (Fig. 243).

The East Surrey Regiment

In silver, on a black-velvet ground, an eight-pointed star; on the star the Arms of Guildford, in silver, on a shield in frosted gilt metal with burnished edges. On the universal scroll *The East Surrey Regt* (Fig. 244).

In 1891, the title on the scroll was altered to *The East Surrey Regiment* but, in 1904, the spelling reverted to *Regt*.

The Duke of Cornwall's Light Infantry

In gilt metal, on a ground of dark-green-velvet, a bugle with strings. On the strings of the bugle two red feathers set in gilt metal. On the stems of the feathers, in silver, a turreted archway. On the universal scroll *The Duke of Cornwall's Lt. Infy* (Fig. 245).

The Duke of Wellington's (West Riding Regiment)

In silver, on a black-velvet ground, the crest of the Duke of Wellington with the motto on a scroll below *Virtutis fortuna comes*. On the universal scroll *The West Riding Regiment* (Fig. 246).

The Border Regiment

On a ground of half white-, half red-enamel, a laurel-wreath in silver. Within the wreath, in silver, the Dragon of China, with a scroll above inscribed *China*. A scroll of special pattern inscribed *The Border Regiment*; below, on another scroll *Arroyo dos Molinos*.

In 1891, the badge was changed to: In silver, a laurel-wreath; on the wreath a Maltese cross with a lion between each division. On the divisions of the cross the battles of the regiment. On the centre of the cross, a raised circle inscribed *Arroyo dos Molinos 1811*. Within the circle, on a ground of red-and-white enamel, the Dragon of China in gilt and the word *China* in gilt on a silver ground. Below the wreath a scroll inscribed *The Border Regiment* (Fig. 247).

In 1911, the scroll was altered to read *The Border Regt*.

The Royal Sussex Regiment

On a black-velvet ground, a Maltese cross, in gilt metal, on a feather in silver; on the cross, a wreath in silver-and-green; on the wreath a raised circle in blue-enamel set with silver. Within the circle, the Cross of St. George in red-enamel, set with silver, on a silver ground. On the universal scroll *The Royal Sussex Regt*. A later version has the spelling *Regiment*.

In 1904, the ground was changed to red-velvet and, in 1911, to scarlet-velvet (Fig. 248).

The Hampshire Regiment

On a black-velvet ground, the Royal Tiger in gilt metal, within a laurel-wreath, in silver. On the universal scroll *The Hampshire Regt* (Fig. 249). A later version has the spelling *Regiment*.

The South Staffordshire Regiment

In silver, on a black-velvet ground, the Sphinx over *Egypt*. On the universal scroll *The South Staffordshire Regiment* (Fig. 250).

249

247

248

250

251

252

253

254

The Dorsetshire Regiment
In silver, on a black-velvet ground, the Castle and Key. A scroll above the Castle inscribed *Primus in Indis* and one below inscribed *Montis Insignia Calpe*. On the universal scroll *The Dorsetshire Regiment* (Fig. 251).
In 1900, in accordance with War Office Instruction of 30th January, the Castle and Key were redesigned (Fig. 252).

The Prince of Wales's Volunteers (South Lancashire Regiment)
In silver, on a black-velvet ground, the Sphinx over *Egypt*. On the universal scroll *South Lancashire Regiment* (Fig. 253).

The Welsh Regiment
In silver, on a black-velvet ground, the Prince of Wales's Plume with scroll below inscribed *Gwell angau neu Chwilydd*. On the universal scroll *The Welsh Regiment* (Fig. 254).
In 1891, the motto was altered to read *Gwell angau na Chywilydd,* and, in 1900, the Coronet to be in gilt or gilding-metal (Fig. 255).

The Black Watch (Royal Highlanders)
For Highland head-dress and white helmet: In silver, the Star of the Order of the Thistle; in gilt metal, on the Star, a thistle-wreath. Within the wreath, in gilt metal, an oval surmounted by the crown. The oval inscribed *Nemo me impune lacessit.* Within the oval, on a recessed seeded ground, St. Andrew and Cross in silver. Below the wreath, the Sphinx, in gilt metal. In silver, a half-scroll to the left of the crown, inscribed *The Royal*; another to the right inscribed *Highlanders*. A half-scroll to the left of the Sphinx inscribed *Black*, another to the right, inscribed *Watch* (Fig. 256).

The Oxfordshire Light Infantry
In silver, on a ground of black-enamel, a bugle with strings. On the universal scroll *The Oxfordshire Lt. Infy.* The plate is of gilding, not gilt, metal (Fig. 257).
In 1911, following the change of title, the universal scroll was altered to read *The Oxfordshire and Buckinghamshire Lt. Infy.*

The Essex Regiment
An oak-leaf wreath is substituted for the universal wreath. In silver, on a black-velvet ground, the Castle and Key, with the Sphinx over *Egypt* above, and a scroll below, inscribed *Montis Insignia Calpe*. On the universal scroll *The Essex Regiment* (Fig. 258).
In 1900, in accordance with War Office Instruction of the 30th January, the Castle and Key were redesigned. After 1911 the universal scroll read *The Essex Regt.*

The Sherwood Foresters (Derbyshire Regiment)
In the helmet-plate, the Garter-with-motto is omitted. Within the universal wreath a Maltese cross, in silver. On the cross, in gilt metal, an oak-leaf wreath; within the wreath, on a ground of blue enamel, a Stag lodged in silver. In gilt metal, on the left division of the cross, the word *The*; on the right division, *Regt*, and on a scroll on the lower division *Derbyshire*. A scroll of special pattern on the bottom of the universal wreath inscribed *Sherwood Foresters*. In 1904, the scroll on the lower division was altered to read *Notts and Derby* (Fig. 259).

256

255

257

258

259

260

261

262

263

The Loyal North Lancashire Regiment

In silver, on a black-velvet ground, the Royal Crest. Below the Crest, the Rose of Lancaster in gilt metal and red-and-green enamel. On the universal scroll *Loyal North Lancashire Regiment* (Fig. 260).

The Northamptonshire Regiment

In silver, on a black-velvet ground, the Castle and Key; on a scroll above, *Gibraltar* and on a scroll below, *Talavera*. On the universal scroll *The Northamptonshire Regiment* (Fig. 261). In 1900, in accordance with War Office Instruction of the 30th January, the Castle and Key were redesigned.

Princess Charlotte of Wales's (Berkshire Regiment)

In silver, on a black-velvet ground, a Stag under an oak. On the universal scroll *The Berkshire Regiment* (Fig. 262).
In 1891, the ground in the centre was altered to scarlet and the title scroll to read *Royal Berkshire Regiment* (Fig. 263).

The Queen's Own (Royal West Kent Regiment)

In silver, on a black-velvet ground, the White Horse of Kent on a scroll inscribed *Invicta*. Above the Horse, another scroll with motto *Quo fas et gloria ducunt*. On the universal scroll *The Royal West Kent Regiment* (Fig. 264).

The King's Own Light Infantry (South Yorkshire Regiment)

In silver, on a black-velvet ground, a French horn with the White Rose in the centre; on the scroll below *Cede Nullis*. On the universal scroll *The South Yorkshire Regiment*. In 1891, the ground of the centre was changed to black-enamel and the scroll reading *Cede Nullis* was omitted. The title on the universal scroll was altered to read *The King's Own Yorkshire Light Infantry* (Fig. 265).

The King's (Shropshire Light Infantry)

In silver, on a ground of dark-green-velvet, a bugle with strings. In gilt metal, within the strings of the bugle, the monogram *KLI*. On the universal scroll *The Shropshire Lt. Infty*. In 1891, the title was altered to read *King's Shropshire Lt. Infty*. In 1900 to *Infy* and, in 1904, back to *Infty* (Fig. 266). Also in 1900, the ground in the centre was altered to dark-green-enamel.

The Duke of Cambridge's Own (Middlesex Regiment)

In silver, on a black-velvet ground, a laurel-wreath; within the wreath, the Prince of Wales's Plume; below the Plume, the Coronet and Cypher of H.R.H. The Duke of Cambridge. On the bottom of the wreath a scroll inscribed *Albuhera*. On the universal scroll *The Middlesex Regt* (Fig. 267). A later version has the spelling *Regiment*.

The King's Royal Rifle Corps

In bronze, a Maltese cross with scroll at the top inscribed *Peninsula*, and another at the bottom inscribed *Celer et audax*. Above the top scroll the Crown. On the cross, a circle inscribed *The King's Royal Rifle Corps*; within the circle on a scarlet cloth ground, a bugle with strings. A lion between each division of the cross; on each division, the battles of the Regiment. The helmet ceased to be worn in 1890.

264

265

266

267

268

269

270

271

In 1900, the badge on the busby was: In blackened metal a Maltese cross surmounted by a tablet inscribed *Celer et Audax,* on the cross a circle inscribed *The King's Royal Rifle Corps*; within the circle, a bugle with strings; on each division of the cross, the battles of the regiment (Fig. 268).

On the white helmet: As for busby badge but surmounted by a crown; and with a scarlet-cloth ground to the centre (Fig. 269).

The Duke of Edinburgh's (Wiltshire Regiment)
On a black-velvet ground, the cross patée in lined gilt metal with burnished edges. On the cross, a round convex burnished plate. On the plate, in silver, the Cypher surmounted by the Coronet. On the universal scroll *The Wiltshire Regiment* (Fig. 270).

The Manchester Regiment
In silver, on a black-velvet ground, the Arms with motto of the City of Manchester. On the universal scroll *The Manchester Regiment* (Fig. 271).

The Prince of Wales's (North Staffordshire Regiment)
In silver, on a black-velvet ground, the Prince of Wales's Plume. On the universal scroll *The North Staffordshire Regiment* (Fig. 272).

The York and Lancaster Regiment
In silver and gilt metal, on a black-velvet ground, The Union Rose. On the universal scroll *The York & Lancaster Regiment* (Fig. 273).

The Durham Light Infantry
In silver, on a black-velvet ground, a bugle with strings. On the universal scroll *The Durham Lt Infy* (Fig. 274). A later version has the spelling *The Durham Light Infantry.*
In 1904, the ground in the centre was altered to dark-green-velvet.

The Highland Light Infantry
The Shako badge: In silver, the Star of the Order of the Thistle. On the star a silver horn. In the centre of the horn the monogram *HLI* in gilt metal. Above the horn in gilt metal the crown as represented in the collar of the Order of the Star of India with the cap of the crown in crimson-velvet. Below the horn, a scroll in gilt metal, inscribed *Assaye*; under the scroll, in gilt metal, the Elephant (Fig. 275).

Seaforth Highlanders (Ross-shire Buffs, the Duke of Albany's)
For Highland head-dress and white helmet: In silver, a stag's head above the Coronet and Cypher of H.R.H. The Duke of Albany; below a scroll inscribed *Cuidich'n Righ* (Fig. 276).

The Gordon Highlanders
For Highland head-dress and white helmet: In silver, the Crest of the Marquis of Huntley within an ivy-wreath. On the bottom of the wreath *Bydand* (Fig. 277).

The Queen's Own Cameron Highlanders
For Highland head-dress and white helmet: In silver, a thistle-wreath; within the wreath the figure of St. Andrew with Cross (Fig. 278).
In 1900, a scroll was added to the lower bend of the wreath inscribed *Cameron* (Fig. 279).

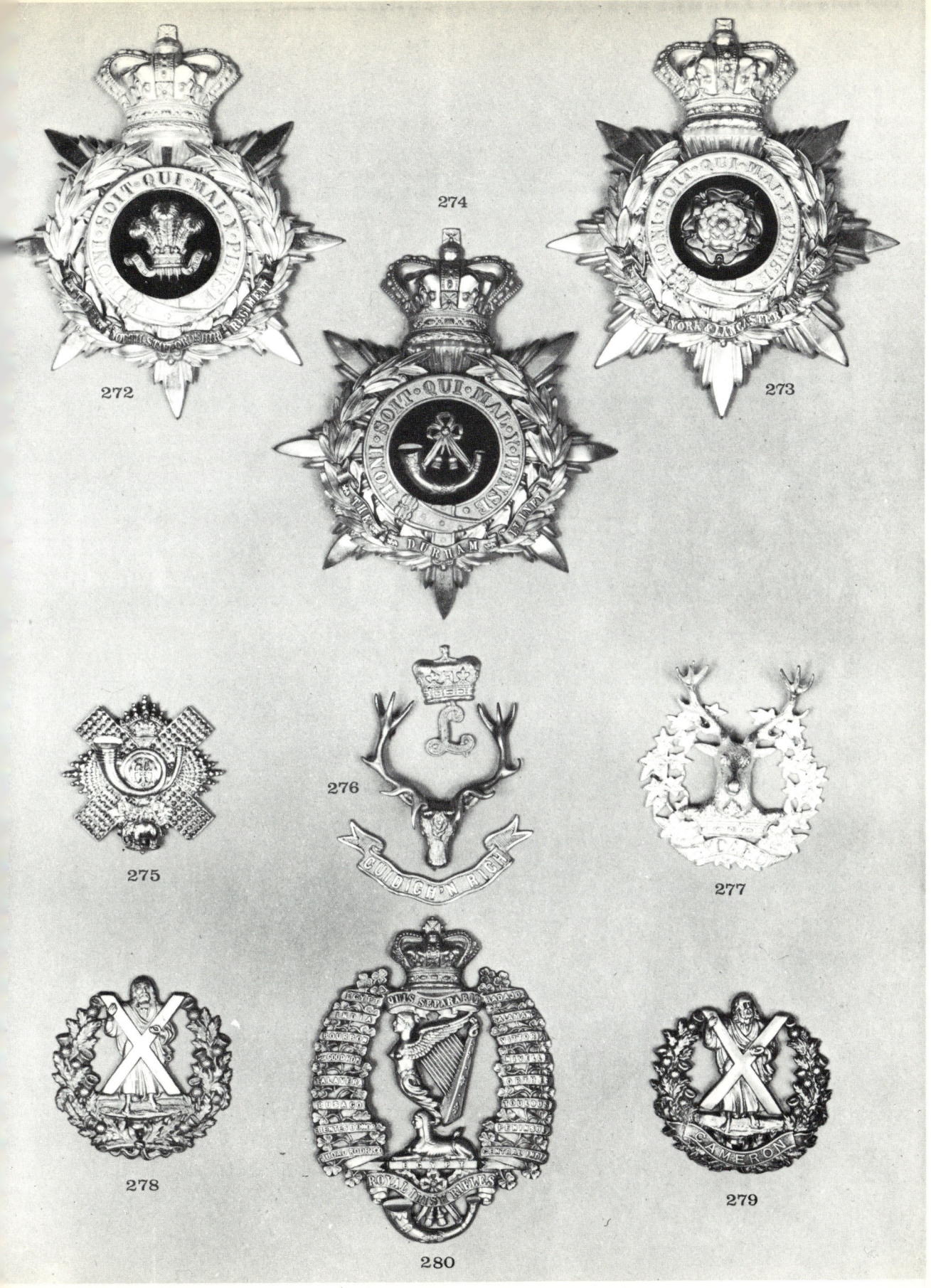

274

272

273

275

276

277

278

280

279

The Royal Irish Rifles

In bronze, a shamrock-wreath intertwined with a scroll bearing the battles of the Regiment; within the wreath, the Harp and Crown. Above the Harp, a scroll inscribed *Quis Separabit*; below the Harp, the Sphinx over *Egypt*; below the Sphinx, a bugle with strings. Over the strings of the bugle, a scroll inscribed *Royal Irish Rifles*. No star behind (Fig. 280). In 1890, the helmet ceased to be worn. The badge on the busby was: in bronze, the Harp and Crown; below the Harp, a scroll inscribed *Quis Separabit*; on the boss, the Sphinx over *Egypt*; below the Sphinx a bugle with strings.

The puggaree badge was the same as for the busby.

The Connaught Rangers

In silver, on a dark-green-velvet ground, the Harp with scroll inscribed *Quis Separabit*. A sprig of laurel issues from either end of the scroll. On the universal scroll *The Connaught Rangers* (Fig. 281).

Princess Louise's (Argyll and Sutherland Highlanders)

For Highland head-dress and white helmet: In silver, a thistle-wreath; within the wreath a circle inscribed *Argyll and Sutherland*. Within the circle, the double Cypher of H.R.H. the Princess Louise. To the left of the Cypher, the Boar's Head; to the right, the Cat. Above the Cypher, and on the circle, the Coronet of the Princess. (Fig. 282.)

The Prince of Wales's Leinster Regiment (Royal Canadians)

In silver, on a black-velvet ground, the Prince of Wales's Plume over two maple-leaves. On a scroll beneath the leaves, *Central India*. On the universal scroll *Prince of Wales's Leinster Regiment* (Fig. 283).

In 1900, the Coronet to be in gilt or gilding-metal.

The Rifle Brigade (The Prince Consort's Own)

In bronze, a wreath of laurel intertwined with a scroll bearing the battles of the Brigade. Within the wreath, a Maltese cross with a Lion between each division. On each division, other battles of the Brigade. On the centre of the cross, a circle inscribed *Rifle Brigade*; within the circle, a bugle with strings, surmounted by the Crown. Above the cross, a crown on a tablet inscribed *Waterloo*; below the cross, a scroll inscribed *Peninsula* and another on the bottom of the wreath inscribed *The Prince Consort's Own* (Fig. 284).

The Brigade ceased to wear the helmet in 1890.

On the astrakhan busby: a blackened-white-metal bugle-horn 3″ wide surmounted by a small Victorian crown in the same metal and mounted on an oval black cord boss.

On the white helmet: In silver, a wreath of laurel intertwined with a scroll bearing some of the battles of the Brigade. Within the wreath a Maltese cross with a Lion between each division. On each division, other battles of the Brigade. On the centre of the cross a circle inscribed *Rifle Brigade*; within the circle a bugle with strings surmounted by the Crown. Above the cross, a Crown on a tablet inscribed *Waterloo*, below the cross a scroll inscribed *Peninsula*. A pattern is also known omitting the scroll inscribed *Peninsula*.

281

283

285

286

Royal Jersey Militia

On the universal plate a circle inscribed *Royal Jersey Light Infantry* is substituted for the Garter. In the centre, in gilt or gilding-metal, the bugle and strings; within the strings the number of the regiment (Fig. 285).

Royal Guernsey Militia

The universal plate, with the Garter inscribed *Pro aris, rege et focis*. In silver, within the Garter, on a black-velvet ground, a shield charged with three lions-leopardé, surmounted by a sprig of laurel; above the Garter a scroll inscribed *Diex Aie*; below the shield, a bugle with strings. Within the strings, the number of the regiment. On the universal wreath at the bottom, a scroll inscribed *Royal Guernsey Militia* (Fig. 286).

282

284

CHAPTER 10

Other-Ranks' Helmet-Plate Centres: 1881 to 1914

The disappearance of regimental numbers and the introduction of territorial titles under the Cardwell Scheme necessitated new designs for the plate on the cloth-helmet.

The basic pattern was a gilding-metal back-plate of an eight-pointed star with the topmost point displaced by the crown. On this was a laurel-wreath which surrounded a voided blank centre. Three oblong holes were placed round this to receive a detachable centre which was usually round and made of gilding-metal.

These centres consisted of a circle inscribed with the title of the regiment above and laurel-sprays below and, within this, the badge in gilding- or white-metal or a combination of both.

On the back of the centre were oblong loops: the three shorter ones secured the centre to the back-plate and the longer central loop penetrated the helmet-wall and made the whole firm in conjunction with the two loops on the back-plate, situated mid-right and mid-left centre, when fitted to the helmet.

For reasons of economy it was intended that the same centres should be worn on the Glengarry undress-cap together with a small crown issued separately for this purpose and, to achieve correct fitting, a blank brass-plate was worn on the inside of the Glengarry (Fig. 289).

Some regiments, however, had Glengarry badges made at their own expense with the helmet-centre and crown struck all in one piece (Figs. 356 and 357) and in a few cases crowns were permanently fixed to the top of the centre.

For use on the puggaree, in India and other hot-weather stations, some centres were made with very long single sliders.

A piece of black cloth was worn behind the centre, except that all Royal regiments had red, *Alexandra, Princess of Wales's Own (Yorkshire Regiment)* had green and *The South Staffordshire Regiment* had a piece of brown holland (although officially described as brown the actual colour is buff).

With the exception of Scottish regiments the Glengarry ceased to be worn after 1895.

In 1901, following the accession of King Edward VII, the back-plate was re-designed. The Imperial crown was substituted for the Victorian crown and a number of centres were also affected by this change.

For a collection of badges of this period it is customary to include a back-plate bearing the Victorian crown (Fig. 287); a back-plate bearing the Imperial crown (Fig. 358); a small Victorian crown (Fig. 288); and a specimen of the blank Glengarry-plate (Fig. 289).

Listed below are the centres worn from 1881 to 1901 followed by those worn from 1902 to 1914.

1881 to 1901

The Royal Scots (Lothian Regiment)
(1) On circlet: *Lothian*. In centre: The Star of the Order of the Thistle; on this an oval inscribed *Nemo me impune lacessit* with thistle-sprays on either side. In the centre of the oval St. Andrew with Cross above which a crown and below, the Sphinx super-scribed *Egypt*. All in gilding-metal (Fig. 290).
This badge was worn only for a very short period.
(2) On circlet: *The Royal Scots*. In centre: Same design as above all in gilding-metal (Fig. 291). Worn from 1882 to 1889.
(3) The Star of the Order of the Thistle. In the centre St. Andrew and Cross. Below this a scroll inscribed *The Royal Scots*. The Star in white-metal, remainder in gilding-metal (Fig. 292).
The 1st Battalion wore a red-cloth backing and the 2nd Battalion a green-cloth backing to the figure of St. Andrew.

The Queen's (Royal West Surrey Regiment)
On circlet: *West Surrey*. In centre: The Paschal Lamb. In gilding-metal with white-metal centre (Fig. 293).

The Buffs (East Kent Regiment)
On circlet: *East Kent*. In centre: The Dragon. All in gilding-metal (Fig. 294).

The King's Own (Royal Lancaster Regiment)
On circlet: *Royal Lancaster*. In centre: The Lion of England. All in gilding-metal (Fig. 295).

The Royal Warwickshire Regiment
On circlet: *Warwickshire*. In centre: The Antelope ducally chained and gorged. Gilding-metal circlet with white-metal centre (Fig. 296).

The King's (Liverpool Regiment)
On circlet: *Liverpool*. In centre: The White Horse of Hanover. Gilding-metal circlet with white-metal centre (Fig. 297).

The Norfolk Regiment
On circlet: *Norfolk*. In centre: The figure of Britannia seated, her right hand holding a sprig of olive and resting on her knee, a trident in her left hand and an oval shield bearing the Great Union resting against her left forearm. Gilding-metal circlet and white-metal centre (Fig. 298).

The Lincolnshire Regiment
On circlet: *Lincolnshire,* In centre: The Sphinx superscribed *Egypt*. Gilding-metal circlet with white-metal centre (Fig. 299).

The Devonshire Regiment
On circlet: *Devonshire,* In centre: The Castle of Exeter above a scroll inscribed *Semper fidelis*. All in gilding-metal (Fig. 300).

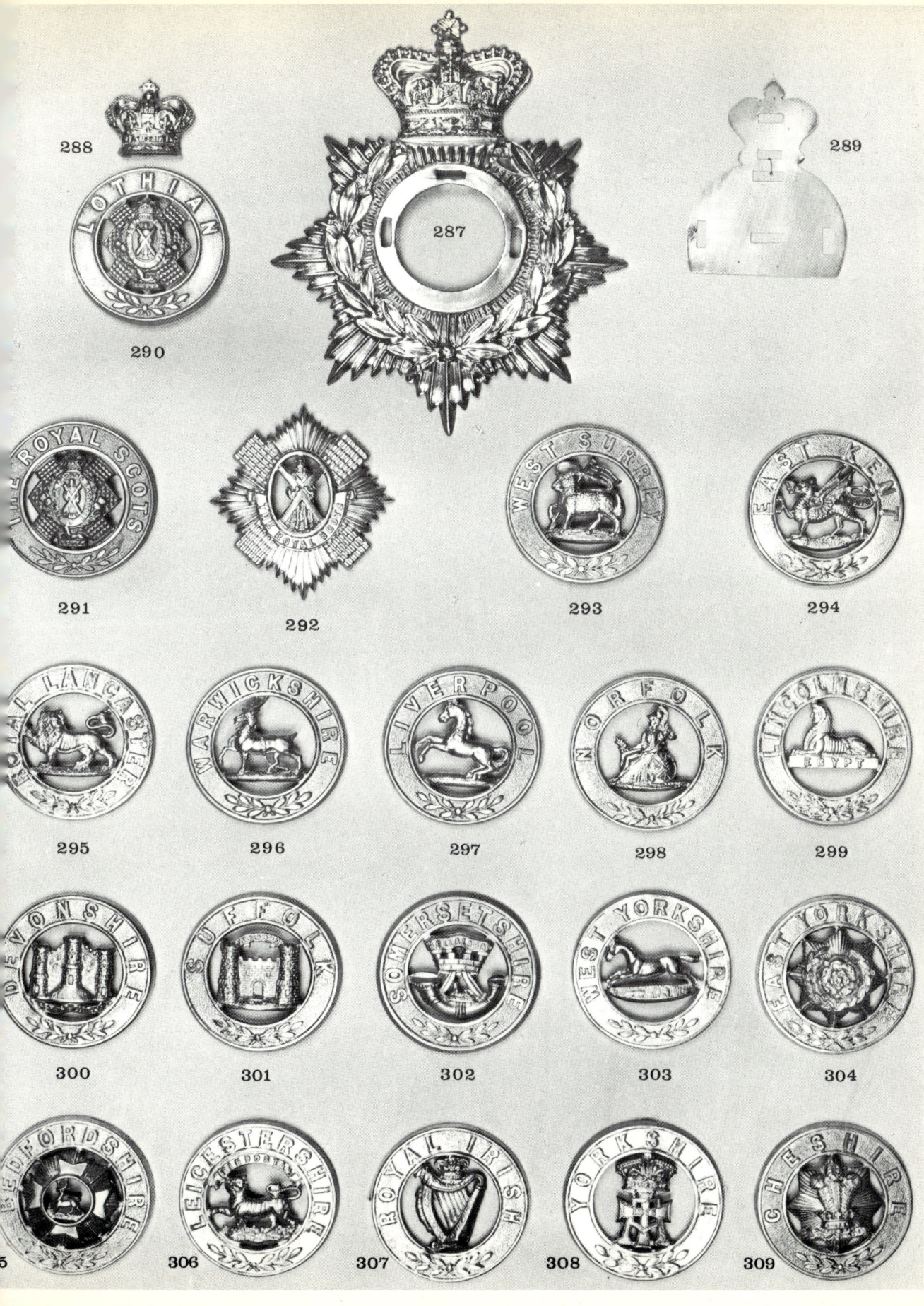

288

289

290

287

291

292

293

294

295

296

297

298

299

300

301

302

303

304

306

307

308

309

The Suffolk Regiment

On circlet: *Suffolk*. In centre: The Castle and Key of Gibraltar. A scroll above inscribed *Gibraltar*. All in gilding-metal (Fig. 301).

Prince Albert's (Somersetshire Light Infantry)

On circlet: *Somersetshire*. In centre: A bugle with strings surmounted by a mural crown. Above a scroll inscribed *Jellalabad* within the strings of the bugle a Sphinx. All in gilding-metal (Fig. 302).

The Prince of Wales's Own (West Yorkshire Regiment)

On circlet: *West Yorkshire*. In centre: The White Horse of Hanover. Gilding-metal circlet with white-metal centre (Fig. 303).

The East Yorkshire Regiment

On circlet: *East Yorkshire*. In centre: An eight-pointed star with the White Rose of York in the centre, the Rose encircled by a laurel-wreath. All in gilding-metal except the Rose which is in white-metal (Fig. 304).

The Bedfordshire Regiment

On circlet: *Bedfordshire*. In centre: A Maltese cross superimposed on an eight-pointed star; in the centre of this a Hart crossing a ford. All in gilding-metal except the Hart which is in white-metal (Fig. 305).

The Leicestershire Regiment

On circlet: *Leicestershire,* In centre: The Royal Tiger superscribed *Hindoostan*. All in gilding-metal (Fig. 306).

The Royal Irish Regiment

On circlet: *Royal Irish*. In centre: A Crowned Harp. All in gilding-metal (Fig. 307).

Alexandra, Princess of Wales's Own (Yorkshire Regiment)

On circlet: *Yorkshire*. In centre: The Cypher of Queen Alexandra interlaced with the Dannebrog inscribed *1875* surmounted by a Coronet. All in gilding-metal (Fig. 308).

The Cheshire Regiment

On circlet: *Cheshire*. In centre: On an eight-pointed star the Prince of Wales's plumes, coronet and motto. All in gilding-metal except the plumes which are in white-metal (Fig. 309).

The South Wales Borderers

On circlet: *South Wales Borderers*. In centre: The Welsh Dragon within a laurel-wreath. All in gilding-metal (Fig. 310).

The King's Own Scottish Borderers

   (1) On circlet: *King's Own Borderers*. In centre: The Castle of Edinburgh and below a scroll inscribed *Nisi Dominus frustra*. All in gilding-metal (Fig. 311). Worn from 1881 to 1884.

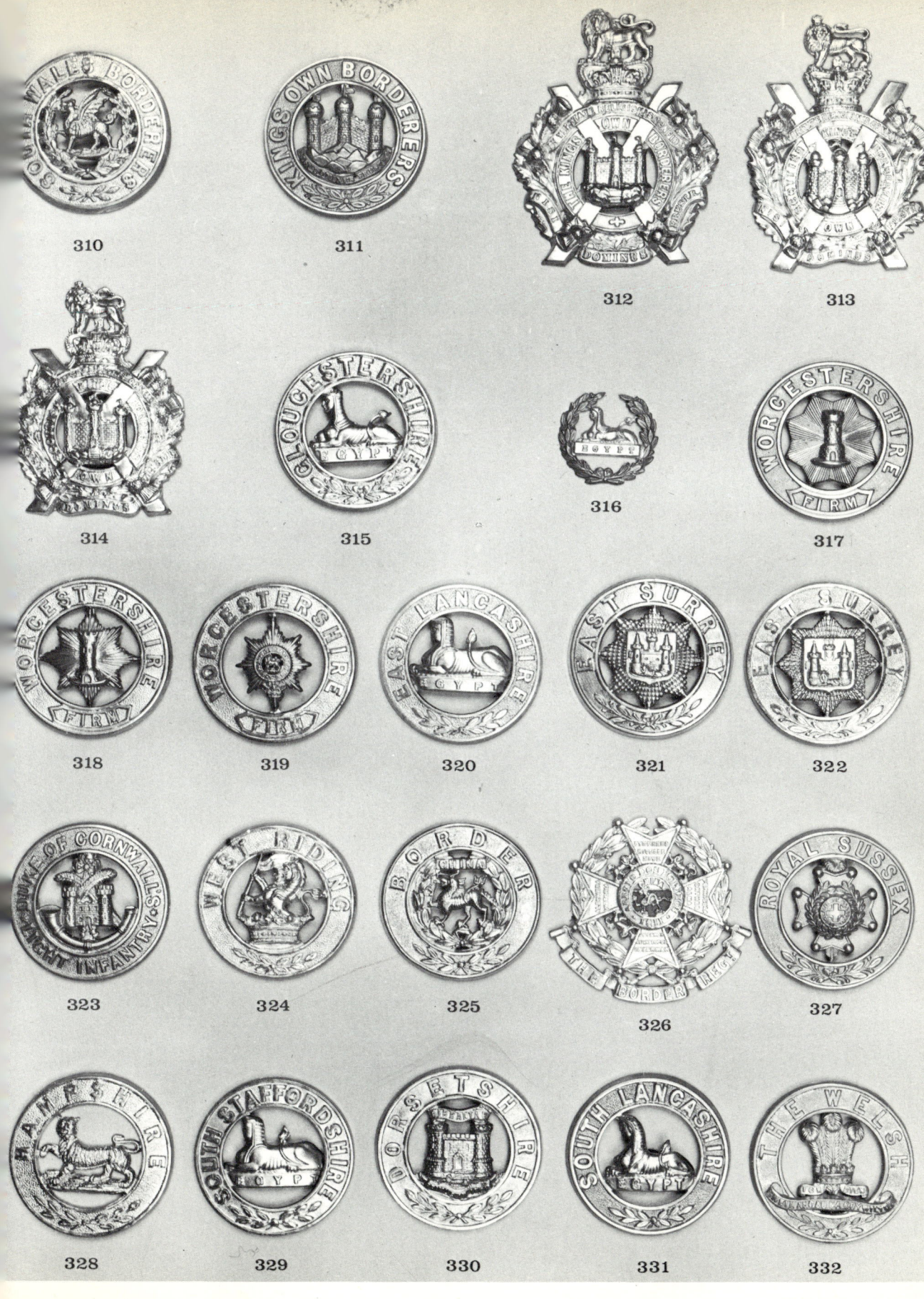

310   311   312   313

314   315   316   317

318 319 320 321 322

323 324 325 326 327

328 329 330 331 332

(2) A circlet inscribed *The King's Own Borderers*. On this St. Andrew's Cross and in the centre the Castle of Edinburgh. Above the circle a scroll inscribed *In veritate religionis confido* and below the circle another scroll inscribed *Nisi Dominus frustra*. Outside the circle a wreath of thistles, the whole ensigned with the Royal Crest. Height 78mm. All in gilding-metal (Fig. 312). Worn from 1884 to 1887.

(3) A similar design to (2) but the circle inscribed *King's Own Scottish Borderers* and the Lion on the Royal Crest is now crowned. Height 78mm. All in white-metal (Fig. 313).

(4) The badge as (3) redesigned with slightly different position of scrolls and thistles and slightly smaller being 77mm in height. All in white-metal (Fig. 314).

The Gloucestershire Regiment

(1) On circlet: *Gloucestershire*. In centre: The Sphinx superscribed *Egypt*. Gilding-metal circlet with white-metal centre (Fig. 315).

(2) The Back Badge: A white-metal Sphinx within a gilding-metal laurel-wreath (Fig. 316).

The Worcestershire Regiment

(1) On circlet: At top *Worcestershire*; at bottom the motto *Firm* replacing the laurel-sprays. In centre: A broad eight-pointed star with two points at top, on this a castle with one turret. All in gilding-metal (Fig. 317). Worn from 1881 to 1885.

(2) As above but the star altered to a more delicate design and with only one point at top. All in gilding-metal (Fig. 318). Worn from 1885 to 1890.

(3) The centre device entirely changed to an eight-pointed elongated star on which a Lion surrounded by the Garter proper. Below the Garter a scroll inscribed *Firm*. All in gilding-metal (Fig. 319). Worn from 1890 to 1901.

The East Lancashire Regiment

On circlet: *East Lancashire*. In centre: The Sphinx superscribed *Egypt*. Gilding-metal circlet with white-metal centre (Fig. 320).

The East Surrey Regiment

(1) On circlet: *East Surrey*. In centre: An eight-pointed star on which a shield bearing the Arms of Guildford—a lion couchant guardant on a mound in front of the castle and a woolpack on either side. Superimposed on the central turret are the Arms of Kingston-upon-Thames—three salmon. All in gilding-metal (Fig. 321).

(2) Same design as above but this specimen is depicted to show the variation in the sprigs of laurel at the base of the circlet. The first pattern has a bow tied at the intersection and this is missing on the second variety (Fig. 322).

The Duke of Cornwall's Light Infantry

On circlet: *Duke of Cornwall's Light Infantry*. In centre: A Bugle with strings, upon which is superimposed a castle. Behind the castle two feathers in saltire. All in gilding-metal (Fig. 323).

The Duke of Wellington's (West Riding Regiment)
On circlet: *West Riding*. In centre: The crest of the Duke of Wellington. The heraldic description of the crest is: Out of a ducal coronet or, a demi-lion rampant gules, holding a forked pennon of the last flowing to the sinister, one-third per pale from the staff argent charged with the Cross of St. George. All in gilding-metal (Fig. 324).

The Border Regiment
  (1) On circlet: *Border*. In centre: The China Dragon within a laurel-wreath; above a scroll inscribed *China*. All in gilding-metal (Fig. 325). Worn from 1881 to 1883.
  (2) A cross similar to that of the Order of the Bath; on the four arms are inscribed eleven battle-honours and superimposed on a laurel-wreath. In the centre a circlet inscribed *Arroyo dos Molinos 1811* and in the centre of this a Dragon with a scroll above inscribed *China*. The lower part of this centre is voided to display a backing of red-cloth. Below the central device is a further scroll inscribed *The Border Regt*. All in white-metal (Fig. 326).

The Royal Sussex Regiment
On circlet: *Royal Sussex*. In centre: A Maltese cross, on this the Garter proper and, in the centre, St. George's Cross. The whole surrounded by a laurel-wreath and with the Roussillon plume behind. All in gilding-metal (Fig. 327).

The Hampshire Regiment
On circlet: *Hampshire*. In centre: The Royal Tiger. All in gilding-metal (Fig. 328).

The South Staffordshire Regiment
On circlet: *South Staffordshire*. In centre: The Sphinx superscribed *Egypt*. Gilding-metal circlet with white-metal centre (Fig. 329).

The Dorsetshire Regiment
On circlet: *Dorsetshire*. In centre: The Castle and Key of Gibraltar. Above, a scroll inscribed *Gibraltar*; below a scroll inscribed *Primus in Indis*. All in gilding-metal (Fig. 330).

The Prince of Wales's Volunteers (South Lancashire Regiment)
On circlet: *South Lancashire*. In centre: The Sphinx superscribed *Egypt*. Gilding-metal circlet with white-metal centre (Fig. 331).

The Welsh Regiment
On circlet: *The Welsh*. In centre: The Prince of Wales's plumes, coronet and motto. Below a scroll inscribed *Gwell angau na chywllydd*. All in gilding-metal except the plumes which are in white-metal. The motto scroll is so long that it extends on to the circlet (Fig. 332).

The Oxfordshire Light Infantry
On circlet: *Oxfordshire*. In centre: A Bugle with strings. All in gilding-metal (Fig. 333).

The Essex Regiment
  (1) On circlet: *Essex*. In centre: The Castle and Key of Gibraltar. Above, the Sphinx

superscribed *Egypt*. Below, a scroll inscribed *Montis Insignia Calpe*. All in gilding-metal (Fig. 334). Worn from 1881 to 1896.
(2) As above but with redesigned castle (Fig. 335).

The Sherwood Foresters (Derbyshire Regiment)
On circlet: *Derbyshire*. In centre: A Maltese cross surmounted by a Victorian crown. In the centre a Stag lodged within a wreath of oak-leaves. On the arms of the cross three scrolls: left inscribed *Sherwood*, right inscribed *Foresters* and bottom inscribed *Derbyshire*. All in gilding-metal (Fig. 336).

The Loyal North Lancashire Regiment
On circlet: *Loyal North Lancashire*. In centre: The Rose of Lancaster surmounted by the Royal Crest (with Victorian crown). Note the reduction in the size of the laurel-sprays in the circlet to accommodate the long title. All in gilding-metal (Fig. 337).

The Northamptonshire Regiment
On circlet: *Northamptonshire*. In centre: The Castle and Key of Gibraltar with a scroll above inscribed *Gibraltar* and one below inscribed *Talavera*. All in gilding-metal (Fig. 338).

Princess Charlotte of Wales's (Royal Berkshire Regiment)
(1) On circlet: *Berkshire*. In centre: The badge of the old *Royal Berkshire Militia*: a stag under an oak tree. All in gilding-metal (Fig. 339).
(2) On circlet: *Royal Berkshire*. In centre: Same device as above. All in gilding-metal (Fig. 340).
This later badge was worn from 1885 onwards, the Regiment having been given the *Royal* title for its conduct at the Battle of Tofrek, 22nd March 1885. (Authority: General Order No. 107 of 1885).

The Queen's Own (Royal West Kent Regiment)
On circlet: *West Kent*. In centre: The White Horse of Kent on a scroll inscribed *Invicta*. Above, a scroll inscribed *Quo fas et gloria ducunt*. The Horse in white-metal, remainder in gilding-metal (Fig. 341).

The King's Own (Yorkshire Light Infantry)
(1) On circlet: *South Yorkshire*. In centre: A bugle with strings. Within the strings, the Rose of York and, below the bugle, a scroll inscribed *Cede Nullis* (this was the motto of the *2nd Madras Light Infantry* which became the 2nd Battalion of the Regiment in 1881). All in gilding-metal (Fig. 342). Worn from 1881 to 1887.
In 1881 the title of the regiment was *The King's Own Light Infantry (South Yorkshire Regiment* but was changed in 1887.
(2) On circlet: *The Yorkshire Light Infantry*. In centre: A French horn with the White Rose of York in the curl. The Rose in white-metal, remainder in gilding-metal (Fig. 343).
Note that, because of the length of the title, the laurel-sprays on the circlet are omitted.

The King's (Shropshire Light Infantry)
On circlet: *Shropshire*. In centre: A Bugle with strings. All in gilding-metal (Fig. 344).

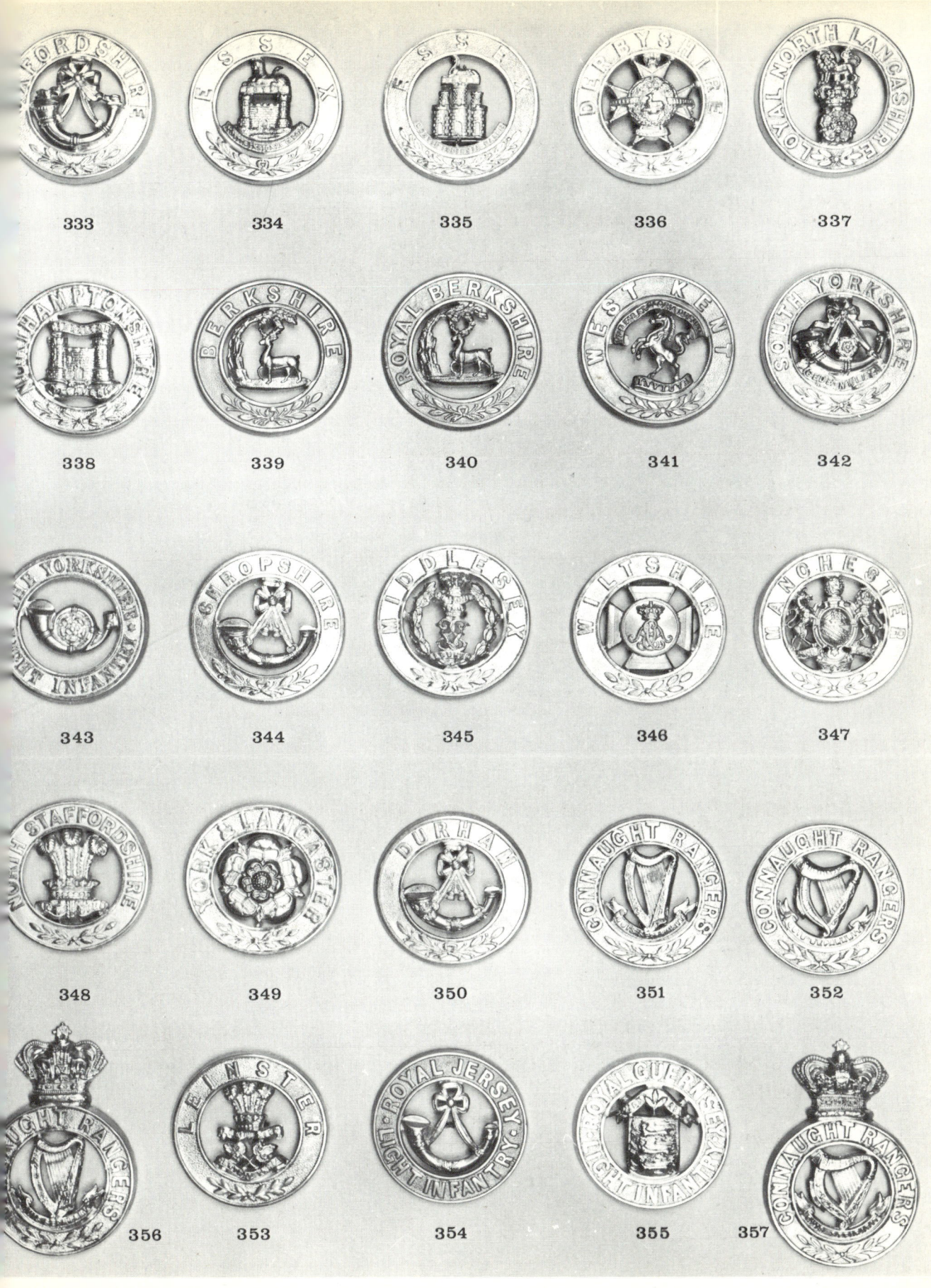

333   334   335   336   337

338   339   340   341   342

343   344   345   346   347

348   349   350   351   352

356   353   354   355   357

The Duke of Cambridge's Own (Middlesex Regiment)

On circlet: *Middlesex*. In centre: Within a laurel-wreath, the Cypher and Coronet of the Duke of Cambridge surmounted by the Prince of Wales's plumes, coronet and motto. At the foot a scroll inscribed *Albuhera*. The Prince of Wales's plumes, coronet and motto in white-metal, remainder in gilding-metal (Fig. 345).

The Duke of Edinburgh's (Wiltshire Regiment)

On circlet: *Wiltshire*. In centre: A cross patée with the Cypher and Coronet of the Duke of Edinburgh in the centre. All in gilding-metal (Fig. 346).

The Manchester Regiment

On circlet: *Manchester*. In centre: The Arms with Crest, Supporters and motto of the City of Manchester. All in gilding-metal (Fig. 347).

The Prince of Wales's (North Staffordshire Regiment)

On circlet: *North Staffordshire*. In centre: The Prince of Wales's plumes, coronet and motto. The plumes and motto in white-metal, remainder in gilding-metal (Fig. 348).

The York and Lancaster Regiment

On circlet: *York & Lancaster*. In centre: The combined Red-and-White Rose. A large white-metal rose with small gilding-metal rose in centre (Fig. 349).

The Durham Light Infantry

On circlet: *Durham*, In centre: A bugle with strings. All in gilding-metal (Fig. 350).

The Connaught Rangers.

(1) On circlet: *Connaught Rangers*. In centre: The Irish Harp; below, a scroll inscribed *Quis Separabit*. All in gilding-metal (Fig. 351).
(2) As above, but the Irish Harp is of a different design. All in gilding-metal (Fig. 352).

The Prince of Wales's Leinster Regiment (Royal Canadians)

On circlet: *Leinster*. In centre: The Prince of Wales's plumes, coronet and motto. Below, two crossed maple-leaves and below these a scroll inscribed *Central India*. The plumes and motto in white-metal, remainder in gilding-metal (Fig. 353).

Rifle Brigade

On the astrakhan busby: A small strung bugle-horn surmounted by a Guelphic crown in blackened-brass on a black cord boss.

The Royal Militia of the Island of Jersey

On circlet: *Royal Jersey Light Infantry*. In centre: A Bugle with strings but without tassels. All in gilding-metal (Fig. 354).

The Royal Guernsey Militia

On circlet: *Royal Guernsey Light Infantry*. In centre: A shield bearing the Arms of Guernsey (three lions leopardé) surmounted by a sprig of laurel. Above the shield a scroll inscribed *Diex Aie*. All in gilding-metal (Fig. 355).

1902 to 1914

The Royal Scots (Lothian Regiment)
The Star of the Order of the Thistle. In the centre St. Andrew and Cross below which is a scroll inscribed *The Royal Scots*. The Star in white-metal, remainder in gilding-metal (Fig. 359).
Worn with a cloth-backing behind St. Andrew. Red for 1st Battalion, green for 2nd Battalion.

The Queen's (Royal West Surrey Regiment)
On circlet: *West Surrey*. In centre: The Paschal Lamb. In gilding-metal with white-metal centre (Fig. 360).

The Buffs (East Kent Regiment)
  (1) On circlet: *East Kent*. In centre: The Dragon. All in gilding-metal (Fig. 361).
  (2) On circlet: *The Buffs East Kent Regiment*. In centre: The Dragon. All in gilding-metal (Fig. 362). Note abbreviation of the laurel-sprays to accommodate the longer title.

The King's Own (Royal Lancaster Regiment)
On circlet: *Royal Lancaster*. In centre: The Lion of England. All in gilding-metal (Fig. 363).

The Royal Warwickshire Regiment
On circlet: *Warwickshire*. In centre: The Antelope ducally chained and gorged. Gilding-metal circlet with white-metal centre (Fig. 364).

The King's (Liverpool Regiment)
On circlet: *Liverpool*. In centre: The White Horse of Hanover. Gilding-metal circlet with white-metal centre (Fig. 365).

The Norfolk Regiment
  (1) On circlet: *Norfolk*. In centre: The figure of Britannia seated; the right hand holding a sprig of olive and resting on the knee, a trident in the left hand, and an oval shield bearing the Great Union resting against the left forearm. Gilding-metal circlet with white-metal centre (Fig. 366).
  (2) As above but Britannia's right arm is raised. Gilding-metal circlet and white-metal centre (Fig. 367).

The Lincolnshire Regiment
On circlet: *Lincolnshire*. In centre: The Sphinx superscribed *Egypt*. Gilding-metal circlet with white-metal centre (Fig. 368).

The Devonshire Regiment
On circlet: *Devonshire*. In centre: The Castle of Exeter. Below, a scroll inscribed *Semper Fidelis*. All in gilding-metal (Fig. 369).
Note the difference in the design of the castle to that worn previously.

The Suffolk Regiment
  (1) On circlet: *Suffolk*. In centre: The Castle and Key of Gibraltar. A scroll above inscribed *Gibraltar*. All in gilding-metal (Fig. 370).
  (2) As above but with redesigned castle. All in gilding-metal (Fig. 371).
The change in the design of the Castle was necessitated by an Instruction from the War Office, dated 30th January 1900, that all Regiments which had a representation of the Castle of Gibraltar in their badges should show the correct pattern as shown upon the seal of Gibraltar, granted in 1502, and subsequently on the coinage of Gibraltar. This design showed the Castle as having three turrets with the key suspended below the central gateway. The order affected the badges of the Suffolk, Dorsetshire, Essex and Northamptonshire, Regiments whose badges were changed accordingly.

Prince Albert's (Somersetshire Light Infantry)
On circlet: *Somersetshire*. In centre: A bugle with strings surmounted by a mural crown above which a scroll inscribed *Jellalabad*. Within the strings of the bugle a Sphinx. All in gilding-metal (Fig. 372).
In 1912 the title of the regiment was altered to *Prince Albert's (Somerset Light Infantry)* and the wording on the circlet was altered to read *Somerset*.

The Prince of Wales's Own (West Yorkshire Regiment)
On circlet: *West Yorkshire*. In centre: The White Horse of Hanover. Gilding-metal circlet with white-metal centre (Fig. 373).

The East Yorkshire Regiment
On circlet: *East Yorkshire*. In centre: An eight-pointed star with the White Rose of York in the centre, the Rose encircled by a laurel-wreath. All in gilding-metal. On the centre of this a smaller white-metal rose is mounted (Fig. 374).

The Bedfordshire Regiment
On circlet: *Bedfordshire*. In centre: A Maltese cross superimposed upon an eight-pointed star. In the centre a Hart crossing a ford. All in gilding-metal except the Hart which is in white-metal (Fig. 375).

The Leicestershire Regiment
On circlet: *Leicestershire*. In centre: The Royal Tiger superscribed *Hindoostan*. All in gilding-metal (Fig. 376).

The Royal Irish Regiment
  (1) On circlet: *Royal Irish*. In centre: The Irish Harp surmounted by an Imperial crown. All in gilding-metal (Fig. 377).
  (2) As above but the Harp is of a different design. All in gilding-metal (Fig. 378).

Alexandra, Princess of Wales's Own (Yorkshire Regiment)
On circlet: *Yorkshire*. In centre: The Cypher of Queen Alexandra interlaced with the Dannebrog inscribed *1875* surmounted by a coronet. All in gilding-metal (Fig. 379).

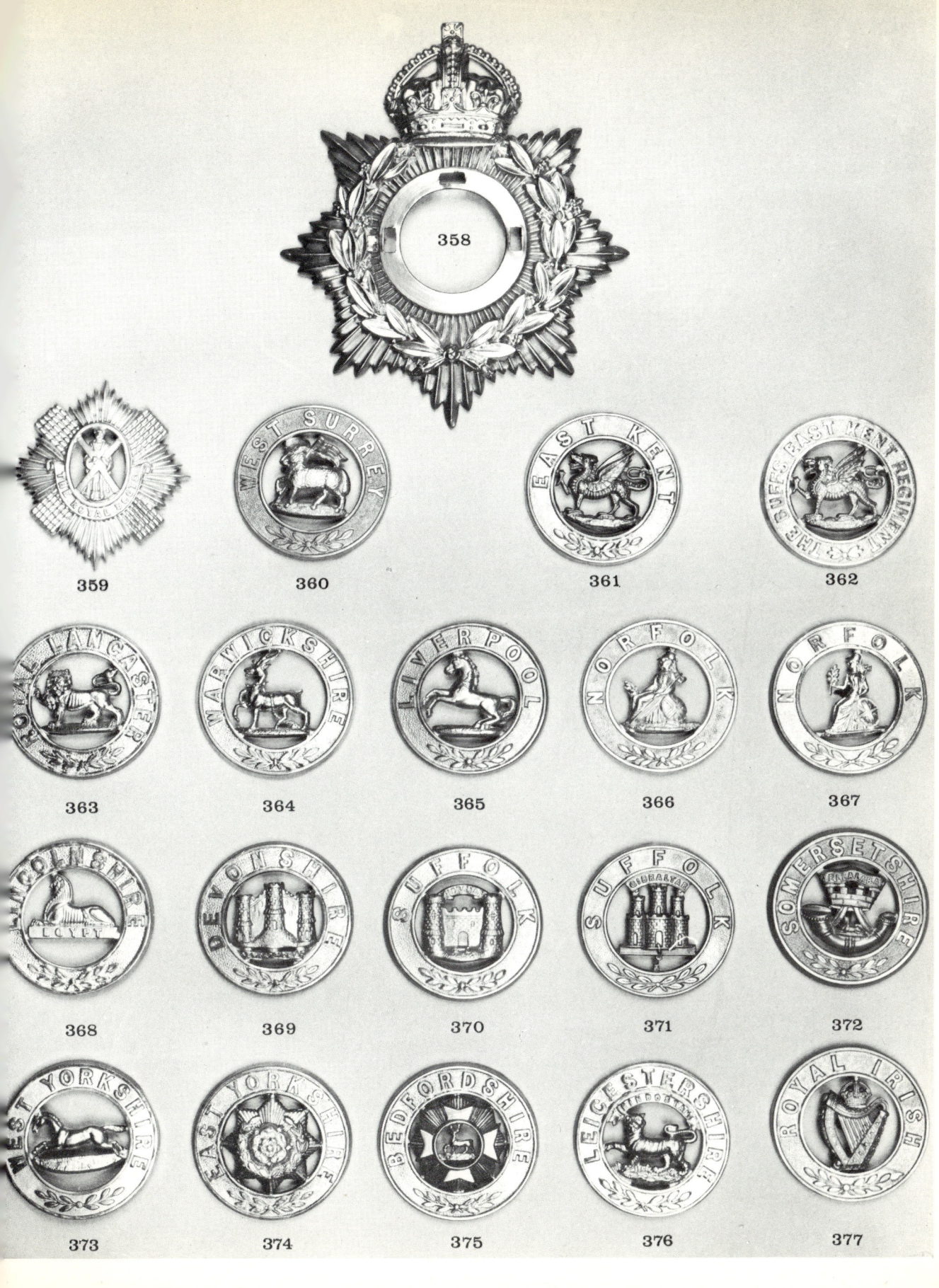

358

359   360   361   362

363   364   365   366   367

368   369   370   371   372

373   374   375   376   377

The Cheshire Regiment

On circlet: *Cheshire*. In centre: On an eight-pointed star the Prince of Wales's plumes, coronet and motto. All in gilding-metal except the plumes which are in white-metal (Fig. 380).

The South Wales Borderers

On circlet: *South Wales Borderers*. In centre: The Welsh Dragon within a laurel-wreath. All in gilding-metal (Fig. 381).

The King's Own Scottish Borderers

(1) A circlet inscribed *King's Own Scottish Borderers*; on this St. Andrew's Cross and in the centre the Castle of Edinburgh, above the circle a scroll inscribed *In veritate religionis confido* and below the circle another scroll inscribed *Nisi Dominus frustra*. Outside the circle a wreath of thistles. The whole ensigned with the Royal Crest with Imperial crown. Height 77mm. All in white-metal (Fig. 382).

(2) A design similar to above but height 64mm. All in white-metal (Fig. 383).

The Gloucestershire Regiment

On circlet: *Gloucestershire*. In centre: The Sphinx superscribed *Egypt*. Gilding-metal circlet with white-metal centre (Fig. 384).

The back-badge was identical with that worn during 1881 to 1901.

The Worcestershire Regiment

On circlet: At top *Worcestershire*, at bottom the motto *Firm* replacing the laurel-sprays. In centre: An eight-pointed elongated star on which the Lion from the Royal Crest surrounded by the Garter proper. Below the Garter a scroll inscribed *Firm*. All in gilding-metal (Fig. 385).

The East Lancashire Regiment

On circlet: *East Lancashire*. In centre: The Sphinx superscribed *Egypt*. Gilding-metal circlet with white-metal centre (Fig. 386).

The East Surrey Regiment

On circlet: *East Surrey*. In centre: An eight-pointed star on which a shield bearing the arms of Guildford. All in gilding-metal (Fig. 387).

The Duke of Cornwall's Light Infantry

On circlet: *Duke of Cornwall's Light Infantry*. In centre: A bugle with strings and, superimposed on this, a castle. Behind the castle two feathers in saltire. All in gilding-metal (Fig. 388).

The Duke of Wellington's (West Riding Regiment)

On circlet: *West Riding*. In centre: The crest of the Duke of Wellington. All in gilding-metal (Fig. 389).

The Border Regiment

A cross, similar to that of the Order of the Bath, on the four arms of which are inscribed eleven battle-honours, superimposed on a laurel-wreath. In the centre, a circlet inscribed *Arroyo dos Molinos 1811* and in the centre of this a Dragon with a scroll above

378

379

380

381

382

383

384

385

386

387

388

389

390

391

392

393

394

395

396

397

inscribed *China*. The lower part of this centre is voided to display a backing of red-cloth. Below the central device is a further scroll inscribed *The Border Regt.* All in white-metal (Fig. 390).

The Royal Sussex Regiment
On circlet: *Royal Sussex.* In centre: A Maltese cross on which the Garter proper and, in the centre, St. George's Cross. The whole surrounded by a laurel-wreath and with the Roussillon plume behind. All in gilding-metal (Fig. 391).

The Hampshire Regiment
On circlet: *Hampshire.* In centre: The Royal Tiger. All in gilding-metal (Fig. 392).

The South Staffordshire Regiment
On circlet: *South Staffordshire.* In centre: The Sphinx superscribed *Egypt*. Gilding-metal circlet with white-metal centre (Fig. 393).

The Dorsetshire Regiment
    (1) On circlet: *Dorsetshire.* In centre: The Castle and Key of Gibraltar. Above, a scroll inscribed *Gibraltar* and below, a scroll inscribed *Primus in Indis.* All in gilding-metal (Fig. 394).
    (2) Similar design to above but with redesigned castle. All in gilding-metal (Fig. 395).

The Prince of Wales's Volunteers (South Lancashire Regiment)
On circlet: *South Lancashire.* In centre: The Sphinx superscribed *Egypt*. Gilding-metal circlet with white-metal centre (Fig. 396).

The Welsh Regiment
On circlet: *The Welsh.* In centre: The Prince of Wales's plumes, coronet and motto. Below, a scroll inscribed *Gwell angau neu chywilydd.* All in gilding-metal except the Prince of Wales's plumes and motto which are in white-metal (Fig. 397).
Note the variation in spelling of the regimental motto from that on the previous badge.

The Oxfordshire and Buckinghamshire Light Infantry
    (1) On circlet: *Oxfordshire.* In centre: A bugle with strings. All in gilding-metal (Fig. 398).
    (2) On circlet: *Oxfordshire & Buckinghamshire.* In centre: A bugle with strings. All in gilding metal (Fig. 399). This pattern was worn from 1908 when the title of the regiment was changed following the disbandment of the *Buckinghamshire Militia* and the desire to perpetuate its title. (Authority: Army Order No. 270 of 1908.)

The Essex Regiment
On circlet: *Essex.* In centre: The Castle and Key of Gibraltar. Above, the Sphinx superscribed *Egypt*, below a scroll inscribed *Montis Insignia Calpe.* All in gilding-metal (Fig. 400).

The Sherwood Foresters (Derbyshire Regiment)
    (1) On circlet: *Derbyshire.* In centre: A Maltese Cross surmounted by an Imperial crown. In the centre, a Stag lodged within a wreath of oak-leaves. On the arms of the cross three scrolls: left inscribed *Sherwood*; right inscribed *Foresters*; and bottom inscribed *Derbyshire.* All in gilding-metal (Fig. 401).

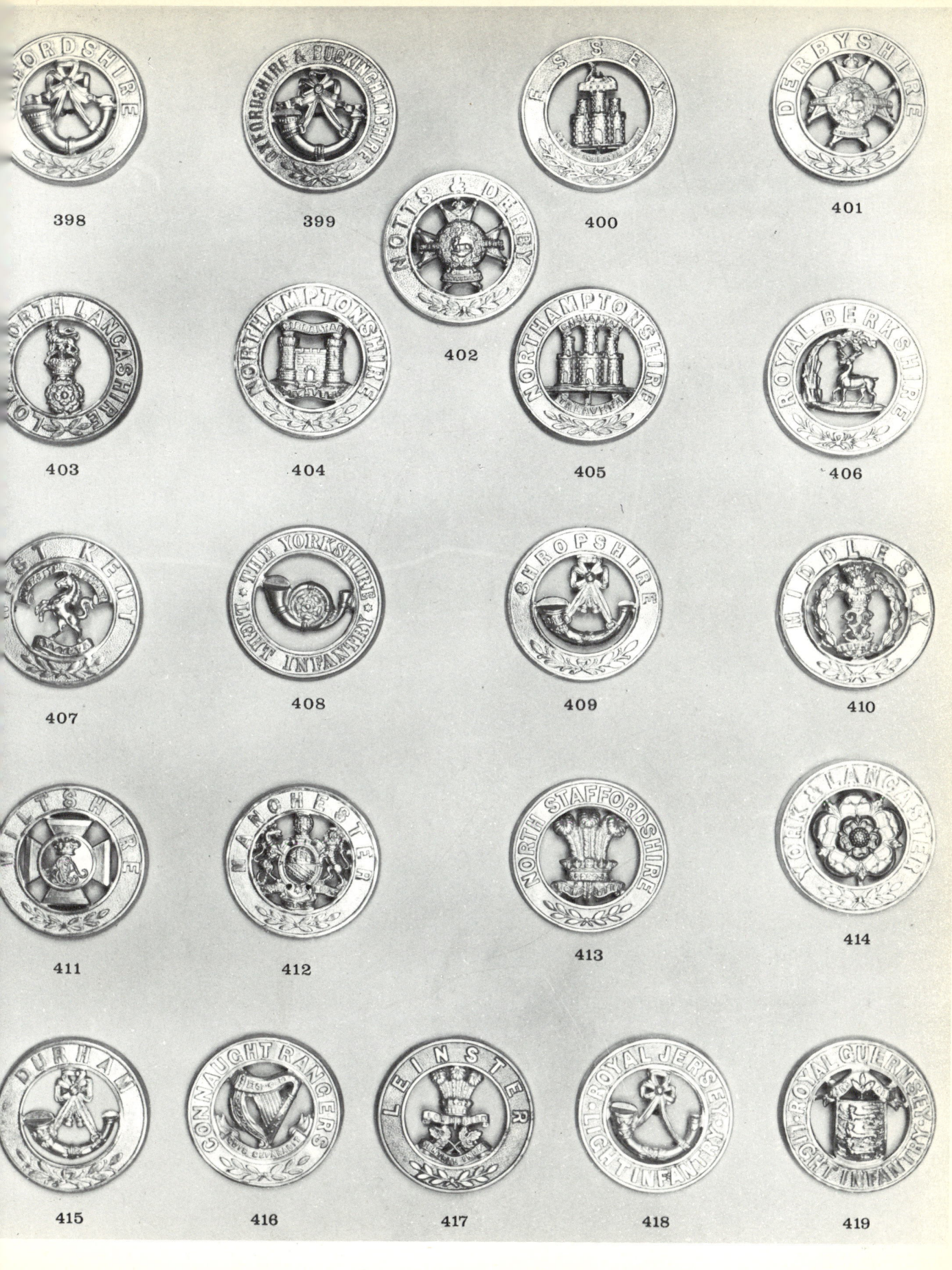

398

399

400

401

402

403

404

405

406

407

408

409

410

411

412

413

414

415

416

417

418

419

(2) On circlet: *Notts & Derby*. In centre: As above but with the bottom scroll inscribed *Notts & Derby*. All in gilding-metal (Fig. 402).

The Loyal North Lancashire Regiment
On circlet: *Loyal North Lancashire*. In centre: The Rose of Lancaster surmounted by the Royal Crest with Imperial crown. All in gilding-metal (Fig. 403).

The Northamptonshire Regiment
(1) On circlet: *Northamptonshire*. In centre: The Castle and Key of Gibraltar with a scroll inscribed *Gibraltar* above and a scroll inscribed *Talavera* below. All in gilding-metal (Fig. 404).
(2) Similar to the above but with redesigned castle and scrolls. All in gilding-metal (Fig. 405).

Princess Charlotte of Wales's (Royal Berkshire Regiment)
On circlet: *Royal Berkshire*. In centre: A Stag under an oak tree. All in gilding-metal (Fig. 406).

The Queen's Own (Royal West Kent Regiment)
On circlet: *West Kent*. In centre: The White Horse of Kent on a scroll inscribed *Invicta*. Above, a second scroll inscribed *Quo fas et gloria ducunt*. The Horse in white-metal, remainder in gilding-metal (Fig. 407).

The King's Own (Yorkshire Light Infantry)
On circlet: *The Yorkshire Light Infantry*. In centre: A French horn with the White Rose of York in the curl. The rose in white-metal, remainder in gilding-metal (Fig. 408).

The King's (Shropshire Light Infantry)
On circlet: *Shropshire*. In centre: A bugle with strings. All in gilding-metal (Fig. 409).

The Duke of Cambridge's Own (Middlesex Regiment)
On circlet: *Middlesex*. In centre: Within a laurel-wreath the Cypher and Coronet of the Duke of Cambridge surmounted by the Prince of Wales's plumes, coronet and motto. At the foot, a scroll inscribed *Albuhera*. The Prince of Wales's plumes, coronet and motto in white-metal, remainder in gilding-metal (Fig. 410).

The Duke of Edinburgh's (Wiltshire Regiment)
On circlet: *Wiltshire*. In centre: A cross patée with the Cypher and Coronet of the Duke of Edinburgh in the centre. All in gilding-metal (Fig. 411).

The Manchester Regiment
On circlet: *Manchester*. In centre: The Arms with crest, supporters and motto of the City of Manchester. All in gilding-metal (Fig. 412).

The Prince of Wales's (North Staffordshire Regiment)
On circlet: *North Staffordshire*. In centre: The Prince of Wales's plumes, coronet and motto. The plumes and motto in white-metal, remainder in gilding-metal (Fig. 413).

The York and Lancaster Regiment

On circlet: *York & Lancaster*. In centre: The combined Red-and-White Rose. A large white-metal rose with a small gilding-metal rose in the centre (Fig. 414).

The Durham Light Infantry

On circlet: *Durham*. In centre: A bugle with strings. All in gilding-metal (Fig. 415).

The Connaught Rangers

On circlet: *Connaught Rangers*. In centre: The Irish Harp. Below, a scroll inscribed *Quis Separabit*. All in gilding-metal (Fig. 416).

The Prince of Wales's Leinster Regiment (Royal Canadians)

On circlet: *Leinster*. In centre: The Prince of Wales's plumes, coronet and motto. Below, two crossed maple-leaves and below these a scroll inscribed *Central India*. The plumes and motto in white-metal, remainder in gilding-metal (Fig. 417).

Rifle Brigade

On the astrakhan busby: A small strung bugle-horn surmounted by an Imperial crown in blackened-brass on a black cord boss.

The Royal Militia of the Island of Jersey

On circlet: *Royal Jersey Light Infantry*. In centre: A Bugle with strings but without tassels. Note that owing to the length of the title, the laurel-sprays are omitted from the circlet. All in gilding-metal (Fig. 418).

The Royal Guernsey Militia

On circlet: *Royal Guernsey Light Infantry*. In centre: A shield bearing the Arms of Guernsey (three lions-leopardé) surmounted by a sprig of laurel. Above the shield a scroll inscribed *Diex Aie*. All in gilding-metal (Fig. 419).

CHAPTER 11

The Glengarry Badges of the Pre-Territorial Era
1874 to 1881

In 1874, a new undress cap for the rank-and-file of the Infantry and certain Departmental Corps was introduced. It was worn until 1895 and, therefore the badges fall into two distinct categories: those worn before and those worn after the reforms of 1881 by which regiments were given territorial designations. This chapter deals with the first period which was the last in which the regimental number was the chief feature of the badge.

They were made in the rather attractive yellow brass of the period and are now quite scarce items. Attachment to the glengarry was by means of two copper loops on the reverse of the badge, usually found at top- and bottom-centre positions.

During the South African War of 1889 to 1902, a Southsea trader obtained a number of the original dies and had them restruck, mostly in gilding-metal and sometimes in an unfinished condition (a catalogue was issued listing these at 6d. each!). Collectors, for whom the re-strikes were made, should note that in many of these, the copper loops at the back were positioned differently, at mid-right and mid-left centre.

Owing to the lapse of time, corrosion had affected some of the dies and this can be seen in the restruck badges—mostly in an imperfect cross-and-orb on the crown.

Although these restrikes were never worn, and in view of the shortage of originals, they can be accepted as representative of the badges of this period.

1st Foot
The Star of the Order of the Thistle in white-metal. In the centre, St. Andrew and Cross in gilding-metal on a domed white-metal plate. Below the figure of St. Andrew a gilt-metal scroll inscribed *The Royal Scots* (Fig. 420).

2nd Foot
A strap inscribed *Queen's Royal* surmounted by the Paschal Lamb standing on a wreathed scroll. In the centre the numeral *2*. All in brass (Fig. 421).

3rd Foot
    (1) A strap inscribed *The Buffs* surmounted by the Victorian crown. In the centre, the Dragon standing on ground above the numeral *3*. In brass (Fig. 422). Also found in white-metal.

    (2) A strap inscribed *Veteri frondescit honore* surmounted by a looped crown. In the centre, the Dragon standing on a wavy scroll. All in brass (Fig. 423).

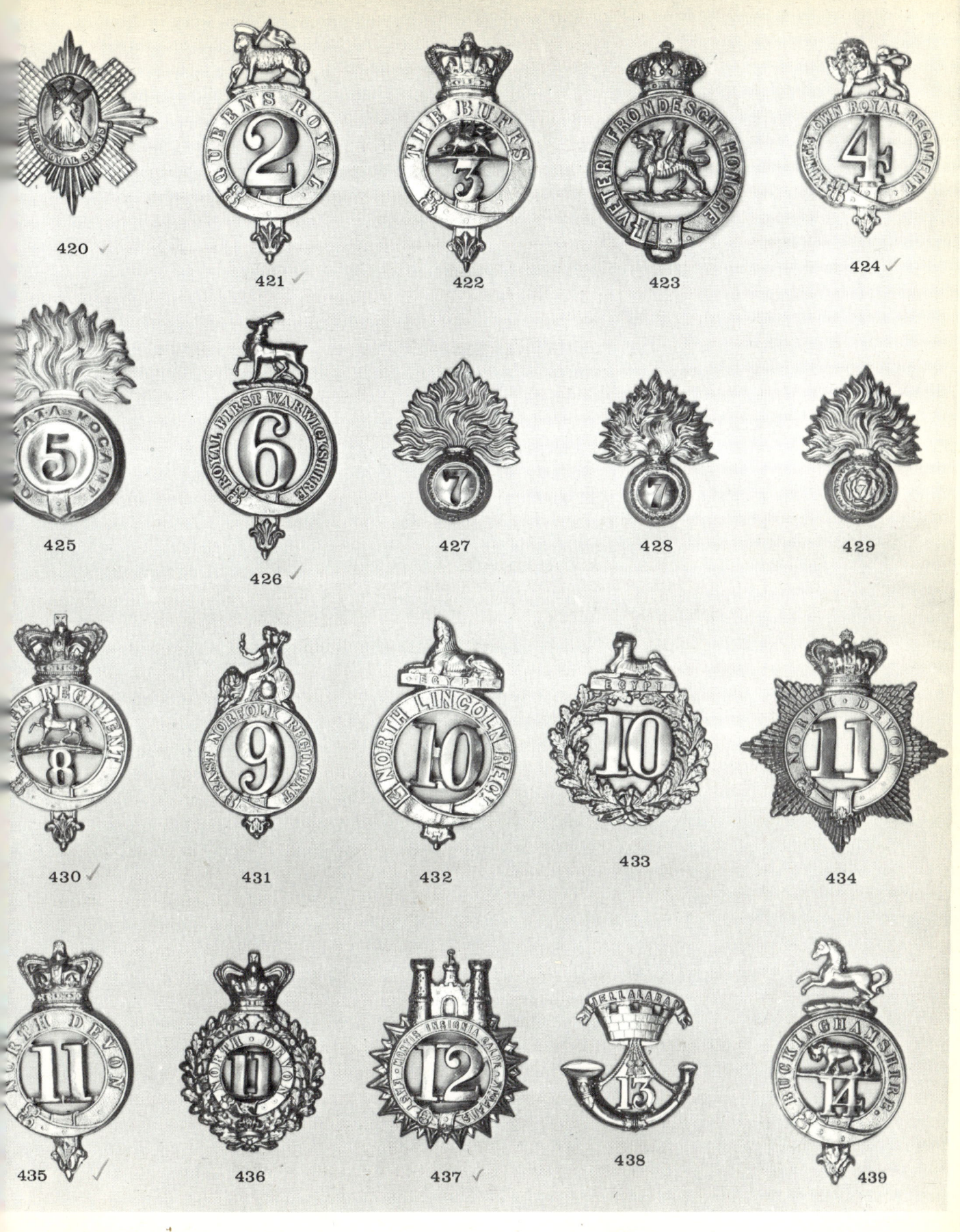

420

421

422

423

424

425

426

427

428

429

430

431

432

433

434

435

436

437

438

439

4th Foot

An oval strap inscribed *King's Own Royal Regiment* surmounted by the Lion of England. In the centre the numeral *4*. All in brass (Fig. 424).

5th Foot

A low-domed fused grenade. On the ball a strap inscribed *Quo fata vocant*. In the centre, the numeral *5* in cut-out form. All in brass (Fig. 425).

6th Foot

(1) A strap inscribed *Royal First Warwickshire* surmounted by the Antelope ducally chained and gorged standing on a wreathed scroll. In the centre the numeral *6*. All in brass (Fig. 426).

(2) A strap inscribed *Royal 1st Warwickshire Regiment* surmounted by a Victorian crown. In the centre the numeral *6*. All in brass.

7th or Royal Fusiliers

(1) A fused grenade. On the ball the Garter proper. In the centre the numeral *7* in cut-out form. All in brass (Fig. 427).

(2) Similar to above but smaller. All in brass (Fig. 428).

(3) Similar to above but smaller still and, in addition, in the centre the Union Rose with a small numeral *7* in the centre. All in brass (Fig. 429).

8th Foot

A strap inscribed *King's Regiment* surmounted by a Victorian crown. In the centre, the White Horse of Hanover standing on ground above the numeral *8*. All in brass except the White Horse which is in white-metal (Fig. 430).

9th Foot

A strap inscribed *East Norfolk Regiment* surmounted by the figure of Britannia holding a sprig of olive in her right hand and with the Lion lying down beside her. In the centre the numeral *9*. All in brass (Fig. 431).

10th Foot

(1) A strap inscribed *North Lincoln Regt* surmounted by the Sphinx superscribed *Egypt*. In the centre the numerals *10* All in brass (Fig. 432).

(2) A wreath of oak surmounted by the Sphinx superscribed *Egypt*. In the centre the numerals *10*. All in brass (Fig. 433).

11th Foot

(1) An eight-pointed star, the top point displaced by a Victorian crown. On this a strap inscribed *North Devon*. In the centre the numerals *11*. All in brass (Fig. 434).

(2) A strap inscribed *North Devon* surmounted by a Victorian crown. In the centre the numerals *11*. All in brass (Fig. 435).

(3) A wreath of oak surmounted by a Victorian crown. Within this a narrow strap inscribed *North Devon*. In the centre the numerals *11*. All in brass (Fig. 436).

440

441

442

443

444

445

446

447

448

449

450

451

452

453

454

455

456

457

458

459

12th Foot

A star of 25 points surmounted by the Castle of Gibraltar with the Key on top of the central turret. On this a strap inscribed at top *Montis Insignia Calpe* and at bottom *East Suffolk*. In the centre the numerals *12*. All in brass (Fig. 437).

13th Light Infantry

A bugle-horn surmounted by a mural crown above which a scroll inscribed *Jellalabad*. In the strings of the bugle the numerals *13*. All in brass (Fig. 438).

14th Foot

   (1) A circular strap inscribed *Buckinghamshire* surmounted by the White Horse of Hanover on a wreathed scroll. In the centre a Tiger over the numerals *14*. All in brass except the White Horse which is in white-metal (Fig. 439).

   (2) A strap inscribed *Prince of Wales's Own* surmounted by the Prince of Wales's plumes, coronet and motto. In the centre the White Horse of Hanover above the numerals *14*. Below the strap, a Tiger standing on a scroll inscribed *India*. The Prince of Wales's plumes, coronet and motto and the White Horse in white-metal, remainder in gilding-metal (Fig. 440).

15th Foot

   (1) A strap inscribed *York East Riding* surmounted by a Victorian crown. In the centre the numerals *15*. All in brass (Fig. 441).

   (2) A star of eight points on which a small circular laurel-wreath. In the centre the numerals *15*. All in brass (Fig. 442).

   (3) Similar to (2) but much smaller and in the centre the figures *XV* in Roman numerals. All in brass (Fig. 443).

16th Foot

   (1) A star of eight points, the top point displaced by a Victorian crown. Superimposed is a Maltese cross on which a laurel-wreath and within this a circular strap inscribed *Bedfordshire*. In the centre the Roman numerals *XVI*. All in brass (Fig. 444).

   (2) A Maltese cross. On this a laurel-wreath surmounted by a Victorian crown. In the centre the numerals *16*. All in brass (Fig. 445).

17th Foot

   (1) A strap inscribed *Leicestershire Regiment* surmounted by a Victorian crown. Within this the Royal Tiger above the numerals *17*. All in brass (Fig. 446).

   (2) The Garter proper surmounted by a Victorian crown. In the centre the numerals *17*. All in brass (Fig. 447).

   (3) A circlet, with laurel-leaves on both edges, inscribed *Leicestershire Regiment* and surmounted by a Victorian crown. In the centre, the Royal Tiger with a scroll above inscribed *Hindoostan* and below, the numerals *17*. All in brass (Fig. 448).

   (4) The Royal Tiger facing right standing on ground above the numerals *17*. All in brass (Fig. 449).

18th Foot

A strap inscribed *Royal Irish* surmounted by the Lion of Nassau standing on a wavy scroll. In the centre the Sphinx superscribed *Egypt*, below which the numerals *18*. All in brass (Fig. 450)

460   461   462   463   464

465   466   467   468   469   470

471   472   473   474   475

476   477   478   479   480

19th Foot

The Rose of York with a cut-out centre surmounted by a Victorian crown. In the centre the numerals *19*. All in brass (Fig. 451).

20th Foot

(1) A laurel-wreath surmounted by a Victorian crown with, at the base of the wreath, a small two-part scroll inscribed *East Devon*. In the centre the numerals *20*. In brass—also found in white-metal (Fig. 452).

(2) An oval-shaped laurel-wreath surmounted by a small Victorian crown. A single scroll at the base of the wreath inscribed *East Devon*. In the centre the numerals *20*. In brass (Fig. 453).

21st Foot

(1) A low-domed fused grenade. On the ball a strap inscribed *Royal North British Fusiliers*. In the centre the numerals *21* in cut-out form. All in brass (Fig. 454). Worn till 1877.

(2) As above but with the strap inscribed *Royal Scots Fusiliers*. Worn from 1877 to 1881.

22nd Foot

A strap inscribed *Cheshire Regiment* surmounted by a Victorian crown. In the centre the numerals *22*. All in brass (Fig. 455).

23rd Foot

(1) A low-domed fused grenade. On the ball a strap inscribed *Royal Welsh Fusiliers*. In the centre the numerals *23* in cut-out form. All in brass (Fig. 456).

(2) Design similar to above but smaller. All in brass (Fig. 457).

24th Foot

(1) A strap inscribed *2nd Warwickshire* surmounted by a Victorian crown. In the centre, the Sphinx superscribed *Egypt* above the numerals *24*. All in brass. Also found in white-metal (Fig. 458).

(2) A circlet inscribed *2nd Warwickshire*. In the centre the Sphinx superscribed *Egypt* above the Roman numerals *XXIV*. All in brass (Fig. 459).

25th Foot

(1) A strap inscribed *Kings Own Borderers* surmounted by the Royal Crest (in this version the Lion is crowned). In the centre the numerals *25*. All in brass (Fig. 460).

(2) A circlet inscribed *The King's Own Borderers* surmounted by the Royal Crest (in this version the Lion is uncrowned). On this St. Andrew's Cross. Within the circlet the Castle of Edinburgh with three turrets and above this a scroll inscribed *In veritate religionis confido* and below a further scroll inscribed *Nisi Dominus frustra*. A wreath of thistles surrounds the circlet and at its base the Roman numerals *XXV*. All in brass; also found in white-metal (Fig. 461).

(3) Similar to (2) but the lion on the Royal Crest is crowned. All in white-metal (Fig. 462).

26th Foot

(1) A bugle-horn with the numerals *26* in the curl.

(2) A mullet within a wreath of thistles. Below this a scroll inscribed *The Cameronians*. All in brass (Fig. 463).

27th Foot

A strap inscribed *Inniskilling Regiment* surmounted by the Castle of Inniskilling with St. George's flag flying. In the centre the numerals *27*. All in brass (Fig. 464).

28th Foot
   (1) A strap inscribed *North Gloucestershire* surmounted by a Victorian crown. In the centre the numerals *28*. All in brass (Fig. 465).
   (2) A strap inscribed *North Gloucestershire* surmounted by the Sphinx superscribed *Egypt*. In the centre the numerals *28*. All in brass (Fig. 466).
   (3) As (2) but smaller. All in brass (Fig. 467).
   (4) Backbadge: An oval with a rope-pattern edging with, in the centre, the numerals *28* in cut-out form. All in brass (Fig. 468).
   (5) Backbadge: Similar design to the above but the numerals are on a solid background. All in brass (Fig. 469).

29th Foot
   (1) A strap inscribed *Worcestershire* surmounted by a Victorian crown. In the centre the numerals *29*. All in brass (Fig. 470).
   (2) An eight-pointed star on which the Garter proper. In the centre the numerals *29*. All in brass (Fig. 471). This pattern is also found with a voided centre.

30th Foot
   (1) A strap inscribed *Spectemur Agendo* surmounted by a Victorian crown. In the centre the Sphinx superscribed *Egypt* with, below, the Roman numerals *XXX*. All in brass (Fig. 472).
   (2) A triple laurel-wreath surmounted by the Sphinx superscribed *Egypt*. Within the wreath an oval inscribed *Spectemur Agendo*. In the centre the Roman numerals *XXX*. All in brass (Fig. 473).

31st Foot
   (1) A strap inscribed *Huntingdonshire* surmounted by a Victorian crown. In the centre the numerals *31*. All in brass (Fig. 474).
   (2) A laurel-wreath surmounted by a Victorian crown. In the centre the numerals *31*. All in brass (Fig. 475).

32nd Light Infantry
   (1) A bugle with strings, the tassels being on the outside, surmounted by a Victorian crown. In the centre the numerals *32*. All in brass (Fig. 476).
   (2) A bugle with strings, the tassels hanging down the centre, surmounted by a bow resting on a three-part scroll inscribed *One and All*. In the centre of the bugle strings the numerals *32*. Below the bugle a scroll inscribed *Cornwall Light Infantry*. All in brass (Fig. 477).

33rd Foot

A strap inscribed *Duke of Wellington's* surmounted by the crest of the Duke of Wellington, *viz.* a demi-lion holding a forked pennon issuant from a ducal coronet. In the centre the numerals *33*. All in brass (Fig. 478).

34th Foot
(1) A laurel-wreath with the numerals *34* in the centre. All in brass (Fig. 479).
(2) A Maltese cross superimposed on a laurel-wreath and surmounted by a Victorian crown. On the arms of the cross are battle-honours as follows: (top) *Pyrenees, Nivelle, Nive*; (left) *Albuhera, Vittoria*; (right) *Peninsula, Orthes*; (bottom) *Sevastopol, Lucknow*. In the centre of the cross a circlet inscribed *Cumberland Regiment*. In the centre of the circlet the numerals *34*. Below the cross a scroll inscribed *Arroyo dos Molinos*. All in brass (Fig. 480).
(3) A Maltese cross superimposed on a laurel-wreath and surmounted by a Victorian crown. On the arms of the cross are battle-honours as follows: (top) *Peninsula, Sevastopol, Lucknow*; (left) *Pyrenees, Nive*; (right) *Vittoria, Orthes*; (bottom) *Nivelle, Albuhera*. In the centre of the cross a circlet inscribed *Cumberland Regt* and in the centre of the circlet the numerals *34*. All in brass (Fig. 481).

35th Foot
A strap inscribed *Royal Sussex* surmounted by a Victorian crown. In the centre the numerals *35*. All in brass; also found in white-metal (Fig. 482).

36th Foot
(1) A figure-of-eight scroll with laurel-ends inscribed *Firm* above the numerals *36*. All in brass (Fig. 483).
(2) A strap inscribed *Herefordshire Regiment* surmounted by a Victorian crown. In the centre the numerals *36* and above these a scroll inscribed *Firm*. All in brass (Fig. 484).
(3) Similar design to (2) but strap and crown are of a different shape. All in brass (Fig. 485).

37th Foot
A laurel-wreath surmounted by a crown. In the centre the numerals *37*. Across the base of the wreath a scroll inscribed *North Hampshire*. All in brass (Fig. 486).

38th Foot
(1) A wreath of laurel (left) and oak (right) surmounted by a crown. In the centre the numerals *38*. At the bottom join of the wreath the Stafford Knot. All in brass (Fig. 487).
(2) A strap inscribed *1st Staffordshire* surmounted by a Victorian crown. In the centre the numerals *38* above which the Stafford Knot. All in brass (Fig. 488).

39th Foot
The Castle of Gibraltar above a scroll inscribed *Gibraltar* and below this is the Key. A further scroll below, inscribed *Primus in Indis*, the ends joining the numerals *39* in the bottom centre. All in brass (Fig. 489).

40th Foot
(1) A laurel-wreath surmounted by the Sphinx superscribed *Egypt*. Within this a strap inscribed *Second Somersetshire*. In the centre the numerals *40*. All in brass (Fig. 490).
(2) Similar design to (1) but smaller. All in brass (Fig. 491).

481

482

483

484

485

486

487

488

489

490 ✓

491

492

493

494

495

496

497 ✓

498

499

500

41st Foot
(1) The numerals *41* surmounted by the Prince of Wales's plumes, coronet and motto. Below, a scroll inscribed *The Welsh Regt.* All in brass (Fig. 492).
(2) Similar design to (1) but the bottom scroll is extended to join the motto-scroll above. All in brass (Fig. 493).

42nd Foot
(1) St. Andrew and Cross standing on a large Sphinx superscribed *Egypt* and, below this, the numerals *42*. A scroll at the top inscribed *Waterloo* and a similar scroll at the bottom inscribed *Peninsula*. Sprays of thistles on either side. All in brass (Fig. 494).
(2) On an eight-pointed star, the figure of St. Andrew and Cross within an oval inscribed *Nemo me impune lacessit* and surmounted by a Victorian crown. Below the oval, the Sphinx superscribed *Egypt*. All in brass (Fig. 495).
(3) Similar design to (2) but larger and all in white-metal (Fig. 496).
(4) An eight-pointed star on which a wreath of thistles surrounding an oval inscribed *Nemo me impune lacessit* surmounted by a crown. In the centre of the oval the numerals *42* and below the oval the Sphinx. The star and numerals in white-metal, remainder in gilding-metal (Fig. 497).

43rd Light Infantry
A bugle with strings. Within the strings the numerals *43*. All in brass (Fig. 498).

44th Foot
(1) The numerals *44* surmounted by the Sphinx superscribed *Egypt*. All in brass (Fig. 499).
(2) A laurel-wreath, on the leaves of which are inscribed eleven battle-honours, surmounted by the Sphinx resting on a blank tablet. In the centre the numerals *44*. All in brass (Fig. 500).

45th Foot
A circlet inscribed *Nottinghamshire* surmounted by a Victorian crown. In the centre the numerals *45*. A scroll inscribed *Sherwood Foresters* is draped across the bottom of the circlet and, in the bottom-centre, a shield bearing the Arms of the City of Nottingham, *viz*: a ragged cross of wood proper between three open crowns of gold, the lowest encircling the bottom limb of the cross. All in brass (Fig. 501).

46th Foot
A strap inscribed *South Devonshire* surmounted by a Victorian crown. In the centre the numerals *46*. All in brass (Fig. 502).

47th Foot
A strap inscribed *Lancashire Regiment* surmounted by a Victorian crown. In the centre the numerals *47*. All in brass (Fig. 503).

48th Foot
A strap inscribed *Northamptonshire* surmounted by a Victorian crown. In the centre the numerals *48*. All in brass (Fig. 504).

501

502

503

504

505

506

507

508

509

510

511

512

513

514

515

516

517

518

519

520

49th Foot
  (1) A three-part scroll inscribed *Princess Charlotte of Wales* surmounted by a further scroll inscribed *Hertfordshire* which is surmounted by a Victorian crown. In the centre, the China Dragon resting on a tablet inscribed *China* and below this the numerals *49*. All in brass (Fig. 505).
  (2) As above but, in this pattern, the centre consists of the China Dragon resting on a tablet inscribed *China* and, above the Dragon, the Roman numerals *XLIX*. All in brass (Fig. 506).

50th Foot
The numerals *50* surmounted by the Royal Crest. All in brass (Fig. 507).

51st Light Infantry
  (1) A strung bugle, within the strings the numerals *51*. All in brass (Fig. 508).
  (2) A laurel-wreath within which a strap inscribed *The King's Own Light Infantry* and surmounted by a crown. In the centre, a bugle with the numerals *51* in the curl. All in brass (Fig. 509).

52nd Light Infantry
A bugle with strings. Within the strings the numerals *52*. All in brass (Fig. 510).

53rd Foot
  (1) A strap inscribed *Shropshire Regiment* surmounted by a crown. In the centre the numerals *53*. All in brass (Fig. 511).
  (2) As above but smaller and with Victorian crown. All in brass (Fig. 512).

54th Foot
A strap inscribed *West Norfolk Regiment* surmounted by a Sphinx resting on a tablet inscribed *Marabout*. In the centre the numerals *54*. All in brass (Fig. 513).

55th Foot
A laurel-wreath surmounted by the China Dragon resting on a tablet inscribed *China*. On the wreath are three battle-honour scrolls inscribed: (left) *Inkerman*, (right) *Sevastopol*, and (bottom) *Alma*. Within the wreath a strap inscribed *Westmoreland*. In the centre the numerals *55*. All in brass (Fig. 514).

56th Foot
  (1) A strap inscribed *Montis Insignia ·Calpe* surmounted by the Castle and Key of Gibraltar. In the centre the numerals *56*; below this a shield bearing the Arms of Essex, *viz.* three Seaxes. All in brass (Fig. 515).
  (2) A strap inscribed *West Essex* surmounted by the Castle of Gibraltar. In the centre the Key resting on a scroll inscribed *Montis Insignia Calpe* and below this the numerals *56*. All in brass (Fig. 516).
  (3) The Castle and Key of Gibraltar resting on a scroll inscribed *Pompadours*. All in brass (Fig. 517).

521   522   523   524   525

526   527   528   529   530

531   532   533   534   535

536   537   538   539   540

57th Foot
(1) A laurel wreath surmounted by a Victorian crown. In the centre the numerals *57*. Below, a scroll inscribed *Albuhera*. All in brass (Fig. 518).
(2) A strap inscribed *West Middlesex* surmounted by a Victorian crown. In the centre the numerals *57*. All in brass.

58th Foot
A strap inscribed *Montis Insignia Calpe* surmounted by the Castle and Key of Gibraltar. In the centre the numerals *58*. All in brass (Fig. 519).

59th Foot
A laurel-wreath surmounted by a Victorian crown. In the centre the numerals *59*. Below, a scroll inscribed *2nd Nottinghamshire*. All in brass (Fig. 520).

60th: King's Royal Rifle Corps
(1) A Maltese cross on the arms of which are inscribed battle-honours. Above, a scroll inscribed *Peninsula* and, below, a similar scroll inscribed *Celer et Audax*; the ends of the scrolls joining the centre arms of the cross and the whole surmounted by a Victorian crown. A circlet in the centre inscribed *The King's Royal Rifle Corps* and within this a strung bugle with the numerals *60* within the strings. All in black-metal (Fig. 521).
(2) Similar design to (1) but the scrolls do not join the arms of the cross, the battle-honours are in a different sequence and there are four lions between the arms of the cross. All in black-metal (Fig. 522).

61st Foot
A strap inscribed *South Gloucestershire* surmounted by a Victorian crown. In the centre, the Sphinx superscribed *Egypt*. Below this the numerals *61*. All in brass (Fig. 523).

62nd Foot
(1) A cross patée. On the ends of the cross four battle-honours: *Sobraon, Ferozeshah, Sevastopol, Nive*. In the centre of the cross, a strap inscribed *Wiltshire* and, in the centre of this, the numerals *62*. All in brass (Fig. 524).
(2) Within a laurel-wreath surmounted by a Victorian crown a strap inscribed *Regiment* with the numerals *62* in the centre. All in brass.

63rd Foot
A strap inscribed *The West Suffolk* surmounted by a Victorian crown. In the centre the numerals *63*. All in brass (Fig. 525). Also in white-metal.

64th Foot
A strap inscribed *2nd Staffordshire* surmounted by a Victorian crown. In the centre, the Stafford Knot above the numerals *64*. All in brass (Fig. 526).

65th Foot
A strap inscribed *Second Yorkshire North Riding* surmounted by a crown. In the centre, the Royal Tiger standing on ground above the numerals *65*. All in brass (Fig. 527).

66th Foot

A laurel-wreath surmounted by a Victorian crown and with a scroll inscribed *Berkshire* across the base of the wreath. In the centre the numerals *66*. All in brass (Fig. 528).

67th Foot

A strap inscribed *South Hampshire* surmounted by the Royal Tiger standing on a wavy scroll. In the centre the numerals *67*. All in brass (Fig. 529).

68th Light Infantry

A bugle with strings. Within the strings the numerals *68*. All in brass (Fig. 530).

69th Foot

A strap inscribed *South Lincolnshire* surmounted by a Victorian crown. In the centre the numerals *69*. All in brass (Fig. 531).

70th Foot

(1) A strap inscribed *The Surrey Regiment* surmounted by a Victorian crown. In the centre the numerals *70*. All in brass (Fig. 532).

(2) The numerals *70* surmounted by a crown and with a scroll under inscribed *The Surrey Regt*. All in brass (Fig. 533).

71st Light Infantry

A bugle-horn with the numerals *71* in the curl. All in brass (Fig. 534).

72nd Highlanders

(1) A raised domed-ball with a chequered design on which the numerals *72*. Above, a scroll inscribed *Duke of Albany's* and surmounted by a Victorian crown. Below the ball, thistle-sprays and below this, on foliage, two scrolls one above the other, the top one reading *Own* and the bottom *Highlanders*. All in brass (Fig. 535).

(2) Similar design to (1) but the foliage surrounding the two bottom scrolls is omitted. All in brass (Fig. 536).

73rd Foot

(1) The numerals *73* with, above, a scroll inscribed *Perthshire* which is surmounted by a Victorian crown. Sprays of thistle either side. On the left, a scroll inscribed *Seringapatam* and on the right, a scroll inscribed *Mangalore*. Below the numerals, a further scroll inscribed *Waterloo*. All in brass (Fig. 537).

(2) A strap inscribed *Perthshire* surmounted by a Victorian crown. In the centre the numerals *73*. All in brass (Fig. 538).

74th Foot

An eight-pointed star on the centre of which a circlet inscribed *Nemo me impune lacessit*. In the centre the numerals *74*. All in brass but also found all in white-metal (Fig. 539).

75th Foot

An oval wreath of thistles. Within this the Royal Tiger standing on ground above the numerals *75*. All in brass but also found all in white-metal (Fig. 540).

76th Foot

(1) A strap inscribed *Hindoostan* surmounted by an Elephant with a howdah on its back and standing on a wavy scroll. In the centre the numerals *76*. All in brass (Fig. 541).

(2) The Elephant standing on ground, below which the numerals *76*. All in brass (Fig. 542).

77th Foot

The numerals *77* surmounted by the Prince of Wales's plumes, coronet and motto. All in brass (Fig. 543).

78th Foot

(1) Within a wreath of thistles an Elephant surmounted by a Victorian crown. Below the Elephant, a scroll inscribed *Cuidigh'n Righ* and below this the numerals *78*. All in brass (Fig. 544).

(2) Similar to (1) but larger and the motto scroll spelt *Cuidigh'n Rhi*. All in brass (Fig. 545).

(3) Identical with (2) except that the motto scroll is now spelt *Cuidigh'n Righ*. All in brass (Fig. 546).

79th Foot

(1) St. Andrew with Cross surrounded by a wreath of thistles. Below, and separate, the numerals *79* with beaded edges. All in white-metal (Fig. 547).

(2) St. Andrew with Cross surrounded by a wreath of thistles. All in brass but also found all in white-metal (Fig. 548).

80th Foot

A strap inscribed *Staffordshire Volunteers* surmounted by a Victorian crown. In the centre the Stafford Knot and below this the numerals *80*. All in brass (Fig. 549).

81st Foot

A strap inscribed *Loyal Lincoln Volunteers* surmounted by a Victorian crown. In the centre the numerals *81*. All in brass (Fig. 550).

82nd Foot

A strap inscribed *Prince of Wales's Volunteers* surmounted by the Prince of Wales's plumes, coronet and motto. In the centre the numerals *82*. All in brass (Fig. 551).

83rd Foot

(1) A strap inscribed *County of Dublin* surmounted by a Victorian crown. In the centre the numerals *83*. All in brass (Fig. 552).

(2) The numerals *83* surmounted by a scroll inscribed *County of Dublin* and a similar scroll below inscribed *Regiment*. The whole ensigned with a Victorian crown. All in brass (Fig. 553).

(3) The numerals *83* with a scroll interwoven with the numerals and inscribed *County of Dublin Regiment*. The whole ensigned with a Victorian crown. All in brass (Fig. 554).

541

542

543

544

545

546

547

548

549

550

551 ✓

552

553

554

555

556

84th Foot

A laurel-wreath surmounted by a coronet. Within this the Union Rose above the numerals *84*. All in brass (Fig. 555).

85th Light Infantry

A bugle with strings. Within the strings the numerals *85*. All in brass (Fig. 556).

86th Foot

A strap inscribed *Royal County Down* surmounted by a Victorian crown. In the centre, the Irish Harp with shamrocks either side resting on a scroll inscribed *Quis Separabit*. Below this the numerals *86*. All in brass (Fig. 557).

87th Foot

A low-domed fused grenade. On the ball a strap inscribed *Royal Irish Fusiliers*. In the centre, the numerals *87* in cut-out form. All in brass (Fig. 558).

88th Foot

   (1) A wreath of shamrock surmounted by the Victorian crown. In the centre the Irish Harp and, below this, the numerals *88*. All in brass (Fig. 559).
   (2) The Irish Harp with a Victorian crown above and the numerals *88* below. The design is in brass but made to resemble embroidery (Fig. 560).

89th Foot

A strap inscribed *Princess Victoria's* surmounted by a coronet. In the centre the numerals *89*. At the base the Sphinx superscribed *Egypt*. All in brass (Fig. 561).

90th Light Infantry

A bugle with strings. Within the strings the numerals *90*. All in brass (Fig. 562).

91st Foot

An eight-pointed star. On this a circlet inscribed *Nemo me impune lacessit*. In the centre the numerals *91*. All in brass (Fig. 563).

92nd Foot

   (1) A complete wreath of thistles. In the centre the Sphinx superscribed *Egypt*. Below this the numerals *92*. All in white-metal (Fig. 564).
   (2) A continuous ivy-wreath joined at the top. Within this, the crest of the Marquis of Huntley, *viz*: a stag's head above a ducal coronet. Below this the numerals *92* resting on a scroll inscribed *Bydand*. All in white-metal (Fig. 565).

93rd Highlanders

   (1) A wreath of thistles surmounted by a Victorian crown. In the centre, a circlet inscribed *Sutherland Highlanders* and in the centre of this the numerals *93*. A scroll at the base of the design inscribed *Cape of Good Hope*. All in brass (Fig. 566).
      This badge was worn on the feather bonnet 1837–1856.
   (2) Design similar to the above but two scrolls at the base; the first inscribed *Cape of Good Hope*, the second *Balaclava*. All in brass (Fig. 567).
      This badge was worn on the feather bonnet 1856–1881.
   (3) A complete wreath of thistles. On this a strap inscribed *Sutherland Highlanders*. In the centre the numerals *93*. All in brass (Fig. 568).

557

558

559

560

561

562

563

564

565

566

567

568

569

570

571

572

94th Foot

A strap inscribed *Regiment* surmounted by a Victorian crown. In the centre the numerals *94*. All in brass (Fig. 569).

95th Foot

A cross patée. On this a circular plate with the numerals *95* thereon. All in brass (Fig. 570).

96th Foot

(1) The Garter proper surmounted by a Victorian crown. In the centre the numerals *96*. All in brass (Fig. 571).

(2) As above but in the centre the numerals *96* above a Sphinx superscribed *Egypt*. All in brass (Fig. 572).

97th Foot

(1) A strap inscribed *The Earl of Ulster's* surmounted by a Victorian crown. In the centre, the numerals *97*. All in brass (Fig. 573).

(2) A strap inscribed *Earl of Ulster's* surmounted by a large Victorian crown. In the centre the numerals *97*. All in brass.

98th Foot

A strap inscribed *Regiment* surmounted by a Victorian crown. In the centre the numerals *98*. All in brass but also found all in white-metal (Fig. 574).

99th Foot

A strap inscribed *Duke of Edinburgh's Regiment*. In the centre the Duke of Edinburgh's coronet and cypher and superimposed on this the numerals *99*. All in brass (Fig. 575).

100th Foot

A strap inscribed *Prince of Wales's* surmounted by the Prince of Wales's plumes, coronet and motto. In the centre the numerals *100*. All in brass (Fig. 576).

101st Fusiliers

A low-domed fused grenade. On the ball a strap inscribed *Royal Bengal Fusiliers*. In the centre the numerals *101* in cut-out form. All in brass (Fig. 577).

102nd Fusiliers

A low-domed fused grenade. On the ball a strap inscribed *Royal Madras Fusiliers*. In the centre the numerals *102* in cut-out form. All in brass (Fig. 578).

103rd Fusiliers

(1) A low-domed fused grenade. On the ball a strap inscribed *Royal Bombay Fusiliers*. In the centre the numerals *103* in cut-out form. All in brass (Fig. 579).

(2) A fused grenade with a plain ball resting on the numerals *103*. All in brass (Fig. 580).

104th Fusiliers

A low-domed fused grenade. On the ball a strap inscribed *Bengal Fusiliers*. In the centre the numerals *104* in cut-out form. All in brass (Fig. 581).

573

574

575

576

577

578

579

580

581

582

583

584

585

586

587

588

105th Light Infantry
A bugle surmounted by a Victorian crown. The numerals *105* in the curl of the bugle. All in brass (Fig. 582).

106th Light Infantry
A wreath of laurel surmounted by a Victorian crown. Within this a bugle with the numerals *106* in the curl. On the base of the wreath a scroll inscribed *Bombay Light Infantry*. All in brass (Fig. 583).

107th Regiment
(1) A strap inscribed *Bengal Infantry* surmounted by a Victorian crown. In the centre the numerals *107*. All in brass (Fig. 584).
(2) A Maltese cross surmounted by a Victorian crown. On the cross a laurel-wreath and within this a strap inscribed *Bengal Infantry*. In the centre the numerals *107*. All in brass (Fig. 585).

108th Regiment
A strap inscribed *Madras Infantry* surmounted by a Victorian crown. In the centre the numerals *108*. All in brass (Fig. 586).

109th Regiment
A strap inscribed *Bombay Infantry* surmounted by a Victorian crown. In the centre the numerals *109*. All in brass (Fig. 587).

Rifle Brigade
A laurel-wreath surmounted by a crown. On the wreath's left-hand side are two scrolls inscribed *Sevas/topol*, the word broken in two; on the right-hand side two scrolls inscribed *Alma* and *Inkerman*. Within the wreath, a cross based on that of the Order of the Bath with battle-honours on the arms, thereon a circlet inscribed *Rifle Brigade* enclosing a strung bugle surmounted by a crown. A tablet inscribed *Waterloo* above the cross and immediately under the crown, and a similar tablet inscribed *Peninsula* at the base of the cross. In black-metal (Fig. 588).

CHAPTER 12

Slouch-Hat and Forage-Cap Badges worn by the Regular Infantry Regiments: 1898 to 1921

The Royal Scots (Lothian Regiment)
The Star of the Order of the Thistle in white-metal. In the centre St. Andrew and Cross above a scroll inscribed *The Royal Scots* in gilding-metal. A voided centre to show a red-cloth backing (Fig. 589).

The Queen's (Royal West Surrey Regiment)
The Paschal Lamb in gilding-metal above a scroll inscribed *The Queen's* in white-metal. In this pattern the flag is swallow-tailed (Fig. 590).

The Buffs (East Kent Regiment)
The Dragon above a scroll inscribed *The Buffs*. All in gilding-metal (Fig. 591).

The King's Own (Royal Lancaster Regiment)
The Lion of England on a bar inscribed *The King's Own*. All in gilding-metal (Fig. 592).

The Northumberland Fusiliers
A fused grenade. On the ball a circlet inscribed *Northumberland Fusiliers*. In the centre St. George killing the Dragon. All in gilding-metal (Fig. 593).

The Royal Warwickshire Regiment
The Antelope ducally chained and gorged standing on a torse (heraldic crest-wreath). Below this a wavy scroll inscribed *Royal Warwickshire*. The Antelope in white-metal, title-scroll in gilding-metal (Fig. 594).

The Royal Fusiliers (City of London Regiment)
  (1) A fused grenade. On the ball, the Garter proper with a Victorian crown super-imposed displacing some of the lettering. In the centre a Rose. All in gilding-metal (Fig. 595).
  (2) As (1), but a different arrangement of flames, an Imperial crown and smaller in size. All in gilding-metal (Fig. 596).
  (3) As (1), but Imperial crown above the Garter showing complete lettering. All in gilding-metal (Fig. 597).

The King's (Liverpool Regiment)
The White Horse of Hanover standing on ground in white-metal. Below, a scroll inscribed *The King's* in gilding-metal (Fig. 598).

The Norfolk Regiment

The figure of Britannia holding a sprig of olive in her right hand, a trident in her left hand resting against her left shoulder; below her left arm an oval shield bearing the Great Union. The whole enclosed by a laurel-wreath. All in white-metal. Below, a scroll inscribed *The Norfolk Regt* in gilding-metal (Fig. 599).

The Lincolnshire Regiment

The Sphinx superscribed *Egypt* in old English characters, in white-metal. Below, a scroll inscribed *Lincolnshire* in gilding-metal (Fig. 600).

The Devonshire Regiment

(1) An eight-pointed star the topmost point displaced by a Victorian crown. On this a circlet inscribed *The Devonshire Regiment*. In the centre the Castle of Exeter. Star and Castle in white-metal, remainder in gilding-metal (Fig. 601).

(2) As above but with Imperial crown (Fig. 602).

The Suffolk Regiment

(1) The Castle and Key of Gibraltar, with a scroll above inscribed *Gibraltar*, within a circlet inscribed *Montis Insignia Calpe* surmounted by a Victorian crown, the whole within a wreath of oak. All in white-metal. Below, a scroll inscribed *The Suffolk Regt* in gilding-metal (Fig. 603).

(2) As above but with Imperial crown (Fig. 604).

(3) As above but with redesigned Castle and Key in accordance with War Office Instruction of 30th January 1900. (Fig. 605.)

Prince Albert's (Somerset Light Infantry)

A bugle surmounted by a mural crown and above this a scroll inscribed *Jellalabad*. Within the strings of the bugle the letters *PA*. In white-metal (Fig. 607).

The Prince of Wales's Own (West Yorkshire Regiment)

The White Horse of Hanover on ground in white-metal. Below, a scroll inscribed *West Yorkshire* in gilding-metal (Fig. 608).

The East Yorkshire Regiment

An eight-pointed star. On this a laurel-wreath and within it a Rose. Below the star a scroll inscribed *East Yorkshire*. The Rose in white-metal, remainder in gilding-metal (Fig. 609).

The Bedfordshire Regiment

(1) A Maltese cross superimposed on an eight-pointed star. On this the Garter proper and in the centre a Hart crossing a ford. Below, a scroll inscribed *Bedfordshire*. Star and scroll in gilding-metal, remainder in white-metal (Fig. 610).

(2) As above but scroll inscribed *Bedfordshire & Hertfordshire* set below bottom point of the star. All in white-metal (Fig. 611).

In 1919, *Hertfordshire* was added to the title in recognition of the fact that many men from Hertfordshire enlisted in The Bedfordshire Regiment during the Great War (Army Order 269 of 1919).

589

590

591

592

593

594

595

596

597

598

599

600

601

602

603

604

605

606

607

608

The Leicestershire Regiment
The Royal Tiger superscribed *Hindoostan* resting on a scroll inscribed *Leicestershire*. The Tiger in gilding-metal, remainder in white-metal (Fig. 612).

The Royal Irish Regiment
   (1) The Irish Harp surmounted by a Victorian crown. Below, a scroll inscribed *The Royal Irish Regiment*. All in gilding-metal (Fig. 613).
   (2) As above but the Harp surmounted by an Imperial crown. All in gilding-metal (Fig. 614).

Alexandra, Princess of Wales's Own (Yorkshire Regiment)
   (1) The letter *A*, cypher of the late Queen Alexandra, thereon the Dannebrog inscribed *1875*, surmounted by a coronet and surrounded by a complete wreath of roses on which are two scrolls: the top inscribed *The Princess of Wales's Own* and the bottom *Yorkshire*. The wreath and scrolls in white-metal, remainder in gilding-metal (Fig. 615).
   (2) The letter *A* and Dannebrog surmounted by a coronet and on these the date *1875* and *Alexandra* all resting on a tablet inscribed *Yorkshire*. Below, a scroll inscribed *The Princess of Wales's Own Regt.* Below the word *of* is a rose. All in white-metal (Fig. 616).
   (3) As (2) but the letter *A* is not voided and is surmounted by an Imperial crown. In white-metal (Fig. 617).

The Lancashire Fusiliers
A fused grenade. On the ball a laurel-wreath and within this the Sphinx superscribed *Egypt*. In gilding-metal. Below, a scroll inscribed *The Lancashire Fusiliers* in white-metal (Fig. 618).

The Royal Scots Fusiliers
   (1) A fused grenade. On the ball the Royal Arms with a Victorian crown. In gilding-metal (Fig. 619).
   (2) As above but the Royal Arms surmounted by the Royal Crest with Imperial crown. In gilding-metal (Fig. 620).

The Cheshire Regiment
On an eight-pointed star in white-metal, an acorn with oak-leaves in gilding-metal. Below, a scroll inscribed *Cheshire* in white-metal (Fig. 621).

The Royal Welsh Fusiliers
   (1) A fused grenade. On the ball a circlet inscribed *Royal Welsh Fusiliers*. In the centre the Prince of Wales's plumes, coronet and motto. The grenade and plumes in gilding-metal, remainder in white-metal (Fig. 622).
   (2) In 1920, the title was altered to read *Royal Welch Fusiliers*. Besides the grenade and plumes the coronet is also in gilding-metal (Fig. 623).

The South Wales Borderers
   (1) An unbroken wreath of Immortelles on the base of which the letters *SWB*. In the

609

610

611

612

613

614

615

616

617

618

619

620

621

622

623

624

625

626

627

628

centre the Sphinx superscribed *Egypt*. The wreath in gilding-metal, remainder in white-metal (Fig. 624).

(2) As above but slightly larger and the tablet inscribed *Egypt* has bolder letters (Fig. 625).

The King's Own Scottish Borderers

(1) A circlet inscribed *King's Own Scottish Borderers*, thereon the Cross of St. Andrew and, within the circlet, the Castle of Edinburgh with three turrets, a flag flying to the left of each; above the circlet a scroll inscribed *In veritate religionis confido* and below the circlet another scroll inscribed *Nisi Dominus frustra*. Outside the circlet a wreath of thistles, the whole ensigned with the Royal Crest with Victorian crown. In white-metal (Fig. 626).

(2) As (1) but smaller (Fig. 627).

(3) As (1) but Royal Crest with Imperial crown (Fig. 628).

(4) As (2) but Royal Crest with Imperial crown (Fig. 629).

The Cameronians (Scottish Rifles)

(1) A mullet above a bugle stringed and enclosed by a spray of thistles. In blackened brass (Fig. 630).

(2) As above but with alterations in the design of the thistle-wreath. In white-metal (Fig. 631).

The Royal Inniskilling Fusiliers

(1) A fused grenade. On the ball the Castle of Inniskilling with St. George's flag flying to the left from the central turret. Below, a scroll inscribed *Inniskilling*. Grenade and flames in gilding-metal, remainder in white-metal (Fig. 632).
Also found with flag flying to the right.

(2) As above, but smaller and with different design of flames and the flag flying to the right (Fig. 633). This was the officers' cap badge.

The Gloucestershire Regiment

(1) The Sphinx superscribed *Egypt* above two sprays of laurel. Below, a scroll inscribed *Gloucestershire*. In white-metal (Fig. 634).

(2) Back-badge: The Sphinx superscribed *Egypt* within a complete laurel-wreath. In gilding-metal (Fig. 635).

The Worcestershire Regiment

An eight-pointed star. On this the Garter proper and within this the Lion of England. At the base of the star a small tablet inscribed *Firm*. Below, a scroll inscribed *Worcestershire*. In gilding-metal (Fig. 636).

The East Lancashire Regiment

(1) The Sphinx superscribed *Egypt* and below this the Rose; the whole within a laurel-wreath surmounted by a Victorian crown. Resting on the lower portion of the wreath a scroll inscribed *East Lancashire*. The Rose in gilding-metal, remainder in white-metal (Fig. 637).

(2) As above but with Imperial crown (Fig. 638).

629

630

631

632

633

634

635

636

637 ✓

638 ✓

639

640

641

642

643

644

645

646

647

648

The East Surrey Regiment

(1) An eight-pointed star, the topmost point displaced by a Victorian crown; which rest on a shield bearing the Arms of Guildford. Below, a scroll inscribed *East Surrey*. Crown, shield and scroll in gilding-metal, remainder in white-metal (Fig. 639).

(2) As above but with Imperial crown (Fig. 640).

The Duke of Cornwall's Light Infantry

(1) A bugle, with a bow at the top of the strings and two tassels, surmounted by a coronet. All in gilding-metal. Also found in white-metal (Fig. 606).

(2) A bugle with strings. Resting on each end of the bugle a scroll inscribed *Cornwall*. Above the scroll a coronet. In white-metal (Fig. 641).

The Duke of Wellington's (West Riding Regiment)

The crest and motto of the Duke of Wellington above a scroll inscribed *The West Riding*. The crest and motto in white-metal, remainder in gilding-metal (Fig. 642).

The Border Regiment

(1) An eight-pointed star, the topmost point displaced by a Victorian crown. On the star a cross, similar to that of the Order of the Bath, on the four arms of which are inscribed battle-honours. The cross is superimposed on a laurel-wreath. In the centre of the cross a circlet inscribed *Arroyo dos Molinos 1811* and in the centre a Dragon superscribed *China* on a ground of one-third white (above) and two-thirds red (below). On the lower points of the star a scroll inscribed *The Border Regt*. In white-metal except the lower two-thirds of the centre which is red cloth (Fig. 643).

(2) As above but with Imperial crown (Fig. 644).

(3) As (2) but larger (Fig. 645).

The Royal Sussex Regiment

The Star of the Order of the Garter over the Roussillon plume with a scroll below inscribed *The Royal Sussex Regt*. The scroll in gilding-metal, remainder in white-metal (Fig. 646).

The Hampshire Regiment

The Hampshire Rose, above which the Royal Tiger standing on an heraldic torse, the whole enclosed by a laurel-wreath. On the lower part of the wreath a scroll inscribed *Hampshire*. The Rose and scroll in gilding-metal, remainder in white-metal (Fig. 647).

The South Staffordshire Regiment

(1) The Stafford Knot surmounted by a Victorian crown. Below the Knot a scroll inscribed *South Staffordshire*. The scroll in gilding-metal, remainder in white-metal (Fig. 648).

(2) As above but with Imperial crown (Fig. 649).

The Dorsetshire Regiment

(1) The Castle and Key of Gibraltar. Above, the Sphinx superscribed *Marabout*. Below the castle, a scroll inscribed *Primus in Indis*. A laurel-wreath enclosing the complete design with, across the top, a scroll inscribed *Dorsetshire*. Wreath and title-scroll in gilding-metal, remainder in white-metal (Fig. 650).

(2) The Castle and Key of Gibraltar. Above, the Sphinx superscribed *Marabout*. Below

649   650   651   652

653   654   655   656

657   658   659   660

661   662   663   664

665   666   667   668

the castle, a scroll inscribed *Primus in Indis*. A laurel-wreath encloses the castle and motto and is continued below the castle by a scroll inscribed *Dorsetshire*. Wreath and title-scroll in gilding-metal, remainder in white-metal (Fig. 651).

The Prince of Wales's Volunteers (South Lancashire Regiment)
The Prince of Wales's plumes, coronet and motto. Below, the Sphinx superscribed *Egypt*. Above the plumes, a scroll inscribed *South Lancashire* and below the Sphinx a scroll inscribed *Prince of Wales's Vols*. Branches of laurel connect the ends of the scrolls. The plumes, motto and Sphinx over *Egypt* in white-metal, remainder in gilding-metal (Fig. 652).

The Welsh Regiment
(1) The Prince of Wales's plumes, coronet and motto. Below, a scroll inscribed *The Welsh*. The plumes and motto in white-metal, remainder in gilding-metal (Fig. 653).
(2) In 1920, the spelling was altered to *The Welch*. (Fig. 654.)

The Black Watch (Royal Highlanders)
(1) The Star of the Order of the Thistle. On the Star a thistle-wreath. Within the wreath, an oval inscribed *Nemo me impune lacesset*, surmounted by a Victorian crown. Within the oval, St. Andrew and Cross. Below the wreath the Sphinx. Across the top of the wreath a scroll inscribed *The Royal Highlanders*. At the base, on either side of the Sphinx, scrolls inscribed *Black Watch*. All in white-metal (Fig. 655).
(2) General design as above but with Imperial crown and the scrolls at top and bottom extended to edge of star and spelling of motto altered to *Lacessit*. St. Andrew and Cross, title-scrolls and Star in white-metal, remainder in gilding-metal (Fig. 656).
(3) General design as above but with Imperial crown and spelling of motto *Lacessit*. All in white-metal (Fig. 657).
(4) Design as (1) but with centre voided. The crown, motto, Sphinx and scroll in one piece in gilding-metal, St. Andrew and Cross and the Star in white-metal.
     Note: all types of badges can be found with the spelling of both *Lacessit* and *Lacesset*.

The Oxfordshire and Buckinghamshire Light Infantry
A Bugle-horn with strings. In white-metal (Fig. 658).

The Essex Regiment
(1) The Castle and Key of Gibraltar. Above the Castle, the Sphinx superscribed *Egypt*. The whole, except the Sphinx, enclosed in a wreath of oak. On the base of the wreath a scroll inscribed *The Essex Regt*. The Sphinx and title-scroll in white-metal, remainder in gilding-metal (Fig. 659).
(2) As above, but with redesigned Castle (Fig. 660).

The Sherwood Foresters (Derbyshire Regiment)
(1) A Maltese cross surmounted by a Victorian crown. In the centre of the cross a wreath of oak, and within the wreath a stag lodged. On the left arm of the cross and across the left branch of the wreath a half-scroll inscribed *Sherwood* and on the right arm of the cross and across the right branch of the wreath a half-scroll inscribed *Foresters*. Below the cross a scroll inscribed *Derbyshire*. Title-scroll in gilding-metal, remainder in white-metal (Fig. 661).
(2) As above but ensigned with the Imperial crown, and title-scroll inscribed *Notts & Derby* (Fig. 662).

669

670

671

672

673

674

675

676

677

678

679

680

681

682

683

684

685

686

687

The Loyal North Lancashire Regiment
(1) The Royal Crest, with Victorian crown, above the Rose of Lancashire. Below the Rose a scroll inscribed *Loyal North Lancashire*. The Royal Crest in white-metal, remainder in gilding-metal (Fig. 663).
(2) As above but the Royal Crest with Imperial crown. (Fig. 664.)
(3) In 1921, following change of title, the scroll altered to read *The Loyal Regiment* (Fig. 665).

The Northamptonshire Regiment
The Castle and Key of Gibraltar within a laurel-wreath. Above the Castle a scroll inscribed *Gibraltar* and below the Castle a scroll inscribed *Talavera*. On the base of the wreath a scroll inscribed *Northamptonshire*. All in white-metal except the title-scroll which is in gilding-metal (Fig. 666).

Princess Charlotte of Wales's (Royal Berkshire Regiment)
The China Dragon on a bar above a scroll inscribed *Royal Berkshire*. In gilding-metal (Fig. 667).

The Queen's Own (Royal West Kent Regiment)
The White Horse of Kent on a scroll inscribed *Invicta* in old English lettering. Below the motto-scroll another scroll inscribed *Royal West Kent*. In white-metal (Fig. 668).

The King's Own (Yorkshire Light Infantry)
(1) A French horn with the White Rose of York in the twist. The Rose in white-metal, the French horn in gilding-metal. Worn on the smasher hat (Fig. 669).
(2) As above but smaller. Worn on the forage-cap (Fig. 670).

The King's (Shropshire Light Infantry).
A strung bugle-horn, the strings tied in three bows. Within the bend of the bugle, and below the strings, on bars the letters *KSLI*. In white-metal with *KSLI* in gilding-metal (Fig. 671).

The Duke of Cambridge's Own (Middlesex Regiment)
The Prince of Wales's plumes, coronet and motto. Below, the coronet and cypher of the Duke of Cambridge interlaced and reversed, all within a laurel-wreath. Across the base of the wreath a scroll inscribed *Albuhera*. Below the wreath a scroll inscribed *Middlesex Regt*. The plumes, motto and title-scroll in white-metal, remainder in gilding-metal (Fig. 672).

The King's Royal Rifle Corps
(1) A Maltese cross. On the top arm a tablet inscribed *Celer et Audax* and above the tablet a Victorian crown. In the centre of the cross a circlet inscribed *The King's Royal Rifle Corps*. Within the circlet a bugle with strings. Battle-honours on each arm of the cross. In black metal on a red-cloth backing (Fig. 673).
(2) As above but with Imperial crown (Fig. 674).
(3) As (2) but larger (Fig. 675).

The Duke of Edinburgh's (Wiltshire Regiment)
A cross patée lined with burnished edges. On the cross a circular convex plate and thereon the cypher of the Duke of Edinburgh. Above the cross a coronet. Below, a scroll inscribed *The Wiltshire Regiment*. All in gilding-metal (Fig. 676).

688

689

.690

691

692

693

694

695

696

697

698

699

700

701

702

703

704

705

The Manchester Regiment
The arms, crest and supporters of the City of Manchester in white-metal. Below, a scroll inscribed *Manchester* in gilding-metal (Fig. 677).

The Prince of Wales's (North Staffordshire Regiment)
The Stafford Knot with the Prince of Wales's plumes, coronet and motto above and a scroll inscribed *North Stafford* below. The coronet and Knot in gilding-metal, remainder in white-metal (Fig. 678).

The York and Lancaster Regiment
The Royal Tiger with the Union Rose above and surmounted by a coronet. Below the Tiger, a scroll inscribed *York and Lancaster* with laurel-sprays continuing the scroll to the coronet. The coronet in white-metal, the Rose in white-metal with gilding-metal centre, remainder in gilding-metal (Fig. 679).

The Durham Light Infantry
(1) A bugle with strings taken upwards into the base of a Victorian crown. Within the strings the letters *DLI*. All in white-metal (Fig. 680).
(2) As above, but with Imperial crown (Fig. 681).

The Highland Light Infantry
(1) The Star of the Order of the Thistle, thereon a bugle-horn. In the twist of the horn the monogram *HLI*. Above the horn a Victorian crown and below it the Elephant superscribed *Assaye* on a scroll. All in white-metal (Fig. 682).
(2) As above but with Imperial crown and with *Assaye* on a very long scroll (Fig. 683).
(3) As (2) but with *Assaye* on a short scroll (Fig. 684).

Seaforth Highlanders (Ross-shire Buffs, The Duke of Albany's)
A stag's head caboshed above a scroll inscribed *Cuidich'n Righ*. In white-metal (Fig. 685).

The Gordon Highlanders
(1) The crest of the Marquis of Huntley, *viz*: A stag's head issuant from a ducal coronet within a wreath of ivy. On the bottom of the wreath a scroll inscribed *By Dand* as two separate words. In white-metal (Fig. 686).
(2) As above but with *Bydand* spelt as one word (Fig. 687).

The Queen's Own Cameron Highlanders
St. Andrew with Cross within a wreath of thistles. On the base of the wreath a scroll inscribed *Cameron*. In white-metal (Fig. 688).

The Royal Irish Rifles
(1) A Harp surmounted by a scroll inscribed *Quis Separabit* with a Victorian crown above. Below the Harp, a tri-part scroll inscribed *Royal Irish Rifles*. In black-metal (Fig. 689). This was probably the Glengarry badge.
(2) A Harp surmounted by an Imperial crown. Below the Harp a scroll inscribed *Quis Separabit*. In black-metal (Fig. 690). Worn until 1913 when a white-metal badge was introduced.
(3) As (2) but in white-metal (Fig. 691).

Princess Victoria's (Royal Irish Fusiliers)

(1) A fused grenade in gilding-metal. On the ball in white-metal an eagle with a laurel wreath on its breast standing on a small tablet inscribed with the numeral *8*. Above this, as a separate badge, the coronet of Queen Victoria when Princess in white-metal (Fig. 692). This is the officers' collar badge.

(2) A fused grenade in gilding-metal. On the ball in white-metal a Harp surmounted by the Prince of Wales's plumes, coronet and motto. Above this, as a separate badge, a Coronet in white-metal (Fig. 693). This badge was not worn with the coronet.

(3) As (2) but smaller and with the coronet joined to the flames of the grenade (Fig. 694).

The Connaught Rangers

(1) A Harp surmounted by a Victorian crown. Below, a scroll inscribed *Connaught Rangers*. In gilding-metal (Fig. 695).

(2) As above but with Imperial crown (Fig. 696).

Princess Louise's (Argyll and Sutherland Highlanders)

(1) A circlet inscribed *Argyll and Sutherland*. Within the circlet the letter *L*, cypher of H.R.H. the late Princess Louise, interlaced and reversed. Within the circlet and on the left of the cypher the Boar's Head and on the right of the cypher the Cat. Above the cypher and resting on the top part of the circlet the Princess's coronet. The whole within a wreath of thistles. In white-metal (Fig. 697).

(2) As above but with the centre voided (Fig. 698).

The Prince of Wales's Leinster Regiment (Royal Canadians)

(1) The Prince of Wales's plumes, coronet and motto. At the base a scroll inscribed *The Leinster*. Coronet and title-scroll in gilding-metal. Plumes and motto in white-metal (Fig. 699).

(2) As above, but with different form of coronet (Fig. 700).

The Royal Munster Fusiliers

A fused grenade in gilding-metal. On the ball in white-metal a Tiger standing on a scroll inscribed *Royal Munster* (Fig. 701).

The Royal Dublin Fusiliers

A fused grenade in gilding-metal. On the ball in white-metal a Tiger above an Elephant. Below the grenade in white-metal a scroll inscribed *Royal Dublin Fusiliers* (Fig. 702).

Rifle Brigade (The Prince Consort's Own)

(1) A cross based on that of the Order of the Bath, thereon a circlet inscribed *Rifle Brigade* enclosing a bugle surmounted by a Victorian crown; the cross enclosed with a laurel wreath on which are four battle-honour scrolls, the upper ends of the wreath connected by a tablet inscribed *Waterloo* surmounted by a Guelphic crown. Battle-honours on each arm of the cross. Below the cross a scroll inscribed *Peninsula*. In white-metal (Fig. 703).

(2) As above but with Imperial crown (Fig. 704).

(3) A larger pattern with the Imperial crown and, on the laurel-wreath, fourteen battle-honour scrolls (Fig. 705).

CHAPTER 13

Cavalry Full-Dress Devices

The Cavalry was unaffected by the Cardwell reforms of 1881 and did not lose its numbers which remained unchanged until the amalgamations following the end of the Great War.

   The earliest badges worn by Cavalry Regiments were those of the Light Dragoons which have been dealt with in Chapter 1.

   During the nineteenth century, the Light Dragoons were converted into either Hussars or Lancers, the last four Regiments becoming Hussars in 1861, and by the end of the century the cavalry consisted of three regiments of Household Cavalry, seven of Dragoon Guards, three of Dragoons, twelve of Hussars and six of Lancers.

706

THE HOUSEHOLD CAVALRY

The badges of the Household Cavalry are the Royal Arms, the Royal Crest and the Star of the Order of the Garter. Early-pattern helmets carried the Royal Cypher while the Garter Star made its appearance in 1842. Except for the inclusion of the Collar of the Order in a later version and the necessary changes of crown there has been practically no change since.

1st Life Guards

Officers: Within a wreath of oak-leaves and laurel, on a frosted-gilt centre surmounted by a crown, the Star of the Order of the Garter. Around the centre, the Collar of the Order with the George upon the lower ends of the stems of the wreath. The colours of the Garter, Cross and Field are displayed in enamel. The Star is silver, the remainder gilt(Fig. 706).
Other Ranks: Same design as officers but all in gilding-metal except the Star which is in white-metal (Fig. 707).

2nd Life Guards

Officers: As for the 1st Life Guards except that the field of the Cross is in silver.

Royal Horse Guards

Same design as Life Guards.

707

709A

DRAGOON GUARDS AND DRAGOONS

In place of the cocked hat, a helmet was introduced for Heavy Cavalry in 1812 and had a reversed Royal Cypher with the title of the regiment on an oval below.

Between 1818 and 1847, the plates on the helmet were of a triangular pointed ray type bearing the Royal Arms of the period with the Regimental title on a metal band below. In later versions some regiments had battle-honours on the plate.

In 1847, a new helmet appeared. It was in gilt or gilding-metal for the seven regiments of Dragoon Guards and in white-metal for the 1st and 6th Dragoons.

The design of the badge was the Royal Cypher, surrounded by a strap bearing the title of the regiment, on a star set upon an ornamental shield. Sprays of laurel and oak either side and the crown over all. That of the 6th (Inniskilling) Dragoons is shown (Fig. 708).

711

712

713

714

717

715

716

In 1871 the design was much simplified, consisting of a twelve-pointed star on which was a strap inscribed with the regimental title and a regimental device in the centre. Except for the change in the Royal Cypher and crown there was little change until full-dress was discontinued.

According to the Dress Regulations for 1900 the designs for the officers' helmets were as follows:

1st (King's) Dragoon Guards
On the Garter Star, in silver, the Garter with motto in gilt or gilding-metal, pierced on a ground of blue-enamel. Within the Garter, on a ground of red-enamel, the Royal Crest in silver. On the puggaree, the Austrian Eagle in gilt or gilding-metal.

2nd Dragoon Guards (Queen's Bays)
On the Garter Star, the Garter with motto pierced on a blue enamel ground; within the Garter the Royal Cypher in silver on a ground of red enamel.

3rd (Prince of Wales's) Dragoon Guards
On the Garter star, in silver, the Garter with motto in gilt or gilding-metal, pierced on a ground of blue enamel. Within the Garter, in silver, the Prince of Wales's plumes on a scarlet-enamel ground (Fig. 709).

4th (Royal Irish) Dragoon Guards
On the Garter star, in silver, a gilt pierced oval inscribed *Quis Separabit MDCCLXXXIII* on a ground of Garter-blue enamel. Within the oval on a silver ground the Cross of St. Patrick in red enamel and on this a shamrock leaf in green enamel with a gilt and red-enamel crown on each petal (Fig. 709A).

5th (Princess Charlotte of Wales's) Dragoon Guards
On the Garter star, in gilt or gilding-metal, an elliptical ring inscribed *P.C.W. Dragoon Guards*. Within the ring *5* in silver.

6th Dragoon Guards (Carabiniers)
In silver, the Garter, with motto in gilt or gilding-metal, pierced on a background of blue-enamel. Within the Garter on a ground of red-enamel, the figure *6* in silver. The Star has plain rays.

7th (Princess Royal's) Dragoon Guards
On the Garter Star, in silver, an elliptical ring with *The Princess Royal's Dragoon Guards* in burnished gilt or gilding-metal on a silver-blue enamel ground. Within, on a ground of red-enamel, the figure *7* in silver.

1st (Royal) Dragoons
In gilt or gilding-metal the Garter Star. On the Star the Crest of England on a burnished silver ground within an elliptical ring, in silver, inscribed *The Royal Dragoons* (Fig. 710).

6th (Inniskilling) Dragoons
On a gilt or gilding-metal beaded Garter Star an elliptical ring inscribed *Inniskilling Dragoons* in burnished letters on a frosted ground. Within the ring, in silver, the Castle over *VI* on a frosted gilt or gilding-metal ground.

The helmet plates for other-ranks were similar in shape to those of the officers, but carried only the regimental number in the centre. To distinguish between the 1st Dragoon Guards and the 1st Dragoons, and the 6th Dragoon Guards and the 6th Dragoons, the metals were reversed.

1st (King's) Dragoon Guards

On a white-metal star a gilt Garter within which a white-metal numeral *1* on a black leather ground (Fig. 711).

3rd (Prince of Wales's) Dragoon Guards

On a white-metal star a gilt Garter within which a white-metal numeral *3* on a black leather ground (Fig. 712).

1st (Royal) Dragoons

On a gilding-metal star a white-metal Garter within which a gilding-metal numeral *1* on a black leather ground (Fig. 713).

6th (Inniskilling) Dragoons

On a gilding-metal star a white-metal Garter within which a gilding-metal numeral *6* on a black leather ground (Fig. 714).

The *2nd Dragoons (Royal Scots Greys)* is not dealt with in the preceding section as its members have worn, for many years, a distinctive head-dress which is unique to English Cavalry—a grenadier-cap of black bear-skin.

On this cap, a fused-grenade badge on the left side holds a white plume and on the back of the cap is a silver or white-metal White Horse of Hanover: a reminder of early days when the Regiment wore grenadier-caps similar to those described in the Royal Warrant of 1751.

2nd Dragoons (Royal Scots Greys)

(1) A fused grenade in gilt or gilding-metal. On the ball the Royal Arms. In the centre below, St. Andrew and Cross between sprays of rose, thistle and shamrock. A scroll beneath inscribed *Waterloo* (Fig. 715).

(2) The White Horse of Hanover (Fig. 716).

LIGHT DRAGOONS

The 11th Light Dragoons were converted to Hussars in 1840 and only four Light Dragoon Regiments then remained, until 1861 when they too became Hussars. These were the 3rd, 4th, 13th and 14th Hussars.

On the last shako, before conversion, the plate was a Maltese cross surmounted by a crown.

3rd (King's Own) Light Dragoons

On the top edge of the cross *King's Own* and on the bottom edge *Light Dragoons*. On the other edges, the following battle-honours: *Salamanca, Vittoria, Toulouse, Peninsula.* In the centre of the cross a laurel-wreath and within this the White Horse of Hanover with *Nec aspera terrent* above. Below the Horse, the Roman numerals *III*.

4th (Queen's Own) Light Dragoons

(1) On the edges of the cross the following battle-honours: *Talavera, Salamanca, Albuhera, Peninsula*. In the centre of the cross, a strap inscribed *The Queen's Own Light Dragoons* and within this a laurel-wreath with the Roman numerals *IV* in the centre. Immediately above the strap, a scroll inscribed *Vittoria* and a scroll below the strap inscribed *Toulouse*.

(2) On the edges of the cross the following battle-honours: *Talavera, Salamanca, Toulouse, Affghanistan, Vittoria, Ghuznee, Albuhera, Peninsula, Alma, Balaklava, Inkerman, Sevastopol*. In the centre of the cross, a strap inscribed *The Queen's Own Lt. Dragoons* with, in the centre, the Roman numerals *IV* in ornamental characters (Fig. 716A).

13th Light Dragoons

On the top edge of the cross *Light* and on the bottom edge *Dragoons*. On the other edges, the following battle-honours: *Peninsula, Waterloo, Alma, Balaklava, Inkerman, Sebastopol*. In the centre of the cross, the Roman numerals *XIII* surrounded by a strap inscribed *Viret in Aeternum*.

716A

14th (The King's) Light Dragoons
On the top edge of the cross *Fourteenth* and on the bottom edge *Light Dragoons*. On the other edges, the following battle-honours: *Orthes, Vittoria, Salamanca, Punjaub, Goojerat, Chillian-wallah, Peninsula, Fuentes d'Onor, Talavera, Douro*. In the centre of the cross, the Garter proper and within this the Royal Crest. Above the Garter a scroll inscribed *Persia*. All in gilt (Fig. 717).

HUSSARS

Badges were not worn on the busby, the colours of the plume and the busby-bag serving to indicate the regiment. When serving in India, Hussars wore the white helmet instead of the busby and certain puggaree-badges were authorised. Those for officers according to the 1900 Dress Regulations were:

7th (Queen's Own) Hussars
In gilt or gilding-metal a circlet inscribed **7***th Queen's Own Hussars* surmounted by a crown. Within the circlet in silver the letters *QO* reversed and intertwined.

11th (Prince Albert's Own) Hussars
In gilt or gilding-metal the crest and motto of the late Prince Consort.

14th (King's) Hussars
The Eagle in silver on a gilt or gilding-metal shield inscribed *14th Hussars*.

LANCERS

Lancer regiments first made their appearance in the British Army in 1816 when four Light Dragoon regiments were converted of which three survive—the 9th, 12th and 16th. The 17th were added in 1822, the 5th in 1858 and the 21st in 1897.

The dress followed closely that of Napoleon's Polish Lancers of the Imperial Guard and the head-dress, of distinctive Polish design, was called the *czapska* after the Polish word for 'cap'. The front was adorned with a triangular metal plate, with scalloped edge, decorated with a pattern of rays dispersing from a central badge or cypher.

The first-pattern lancer-cap was superseded in 1826 and yet another version appeared in 1846. The final pattern, worn until full-dress was discontinued, was authorised in 1856.

The early plates were not quite so elaborate as later patterns which incorporated the various battle-honours subsequently awarded.

They are triangular in shape with scalloped top edges and the traditional rays dispersing from the bottom-centre upon which are superimposed the Royal Arms, the title of the regiment and its battle-honours. The only variation in this basic pattern is the 9th Lancers who have always differed from the others.

Plates worn after the death of Queen Victoria had the Imperial crown substituted for the Victorian crown. Officers' plates were in gilt-and-silver but other-ranks had plates of the same design in gilding-metal ranging from a light yellow brass to a deep bronze.

5th (Royal Irish) Lancers
(1) On a gilt or gilding-metal plate of universal pattern, in silver: the Royal Arms with,

below, the Harp between sprays of shamrock. Across the bottom of the plate, a scroll inscribed *Fifth Royal Irish Lancers*.

(2) As above, but with two scrolls inscribed *Blenheim, Oudenarde* above *Fifth* and two scrolls inscribed *Ramillies, Malplaquet* above *Lancers*.

(3) As (2) but with the addition of a scroll inscribed *Suakin* above *Blenheim* and *1885* above *Ramillies* (Fig. 718).

(4) As (2) but with scroll inscribed *Suakin, 1885* above the Harp and two additional scrolls on the bottom of the plate inscribed *Defence of Ladysmith* and *South Africa, 1899–1902*.

(5) On the puggaree: On crossed lances a circlet inscribed *Quis Separabit*. Within the circlet the figure *5*.

9th (Queen's Royal) Lancers

(1) In gilt or gilding-metal the universal plate with, on the Royal Arms, two oval shields; on the left the Royal Arms and on the right that of Queen Adelaide. Two pairs of crossed lances behind. Below the Arms in silver, the Cypher of Queen Adelaide reversed and intertwined. On either side sprays of laurel. Below the Cypher a scroll inscribed *Royal Lancers*.

(2) As above but with battle-honour scrolls added to the laurel-sprays: (left) *Punniar, Sobraon, Peninsula, Delhi*; (right) *Chillianwallah, Goojerat, Punjaub, Lucknow* (Fig. 719).

(3) As (1) but with six honour-scrolls either side: (left) *Peninsula, Sobraon, Chillianwallah, Delhi, Charasiah, Kandahar*; (right) *Punniar, Punjaub, Goojerat, Lucknow, Kabul, Afghanistan*.

(4) As (3) but with dates added as follows: *Kabul, 1879, Kandahar, 1880, Afghanistan, 1878–80*.

(5) As (4) but with four additional scrolls: (bottom left) *Relief of Kimberley*; (bottom right) *South Africa, 1899–1902*; (above title scroll) *Modder River, Paardeberg* (Fig. 720).

12th (Prince of Wales's Royal) Lancers

(1) In silver the Royal Arms, with the Prince of Wales's plumes, coronet and motto above and the Sphinx superscribed *Egypt* below; the scroll inscribed *Dieu et mon Droit* resting on two sprays of rose, thistle and shamrock intertwined. Below on two gilt or gilding-metal scrolls the battle-honour scrolls *Peninsula* and *Waterloo* finished with sprays of laurel.

(2) As above, but with three scrolls *Peninsula, Waterloo* and *South Africa, 1851–2–3*.

(3) As above but with, on the left, two scrolls *South Africa, 1851–2–3* and *Peninsula*; on the right *Central India* and *Waterloo*. Below the Sphinx, *Sevastopol*.

(4) As above, but with the addition on left of *South Africa 1899–1902*; on right, *Relief of Kimberley*; below, *Sevastopol Paardeberg* (Fig. 721).

16th (Queen's) Lancers

(1) The universal plate in gilt or gilding-metal. On the plate in silver the Royal Arms surmounted by the Sovereign's helm on which rests the Royal Crest. Above the Royal Arms a scroll inscribed *Queen's*. Below the Royal Arms on scrolls the following battle-honours: (left) *Peninsula, Bhurtpore, Maharajpore*; (right) *Waterloo, Affghanistan, Sobraon*; (centre) *Ghuznee, Aliwal*. Bottom centre the numerals *16*.
This is an extra large plate being $11'' \times 5\frac{1}{2}''$ instead of the usual $9'' \times 5''$.

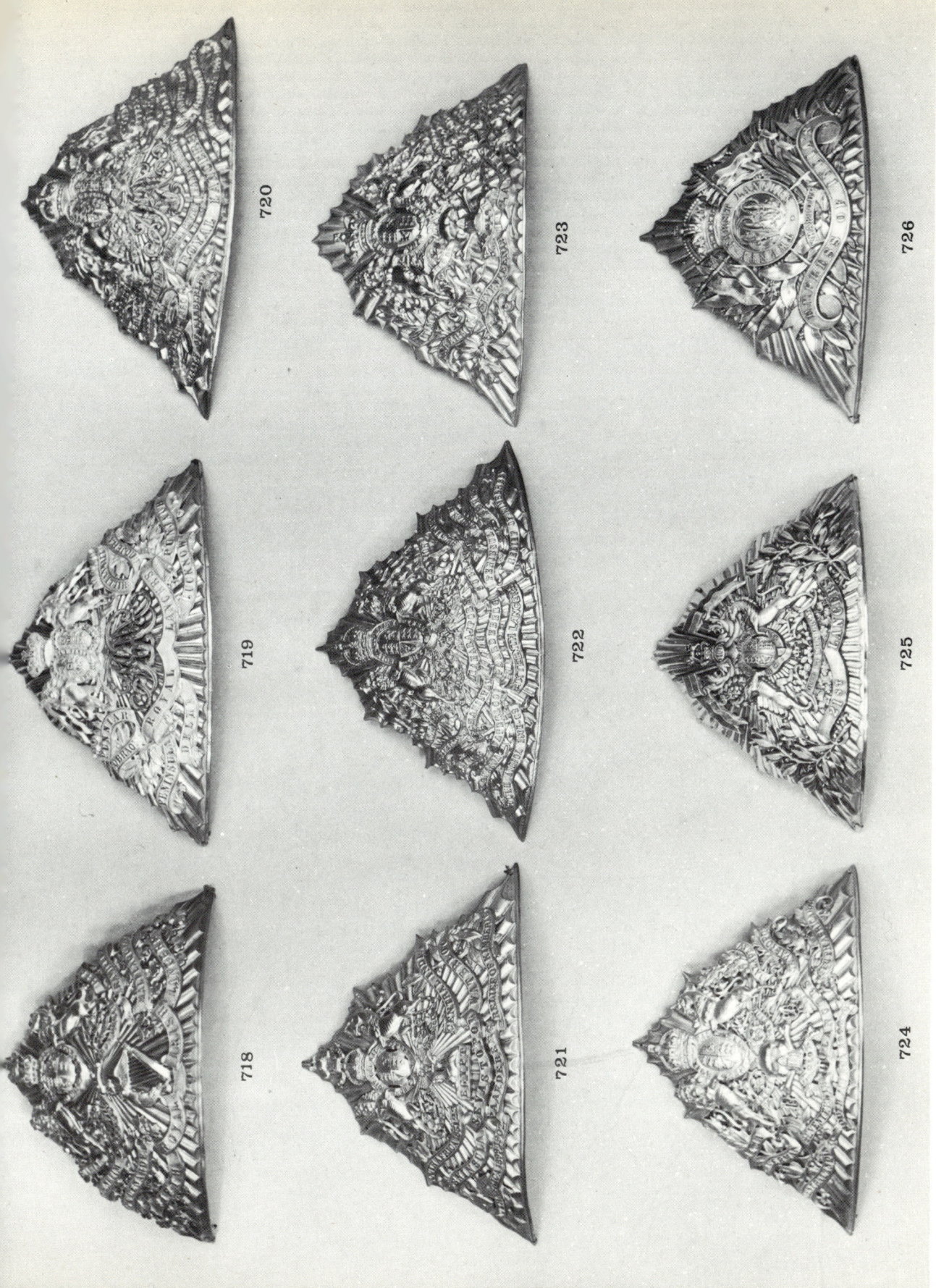

718

719

720

721

722

723

724

725

726

(2) The universal plate in gilt or gilding-metal. On the plate in silver the Royal Arms superimposed on crossed lances. Below the Royal Arms a scroll inscribed *Maharajpore* and below this a scroll inscribed *Sixteenth Lancers*. On laurel-sprays, the following battle-honours: left, *Talavera, Fuentes d'Onor, Nive, Salamanca, Afghanistan, Waterloo;* right, *Sobraon, Peninsula, Vittoria, Bhurtpore, Ghuznee, Aliwal.*

(3) As above but with the addition, at the base, of three more scrolls inscribed *South Africa, 1900–02, Paardeberg, Relief of Kimberley* (Fig. 722).

17th (Duke of Cambridge's Own) Lancers

(1) In silver the Royal Arms with, below, the Death's Head and scroll inscribed *Or Glory*. In old English characters on the left the letter *D*, below the letter *C* and on the right the letter *O*. On the left a branch of laurel on the right a branch of oak. On the left, two scrolls inscribed *Alma, Inkerman* and on the right, two scrolls inscribed *Balaclava, Sevastopol*. At the bottom of the plate a scroll inscribed *Seventeenth Lancers* (Fig. 723).

(2) As above but with additional scroll *Central India*.

(3) As above but with three scrolls on left *Alma, Inkerman, Central India* and three scrolls on right *Balaclava, Sevastopol, South Africa, 1879*.

(4) As (3) but with the addition of a scroll inscribed *South Africa, 1900–02* below the title scroll (Fig. 724).

21st (Empress of India's) Lancers

(1) In silver, on crossed lances, the Royal Arms with a scroll below inscribed *21st Lancers*. Laurel-sprays either side (Fig. 725).

(2) In silver in the centre the Royal Cypher *VRI* within a circlet inscribed *Twenty First Lancers* surmounted by a crown and superimposed on crossed lances. Beneath the circlet a scroll inscribed *Khartoum* and a further scroll below *Empress of India's*. On the left a spray of laurel, on the right a spray of palm (Fig. 726).

(3) On crossed lances the Royal Arms with a scroll below inscribed *Khartoum*. Below the scroll the Imperial Cypher. On the left a spray of laurel with a scroll below it inscribed *21st (Empress of*; and on the right palm leaves with a scroll below them inscribed *India's) Lancers*.

CHAPTER 14

Cavalry Field-Service Caps: 1896 to 1922

THE HOUSEHOLD CAVALRY

On the 1913 Manoeuvres the Household Cavalry wore khaki for the first time on home service. King George v commented to Lieutenant-Colonel Wilson of The Blues that his Household Cavalry, alone in the British Army, had no cap badge. He offered, if the three regiments so wished, to supply the deficiency.

Two distinct types of badges were produced. One for the Service Dress cap and one for the Forage cap. These were:

(1) For the Service Dress cap: The Royal Cypher surrounded by a circlet and ensigned with the Imperial crown. The circlet bearing in each case the title of the regiment. These badges were issued on the outbreak of war in 1914.

(2) For the Forage cap: The Royal Cypher surrounded by the Garter and ensigned with the Imperial crown. This badge was common to all three regiments and not taken into wear until the Forage cap was re-issued in 1919.

During the Great War there were in the Guards Division one divisional mounted Cavalry squadron from the 1st Life Guards and two squadrons Cyclists supplied by the 2nd Life Guards and Royal Horse Guards respectively. These all wore their own regimental cap badge.

Details of these various badges are as follows:

1st Life Guards
The Royal Cypher of King George v pierced: within a circlet inscribed *First Life Guards* and surmounted by an Imperial crown. In bronze (Fig. 727).
Also an Officers' pattern in gilt with red- and blue-enamel backing.

2nd Life Guards
The Royal Cypher of King George v pierced; within a circlet inscribed *Second Life Guards* and surmounted by an Imperial Crown. In brass (Fig. 728).
Also an Officers' pattern in gilt with red- and blue-enamel backing.

The Life Guards
The 1st and 2nd Life Guards were amalgamated in 1922.

(1) The Royal Cypher of King George v pierced; within a circlet inscribed *Life Guards 1st and 2nd* and surmounted by an Imperial crown. In bronze only (Fig. 729).

(2) The Royal Cypher of King George v pierced; within a circlet inscribed *The Life Guards* and surmounted by an Imperial crown. In brass, also in bronze (Fig. 730).

Royal Horse Guards (The Blues)

The Royal Cypher of King George v pierced; within a circlet inscribed *Royal Horse Guards* and surmounted by an Imperial crown. In bronze (Fig. 731).

Also an Officers' pattern in gilt with red- and blue-enamel backing.

The Household Cavalry

The Royal Cypher of King George v pierced; within the Garter, and surmounted by an Imperial crown. In brass, also in bronze (Fig. 732).

The Household Battalion

In September 1916, a battalion of Infantry was raised from the three Reserve Regiments of Household Cavalry. Designated the Household Battalion, it proceeded to France and joined the 4th Division.

Badge: the Royal Cypher of King George v on a solid background within the Garter, and surmounted by an Imperial crown. In brass or bronze (Fig. 733).

CAVALRY OF THE LINE

All titles are as carried before 1920, at which date changes were made in the designation of all cavalry regiments.

1st (King's) Dragoon Guards

(1) The double-headed Eagle of the Emperor Francis Joseph II of Austria on a scroll inscribed *King's Dragoon Guards*. Other-ranks' in brass. Officers' in gilt, or bronze for service dress (Fig. 734).

The wearing of this badge was discontinued in 1915 but resumed in 1937.

(2) An eight-pointed star, the topmost point displaced by an Imperial crown. On the star, the letter *K* above the letters *DG* within the Garter (Fig. 735). The star and crown in white-metal, remainder in gilding-metal. Also an economy issue during the Great War in all-brass. Officers' pattern: gilt crown, gilt centre and voided Garter, star in silver, blue background to Garter, and letters *KDG* in silver. Also in bronze for service dress.

2nd Dragoon Guards (Queen's Bays)

(1) The word *Bays* in old-English lettering within a laurel-wreath surmounted by a Victorian crown (Fig. 736).

In brass. For officers: gilt and also bronze.

(2) As above but with Imperial crown (Fig. 737).

In brass. For officers: gilt and also bronze.

3rd (Prince of Wales's) Dragoon Guards

(1) The Prince of Wales's plumes, coronet and motto above a scroll inscribed *3rd Dragoon Guards* (Fig. 738). The coronet and scroll in gilding-metal, remainder in white-metal. Officers: in gilt-and-silver, also in bronze.

(2) As above but with slight difference in design to *3rd* on title-scroll. The coronet and title-scroll in gilding-metal, remainder in white-metal. Also economy issue in all brass (Fig. 739).

Note: Although amalgamated with the 6th Dragoon Guards in 1920 to form the *3rd/6th Dragoon Guards*, each squadron retained its separate regimental badge until the regiment received the title of *3rd Carabiniers (Prince of Wales's Dragoon Guards)* in 1928. The new combined badge was not worn until 1929.

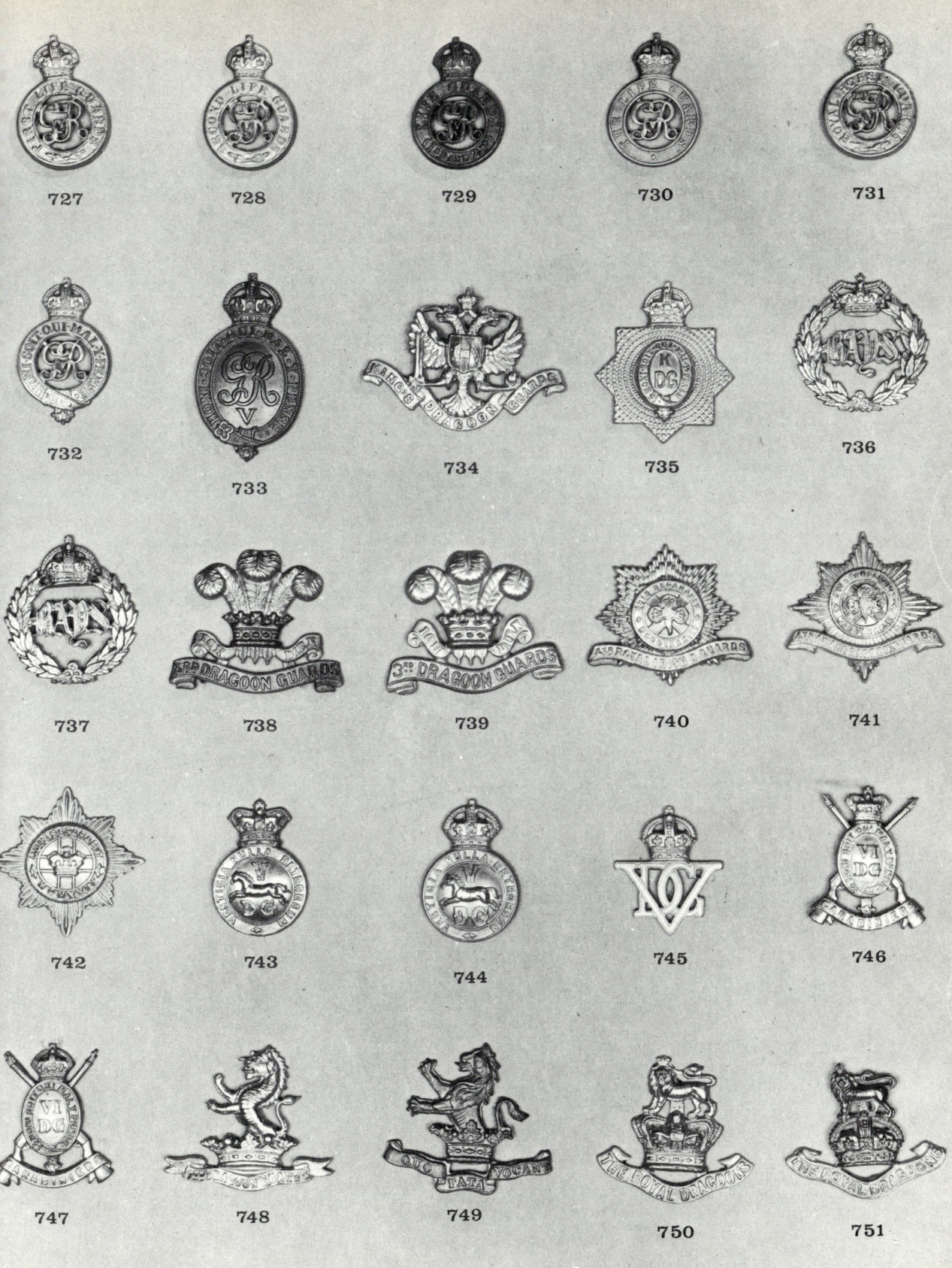

727   728   729   730   731

732   733   734   735   736

737   738   739   740   741

742   743   744   745   746

747   748   749   750   751

The 4th Royal Irish Dragoon Guards

(1) The Star of the Order of St. Patrick. Below, a scroll inscribed *4th Royal Irish D. Guards*. The star in white-metal, scroll in gilding-metal. War economy issue all-brass. Officers: in silver-and-gilt, also in bronze (Fig. 740).

(2) The Star of the Order of St. Patrick. Below, a scroll inscribed *4th (RI) Dragoon Guards*. Officers' pattern: in silver with gilt scroll. Also in bronze (Fig. 741). No other-ranks' found in this pattern.

4th/7th Dragoon Guards

The 4th and 7th Dragoon Guards were amalgamated in 1922.

An eight-pointed star, thereon a circlet inscribed *Quis Separabit MCMXXII*. Within the circlet St. George's Cross with the Princess Royal's coronet superimposed thereon (Fig. 742). In white-metal. Officers: in silver and also in bronze. Another pattern exists with the star in silver, the motto voided, the centre having a red-enamel cross on a white-enamel ground, red-enamel in the coronet and green behind the motto.

The 5th (Princess Charlotte of Wales's) Dragoon Guards

(1) A circlet inscribed *Vestigia nulla retrorsum* surmounted by a Victorian crown. In the centre the White Horse of Hanover with the Roman numeral *V* above and the letters *DG* below. The centre in white-metal, remainder in gilding-metal. Officers: in silver-and-gilt, also in bronze (Fig. 743).

(2) As above but with Imperial crown (Fig. 744).
In same metals and also an economy issue in all-brass.

(3) The monogram *VDG* surmounted by an Imperial crown. In white-metal. Officers: in silver, also in bronze (Fig. 745).

The 6th Dragoon Guards (Carabiniers)

(1) On the crossed carbines the Garter surmounted by a Victorian crown. In the centre the Roman numerals *VI* over the letters *DG*. Below the Garter a scroll inscribed *Carabiniers*. The centre and scroll in white-metal, remainder in gilding-metal. Officers: in gilt-and-silver, also in bronze (Fig. 746).

(2) As above but with Imperial crown. In same metals (Fig. 747). Also an economy issue in all brass.

7th (the Princess Royal's) Dragoon Guards

(1) The crest of Earl Ligonier: A demi-lion issuant from a coronet. Below, a scroll inscribed *7th Dragoon Guards*. In white-metal. Officers: in silver, also in bronze (Fig. 748).

(2) The crest of Earl Ligonier above a scroll inscribed with the Earl's motto: *Quo fata vocant*. In brass. Officers: in gilt, also in bronze (Fig. 749).

1st (Royal) Dragoons

(1) The Royal Crest with Victorian crown above a scroll inscribed *The Royal Dragoons*. The Royal Crest in gilding-metal, scroll in white-metal. Officers: in gilt-and-silver, also in bronze (Fig. 750).

(2) As above but with Imperial crown. In same metals (Fig. 751).
Although the above was the official badge, the small eagle collar badge was worn in the head-dress during the Great War by both Officers and men as shown in contemporary photographs.

752   753   754   755   756

757   758   759   760   761

762   763   764   765   766

767   768   769   770   771

772   773   774   775   776

2nd Dragoons (Royal Scots Greys)

An Eagle with a laurel-wreath round its neck standing on a tablet inscribed *Waterloo*. Below, a scroll inscribed *Royal Scots Greys*. The Eagle in white-metal, scroll in gilding-metal. Officers: in silver-and-gilt, also in bronze (Fig. 752).

The 3rd (King's Own) Hussars

The White Horse of Hanover on ground. Below this a scroll inscribed *3rd King's Own Hussars*. The Horse and ground in white-metal, the scroll in gilding-metal. Officers: in silver-and-gilt, also in bronze (Fig. 753).

The 4th (Queen's Own) Hussars

(1) A circlet inscribed *Queen's Own Hussars* with a spray of laurel in the bottom-centre of the circlet. In the centre the Roman numerals *IV* in ornamental characters. The whole surmounted by a Victorian crown. The numerals in white-metal, remainder in gilding-metal. Officers: in silver-and-gilt, also in bronze (Fig. 754).

(2) As above but with Imperial crown. In same metals (Fig. 755).

(3) As (2) but with the addition of a scroll below inscribed *Mente et Manu* in white-metal. Officers: in silver. There was also an all-brass economy issue of this pattern in 1916 (Fig. 756).

The 5th (Royal Irish) Lancers

On crossed lances a circlet inscribed *Quis Separabit* with a spray of laurel in the bottom-centre of the circlet. In the centre the numeral *5* (Fig. 757).

The numeral and bottom-half of the lance-pennon in white-metal, remainder in gilding-metal. The 1916 economy issue was all-brass. Another version has only the numeral in white-metal, the pennons being all-brass. Officers: in silver-and-gilt, also in bronze.

6th (Inniskilling) Dragoons

The Castle of Inniskilling with St. George's flag flying from the central turret. Below, a scroll inscribed *Inniskilling*. The Castle in white-metal, scroll in gilding-metal, also found in bronzed-brass. Officers: in silver-and-gilt, also in bronze (Fig. 758).

7th The Queen's Own Hussars

(1) A circlet inscribed **7**th *Queen's Own Hussars* surmounted by a Victorian crown. In the centre the monogram *QO* reversed and intertwined. The monogram in white-metal, remainder in gilding-metal. Officers: in silver-and-gilt, also in bronze (Fig. 759).

(2) As above but with Imperial crown. In same metals. (Fig. 760.) There was also an all-brass economy issue in 1916.

8th (King's Royal Irish) Hussars

(1) The Irish Harp surmounted by a Victorian crown. Below, a scroll inscribed *8th King's Royal Irish Hussars* (Fig. 761). The Harp in white-metal, remainder in gilding-metal. Officers: in gilt-and-silver, also in bronze.

(2) As above but with Imperial crown (Fig. 762).
In same metals but also in all-brass economy issue in 1916.

9th (Queen's Royal) Lancers

(1) On crossed lances, the numeral *9* surmounted by a Victorian crown. Across the butts of the lances a scroll inscribed *Lancers* (Fig. 763).
In white-metal. Officers: in silver, also in bronze.

(2) As above but with Imperial crown (Fig. 764).
Metals as above but a pattern is known in silver with the top half of the lance-pennons and the crown in gilt. There was also an economy issue in brass.

10th (The Prince of Wales's Own Royal Regiment) Hussars

The Prince of Wales's plumes, coronet and motto resting on a scroll inscribed *10th Royal Hussars* (Fig. 765).
The coronet and scroll in gilding-metal, remainder in white-metal. The 1916 war economy issue is all-brass. Officers: in gilt-and-silver, also in bronze.

The 11th (Prince Albert's Own) Hussars

The crest of the late Prince Consort, Prince Albert of Saxe-Coburg-Gotha, with a scroll below inscribed with his motto *Treu und Fest*. In gilding-metal. Officers: in gilt, also in bronze (Fig. 766).

The 12th (Prince of Wales's Royal) Lancers

(1) The Prince of Wales's plumes, coronet and motto resting on a scroll inscribed *XII Royal Lancers* (Fig. 767). The coronet and scroll in gilding-metal, remainder in white-metal. Officers: in gilt-and-silver, also in bronze.

(2) On crossed lances the Prince of Wales's plumes, coronet and motto. Above these the Imperial crown. Below, the Roman numerals *XII* (Fig. 768). The plumes, motto and lower-half of the lance-pennons in white-metal, remainder in gilding-metal. Also all-brass economy issue. Officers: in silver-and-gilt, also in bronze.

13th Hussars

(1) Within a laurel-wreath, a circlet inscribed *Viret in Æternum* surmounted by a Victorian crown. In the centre the Roman numerals *XIII*. Below the circlet a scroll inscribed *Hussars* (Fig. 769). The numerals in white-metal, remainder in gilding-metal. Officers: in silver-and-gilt, also in bronze.

(2) As above but with Imperial crown (Fig. 770). In same metals but also the 1916 war economy issue in all-brass.

(3) On the numerals *13* a Z-shaped scroll inscribed *Hussars* and surmounted by an Imperial crown (Fig. 771). In gilding-metal. Officers: in gilt, also in bronze.

14th (King's) Hussars

(1) On an oval the Prussian Eagle, below this the wording *14th King's Hussars* (Fig. 772). The Eagle in white-metal, remainder in gilding-metal. Officers: in gilt-and-silver. This badge was discontinued in 1915 but the Eagle was restored to the regiment in 1931.

(2) Within the Garter the Royal Crest. Below the Garter a scroll inscribed *14th King's Hussars* (Fig. 773). In gilding-metal. Officers: in gilt, also in bronze with voided centre.

(3) As (2) but smaller (Fig. 774). In gilding-metal and also in gilding-metal with voided centre. Officers: in gilt non-voided and also in bronze.

(4) As (3) but with voided centre and with scroll inscribed *14th/20th Hussars* (Fig. 775). In gilding-metal. Officers: in gilt, also in bronze.

15th (the King's) Hussars

(1) The Royal Crest with Victorian crown within the Garter. Below the Garter *XVKH* resting on a scroll inscribed *Merebimur* (Fig. 776). The Royal Crest in white-metal, remainder in gilding-metal. Officers: in silver-and-gilt, also in bronze. Another pattern has silver letters on a blue-enamel ground.

(2) As above but with Imperial crown (Fig. 777). In same metals as above. Also an all-brass economy issue in 1916.

(3) As (2) but with *XV.XIX* between the Garter and the scroll on amalgamation (Fig. 778). In same metals as above.

16th (The Queen's) Lancers

(1) On crossed lances the numerals *16* surmounted by a Victorian crown. Below, a scroll inscribed *Queen's Lancers* (Fig. 779). The lower half of the lance-pennons, the numerals and the scroll in white-metal, remainder in gilding-metal. Officers: in silver-and-gilt.

(2) As above but with Imperial crown (Fig. 780). In same metals, also in bronze.

(3) As (2) but with the scroll inscribed *The Queen's Lancers* (Fig. 781). In same metals as above, also an economy issue in 1916 in all-brass.

The 17th (Duke of Cambridge's Own) Lancers

A skull and crossed bones with a scroll resting on the lower part of the bones inscribed *Or Glory* (Fig. 782). In white-metal. Officers in silver, also in bronze. An economy issue in bronzed-brass was issued in 1916.

The 18th (Queen Mary's Own) Royal Hussars

(1) A circlet inscribed *Pro Patria Conamur* surmounted by a Victorian crown and surrounded by a laurel-wreath. On the wreath on the left a scroll inscribed *Peninsula* and on the right a scroll inscribed *Waterloo*. In the centre the numerals *18* above the letter *H* (Fig. 783). *18H* in white-metal, remainder in gilding-metal. Officers: in silver-and-gilt, also in bronze.

(2) As above but with Imperial crown (Fig. 784). In same metals.

(3) An oval inscribed *Pro Rege Pro Lege Pro Patria Conamur* surmounted by an Imperial crown and surrounded by a laurel-wreath. On the wreath on the left a scroll inscribed *Peninsula* and on the right a scroll inscribed *Waterloo*. In the centre on a solid background the Roman numerals *XVIII* above the letter *H* (Fig. 785). For officers, only in gilt.

(4) As (3) but with the addition of a scroll inscribed *Princess of Wales's* (Fig. 786). For other-ranks only, in brass.

(5) As (4) but the scroll altered to read *Princess of Wales's Own* (Fig. 787). In gilt for officers, also in bronze.

(6) A circlet inscribed *Queen Mary's Own* surmounted by an Imperial crown. Below the circlet two sprigs of laurel. In the centre the Roman numerals *XVIII* (Fig. 788). In white-metal. Officers: in silver, also in bronze.

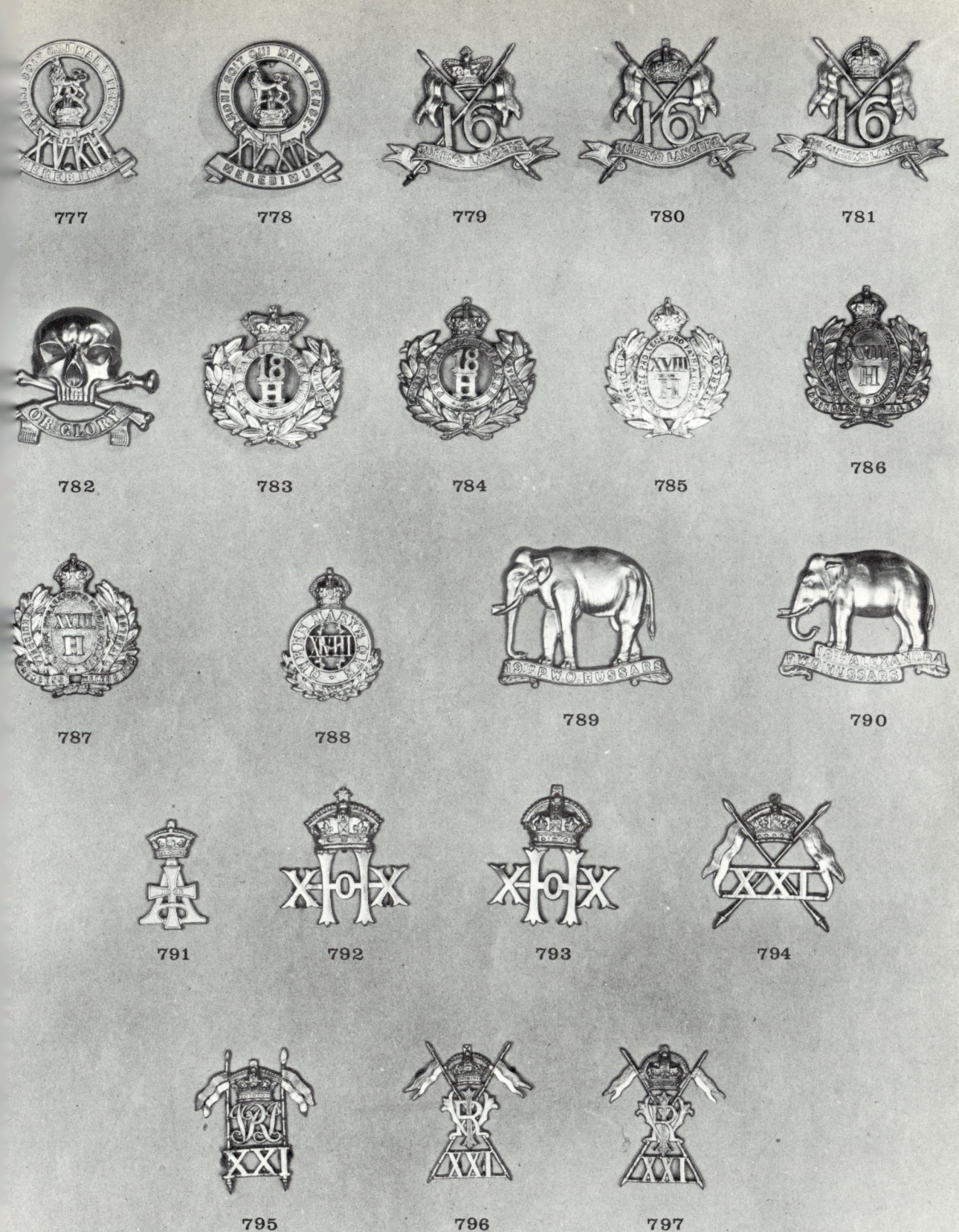

777   778   779   780   781

782   783   784   785   786

787   788   789   790

791   792   793   794

795   796   797

19th (Queen Alexandra's Own Royal) Hussars

(1) An Elephant standing on a scroll inscribed *19th PWO Hussars* (Fig. 789). In white-metal. Officers: in silver.

(2) An Elephant standing on a double scroll, the top inscribed *19th Alexandra* and the bottom *PWO Hussars* (Fig. 790).

(3) The letter *A*, cypher of the late Queen Alexandra ensigned with a crown. Interwoven with the cypher, the Dannebrog and in the centre of this the date *1885* (Fig. 791). In white-metal. Officers: gilt cypher and crown, silver cross and date. Also in bronze.

20th Hussars

(1) The letter *H* surmounted by a crown with the Roman numeral *X* on either side (Fig. 792). In gilding-metal. Officers: in gilt, also in bronze.

(2) As above but with Imperial crown. In same metals (Fig. 793).

21st (Empress of India's) Lancers

(1) On crossed lances, the Roman numerals *XXI* surmounted by a crown (Fig. 794). The lower half of the lance-pennons in white-metal, remainder in gilding-metal. Officers: in gilt-and-silver.

(2) Within two upright lances, the cypher *VRI* of Queen Victoria, as Empress of India, surmounted by a Victorian crown. Below, the Roman numerals *XXI* (Fig. 795). The lower half of the lance-pennons in white-metal, remainder in gilding-metal. Officers: in gilt-and-silver.

(3) On crossed lances, the cypher of Queen Victoria as Empress of India surmounted by a crown. Below, the Roman numerals *XXI* (Fig. 796). In same metals as above, also in bronze.

(4) As (3) but with Imperial crown (Fig. 797). In same metals as above, and also an all-brass economy issue.

CHAPTER 15

The Royal Regiment of Artillery

Similar changes of head-dress occurred in the Royal Artillery as in the other Arms and their badges followed the same general design.

In 1832, they were granted two mottoes: *Ubique* (Everywhere) and *Quo fas et gloria ducunt* (Whither right and glory lead), which feature prominently in their badges from that date. However, these were not permitted to the Militia, Volunteers or the Territorial Force and, in consequence, there are a very large number of non-Regular Artillery badges in which, usually, the principal motto is replaced by a laurel leaf and the secondary motto by the unit's title.

REGULARS

Tarleton helmet: c. 1795
A strap inscribed *Royal Regt. of Artillery* surmounted by a crown. In the centre, the Royal Cypher *GR*. In gilding-metal (Fig. 798).

Stove-pipe shako: 1800–1812
As the general style of the Infantry pattern but the Garter replaced by a strap inscribed *Royal Reg. of Artillery*. Below the strap a mortar with piles of shot either side. In brass (Fig. 798A).

Waterloo shako: 1812–1816
The universal shield-and-crown plate. On this, a strap inscribed *Royal Regt. of Artillery* within which the Royal Cypher *GR* reversed. Below the strap, a mortar with a fused grenade either side. In gilding-metal (Fig. 799).

Royal Horse Artillery helmet: c. 1827
A strap inscribed *Royal Horse Artillery* and surmounted by a crown. In the centre the Royal Cypher. In gilt (Fig. 800A).

Regency shako: 1816–1828
On a circular ring, a strap inscribed *Royal Regt. of Artillery* surmounted by a crown. In the centre the Royal Cypher *GR* reversed. In gilt (Fig. 800).

799

798

798A

800

800A

Bell-topped shako: 1828–1832
On the universal plate: a laurel-wreath, with in the centre, three guns in pale.

Bell-topped shako: 1832–1839
On an eight-pointed star the Royal Arms with, below this, a gun and below the gun a scroll inscribed *Ubique*. Across the base a further scroll inscribed *Quo fas et gloriä ducunt*.

Bell-topped shako: 1839–1846
   (1) An eight-pointed star, the topmost point displaced by a crown. On this a gun and, below the gun, a scroll inscribed *Ubique*. Officers' pattern in gilt (Fig. 801).
   (2) Similar design to above. Other-ranks pattern. All in brass (Fig. 801A).

Albert shako: 1846–1855
   (1) On an eight-pointed star the Royal Arms with, below this, a gun and below the gun a scroll inscribed *Ubique*. Across the base, a further scroll inscribed *Quo fas et gloria ducunt*. Officers' pattern in gilt (Fig. 803).
   (2) Similar design to above. Other-ranks pattern. All in brass (Fig. 803A).

801

803

801ᴬ

803ᴬ

804

810

808

805

806

809

807

Fur Busby
The busby was authorised in 1855, taken into wear in 1856 and worn until replaced by the cloth helmet in 1878.
   (1) On the ball of a fused grenade the Royal Arms with a scroll below inscribed *Ubique*. Below this a gun and below the gun a scroll inscribed *Quo fas et gloria ducunt*. In gilt (Fig. 804).
   (2) As above but with Imperial crown. In gilding-metal (Fig. 805).

Cloth Helmet
On May 1st 1878, a cloth helmet with spike was authorised for the *RFA* and *RGA*. The spike was replaced by a ball-in-cup pattern on August 1st 1881.
   (1) The Royal Arms with a scroll below inscribed *Ubique*. Below this a gun and below the gun a scroll inscribed *Quo fas et gloria ducunt*. In gilt (Fig. 806).
   (2) As above but with Imperial crown (Fig. 807).

Forage cap
A gun surmounted by a scroll inscribed *Ubique* above which an Imperial crown. Below the gun a scroll inscribed *Quo fas et gloria ducunt*. In gilding-metal (Fig. 808). Also in gilt, and bronze, and with the wheel of the gun mounted separately.

CADETS

Helmet plate
The Royal Arms with a scroll below inscribed *Ubique*. Below this a gun and below the gun a scroll inscribed *Cadet Company*. In gilt (Fig. 809).

Forage cap
A gun surmounted by a scroll inscribed *Cadet*. Above this an Imperial crown. Below the gun a scroll inscribed *Quo fas et gloria ducunt*. In gilding-metal (Fig. 810).

MILITIA

Helmet plates
   (1) The Royal Arms with a gun below, and below the gun a scroll inscribed *Artillery Militia*. In silver-plate or white-metal (Fig. 811).
   (2) As above but scroll inscribed *Militia Artillery*. In gilt (Fig. 812). In 1891 the title was changed from *Artillery Militia* to *Militia Artillery*.
   (3) As Regular badge but with white-metal *M* below the gun.
   (4) The Royal Arms with a scroll engraved with a laurel-spray instead of *Ubique*. Below this a gun with a scroll below inscribed *Antrim Artillery*. In gilt (Fig. 813).
   (5) As (4) but scroll inscribed *Hants Artillery*. In gilt (Fig. 814).
   (6) As (4) but scroll inscribed *Northern Division*. In gilt (Fig. 815).
   (7) As (4) but scroll inscribed *Eastern Division*. In gilt (Fig. 816).
Note the slight variations in size and design.

Busby
A fused grenade with, on the ball, a laurel-wreath and within the wreath a gun. In gilding-metal (Fig. 817).

813

836

815

814

837

817

811

812

818

816

Forage cap

The same badge as for Regulars in gilding-metal with a silver *M* mounted at the base of the gun-wheel (Fig. 818).

TERRITORIAL FORCE

Helmet plates

    (1) The Royal Arms with a scroll engraved with a laurel-spray in place of *Ubique*. Below the gun a scroll inscribed *Quo fas et gloria ducunt*. In gilt for officers (Fig. 819).

    (2) As above in gilding-metal for other-ranks (Fig. 820).

Forage cap

General pattern

As for Regulars but with laurel-spray in place of *Ubique*. In gilding-metal (Fig. 821).

5th London Brigade, Royal Field Artillery

Above a gun, a scroll inscribed *Fifth* surmounted by an Imperial crown. Below the gun a scroll inscribed *London RFA Brigade*. In gilding-metal (Fig. 822).

Warwickshire Royal Horse Artillery

Above a gun, a scroll inscribed *Warwickshire* surmounted by an Imperial crown. Below the gun a scroll inscribed *Royal Horse Artillery*. In gilding-metal (Fig. 823).

VOLUNTEERS

Shako plate

General pattern

An eight-pointed star. On this a laurel-wreath surmounted by a Victorian crown. In the centre three guns in pale. In silver (Fig. 824).

Busby grenades

General pattern

    (1) On the ball, below the Royal Arms, a blank scroll. Below this the gun and below the gun a scroll inscribed *Quo fas et gloria ducunt*. In silver (Fig. 825).

    (2) On the ball a laurel-wreath and within this a gun. In white-metal (Fig. 826).

1st Edinburgh City Artillery Volunteers

On the ball, a strap inscribed *Edinburgh City Artillery* with the arms, crest, supporters and motto of the City of Edinburgh in the centre. Below the ball, a scroll inscribed *Volunteers*. In white-metal (Fig. 827).

1st Brigade, Glamorgan Artillery Volunteers

On the ball, the lettering *1st Brigade Glamorgan Artillery Volrs* engraved direct in a circle with a scroll at the top to complete the circle inscribed *Ready Aye Ready*. In the centre, a gun surmounted by the Prince of Wales's plumes, coronet and motto. In white-metal (Fig. 828).

Kent Artillery Volunteers

On the ball a laurel-wreath and within this the White Horse of Kent standing on a scroll inscribed *Invicta*. In white-metal (Fig. 828A).

819

821

820

822

840

841

823

842

843

825

838

824

839

826

827

828

828ᴬ

829

Lancashire Volunteer Artillery

On the ball, a circlet inscribed *Lancashire Volunteer Artillery*. In the centre a gun surmounted by a rose. In white-metal or silver-plate (Fig. 829).

Note: The above is a small selection only from a very large number of units.

Helmet plates

Officers' plates in silver-plate; other ranks in white-metal. Officers' plates usually had an extra wheel on the gun.

General pattern

The Royal Arms with a scroll engraved with a laurel spray in place of *Ubique*. Below the gun a scroll inscribed *Artillery Volunteers* (Fig. 829A).

1st Norfolk Artillery Volunteers

As for general pattern but with *First* replacing the laurel-spray and *Norfolk Artillery* on the title-scroll. In silver-plate (Fig. 830).

1st Northumberland Artillery Volunteers

As for general pattern but with *First* replacing the laurel-spray and *Northumberland Artillery Vols* on the title-scroll (Fig. 831).

1st Ayrshire and Galloway Artillery Volunteers

As for general pattern but with *1st* replacing the laurel-spray and *Ayrshire & Galloway Artillery Vols* on the title-scroll (Fig. 832).

In 1891, the title for all units was changed from *Artillery Volunteers* to *Volunteer Artillery*.

5th Lancashire Volunteer Artillery

As for general pattern but with *5th* replacing the laurel-spray and *Lancashire Volunteer Artillery* on the title-scroll (Fig. 833).

The designation *Royal Garrison Artillery (Volunteers)* was adopted in 1902.

2nd East Riding of Yorkshire R.G.A. (Volunteers)

As for general pattern but with Imperial crown and *Second* replacing the laurel-spray and *East Yorks R.G.A. Volunteers* on the title-scroll (Fig. 834).

2nd Lincolnshire Artillery Volunteers

Head-dress worn prior to 1891.

A gun with a scroll inscribed *Second Lincolnshire Volunteers* extending from the left base over the gun and down to the right base. The scroll surmounted by a coronet. In silver-plate (Fig. 835).

Fifeshire Artillery Volunteers

(1) An eight-pointed gilt star. On this, in silver, the Thane of Fife with a scroll above inscribed *Deo Juvante*. Below the Thane, a scroll inscribed *Nemo me impune lacessit* on which is superimposed a gun. Below the gun, another scroll inscribed *Fifeshire Artillery* with a spray of thistles at either end (Fig. 836).

(2) Within a wreath of thistles a circlet inscribed *Virtute et Opera* and surmounted by a Victorian crown. In the centre, the Thane of Fife. In silver (Fig. 837).

829ᴬ

835

830

831

845

833

846 X 847

832 844 834

Forage caps (pre-1902)

General pattern
(1) A fused grenade in the same shape as for the Grenadier Guards. In white-metal (Fig. 838).
(2) A fused grenade with seven flames. In white-metal (Fig. 839).

1st (City) Edinburgh Artillery Volunteers
(1) On an eight-pointed star a winged torch-of-learning with, on the left the letters *EA* intertwined and, on the right, the letters *VC* intertwined. In gilding-metal (Fig. 840).
(2) Superimposed on crossed gun-barrels, a shield bearing a Scottish Lion with the Crown of Scotland above. On the left side of the shield the letters *EA* intertwined and, on the right, the letters *VC*. At the base, below the shield, a scroll inscribed *Nemo me impune lacessit*. In gilding-metal (Fig. 841).

3rd Sussex Artillery Volunteers
An oval inscribed in old English lettering *S.A. III VC* at the top and *HIC* at the bottom. In the centre a tree. The oval surmounted by a Victorian crown. In white-metal (Fig. 842).

3rd North Riding of Yorkshire Artillery Volunteers
A strap inscribed *3rd NR Yorks Artillery Volunteers* surmounted by a Victorian crown. In the centre a Rose. In white-metal (Fig. 843).

Forage caps (1902–1908)

General pattern
(1) A gun surmounted by a scroll on which a spray of laurel. Above the scroll an Imperial crown. Below the gun, a scroll inscribed *Quo fas et gloria ducunt*. In white-metal (Fig. 844).
(2) As above but the word *Volunteers* replacing the laurel-spray. In white-metal (Fig. 845).

1st Hampshire R.G.A. (Volunteers)
As general pattern but with the top scroll inscribed *First* and the bottom scroll inscribed *Hants RGA Volunteers*. In white-metal (Fig. 846).

3rd Middlesex R.G.A. (Volunteers)
As general pattern but with the top scroll inscribed *Third* and the bottom scroll inscribed *Middlesex R.G.A. Volunteers*. In white-metal and in bronze (Fig. 847).

CHAPTER 16

The Corps of Royal Engineers

Engineer Officers of the Army received the title *Royal* in 1787 and were styled *The Corps of Royal Engineers* – an 'officers only' Corps. As regards other-ranks, a Company of Military Artificers was formed in Gibraltar in 1772 and was amalgamated with the *Corps of Royal Military Artificers* in 1797, the latter having been formed ten years earlier. In 1812, the title was changed to *Royal Sappers and Miners*.

In 1856, officers and other-ranks were combined to form *The Corps of Royal Engineers*. The mottoes *Ubique* and *Quo fas et gloria ducunt* were authorised in 1832.

REGULARS

Fur busby
On the ball of a fused grenade the Royal Arms with a scroll below inscribed *Ubique*. Below this a further scroll inscribed *Quo fas et gloria ducunt*. In gilt and for officers only (Fig. 848).

Cloth helmet
The Royal Arms with a scroll below inscribed *Ubique*. Below this a further scroll inscribed *Quo fas et gloria ducunt* (Fig. 849). In gilt for officers, gilding-metal for other ranks.
On the accession of King Edward VII, the crown was changed to the Imperial pattern. The illustration depicts the later type.

Forage cap
(1) With a wreath of laurel, surmounted by a Victorian crown, a strap inscribed *Royal Engineers*. In the centre, the Royal Cypher *VR* (Fig. 850).
In gilding-metal for other ranks. Worn c. 1898.
(2) As above but with cypher of King Edward VII and Imperial crown (Fig. 851).
In gilt for officers. Other-ranks did not wear this pattern.
(3) A laurel-wreath surmounted by an Imperial crown. Within this the Garter and, in the centre, the cypher of King Edward VII. Across the base of the wreath a scroll inscribed *Royal Engineers* (Fig. 852). In gilt for officers and in gilding-metal for other-ranks.
(4) As (3) but with cypher of King George V (Fig. 853).
In gilt, gilding-metal and bronze. There was also an economy issue in 1916 with a solid, instead of voided, centre.

MILITIA

Helmet plates
  (1) Below the Royal Arms a scroll inscribed *Militia Engineers* (Fig. 854). In gilt for officers and gilding-metal for other-ranks.
  (2) Similar to above but with a scroll engraved with a laurel-spray above the title scroll (Fig. 855). In gilt for officers.
  (3) Below the Royal Arms a scroll inscribed *Royal Engineers* with a laurel-spray in the centre and below this a further scroll inscribed *Militia* (Fig. 856). In gilt for officers.

Forage cap
  (1) A laurel-wreath surmounted by an Imperial crown, within this the Garter with the cypher of King Edward VII in the centre. Across the base of the wreath a scroll inscribed *Royal Engineers Militia* (Fig. 857). In gilt for officers.
  (2) Similar badge to Regulars with cypher of King Edward VII and with a white-metal letter *M* on the base of the Garter (Fig. 858). In gilding-metal for other ranks.
  (3) As (2) above but with the cypher of King George V (Fig. 859). In gilding-metal for other ranks.

TERRITORIAL FORCE

Helmet plates

General pattern
Below the Royal Arms a scroll engraved with a laurel-spray and beneath this a scroll inscribed *Quo fas et gloria ducunt* (Fig. 860). In gilt.

Tyne Electrical Engineers
As general pattern but with *Tyne* replacing the laurel-spray (Fig. 861). In gilt.

CADETS

Forage cap

Manchester Engineer Cadet Corps
A strap inscribed *Engineer Cadet Corps* and within this a Rose. Beneath the strap a scroll inscribed *Manchester* (Fig. 862). In gilding-metal.

VOLUNTEERS

The Volunteer Force in Great Britain was sanctioned by a War Office Circular letter of the 12th May 1859, but this covered Artillery and Rifle Volunteers only. However, offers were made for the formation of Engineer and Mounted Corps and these were then authorised. By 1860, several corps of Volunteer Engineers had been formed, the first commissioned being the Middlesex followed by the 1st Lanarkshire.

The Engineer Volunteers had a variety of head-dresses; some a fur busby, others a tall shako with drooping plume or a French-type low shako. After the introduction of the cloth helmet this also was worn.

A small selection of the many Volunteer badges follows:

850

848

851

852

853

854

849

855

858

859

857

856

862

861

888

860

Shako badges

General pattern

A strap inscribed *Engineer Volunteers* surmounted by a Victorian crown. In the centre the Royal Cypher *VR* (Fig. 863). In white-metal for other-ranks.

Tower Hamlets Engineer Volunteers

(1) An eight-pointed star, the topmost point displaced by a Victorian crown. On this a strap inscribed *Peritia Potius Quam Vi* with, in the centre, the Royal Cypher *VR* (Fig. 864). Star, crown and cypher in silver-plate, remainder in gilt. For officers.

(2) Similar to above but the cypher reversed and intertwined. (Fig. 865.) All in white-metal for other-ranks.

Busby grenades

General pattern

On the ball of a fused grenade, the Royal Arms (Fig. 866). In silver-plate.

Tower Hamlets Engineer Volunteers

On the ball of a fused grenade a strap inscribed *Peritia Potius Quam Vi* with, in the centre, a shield bearing the Royal Arms (Fig. 867). In white-metal.

1st Middlesex Engineer Volunteers

A fused grenade. Superimposed on the flames a heart-shaped shield bearing the letters *EV*. Behind the shield a trident. On the ball of the grenade a plan of a fortification on which is superimposed a helmeted head (Fig. 868). In white-metal for rank-and-file.

Helmet plates

General pattern

(1) The Royal Arms with a blank scroll below and beneath this a scroll inscribed *Quo fas et gloria ducunt*. In white-metal for other-ranks (Fig. 869).

(2) As above but with Imperial crown (Fig. 870).

(3) The Royal Arms with an ornamental scroll below and beneath this a scroll inscribed *Engineer Volunteers* with an ornamental section between the two words. In silver-plate (Fig. 871).

(4) Similar to (3) but bottom scroll inscribed *Engineer Volunteer* and without the ornamentation between the two parts of the title. In silver-plate (Fig. 872).

(5) The Royal Arms beneath which a scroll engraved with a laurel-spray. Below this a scroll inscribed *Quo fas et gloria ducunt*. In white-metal (Fig. 873).
This was the last pattern worn.

Royal Engineers Submarine Miners

Submarine Miners were employed at defended ports. First raised in 1863, they were abolished by Army Order 130 of June 1907.
The Royal Arms with a scroll below inscribed *Royal Engineers*, beneath which a scroll inscribed *Submarine Miners*. In white-metal (Fig. 874).

864

867

865

866

884

883

868

885

886

863

869

875

870

1st Cheshire Engineer Volunteers
The Royal Arms, but the shield bearing the Royal Arms in the centre is replaced by a shield bearing three lions on the left and two garbs on the right. Below the Arms a scroll inscribed *First* and beneath this a scroll inscribed *Cheshire Engineer Volunteers*. In silver-plate (Fig. 875).

1st Gloucestershire Volunteer Engineers
The Royal Arms beneath which a scroll inscribed *1st Glou. VE* and below this a scroll inscribed *Cheltenham College Cadets*. In white-metal (Fig. 876).

1st Administrative Battalion, 2nd Gloucestershire Engineer Volunteers
The Royal Arms beneath which a scroll inscribed *1st AB* and below this a scroll inscribed *2nd Gloster Engineer Volunteers*. In white-metal (Fig. 877).

2nd Gloucestershire Engineer Volunteers
The Royal Arms beneath which a scroll inscribed *2nd Gloster* and below this a scroll inscribed *Bristol Engineer Volunteers*. In white-metal (Fig. 878).

1st Bedfordshire Royal Engineers Volunteers
The Royal Arms beneath which a scroll inscribed *1st Bedfordshire* and below this a scroll inscribed *Royal Engineers Volunteers*. In white-metal (Fig. 879).

Forage caps

General pattern
   (1) A laurel-wreath surmounted by an Imperial crown. Within this the Garter and in the centre the cypher of King Edward VII. Across the base of the wreath a scroll inscribed *Royal Engineers*. In white-metal (Fig. 880). Silver-plate for officers.
   (2) As above but scroll inscribed *Royal Engineers (Volunteers)*. In white-metal (Fig. 881). Silver-plated for officers, also found in gilding-metal and in bronze.
   (3) As (2) but with the cypher of King George V. In white-metal (Fig. 882). Silver-plated for officers.

Other head-dress badges

1st Middlesex Engineer Volunteers
Within a scroll inscribed *1st Middlesex Engineer Vols* a shamrock, rose and thistle on stalks with the letters *VR* flanking the stalks. The whole surmounted by a crown. In white-metal (Fig. 883).

Sheffield Engineer Volunteers
Within a scroll inscribed *Sheffield Engineer Vols* a shamrock, rose and thistle on stalks with the letters *VR* flanking the stalks. The whole surmounted by a crown. In white-metal (Fig. 884).

1st City of Edinburgh Engineer Volunteers
Although this unit did not wear a busby, the badge is affixed to a plume-holder. Within a wreath of thistles surmounted by a crown an ornamental strap inscribed *Nemo me impune lacessit*. In the centre a lion. Below the strap within an oval St. Andrew and Cross. In silver-plate (Fig. 885).

876

872

877

879

871

874

880

878

881

882

887

873

1st City of London Engineer Volunteers
Within a circlet inscribed *1st City of London Engineers* a shield bearing the Arms of the City of London; supporters either side of the circlet which is surmounted by a crown. At the base a scroll inscribed *Domine Dirige Nos*. In white-metal (Fig. 886).

2nd Cheshire Engineer Volunteers
A steam locomotive. In silver-plate or white-metal (Fig. 887).

ROYAL CORPS OF SIGNALS

On the 28th June 1920, King George v gave his consent to the creation of the Corps of Signals as a separate Corps distinct from the Royal Engineers and the order giving effect to this was promulgated by Royal Warrant of the 2nd July 1920.

On the 5th August in the same year, the King granted the Corps the distinction of the title *Royal Corps of Signals*.

Forage cap
An oval inscribed *Royal Corps of Signals* with, in the bottom centre, the Globe with a sprig of laurel either side. The oval surmounted by an Imperial crown. In the centre the figure of Mercury, holding a caduceus in his left hand, his right hand held aloft, poised on the globe with his left foot. Oval and crown in gilding-metal, remainder in white-metal. Officers' in gilt-and-silver-plate, also in bronze (Fig. 888).

888

CHAPTER 17

The Brigade of Guards

As the full-dress head-dress of the Foot Guards is the bearskin, on which the distinction between regiments is shown by the plume, metal badges are worn only on the forage or field-service caps, or the puggaree when serving in hot-weather stations.

Practically no change has been made in the design; Grenadier Guards having the fused grenade with change of the Royal Cypher where appropriate, Coldstream Guards the Star of the Order of the Garter, Scots Guards the Star of the Order of the Thistle, Irish Guards the Star of the Order of St. Patrick and Welsh Guards a leek.

GRENADIER GUARDS

Officers' bearskin cap-plate: c. 1834

The Garter surmounted by a crown and within the Garter the Royal Arms of the period. On the left of the Garter, a Lion and on the right, a Unicorn. Just visible below the Garter are the ends of the Prince of Wales's plumes, coronet and motto *Ich Dien*. At the base, a scroll inscribed *Dieu et mon droit*. All in gilt. The plate is 6″ wide and 2½″ high at its highest point.

Forage cap: 1896

Officers: A fused grenade with the Royal Cypher *VR* mounted on the ball. In gilt (Fig. 889). Also worn by Warrant Officers but with the cypher struck on the ball and not mounted. Sergeants and Musicians, the same badge but in gilding-metal.

Commissioned Quartermasters: A fused grenade in gilt with the Royal Cypher, surmounted by a crown in silver, on the ball (Fig. 890).

All other ranks: A fused grenade with a plain ball. In gilding-metal (Fig. 891).

This pattern also found in bronze.

Forage cap: 1902

As above but with the cypher of King Edward VII. Sergeants' pattern shown (Fig. 892).

Forage cap: 1911

As above but with the cypher of King George V. Sergeants' pattern shown (Fig. 893).

Officers' puggaree badges

(1) A pierced Garter with blue-enamel backing surmounted by a Victorian crown. In the centre the Royal Cypher *VR* interlaced and reversed with red-enamel backing. All in gilt.

(2) As above, but with the cypher of King Edward VII and with Imperial crown.

(3) As above, but with the cypher of King George V and with Imperial crown (Fig. 894).

Other-ranks' puggaree badges
(These formed part of the shoulder-titles.)
    (1) The Garter surmounted by a Victorian crown. In a voided centre the Royal cypher interlaced and reversed. In gilding-metal (Fig. 895).
    (2) As above but with the cypher of King Edward VII and with Imperial crown.
    (3) As above but with the cypher of King George V and with Imperial crown (Fig. 896).

COLDSTREAM GUARDS

Officers' Field cap: 1896–
The Garter Star in silver with blue-enamel backing to the Garter and red-enamel backing to St. George's Cross (Fig. 897).

Officers' service-dress cap
As above, but smaller (Fig. 898).

Warrant Officers' and Staff Sergeants' forage cap: 1896–
The Garter Star in white-metal with blue-enamel backing to the Garter and red-enamel to St. George's Cross (Fig. 899).

Other-ranks' forage cap: 1902
    (1) The Garter Star in gilding-metal (worn on the Broderick cap, 1902 to 05). (Fig. 900.)
    (2) As above, in gilding-metal (as worn since 1905). (Fig. 901.)

Puggaree badges
Officers: The Garter Star in silver with blue-enamel backing to the Garter and red-enamel backing to St. George's Cross (Fig. 902).
Warrant Officers' and Staff Sergeants': As above but in white-metal (Fig. 903).
Other ranks: As above but all in gilding-metal (Fig. 904).

SCOTS GUARDS

Forage cap and puggaree
Officers: The Star of the Order of the Thistle in silver. The circlet inscribed with the motto and the thistle with two leaves in the centre in gilt. Green-enamel background to the centre (Fig. 905).
Warrant Officers', Regimental and Battalion Staff: Similar to officers but the star is of a slightly different shape (Fig. 906).
Colour Sergeants, Sergeants and Musicians: Similar to above but with star in white-metal, motto circlet and thistle-centre in gilding-metal (Fig. 907).
Lance Sergeants and below: Similar to above but all in gilding-metal (Fig. 908).

Other-ranks' Broderick cap: 1902–05
The Star of the Order of the Thistle in brass (Fig. 909).

891

890

892

889

894

893

895

896

898

901

900

899

897

903

902

904

Officers' service dress cap
The Star of the Order of the Thistle in silver. The circlet and centre in gilt. Green-enamel ground to centre (Fig. 910).

Pipers' badges

Pre-1865
The Star of the Order of the Thistle in elongated form, 4″ high. In white-metal.

1865–77
Within a strap inscribed *Scots Fusilier Guards* the Star of the Order of the Thistle.

1877–
Within a strap inscribed *Scots Guards* the Star of the Order of the Thistle (Fig. 911). (Sergeant pipers wear a sergeant's star and pipe-majors, a warrant officer's star within the strap.)

IRISH GUARDS
(Formed by Army Order 77 of 1900)

Forage cap
Officers: The Star of the Order of St. Patrick. The star in silver, the pierced circlet with the motto of the Order *Quis separabit* and the Roman numerals *MDCCLXXXIII* (the date of the foundation of the Order) in gilt with light-blue-enamel backing. In a voided centre, St. Patrick's Cross in red-enamel; superimposed on this a gilt and green-enamel shamrock-leaf with three gilt crowns on the leaf (Fig. 912).
Warrant Officers and Staff Sergeants: Similar to officers' but the centre portion is not raised so high (Fig. 913).
Other-ranks: Similar to above but in gilding-metal only (Fig. 914).

Officers' service-dress cap
As the forage cap but smaller (Fig. 915).

Puggaree badge
Officers: The Star of the Order of St. Patrick in gilt with silver centre (Fig. 916).
Other-ranks: As above but all in bronze (Fig. 917).

Pipe-major's caubeen badge
The Star of the Order of St. Patrick in silver. A gilt circlet with motto voided on a light-blue-enamel ground. In the centre a red-enamel edged gold St. Patrick's Cross on a white-enamel ground. On this a green shamrock-leaf with three red crowns on the leaf (Fig. 918).

Pipers' caubeen badge
As above but all in white-metal (Fig. 919).

WELSH GUARDS
(Formed 26th February, 1915 by Army Order 124 of 1915)

Forage cap
A leek. In gilding-metal (Fig. 920).

905

906

907

911

909

910

908

919

916

918

913

914

912

915

917

920

921

922

924

923

Puggaree badge

A circlet inscribed *Cymru am byth* surmounted by an Imperial crown. In a voided centre a leek. Red cloth backing to the badge (Fig. 921).

GUARDS MACHINE GUN REGIMENT

Formed in February 1918, from the three regiments of Household Cavalry and the Guards Machine Gun Battalion. The 1st Life Guards became the 1st Battalion, the 2nd Life Guards the 2nd Battalion, the Royal Horse Guards the 3rd Battalion, and the Guards Machine Gun Battalion the 4th Battalion. There was also a 5th Reserve Battalion.

The three Household Cavalry regiments retained their own cap badges but recognised their temporary employment by wearing crossed machine-guns collar badges. These three regiments returned to England in March 1919 and each went to its own barracks and resumed its normal function.

The 4th Battalion on its return was known as the 6th or Machine Gun Regiment of Foot Guards or Guards Machine Gun Regiment and had its own Regimental Headquarters and Regimental Lieutenant-Colonel, taking its turn to provide Public Duties with the other regiments of Foot Guards. It also took part in the first Trooping the Colour in Hyde Park after the war. It was disbanded in 1920.

The date *1916* on the badge refers to the formation of the Guards Machine Gun Battalion in the Guards Division.

(1) Superimposed on crossed machine-guns The Garter surmounted by an Imperial crown. In the centre the Cypher of King George v interlaced and reversed. Below, a scroll inscribed *Guards M.G. Regiment*. For other ranks in gilding-metal (Fig. 922). In gilt for officers, also in bronze.

(2) A five-pointed star on which a circlet inscribed *Quinque juncta in Uno 1916* with, in the centre, the monogram *MGR* surmounted by an Imperial crown. Radiating from the circlet, five machine-gun bullets with between them a grenade, rose, thistle, shamrock and leek. In white-metal (Fig. 923).

HOUSEHOLD BRIGADE OFFICER CADET BATTALION
(Formed 10th February 1917 by A.C.I. 241. Disbanded 1919)

A circlet of white enamel with gilt edges. On this reading from right to left in script characters *1LG2LGRHGGGCGSGIGWG*. In the centre, in gilt-metal, the cypher of King George v surrounded by a chain and surmounted by an Imperial crown (Fig. 924).

CHAPTER 18

The Grenade Badges of the Fusilier Regiments

A fur cap made of racoon-skin was authorised for Fusilier Regiments in 1865 and taken into use soon afterwards. It remained the head-dress for full-dress until the wearing of full-dress ceased.

The badges worn were, in every case, a fused grenade—in gilt for officers and gilding-metal for other-ranks. With different devices on the ball of the grenade.

As the general format was identical, only the designs on the ball of the grenade are shown in the descriptions which follow.

OFFICERS' HEAD-DRESS BADGES

The Northumberland Fusiliers

On racoon-skin cap
(1) Within a strap inscribed *Quo fata vocant* St. George and the Dragon, with a small Roman *V* below. Worn 1874 to 1881 (Fig. 925).
(2) As above but without the *V*. Worn 1881 to 1904 (Fig. 926).
(3) As (2) but with a circlet instead of a strap (Fig. 927).

On white F. S. Helmet and forage cap
St. George and the Dragon within a circlet inscribed *Northumberland Fusiliers*. All in silver.

The Royal Fusiliers (City of London Regiment)

On racoon-skin cap
(1) The Garter pierced with the motto on a ground of blue-enamel. Within the Garter the Rose. Below the Garter in silver the White Horse of Hanover (Fig. 927A). This was the first pattern worn. Note the absence of the Crown above the Garter.
(2) The Garter surmounted by a Victorian crown. The Garter pierced with the motto; the ground of blue-enamel. Within the Garter, the Rose. Below the Garter, in silver the White Horse of Hanover (Fig. 928).
(3) As above but with the Imperial crown (Fig. 929).

On white F. S. Helmet and forage cap
As for full-dress head-dress but smaller. The Rose in silver and the White Horse omitted.

927ᴬ

The Lancashire Fusiliers

On racoon-skin cap

(1) In silver the Sphinx superscribed *Egypt* within a laurel wreath.
(2) As above but larger (Fig. 930).

On white F. S. Helmet and forage cap

In gilt the Sphinx superscribed *Egypt* within a laurel-wreath. Below the grenade, a scroll in silver inscribed *Lancashire Fusiliers*.

The Royal Scots Fusiliers

On racoon-skin cap and F. S. Helmet

(1) The Royal Arms with Victorian crown (Fig. 931).
(2) As above but with Victorian Royal Crest (Fig. 932).
(3) As above but with Imperial Royal Crest (Fig. 933).

On glengarry cap and Tam o'Shanter bonnet

As above but smaller.

The Royal Welsh Fusiliers

On racoon-skin cap

The Prince of Wales's plumes, coronet and motto. The coronet in gilt, remainder in silver (Fig. 934).
Also found with the coronet in silver.

On white F. S. Helmet and forage-cap

In frosted silver a circlet inscribed *Royal Welsh Fusiliers*. Within the circlet the Prince of Wales's plumes, coronet and motto in silver.

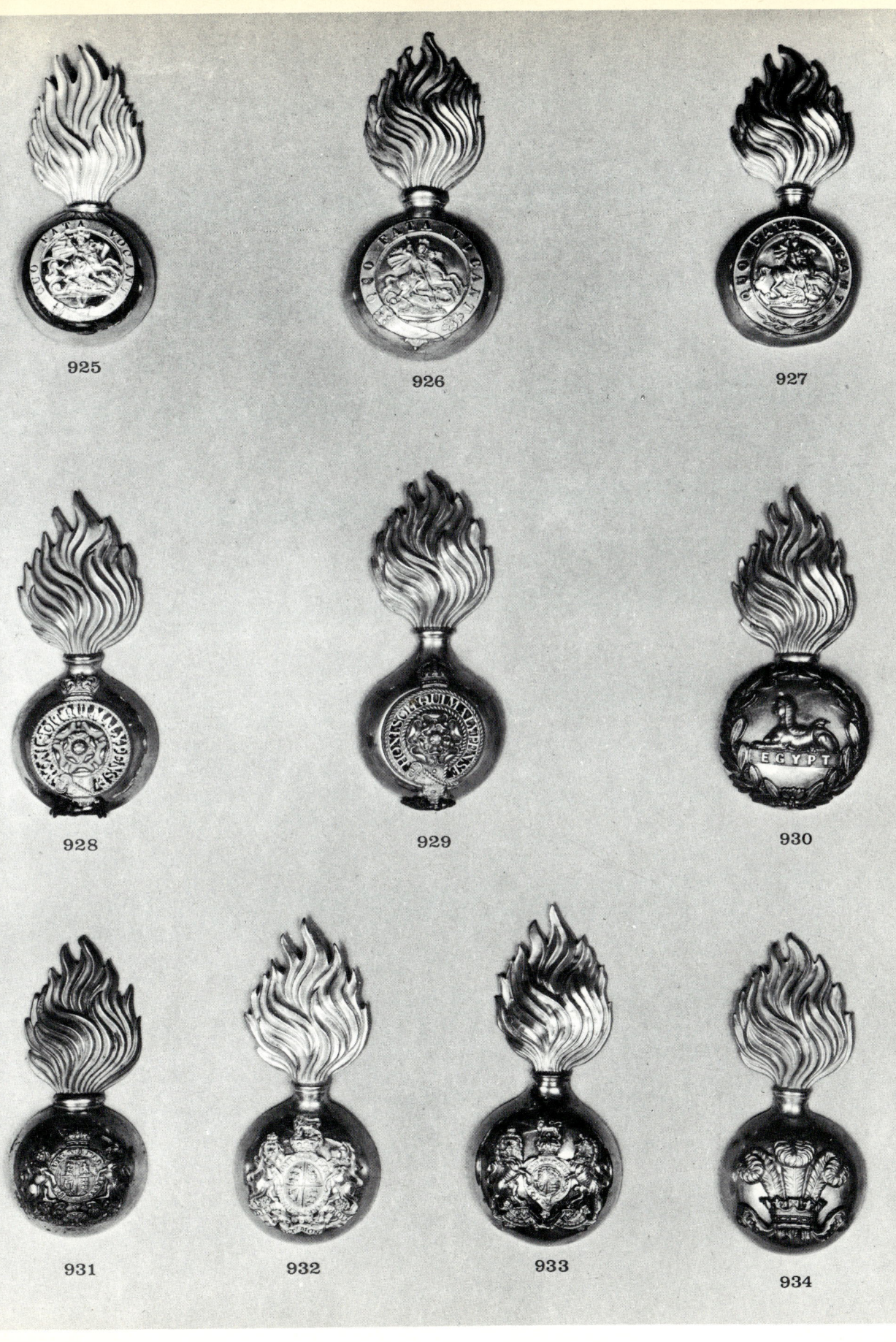

925   926   927

928   929   930

931   932   933   934

The Royal Inniskilling Fusiliers

On racoon-skin cap
The Castle of Inniskilling in silver (Fig. 935).

On white F. S. Helmet and forage-cap.
As for full-dress head-dress but smaller. Below the Castle, a scroll in silver inscribed *Inniskilling*.

The Royal Irish Fusiliers (Princess Victoria's)

On racoon-skin cap
In silver the Eagle within a wreath of laurel. Below the Eagle a small tablet inscribed with the numeral *8* (Fig. 936).

On white F. S. Helmet and forage-cap
   (1) 1st badge: The coronet of H.R.H. The Princess Victoria.
         2nd badge: As for racoon-skin cap but smaller.
   (2) 1st badge: The coronet of H.R.H. The Princess Victoria.
         2nd badge: The Harp surmounted by the Prince of Wales's plumes, coronet and motto in silver.
The 1st badge is worn above the 2nd badge.

The Royal Munster Fusiliers

1st Battalion: 101st Royal Bengal Fusiliers

On racoon-skin cap
A laurel-wreath bearing scrolls inscribed with battle-honours: (left) *Buxar, Plassey, Ghuznee, Ferozeshah*; (right) *Deig, Guzerat, Bhurtpore, Affghanistan*; across the base of the wreath *Sobraon* and below this *Pegu* with bottom-left *Lucknow* and bottom-right *Delhi*. Within the wreath in silver a strap inscribed *Royal Bengal Fusiliers* surmounted by a Victorian crown. In the centre the numerals *101*. (Fig. 937).

2nd Battalion: 104th Bengal Fusiliers

On racoon-skin cap
   (1) A laurel-wreath with scrolls, (left) inscribed *Punjaub* and (right) *Goojerat* with across the base *Chillianwallah*. Above this a two-part scroll inscribed *Pegu, Delhi*. Within the wreath in silver a monogram of the letters *BF* (Fig. 938).
   (2) A laurel-wreath with scrolls, (left) inscribed *Punjaub* and (right) *Goojerat* with across the base *Chillianwallah*. Above this a scroll inscribed *Pegu*. Within the wreath a strap inscribed *Bengal Fusiliers* surmounted by a Victorian crown. In the centre the numerals *104* (Fig. 939).
   (3) A laurel-wreath with scrolls, (left) inscribed *Punjaub* and (right) *Goojerat* with across the base *Chillianwallah*. Above this a two-part scroll inscribed *Pegu, Delhi*. Within the wreath a strap inscribed *Bengal Fusiliers* surmounted by a Victorian crown. In the centre the numerals *104* (Fig. 940).

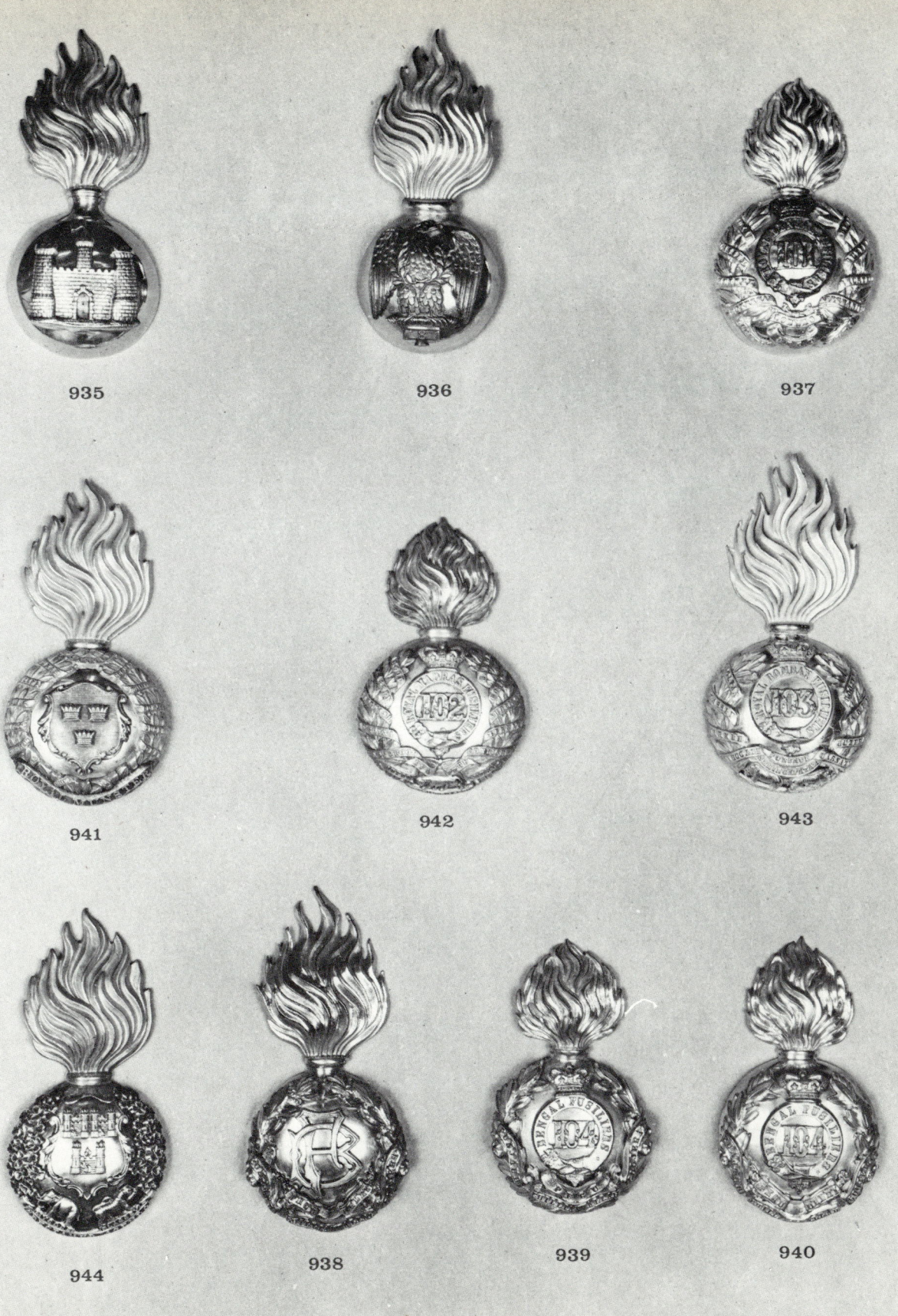

935   936   937

941   942   943

944   938   939   940

1st and 2nd Battalions after 1881

On racoon-skin cap

A laurel-wreath bearing scrolls inscribed with battle-honours: across the top of the wreath *Plassey*; (left) *Buxar, Guzerat*; *Deig, Bhurtpore, Affghanistan*; (right) *Goojerat, Chillianwallah, Punjaub, Lucknow, Delhi*. Across the base of the wreath a silver scroll inscribed *Royal Munster*. Within the wreath a silver shield bearing the Arms of the Province of Munster (Three crowns) in gilt (Fig. 941).

On forage cap

   (1) A silver shield bearing the Arms of the Province of Munster.
   (2) In silver The Tiger with a scroll below inscribed *Royal Munster*.

The Royal Dublin Fusiliers

1st Battalion: 102nd Royal Madras Fusiliers

On racoon-skin cap

A laurel-wreath bearing scrolls inscribed with battle-honours: (left) *Arcot, Plassey, Wyndewash, Amboyna, Nundy Droog, Maheidpore*; (right) *Banda, Condore, Sholingur, Ternate, Pondichery, Lucknow*. At the base two scrolls inscribed *Ava, Pegu*, with below these the Tiger resting on a scroll inscribed *Spectamur Agendo*. Within the wreath a strap inscribed *Royal Madras Fusiliers* surmounted by a Victorian crown. In the centre the numerals *102* (Fig. 942).

2nd Battalion: 103rd Royal Bombay Fusiliers

On racoon-skin cap

A laurel-wreath bearing scrolls inscribed with battle-honours: *Mooltan, Plassey, Kirkee, Beni Boo Ali, Punjaub, Seringapatam, Carnatic, Guzerat, Aden, Goojerat*; at the base (left) an Elephant resting on *Mysore* and (right) a Tiger resting on *Buxar*. Within the wreath a strap inscribed *Royal Bombay Fusiliers* surmounted by a Victorian crown. In the centre the numerals *103* (Fig. 943).

1st and 2nd Battalions after 1881

On racoon-skin cap

In silver a wreath of shamrock broken at the base with (left) an Elephant resting on a tablet inscribed *Mysore* and (right) a Tiger resting on a tablet inscribed *Plassey* with, below these, a scroll inscribed *Spectamur Agendo*. Within the wreath a shield bearing the Arms of the City of Dublin (three silver castles). (Fig. 944.)

On forage cap

In silver the Tiger. Below the Tiger the Elephant. Below the grenade a scroll in silver inscribed *Royal Dublin Fusiliers*.

OTHER-RANKS' HEAD-DRESS BADGES

On racoon-skin cap

The Northumberland Fusiliers

Within a strap inscribed *Quo fata vocant* St. George and the Dragon (Fig. 945).

945

946

947

948

949

950

951

952

953

954

957

960

955

958

959

956

The Royal Fusiliers (City of London Regiment)
(1) The Garter surmounted by a Victorian crown. Within the Garter a Rose (Fig. 946).
(2) As above but with the Imperial crown (Fig. 947).
In both patterns there are various sizes of the crown above the Garter.

The Lancashire Fusiliers
Within a circlet inscribed *Lancashire* the Sphinx superscribed *Egypt* within a laurel-wreath (Fig. 948).

The Royal Scots Fusiliers
(1) The Royal Arms with a Victorian crown (Fig. 949).
(2) As above but with the Imperial Royal Crest (Fig. 950).
There are variations in the size of the Royal Arms for both periods.

The Royal Welsh Fusiliers
The Prince of Wales's plumes, coronet and motto (Fig. 951).

The Royal Inniskilling Fusiliers
Within a circlet inscribed *Inniskilling* the Castle of Inniskilling (Fig. 952).

The Royal Irish Fusiliers (Princess Victoria's)
(1) Within a circlet inscribed *Royal Irish Fusiliers* the Eagle, with the numeral *8* below (Fig. 953).
(2) The Eagle with a wreath of laurel. Below the Eagle a small tablet inscribed with the numeral *8* (Fig. 954).

The Royal Munster Fusiliers
(1) A strap inscribed *Royal Bengal Fusiliers*. In the centre the numerals *101* (Fig. 955).
(2) A strap inscribed *Bengal Fusiliers*. In the centre the numerals *104* (Fig. 956).
(3) Within a laurel-wreath a shield bearing the Arms of the Province of Munster (Fig. 957).

The Royal Dublin Fusiliers
(1) A strap inscribed *Royal Madras Fusiliers*. In the centre a Tiger (Fig. 958).
(2) A strap inscribed *Royal Bombay Fusiliers*. In the centre an Elephant (Fig. 959).
(3) A shield bearing the Arms of the City of Dublin (Fig. 960).

On the glengarry
With the exception of The Royal Scots Fusiliers this head-dress was discontinued in 1898.

The Northumberland Fusiliers
(1) Within a strap inscribed *Quo fata vocant* St. George and the Dragon (Fig. 961).
(2) As above but with a circlet instead of a strap (Fig. 962).

The Royal Fusiliers (City of London Regiment)
The Garter surmounted by a Victorian crown. Within the Garter a Rose (Fig. 963).

961    962    963    964

965    966    967    968

969    970    971    972

The Lancashire Fusiliers
Within a circlet inscribed *Lancashire* the Sphinx superscribed *Egypt* within a laurel-wreath (Fig. 964).

The Royal Scots Fusiliers
(1) The Royal Arms with Victorian crown (Fig. 965).
(2) As above but with Imperial Royal Crest (Fig. 966).

The Royal Welsh Fusiliers
The Prince of Wales's plumes, coronet and motto (Fig. 967).

The Royal Inniskilling Fusiliers
Within a circlet inscribed *Inniskilling* the Castle of Inniskilling (Fig. 968).

The Royal Irish Fusiliers (Princess Victoria's)
(1) Within a circlet inscribed *Royal Irish Fusiliers* the Eagle (Fig. 969).
(2) The Eagle with a wreath of laurel. Below the Eagle a small tablet inscribed with the numeral *8* (Fig. 970).

The Royal Munster Fusiliers
Within a laurel-wreath a shield bearing the Arms of the Province of Munster (Fig. 971).

The Royal Dublin Fusiliers
A shield bearing the Arms of the City of Dublin (Fig. 972).

CHAPTER 19

Departments, Corps and Miscellaneous Badges

ROYAL ARMY CHAPLAINS DEPARTMENT

'His Majesty The King, in view of the splendid work which has been performed by the Army Chaplains Department during the present War, has been graciously pleased to approve of the department being in future designated the *Royal Army Chaplains Department*.'—Army Order 92 of 1919.

Christian Chaplains
(1) A cross surmounted by an Imperial crown. In silver. Pattern worn up to 1922. (Fig. 973).
(2) A cross surmounted by an Imperial crown voided between the arms of the cross. In gilt, also in black-metal (Fig. 974).

Jewish Chaplains
Jewish Chaplains did not wear uniform until the outbreak of the Great War.
(1) The Star of David in black-metal: Unofficial badge worn in 1914 (Fig. 975).
(2) The Star of David surmounted by an Imperial crown in black-metal. Official badge worn during the Great War (Fig. 976).

ROYAL FLYING CORPS

The Royal Flying Corps (Military Wing) was formed by Army Order 130 of 1912 and took precedence immediately following the Corps of Royal Engineers.

On the 1st April 1918 together with the Royal Naval Air Service it formed the Royal Air Force.

Cap-badge
Within a laurel-wreath surmounted by an Imperial crown the monogram *RFC*. In gilding-metal (Fig. 977).
Officers: in gilt, also in bronze.

973   **974**   **975**   **976**   **977**

ROYAL ARMY SERVICE CORPS

The Royal Wagon Train was raised in 1799 and disbanded in 1833. An Ambulance Corps, for service in the Crimean War, was raised in 1854 but was merged into the Land Transport Corps raised by Royal Warrant of 24th January 1855.

In 1856 the Land Transport Corps was remodelled and designated the *Military Train* by Royal Warrant of 14th August 1856.

1st Battalion, Military Train

Shako-plate: 1859–65
Within an oak-wreath a strap inscribed *Military Train* surmounted by a Victorian crown. In the centre the numeral *1*. In brass with the numeral in black (Fig. 978).

978

In 1870, a Control Department was formed which absorbed the officers of the Military Train. The other-ranks went into the first Army Service Corps.

The other-ranks' plate worn on the last shako is shown in Fig. 182, Chapter 7. Junior officers of the Control Department wore a similar plate but with slightly different lettering from 1870 to 1875 and by those of the Commissariat and Transport Department from 1875 to 1878 (see Fig. 181 in the same Chapter).

On the introduction of the cloth helmet in 1878 the standard-pattern plate was worn.
Officers: In the centre in gilt, script letters *ASC* on a black background (Fig. 979).
Other-ranks: The centre of the plate voided and the letters *ASC* on a separate piece of metal inserted therein. All in gilding-metal (Fig. 980).

In 1881 the title was changed to *Commissariat and Transport Corps* and the centre-device was changed to agree with the new title.
Other ranks: As the previous plate but with the letters *CTC* on a separate bar. In gilding-metal (Fig. 981).

This title was only in use for seven years and by Army Order 3 of 1889 the previous designation of *Army Service Corps* was resumed.
Officers: As the previous plate but the letters *ASC* now in the form of a monogram and in silver-plate on a red-velvet ground, remainder in gilt (Fig. 982).

Following the accession of King Edward VII the design of the crown was altered and this was worn until the helmet was discontinued.

980

987

986

988

989

990

981

979

991

992

982

984

983

985

Officers: In the centre a silver-plated monogram on a red-velvet ground, remainder of the badge in gilt (Fig. 983).

Other ranks: In the centre the letters *ASC* in the same design as the previous pattern with detachable centre (Fig. 984).

There was also a pattern with the letters in the centre fixed and not detachable (Fig. 985).

Forage cap badges

The first type of forage cap badge was an eight-pointed star, the topmost point displaced by a Victorian crown. On this a laurel-wreath and within the wreath the Garter. In a voided centre the monogram *ASC*.

Officers: All in silver with the monogram on a black-enamel ground (Fig. 986).

Other-ranks: Same design as for the officers but all in gilding-metal (Fig. 987).

In 1902 the new badge was of the same basic design except for the change in the crown.

Officers: The star in gilt, remainder in silver-plate (Fig. 988). Also in bronze.

Other-ranks: Same design as for officers but all in gilding-metal.

Certainly not later than 1911 the design was modified with broader letters in the monogram, a wider laurel-wreath and a change in the shape of the star.

Officers: In gilt and silver-plate (Fig. 989).

Other ranks: In gilding-metal (Fig. 990).

An all-brass economy issue with solid background to the centre was made in 1916.

The Corps was granted the prefix *Royal* for services during the Great War by Army Order 362 of 25th November 1918 and the badge was altered accordingly.

Officers: An eight-pointed star, the topmost point displaced by an Imperial crown. On this a pierced Garter and within a voided centre the Royal Cypher of King George v. Below the Garter a scroll inscribed *Royal Army Service Corps* with laurel-sprays from each end of the scroll to meet the crown. In gilt with blue-enamel ground to the Garter and red-enamel to the cypher (Fig. 991).

Other-ranks: As for the officers but all in gilding-metal (Fig. 992).

Army Service Corps Volunteers

The helmet-plates for the Volunteers were in silver-plate or white-metal. Three examples are shown:

Supply Detachment, Harwich Infantry Volunteer Brigade

Standard-pattern crown, star and laurel-wreath. Within the wreath a circlet inscribed *Harwich Inf. Vol. Bde. Supply Detachment*. In a voided centre, and in script letters, *SD* on a bar (Fig. 993).

Sussex and Kent Volunteer Brigade, Army Service Corps

Standard-pattern crown, star and laurel-wreath. Within the wreath a circlet inscribed *Sussex & Kent Volr Brigade*. In a voided centre, in script, the letters *ASC* (Fig. 994).

General Pattern

Standard-pattern crown, star and laurel-wreath. Within the wreath the Garter. In the centre the letters *ASC* in script (Fig. 995).

Forage cap badges

(1) As A.S.C. with Victorian crown. In white-metal (Fig. 996).
(2) As A.S.C. with Imperial crown. In white-metal (Fig. 997).

996   997

993

994   995

ROYAL ARMY MEDICAL CORPS

The Army has always had medical officers in attendance but the formation of the R.A.M.C. is comparatively recent.

At the commencement of the Crimean War, apart from the Regimental Establishment, the Army Medical Department consisted of a Director-General, four Inspectors-General, eleven Deputy Inspectors and some 163 Officer-Surgeons distributed in garrisons all over the world. There were no trained stretcher-bearers and the wounded were brought out of action by the regimental surgeons, their orderlies, and bandsmen.

This situation led to the formation of a Medical Staff Corps in 1855, which was renamed *The Army Hospital Corps* in 1857 and, again, *Medical Staff Corps* by Warrant of 20th September 1884.

In 1873 all Medical Officers ceased to be regimental officers and came under the Medical Department and in 1884 all Army Medical Department officers and quartermasters were designated *Army Medical Staff* and given command over the other-ranks of the *Medical Staff Corps* as the Army Hospital Corps was now designated.

Finally, by the Royal Warrant of the 23rd June 1898, officers and other-ranks were merged into one Corps entitled *The Royal Army Medical Corps*.

Medical Staff Corps
An eight-pointed star, the topmost point displaced by a Victorian crown. On this a laurel-wreath within which the Garter, and in the centre a cut-out cross with red-cloth backing. Below the wreath a three-part scroll inscribed *Medical Staff Corps*. In gilding-metal (Fig. 998).

Army Hospital Corps
Similar badge to the above but the scroll at base inscribed *Army Hospital Corps*. In gilding-metal (Fig. 999).

Army Medical Department
Within a laurel-wreath, surmounted by a Victorian crown, a rope circle. Within this a cross of red-enamel on a background of white-enamel. Remainder in gilt. Worn from 1869 to 1878 (Fig. 1000).

Army Medical Staff
An eight-pointed star surmounted by a Victorian crown. On this a strap inscribed *Army Medical Staff* and in the centre the cypher *VR*. In silver. Worn on the puggaree in India (Fig. 1001).

Royal Army Medical Corps
Officers' helmet-plate:
(1) The Royal Arms with a scroll below inscribed *Royal Army Medical Corps*. In gilt (Fig. 1002).
(2) As above but with Imperial crown in the Royal Crest. In gilt (Fig. 1003).
Other-ranks' helmet-plate:
(1) An eight-pointed star, the topmost point displaced by a Victorian crown. On this a laurel-wreath and within the wreath the Garter. A white-metal centre having a cut-out cross with red-cloth backing. Remainder in gilding-metal (Fig. 1004).
(2) As above but with Imperial crown (Fig. 1005).

Forage cap (Officers and other-ranks)
(1) A laurel-wreath surmounted by a Victorian crown. In the centre the rod of Aesculapius with a serpent twined round it. Below, a scroll inscribed *Royal Army Medical Corps*. In gilding-metal (Fig. 1006). Officers: in gilt, also in bronze.
(2) As above but with Imperial crown. (Fig. 1007).

Royal Army Medical Corps Militia
The same badges as for the Royal Army Medical Corps but with a small silver, or white-metal, letter *M* at the base.

In the Volunteer Movement which commenced in 1859 the Volunteer Rifle Companies had sections of stretcher-bearers and these were the nuclei of the Medical Volunteers.

Their badges can be divided into two categories; firstly the general pattern and later, when the Volunteers were formed into brigades, the badges of the Bearer Companies. These were mostly of a standard design, the only difference being the title of the unit on the circlet. As there were many Volunteer Infantry Brigades there are consequently a large number of these badges. Four representative badges are shown: one with Victorian crown, one with large, and one with small, Imperial crown and one badge which is of a different design.

As is customary, all Volunteer badges are in silver-plate for officers and white-metal for other-ranks.

998

1000

999

1002

1001

1003

1006

1004

1007

1005

Volunteer Medical Staff Corps

Shako-plate
An eight-pointed star, the topmost point displaced by a Victorian crown. On this a laurel-wreath and within this the Garter. In the centre a cut-out cross with a backing of red-cloth. Below the wreath a three-part scroll inscribed *Medical Staff Corps* (Fig. 1008).

Helmet-plate
An eight-pointed star the topmost point displaced by a Victorian crown. On this a laurel-wreath and within this a circlet inscribed *Volunteer Medical Staff Corps*. In the centre a cut-out cross with a backing of red-cloth (Fig. 1009).

Forage cap
A laurel-wreath surmounted by a Victorian crown. Within this the rod of Aesculapius with a serpent twined round it. Below the wreath a scroll inscribed *Volr. Medical Staff Corps* (Fig. 1010).

Royal Army Medical Corps Volunteers (Officers)

Helmet-plate
The Royal Arms with a scroll below inscribed *Royal Army Medical Corps* (Fig. 1011).

Forage cap
A laurel-wreath surmounted by an Imperial crown. In the centre the rod of Aesculapius with a serpent twined round it. At the base of the rod a scroll inscribed *Vols*;. Below the wreath, a scroll inscribed *Royal Army Medical Corps* (Fig. 1012). In bronze, also in silver-plate.

Royal Army Medical Corps Volunteers (Other-ranks)

Helmet-plate
(1) An eight-pointed star, the topmost point displaced by an Imperial crown. On this a laurel-wreath and within the wreath a circlet inscribed *Royal Army Medical Corps Volunteers*. In the centre, a cut-out cross with a backing of red-cloth (Fig. 1013).
(2) Star, crown and laurel-wreath as above. Within the laurel-wreath the Garter. In the centre a white-metal disc with a painted red cross (Fig. 1014).

Forage cap
A laurel-wreath surmounted by an Imperial crown. In the centre the rod of Aesculapius with a serpent twined round it. Below, a scroll inscribed *Royal Army Medical Corps* (Fig. 1015).

Bearer Companies (Other-ranks badges)

3rd London Volunteer Infantry Brigade Bearer Company

Forage cap
A circlet inscribed *3rd London Vol. Infy. Brigade Bearer Co.* surmounted by an Imperial crown. In the centre, a cut-out cross with a backing of red-cloth. Below the circlet a scroll inscribed *In arduis fidelis* (Fig. 1016).

Forth Volunteer Infantry Brigade Bearer Company

Helmet-plate
Standard design with Victorian crown. The circlet inscribed *Forth V.I.B. Bearer Company* (Fig. 1017).

1008

1009

1013

1016

1010   1015

1017   1014

1011

1012

1018   1019

Leicestershire and Lincolnshire Volunteer Infantry Brigade Bearer Company

Helmet-plate

Standard design with Imperial crown. The circlet inscribed *Leic. & Linc. Vol. Bde. Bearer Company* (Fig. 1018).

Liverpool Volunteer Infantry Brigade Bearer Company

Helmet-plate

Standard design with small Imperial crown. The circlet inscribed *I B Bearer Company (Vol.) Liverpool* (Fig. 1019).

When, in 1908, the Volunteers became the Territorial Force, the R.A.M.C. (T.F.) wore the same badges as the Regulars except that they were in white-metal.

ROYAL ARMY ORDNANCE CORPS

Officers and men did not come together to form one Corps until they were amalgamated in 1918 by Army Order 363 to form the Royal Army Ordnance Corps.

Officers: Ordnance Store Department formed from Control Department by Royal Warrant 27th November 1875, changed to Army Ordnance Department by Special Army Order 20th June 1896.

Men: Ordnance Store Branch formed from Army Service Corps in 1877, renamed Ordnance Store Corps in 1881 and Army Ordnance Corps by Special Army Order 20th June, 1896.

It absorbed the Corps of Armourer Sergeants (which had been formed by Royal Warrant of 24th June 1858) by Army Order 96 of 1895 and also The Armament Artificers R.A. (formed by Army Order 89 of 1893 from the Corps of Ordnance Artificers which had been formed in 1882 by General Order 3225).

Ordnance Store Corps

Helmet-plate: 1881

An eight-pointed star, the topmost point displaced by a Victorian crown. On this a laurel-wreath and within the wreath the Garter. In the centre the letters *OSC* on a black-velvet ground.

Army Ordnance Department

Helmet-plate: 1896

An eight-pointed star the topmost point displaced by a Victorian crown. On this a laurel wreath. Within the wreath the Garter. In the centre the monogram *AOD*. All in gilt except the monogram which is silver. Black-velvet backing to the centre (Fig. 1020).

Army Ordnance Corps

Helmet-plate: 1896

As above but, in the centre, a shield bearing the Ordnance Arms in white-metal on a black-cloth ground. Other-ranks' pattern Fig. 1021. For officers: the Ordnance Arms in silver on a black-velvet ground.

1023

1020

1026   1025

1022ᴬ

1024

1021

1027

1022

1028   1029

1030   1031   1028ᴬ

Helmet-plate: 1902
As above but with Imperial crown. Other-ranks' pattern (Fig. 1022). Officers' pattern (Fig. 1022A).

Field-service cap: 1896
   (1) A shield bearing the Ordnance Arms resting on a scroll inscribed *Army Ordnance Corps*. In gilding-metal (Fig. 1023).
   (2) As above, but smaller (Fig. 1024).

Royal Army Ordnance Corps

Other-ranks' forage-cap: c. 1920
The Garter surmounted by an Imperial crown. Within the Garter a shield bearing the Ordnance Arms. Below the Garter a scroll inscribed *Royal Army Ordnance Corps*. In gilding-metal (Fig. 1025).

Officers' forage-cap: c. 1920
A gilt pierced-Garter with a blue-enamel ground surmounted by an Imperial crown. Within the Garter a shield bearing the Ordnance Arms on a red-enamel ground. Below the Garter a scroll inscribed *Royal Army Ordnance Corps* (Fig. 1026).

CORPS OF MILITARY POLICE

Except for the Quartermaster no officers were gazetted to the Corps until after the Second World War. Officers were seconded from other regiments and retained their own badges.

In 1885, the Military Police was divided into the Military Mounted Police and the Military Foot Police and these remained separate until the 27th February 1926 when they were merged into one Corps under the title of the *Corps of Military Police*.
All badges are those of other-ranks.

Helmet-plates
Standard-pattern of star, crown, laurel-wreath and Garter.
   (1) In the centre the cypher of Queen Victoria on a red-cloth ground. All in gilding-metal (Fig. 1027).
   (2) In the centre the cypher of King Edward VII on a red-cloth ground. All in gilding-metal (Fig. 1028).
      Note: Although the cypher is that of King Edward VII the plate has a Victorian crown.
   (3) As (2) but with Imperial crown (Fig. 1028A).

Forage-cap badges
   (1) The Royal Crest resting on a scroll inscribed *Military Foot Police*. In gilding-metal (Fig. 1029).
   (2) Within a laurel-wreath the cypher of King Edward VII surmounted by an Imperial crown. Below the wreath a scroll inscribed *Military Police*. In gilding-metal (Fig. 1030).
   (3) As (2) but with the cypher of King George V. In gilding-metal (Fig. 1031).

ROYAL ARMY PAY CORPS

Officers: A Pay Sub-Department of the Control Department was formed in 1870 and in 1878 was designated the *Army Pay Department*. By Army Order 86 of 1905 the title was changed to

1033 1036

1034 1032 1035

Army Accounts Department but reverted to *Army Pay Department* in 1909 by Army Order 294,
In 1920 it became the *Royal Army Pay Department* by Army Order 146.
Men: The *Army Pay Corps* was formed by Army Order 134 of 1893 and became *Royal Army Pay Corps* by Army Order 146 of 1920.
The Royal Army Pay Department and the Royal Army Pay Corps were amalgamated to form the Royal Army Pay Corps by Army Order 498 of 1920.

Helmet-plate: 1902
An eight-pointed star, the topmost point displaced by an Imperial crown. On this a laurel-wreath. Within the wreath the Garter. In the centre, on a bar in script, the letters *APC* with green-cloth backing. In gilding-metal (Fig. 1032).
The same pattern badge but with Victorian crown was worn from 1893 to 1902.

Forage-cap
   (1) The monogram *APC*. In gilding-metal. Worn from 1898 to 1900 (Fig. 1033).
   (2) The monogram *APC* surmounted by a Victorian crown. In gilding-metal. Worn from 1900 to 1901 (Fig. 1034).
   (3) The monogram *APC* surmounted by an Imperial crown. In gilding-metal. Worn from 1902 to 1920 (Fig. 1035).
   (4) The monogram *RAPC* surmounted by the Royal Crest. In gilding-metal. Worn from 1920 (Fig. 1036). For officers: in gilt, also in bronze.

CORPS OF MILITARY ACCOUNTANTS

Was formed by Army Order 409 of 1919 and disbanded by Army Order 137 of 1927.

Forage-cap
An oval inscribed *Corps of Military Accountants* with, in the centre, the cypher of King George v surmounted by an Imperial crown. In gilding-metal (Fig. 1037). For officers: in gilt, also in bronze.

1037

ROYAL ARMY VETERINARY CORPS

On the 1st April 1881, the regimental veterinary system in the cavalry was abolished and henceforth the Veterinary Service was known as the *Army Veterinary Department*. All officers except those of the Household Cavalry being transferred to one list and wearing one uniform.

The Royal Warrant of 5th October 1903 created the *Army Veterinary Corps* from among the non-commissioned officers and men already employed on Army Veterinary Services.

In March 1906, the officers of the Army Veterinary Department and the N.C.O.s and men of the Army Veterinary Corps were amalgamated into one unit named the *Army Veterinary Corps* by Army Order 48 of 1906.

For its services in the Great War the Corps was granted the prefix *Royal* on the 27th November 1918 by Army Order 362 of 1918.

Helmet-plate (Officers)
Standard-pattern of star, crown, wreath and Garter.
  (1) In gilt with Victorian crown, the monogram *AVD* in silver on a white-metal ground (Fig. 1038).
  (2) In gilt with Imperial crown, the monogram *AVD* in silver on a black-leather ground (Fig. 1039).
  (3) In gilt with Imperial crown, the monogram *AVC* in silver on a black-leather ground (Fig. 1040).

1041

Helmet-plate (Other-ranks)
Standard-pattern of star, crown, laurel-wreath and Garter. In the centre, on a detachable bar in script letters, *AVC* (Fig. 1041).

Forage-cap
(1) In gilt a laurel-wreath surmounted by an Imperial crown. Within the wreath the monogram *AVD* in silver plate (Fig. 1042). Also in bronze.
(2) As above but with the monogram *AVC* (Fig. 1043). Also in bronze. Other-ranks' in gilding-metal and white-metal. There was also an all-brass economy issue in 1916.
(3) Within a laurel-wreath surmounted by an Imperial crown, a centaur. Below the wreath, a scroll inscribed *Royal Army Veterinary Corps*. The centaur in silver-plate, remainder in gilt (Fig. 1044). Also in bronze. Other-ranks' in gilding-metal and white-metal.

ARMY REMOUNT SERVICE

Forage-cap
(1) Superimposed on crossed whips a horseshoe with, in the centre, a horse standing on a scroll inscribed *Remounts*. In gilding-metal (Fig. 1045).
(2) An oval inscribed *Army Remount Service* surmounted by an Imperial crown. In the centre a horse rampant. In gilding-metal (Fig. 1046). Also in bronze.
(3) A strap inscribed *Army Remount Service* surmounted by the cypher of King George V and above this an Imperial crown. In the centre a horse rampant. The horse in white-metal, remainder in gilding-metal (Fig. 1047).

1045   1046   1047

SCHOOL OF MUSKETRY

The School of Musketry was formed in 1854 and in 1919 was designated Small Arms School Hythe. In 1926 it was amalgamated with the Machine Gun School Netheravon and in 1929 the amalgamated schools were formed into a Corps and designated *Small Arms School Corps*.

Helmet-plate: 1878 to 1901
An eight-pointed star the topmost point displaced by a Victorian crown. On this a laurel-wreath. Within the wreath the Garter and, in a voided centre, crossed rifles. In gilding-metal (Fig. 1048).

Helmet-plate: 1902 to 1914
As above but with Imperial crown. In gilding-metal (Fig. 1049).

Forage-cap: 1902 to 1919
Crossed rifles surmounted by an Imperial crown. In gilding-metal (Fig. 1050).
The badge worn prior to this was the same but with a Victorian crown.

MILITARY PROVOST STAFF CORPS

The Military Prison Staff Corps was formed under Army Order 241 of 1901 and redesignated *Military Provost Staff Corps* in 1906.

Helmet-plate
Worn by Governors and Inspectors of Military Prisons.
The Royal Arms in gilt.
   (1) With Victorian crown (Fig. 1051).
   (2) With Imperial crown (Fig. 1052).

Forage-cap
   (1) The cypher of King Edward VII surmounted by an Imperial crown. In gilding-metal (Fig. 1053).
   (2) A laurel-wreath surmounted by an Imperial crown. Within this the cypher of King George v (Fig. 1054).

ARMY EDUCATIONAL CORPS

The Corps of Army Schoolmasters was formed by Royal Warrant of 2nd July 1846. The Army Educational Corps was formed by Royal Warrant of 15th June 1920. At the same time the Corps of Army Schoolmasters was disbanded and the Inspectors and Instructors transferred to the new Corps.

Helmet-plate: 1881 to 1902
Inspector of Army Schools: An eight-pointed star, the topmost point displaced by a Victorian crown. On this a laurel-wreath. Within the wreath the Garter and in the centre the Royal Cypher *VR*. In gilt with the cypher in silver on a light-blue-enamel ground (Fig. 1055).

Forage cap: 1920
An open book superimposed on crossed lances and rifles. Below, a scroll inscribed *Army Educational Corps*. In gilding-metal (Fig. 1056).
Officers: in gilt, also in bronze.

1048

1050

1049

1056

1055

1057

1051

1053

1054

1052

ARMY DENTAL CORPS

The Army Dental Corps was formed by Royal Warrant dated 4th January 1921 (Army Order 4 of 1921).

Forage cap
A laurel-wreath surmounted by an Imperial crown. Within the wreath the monogram *ADC*. In gilding-metal (Fig. 1057). Officers: in gilt, also in bronze.

ARMY PHYSICAL TRAINING STAFF

The Army Gymnastic Staff, as it was designated first, was formed in September 1860. It did not become the Army Physical Training Corps until September 1940.

Shako-plate: 1869 to 1878
A laurel-wreath surmounted by a Victorian crown. Within the wreath the Garter and, in the centre, crossed swords with a black-leather ground. In gilt (Fig. 1058).

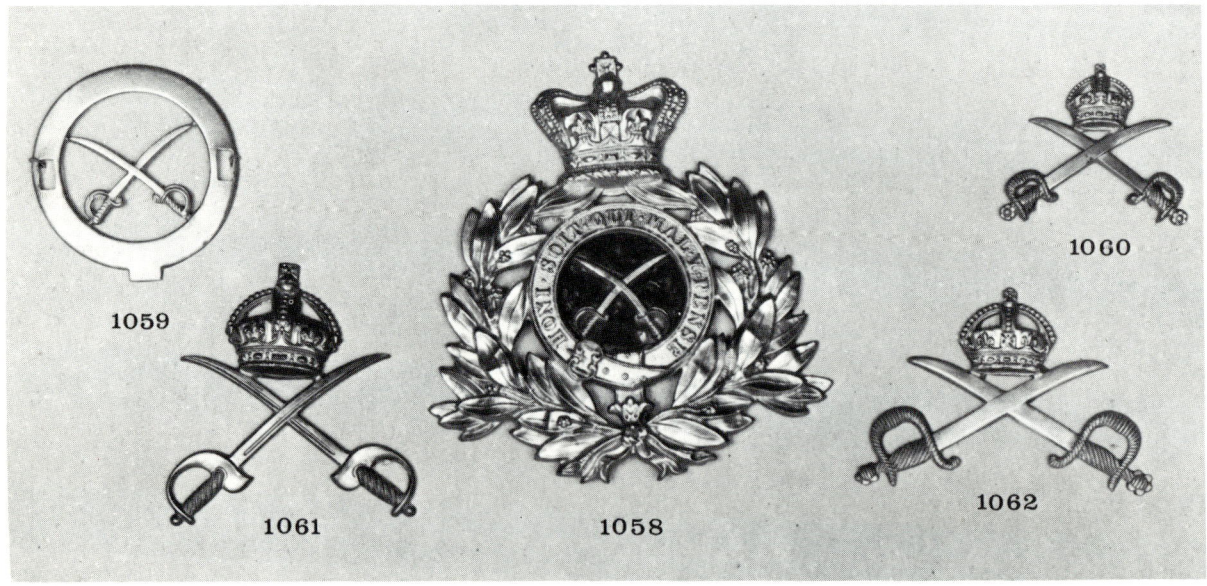

Helmet-plate centre
Crossed swords in gilding-metal (Fig. 1059).
Worn in the centre of the standard-pattern with Victorian crown from 1878 to 1901 and with the Imperial crown from 1902 to 1914.

Forage-cap: 1902–
    (1) Crossed swords surmounted by an Imperial crown. Small size. In gilding-metal (Fig. 1060).
    (2) As above but larger (Fig. 1061).
    (3) As above but different pattern swords and smaller crown (Fig. 1062).

ROYAL DEFENCE CORPS

The Royal Defence Corps was authorised by Royal Warrant of the 12th March 1916 published in Army Order 115 of 1st April 1916.

Cap-badge
  (1) The cypher of King George v surmounted by an Imperial crown. Below the cypher a scroll inscribed *Royal Defence Corps*. In gilding-metal.
  (2) A circlet inscribed *Royal Defence Corps*. In the centre the cypher of King George v surmounted by an Imperial crown (Fig. 1063).

FIRST AID NURSING YEOMANRY

This organisation was formed in 1907 as a corps of horsewomen trained in first aid for mobile service. By 1914 it had become mechanized and during the Great War served in France and Flanders with the British, French and Belgian Armies. It was the first women's service to be mechanized, and staffed, and ran self-contained motor-ambulance units.

By Army Order 94 of 31st March 1927 it was designated *First Aid Nursing Yeomanry (Ambulance Car Corps)*.

Cap-badge
A circlet inscribed *First Aid Nursing Yeomanry* with, in the centre, a cross moliné. In bronze (Fig. 1064).

THE WOMEN'S LEGION

Owing to a shortage of cooks in the New Armies raised during 1914–15, the Women's Legion was formed by Lady Londonderry and first commenced duties on the 3rd August 1915. Later the Legion was employed in other capacities and the Motor Transport Section was officially employed with the Army in February 1917.

When the Women's Army Auxiliary Corps was formed in 1917 the Cooking and General Service Sections enrolled in it; but the M. T. Section continued as the Women's Legion and served overseas until 1919 thereby speeding demobilization of men for work at home.

Cap-badge
The figure of Victory holding a sword in the left hand and a wreath of laurel in the right hand surrounded by a wreath of laurel having a rose in the centre on either side. At the top of the wreath the letters *WL* and across the base a scroll inscribed *Ora et labora*. In bronze (Fig. 1065). Motor-drivers wore a claret background to the badge.

WOMEN'S ARMY AUXILIARY CORPS

The Women's Army Auxiliary Corps was formed in March 1917. About 7,000 members of the General Service and Clerical Sections of the Women's Legion enrolled in the new Corps, and the first contingent was soon serving in France.

Cap-badge
Within a laurel-wreath the letters *WAAC*. In gilding-metal (Fig. 1066). Officers: in gilt, also in bronze.

1063

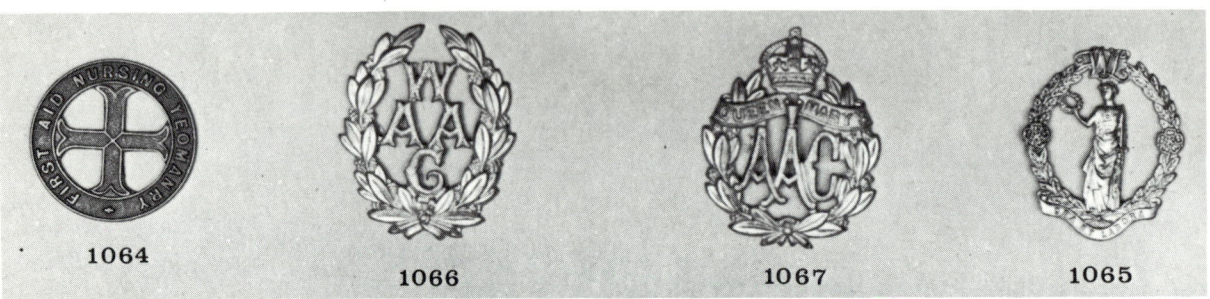

1064   1066   1067   1065

QUEEN MARY'S ARMY AUXILIARY CORPS

In May, 1918, Queen Mary became Colonel-in-Chief of the Women's Army Auxiliary Corps and the title was changed to Queen Mary's Army Auxiliary Corps (Army Order 137 of 1918).

On the conclusion of the war, a unit was retained with the Graves Registration Commission at St. Pol. It was demobilized in London on 27th September 1921.

Cap-badge

A laurel-wreath surmounted by an Imperial crown. Across the top of the wreath a scroll inscribed Queen Mary's and, within the wreath, the letters *AAC*. In gilding-metal (Fig. 1067). Officers: in gilt, also in bronze.

WOMEN'S FORAGE CORPS

This unit was formed during the Great War and, as its name implies, dealt solely with forage for the Armed Forces.

Cap-badge

An eight-pointed star with, in a voided centre, the letters *FC*. In bronze.

ROYAL MILITARY ACADEMY

The Academy was established by Royal Warrant of 30th April 1741 and trained Officer-Cadets for the Royal Regiment of Artillery and the Corps of Royal Engineers.

Officer-Cadets' cap-badge: 1902–

A circlet inscribed *Royal Military Academy* surmounted by an Imperial crown. In the centre a gun. In gilding-metal (Fig. 1068). Also in gilt and bronze.

ROYAL MILITARY COLLEGE

In 1802 the first college for Army Cadets was opened at Great Marlow. Meanwhile the permanent home at Sandhurst was being built and was completed in 1812. Officer-Cadets from Sandhurst were commissioned into the Cavalry, Foot Guards, Infantry and the Departmental Corps.

Shako-plate, Officer-Cadets: prior to 1878

An eight-pointed silver star. On this a gilt pierced strap inscribed *Nec aspera terrent* with a blue-enamel ground and surmounted by a gilt Guelphic crown. In the centre the Royal Cypher *VR* in gilt on a red-enamel ground (Fig. 1069).

Helmet-plate, Officer-Cadets: 1881 to 1901

A gilt eight-pointed star the topmost point displaced by a Victorian crown. On this a gilt laurel-wreath. Within the wreath a gilt pierced strap inscribed *Nec aspera terrent* with a blue-enamel ground. In the centre the Royal Cypher *VR* in gilt on a red-enamel ground (Fig. 1070).

Instructional Staff Cap: 1896–

The monogram *RMC* in gilt, finished as if made in embroidery (Fig. 1071).

1069

1071

1072

1074

1076

1070

1073

1075

1068

Officer-Cadets' cap-badge prior to 1901

A gilt pierced circlet inscribed *Nec aspera terrent* with a blue-enamel ground surmounted by a gilt Victorian crown. In the centre the Royal Cypher *VR* in silver on a red-enamel ground (Fig. 1072).

Officer-Cadets' cap-badge: 1902 to 1910

  (1) A gilt pierced circlet inscribed *Nec aspera terrent* with a blue-enamel ground surmounted by a gilt Imperial crown. In the centre the cypher of King Edward VII in silver on a red-enamel ground (Fig. 1073).

  (2) A circlet inscribed *Vires acquirit eundo* surmounted by an Imperial crown. In the centre the cypher of King Edward VII. In gilding-metal with the cypher in white-metal (Fig. 1074). Also all in gilding-metal, and in bronze.

Officer-Cadets' cap-badge: 1911–

  (1) A circlet inscribed *Vires acquirit eundo* surmounted by an Imperial crown. In the centre the cypher of King George V. In gilding-metal with the cypher in white-metal (Fig. 1075). Also in bronze.

  (2) As above but all in white-metal (Fig. 1076).

ROYAL MILITARY SCHOOL OF MUSIC

A Military Music Class was established at Kneller Hall in March 1857. It was designated *The Military School of Music* and granted the title *Royal* in 1887.

Student Bandmasters cease to wear their regimental badges on joining the school and wear the badge described below which was taken into use on 10th October 1907:

The monogram *RMSM* surmounted by an Imperial crown. In gilding-metal (Fig. 1077).

1077

1078

1079

1080

DUKE OF YORK'S ROYAL MILITARY SCHOOL

Situated in Chelsea from 1803 until 1909, when it moved to Dover.

Cap-badge: 1898–1901

A circlet inscribed *Royal Military School* surmounted by a Victorian crown. In the centre the cypher of Queen Victoria. In gilding-metal with the cypher in white-metal (Fig. 1078).

Cap-badge: 1902–10

As above but with the Imperial crown and the cypher of King Edward VII (Fig. 1079).

Cap-badge: 1911–

As above but with the Imperial crown and the cypher of King George V (Fig. 1080).
Prior to 1898 the badge was the Prince of Wales's plumes, coronet and motto in gilding-metal. It also had a single letter and numeral on the reverse.

1081   1082

QUEEN VICTORIA SCHOOL, DUNBLANE

The School was founded in 1903 as a memorial to Queen Victoria and to the Scottish servicemen who fell in the South African War of 1899 to 1902.

Cap-badge
Within a wreath of mixed thistle and oak a lion sejant, as used in the Royal Arms of Scotland, upon an Imperial crown. Across the base of the wreath a scroll inscribed *Queen Victoria School*. In white-metal (Fig. 1081).

ROYAL HIBERNIAN MILITARY SCHOOL

Situated in Dublin. On the formation of the Irish Free State in 1921 it was closed and the staff and pupils transferred to Dover.

Cap-badge: 1902–21
An oval inscribed *Royal Hibernian Military School 1769* surmounted by an Imperial crown. In the centre the Irish Harp. Below the oval, a scroll inscribed *Fear God, Honour the King*. In gilding-metal (Fig. 1082).

EXTRA-REGIMENTALLY EMPLOYED LIST

The Extra-Regimentally Employed List originated as part of the reorganisation of the Staff of the Army resulting from the report of the Esher Committee in 1904.

The List was in two parts. Part I included the names of officers of the Judge Advocate's Staff and Staff Quartermasters, the latter being officers employed at Training Establishments, etc., or on establishments not applicable to any particular Arm of the Service. Part II included the names of Quartermasters supernumerary to their regimental establishment.

The E.R.E. List was reorganised and divided into three categories in 1953.

Cap-badge
The Royal Crest in gilt (Fig. 1083).
Also in bronze.

1083

GENERAL LIST

The General List first appeared in the Army List in October 1914, its title then being *General List, Infantry, for Service Battalions*, and it included the names of 'officers who have been gazetted to the General List for service with Service Battalions, but whose allocation is not included in this issue'. To this was added, in February 1915, the names of officers 'who are holding other appointments'.

Cap-badge
The Royal Arms in gilt (Fig. 1084). Also in bronze.

1084

1085

1087

CHAPTER 20

The Royal Marines

Hat-plate: 1816 (R.M.A.)
As the general style of the 1800 Infantry pattern but the Garter replaced by a strap inscribed *Royal Marine Artillery* with the 'Fouled Anchor' in the centre. Below the strap a mortar with piles of shot either side. In brass (Fig. 1084A).

Shako-plate: 1821 to 1830
A circular domed plate with rope border surmounted by the Royal Crest. In the centre the 'Fouled Anchor' surrounded by a laurel-wreath. Above this a scroll inscribed *Royal Marines*. For officers: in gilt with silver anchor. Other-ranks: in brass (Fig. 1084B).

Officers' shako-plate: 1840 to 1845

An eight-pointed star the topmost point displaced by a Victorian crown. In the centre of the star the 'Fouled Anchor' with a scroll above inscribed *Gibraltar*. To the left of the Anchor a scroll inscribed *Per mare* and to the right a similar scroll inscribed *Per terram*. In gilt with a silver anchor (Fig. 1085).

1084A

1084B

Other-ranks' shako-plate: 1839 to 1855

A circular plate with a border of oak on the left and laurel on the right surmounted by a Victorian crown. On a lined centre the Globe with a scroll above inscribed *Gibraltar*. Laurel-sprays below the Globe and below this the 'Fouled Anchor' with a scroll intertwined and inscribed *Per mare per terram*. In brass (Fig. 1086).

Shako-plate: 1845 to 1855

An eight-pointed star, the topmost point displaced by a Victorian crown. On this a complete laurel-wreath with a scroll across the top inscribed *Gibraltar*. On the left side of the wreath a scroll inscribed *Per mare* and on the right a similar scroll inscribed *Per terram*. In the centre the Globe. Below the wreath the 'Fouled Anchor'. For officers only. All gilt except the Globe and Anchor which are in silver (Fig. 1087). Some plates are known to have the spelling *Gibralter*.

Shako-plate: 1855 to 1866 (R.M.L.I.)

An eight-pointed star, the topmost point displaced by a Victorian crown. On this a laurel-wreath and within this a strap inscribed *Per mare per terram*. In the centre the Globe. At the top-join of the wreath the 'Fouled Anchor' and at the base a bugle with strings. For officers only. Globe, Anchor and bugle in silver, remainder in gilt (Fig. 1088).
There are several variations, some with the design all-gilt, others with only the bugle-horn in silver. Other-ranks wore a similar pattern in all-brass.

Shako-plate: 1855 to 1866 (R.M.A.)

An eight-pointed star, the topmost point displaced by a Victorian crown. On this a laurel-wreath and within this a strap inscribed *Per mare per terram*. In the centre the Globe. At the top join of the wreath the 'Fouled Anchor' and on the bottom point of the star a grenade. For officers only. Globe, Anchor and Grenade in silver, remainder in gilt (Fig. 1088A).

1088A

1088

1086

1089

1091

1090

1092

1093

1094

1096

1097

1098

1095

Shako-plate: 1866 to 1878
An eight-pointed star, the topmost point displaced by a Victorian crown. On this a laurel-wreath surmounted by a scroll inscribed *Gibraltar* with the 'Fouled Anchor' at the bottom of the wreath. Within the wreath a voided strap inscribed *Per mare per terram* with a backing of blue-enamel. In the centre the Globe. For officers only. All in gilt (Fig. 1089).

Shako-plate: 1866 to 1878 (R.M.L.I.)
An eight-pointed star, the topmost point displaced by a Victorian crown. On this a laurel-wreath surmounted by a scroll inscribed *Gibraltar*. Within the wreath a circlet inscribed *Per mare per terram*. In the centre the Globe. At the base of the wreath the 'Fouled Anchor' above a bugle with strings. For other-ranks only. In brass (Fig. 1090).

Helmet-plate: 1878 to 1902 (R.M.L.I.)
Officers: An eight-pointed star, the topmost point displaced by a Victorian crown. On this a laurel-wreath and within this a voided strap inscribed *Per mare per terram*. In the centre the Globe. Above the strap a scroll inscribed *Gibraltar*. On the bottom-join of the wreath the 'Fouled Anchor' and below this a bugle with strings. Blue-enamel backing to the strap, the Globe and bugle in silver, remainder in gilt (Fig. 1091).
Other-ranks: Similar design to the officers' pattern but the motto is on a circlet instead of a strap and the 'Fouled Anchor' at the base is superimposed on the strings of the bugle. In gilding-metal (Fig. 1092).

Glengarry: 1870 to 1897/8 (R.ML.I.)
Officers: A laurel-wreath with a scroll inscribed *Gibraltar* above and the scroll surmounted by a bugle with strings. On the base of the wreath the 'Fouled Anchor'. Within the wreath a voided strap inscribed *Per mare per terram* and, in the centre, the Globe. Silver bugle-horn and Globe, blue-enamel backing to strap, remainder in gilt (Fig. 1093).
Other-ranks: A complete laurel-wreath with, in the centre, the Globe. Worn separately above, a bugle-horn with strings. In gilt for Senior N.C.O.s and in brass for rank-and-file (Fig. 1094).
The glengarry was authorised for wear by both the R.M.L.I. and the R.M.A. on 24th January 1870.

Forage-cap: 1880 (R.M.L.I.)
Officers: An embroidered laurel-wreath with a gilt-and-silver Globe in the centre. Above, and separate, a bugle with strings in gilt.

Helmet-plate: 1902 to 1905 (R.M.L.I.)
Officers: As plate for 1878–1902 but with Imperial crown (Fig. 1095).
Other-ranks: As plate for 1878–1902 but with Imperial crown (Fig. 1096).

Forage-cap: 1898 to 1923 (R.M.L.I.)
Within a laurel-wreath the Globe surmounted by a bugle with strings. Senior N.C.O.s in gilt; rank-and-file in brass or gilding-metal (Fig. 1097).

Forage-cap, Royal Marines Labour Corps
Within a laurel-wreath the Globe surmounted by a ship, bows-on, resting on a wreathed-scroll. In brass (Fig. 1098). This Corps was formed on 2nd February 1917 from two companies of the Army Service Corps. It was disbanded at the conclusion of the First World War.

1099

1101

1100

1102

1106

1103

1104

1107

1105

Helmet-plate: 1905 (R.M.L.I.)

Officers: An eight-pointed star the topmost point displaced by an Imperial crown. On this a laurel-wreath and within this a voided strap inscribed *Per mare per terram*. In the centre the Globe. Above the strap a scroll inscribed *Gibraltar*. Below the wreath the 'Fouled Anchor'. Blue-enamel backing to the strap, the Globe in silver-and-gilt, remainder in gilt (Fig. 1099). Other-ranks: Similar design to the officers' pattern but with the motto on a circlet instead of a strap. All in gilding-metal (Fig. 1100).

Busby: 1866 to 1879 (R.M.A.)

Officers: A fused grenade. On the ball a laurel-wreath with, above, a scroll inscribed *Gibraltar*. Within the wreath a voided strap inscribed *Per mare per terram*. In the centre the Globe. On the bottom-join of the wreath a 'Fouled Anchor'. Blue-enamel backing to the strap, the Globe in silver-and-gilt, remainder in gilt (Fig. 1101). A pattern similar to above but with a grenade replacing the 'Fouled Anchor' (Fig. 1101A).

Warrant Officers: Same general design as for officers but strap not voided and with different arrangement of flames. All in gilt (Fig. 1102).

Rank-and-file: A fused grenade. On the ball a scroll inscribed *Per mare per terram* broken in the centre by the 'Fouled Anchor'. Below the neck of the grenade a scroll inscribed *Gibraltar*. In the centre the Globe. All in brass (Fig. 1103). A red horse-hair plume was held in the plume-holder.

Helmet-plate: 1879 to 1905 (R.M.A.)

Officers: A fused grenade with eighteen points to the flames and with a narrow neck. On the ball a laurel-wreath with, above, a scroll inscribed *Gibraltar* and with the 'Fouled Anchor' at the bottom-join of the wreath. Within the wreath a voided strap inscribed *Per mare per terram* and, in the centre, the Globe. Blue-enamel backing to the strap, the Globe in silver, remainder in gilt (Fig. 1104).

Helmet-plate: Officers', 1879 to 1905; Other-ranks, 1879 to 1923 (R.M.A.)

Officers: A fused grenade with nine points to the flames and with a wide neck. Other details as per previous pattern. Blue-enamel backing to the strap, the Globe in silver-and-gilt, remainder in gilt (Fig. 1105). Other-ranks: Same design as for officers but all in gilding-metal (Fig. 1106).

Forage-cap: 1902 (R.M.A.)

Officers: On a red-cloth ground a gold embroidered laurel-wreath with, in the centre, a silver Globe. Above, and separate, crossed gun-barrels in gilt (Fig. 1107).

Brodrick cap: 1902 to 1921 (R.M.A.)

A fused grenade with a plain ball. Senior N.C.O.s in gilt, rank-and-file in brass (Fig. 1108). This badge was worn on various head-dresses by other-ranks until 1922.

1101A

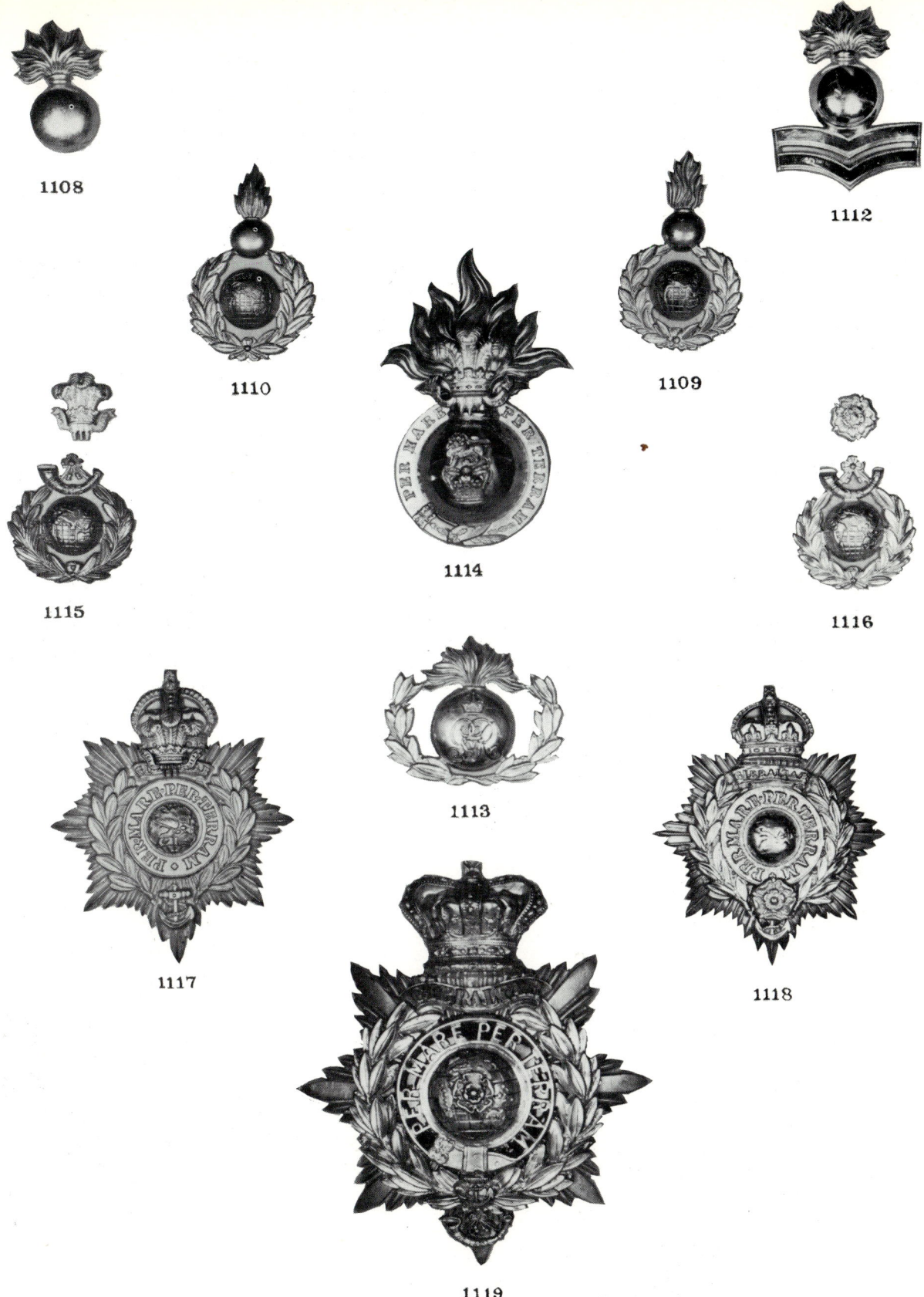

1108

1112

1110

1109

1114

1115

1116

1117

1113

1118

1119

Forage-cap: 1921 (R.M.A.)

Sergeants: The Globe surrounded by a laurel-wreath and surmounted by a fused grenade. In gilt (Fig. 1109).

Bombardiers and below: The same basic design but the laurel-wreath is not so close to the Globe and the flames of the grenade are arranged differently. In gilding-metal (Fig. 1110). Quartermaster Sergeants wore a small grenade separately from the Globe and laurel.

Undress-cap (February 1855 to February 1857)

Lance-Sergeants: A fused grenade above three chevrons. (Full Sergeants wore a band of lace on their pillbox.)

Bombardiers: A fused grenade above two chevrons (Fig. 1112).
Lance-Bombardiers: A fused grenade above a single chevron.

THE ROYAL MARINES BANDS

R.M.A.: 1912 to 1923

Within a laurel-wreath a fused grenade with the Royal Cypher of King George v on the ball. The cypher in silver, remainder in gilt (Fig. 1113).

The band was authorised to wear the Royal Cypher by General Order, Royal Marines 44 of 1912 to commemorate their attendance on King George v on his voyage to India. On the helmet-plate a silver cypher of King George v was mounted above the 'Fouled Anchor' and below the Globe, the plate itself being brass.

Note: A badge of this type bearing the cypher of King Edward vii is also known.

Bandmaster's badge, R.M.L.I. Portsmouth Division: 1876 to 1878

A circlet inscribed *Per mare per terram*. Within this a fused grenade. On the ball the Royal Crest. On the flames the Prince of Wales's plumes, coronet and motto. Circlet, Royal Crest and the plumes in silver, remainder in gilt (Fig. 1114).

In 1868 the band of the Portsmouth Division adopted a new head-dress. It was a black seal-skin cap, somewhat similar to the Fusilier cap. The Prince of Wales's plumes would have been added to the badge in 1876.

R.M.L.I. Portsmouth Division: 1905 to 1923

Within a laurel-wreath surmounted by a bugle with strings the Globe. All in brass. (Senior N.C.O.s in gilt.) Above, and separate, the Prince of Wales's plumes, coronet and motto in silver (Fig. 1115).

On the 5th July 1876, the band was authorised to wear the Prince of Wales's plumes on their helmet-plates and cap-badges to commemorate their attendance on H.R.H. The Prince of Wales (late King Edward vii) during his voyage to India in 1875–1876. From 1905 to 1923, to differentiate from the Plymouth Division who also had been granted this same distinction, the plumes in silver were placed between the 'Fouled Anchor' and the Globe on the helmet-plate. Gilt-plate for Senior N.C.O.s, brass for rank-and-file.

R.M.L.I. Chatham Division: 1902 to 1923
Within a laurel-wreath surmounted by a bugle with strings the Globe. Above, and separate, a rose. In gilt with silver rose for Senior N.C.O.s, in brass with silver rose for rank-and-file (Fig. 1116).
General Order, Royal Marines 31 of 1902, authorised the wearing of the White Rose of York to commemorate the bands' attendance on H.R.H. The Duke of York (later King George v) on his voyage to the Colonies in 1901.

Helmet-plates

R.M.L.I. Plymouth Division: 1920 to 1923
The same pattern as shown in Fig. 1100. On this, above the circlet, the Prince of Wales's plumes, coronet and motto. In gilt with silver plumes for Senior N.C.O.s, in brass with silver plumes for the rank-and-file (Fig. 1117).
General Order, Royal Marines 206 of 1920, authorised the wearing of the Prince of Wales's plume for their attendance on H.R.H. The Prince of Wales on his voyage to Canada, Australia, New Zealand and other British Possessions.

R.M.L.I. Chatham Division: 1905 to 1923
The same pattern as shown in Fig. 1100. On this, between the Globe and the 'Fouled Anchor', a Rose. In gilt with silver rose for Senior N.C.O.s, in brass with silver rose for the rank-and-file (Fig. 1118).

R.M.L.I. Chatham Division
Commissioned Bandmaster: Similar to Fig. 1091 but the 'Fouled Anchor' is smaller and consequently the bugle-horn is in a slightly higher position. Superimposed on the centre of the Globe a silver rose (Fig. 1119).

Royal Naval School of Music
The Royal Naval School of Music was subsequently amalgamated with the Royal Marines and designated The Royal Marines School of Music. Its helmet plate was the same as Fig. 1096 but without the bugle-horn below the anchor.

CHAPTER 21

The Reserve Regiments of the South African War

During the South African War of 1899 to 1902, Reserve Regiments were formed and Army Orders 77, 78 and 79 (April) and 129 (June) of 1900 give details of the method of enlistment, terms of service, dress, etc.

Her Majesty's Reserve Regiment of Dragoon Guards

Officers' full-dress helmet
On the Garter Star the Garter with the motto pierced on a blue-enamel ground. Within the Garter the letters *RR* in silver on a red-enamel ground.

Officers' and other ranks' field cap
The letters *HMRR* surmounted by a Victorian crown. Beneath the letters a scroll inscribed *Dragoon Guards*. In gilt or gilding-metal (Fig. 1122).

Her Majesty's Reserve Regiment of Dragoons

Officers' full-dress helmet
As Dragoon Guards. See above.

Officers' and other-ranks' field-cap
The letters *HMRR* surmounted by a Victorian crown. Beneath the letters a scroll inscribed *Dragoons*. In gilt or gilding-metal (Fig. 1124).

Her Majesty's Reserve Regiment of Hussars

Officers' and other-ranks' field-cap
The letters *HMRR* surmounted by a Victorian crown. Beneath the letters a scroll inscribed *Hussars*. In gilt or gilding-metal (Fig. 1125).

Her Majesty's Reserve Regiment of Lancers

Officers' lance-cap
In gilt-metal the universal plate. On the plate in silver the Royal Arms upon crossed lances. Below the Royal Arms the letters *RR*. Above, a scroll inscribed *Lancers*. On either side a spray of laurel.

1120

1122

1121

1124

1125

1127

1123

1128

1126

1129

1130

1131

1132

1133

Officers' and other-ranks' field-cap
A pair of crossed lances. On these the letters *RR* surmounted by a Victorian crown. Below the letters a scroll inscribed *Lancers*. In gilt or gilding-metal. Also found with the lower half of the lance-pennon in white-metal (Fig. 1127).

Cavalry Foreign Service Helmet
Other Ranks of Reserve Regiments of Cavalry did not wear a full-dress helmet but Cavalry Regiments serving abroad wore a badge on the foreign service helmet. Specimens of these are shown in Figs. 1120, 1121, 1123 and 1126, the latter being worn by all Lancer regiments.
  (1) On a twelve-pointed star the Garter. Within a voided centre the cypher of Queen Victoria. In gilding-metal with black leather backing to the cypher (Fig. 1120).
  (2) As above but with the cypher of King Edward VII (Fig. 1121).
  (3) On a twelve-pointed star the Garter. Within a voided centre the Royal Crest. In gilding-metal with black leather backing to the Royal Crest (Fig. 1123).
  (4) On a twelve-pointed star crossed lances, and superimposed on these the Garter. Within a voided centre a Victorian crown. In gilding-metal with black leather backing to the crown (Fig. 1126).

Royal Guards Reserve Regiment
Same badges as other Guards regiments.

Royal Home Counties Reserve Regiment

Officers' full-dress
On the helmet-plate, the Royal Crest in silver on a gilt-metal ground. No scroll on the helmet-plate.

Officers' and other-ranks' field-cap
The Royal Arms (Fig. 1128).
In gilt, gilding-metal or black-metal.

Royal Northern Reserve Regiment
Same badges as Royal Home Counties Reserve Regiment.

Royal Rifles Reserve Regiment

Officers' full-dress
A bugle on the busby boss.

Officers' and other-ranks' field-cap
A bugle (Fig. 1129).
In bronze for officers. In blackened-brass for other-ranks.

Royal Southern Reserve Regiment
Same badges as Royal Home Counties Reserve Regiment.

Royal Lancashire Reserve Regiment

Officers' full-dress
On the helmet-plate the Rose of Lancaster in gilt.
No scroll on the helmet-plate.

Officers' and other-ranks' field-cap
The Rose of Lancaster. In gilt or gilding-metal (Fig. 1130).

Royal Scottish Reserve Regiment

Officers' full-dress
A thistle in silver.

Officers' and other-ranks' field-cap
A thistle in silver or white-metal (Fig. 1131).

Royal Eastern Reserve Regiment
Same badges as Royal Home Counties Reserve Regiment.

Royal Irish Reserve Regiment

Officers' full-dress
On the helmet-plate the Harp and Crown within a shamrock-wreath in silver. No scroll on the helmet-plate.

Officers' and other-ranks' field-cap
The Harp and Crown. In gilt, gilding-metal and black-metal (Fig. 1132).

Royal Irish Fusilier Reserve Regiment

Officers' full-dress
A fused grenade with the Royal Arms on the ball. In gilt.

Officers' and other-ranks' field-cap
A fused grenade with a shamrock leaf on the ball (Fig. 1133).
Officers: the grenade in gilt and shamrock leaf in silver.
Other-ranks: in gilt or gilding-metal.

CHAPTER 22

Units raised during the Great War of 1914 to 1918

The war occasioned an enormous increase in the strength of the Armed Forces but the vast majority of the new units raised wore the badges of their parent regiment.

There were a few, however, that wore special badges, particularly the 'Pals' battalions that were raised in the big cities.

Some units formed during the war adopted distinctive collar-badges or shoulder-titles, but these are outside the scope of the present work.

All were disbanded on the conclusion of hostilities except the *Tank Corps* which became the *Royal Tank Corps* on 18th October 1923.

2nd King Edward's Horse

A wreath of laurel on left and oak on right, surmounted by an Imperial crown. Across the top of the wreath a scroll inscribed *King Edward's Horse*, with a small label between the centre of the scroll and the crown inscribed *2nd*. Scrolls on the wreath inscribed: (left) *Canada, N. Zealand* and (right) *Australia, S. Africa*. In the centre a shield bearing the Royal Arms, and below this three scrolls inscribed: (top) *India*, (centre) *Crown Colonies* and (bottom) *1914*. Below the wreath a scroll inscribed *Empire and Liberty*. In gilding-metal (Fig. 1134). Also in bronze.

The Northumberland Fusiliers

20th, 21st, 22nd, 23rd and 29th Battalions (Tyneside Scottish)

(1) A circular strap inscribed *Quo fata vocant*. Across the base of the strap a scroll inscribed *Tyneside Scottish* and resting thereon a tower. Issuing from the tower a lion holding a forked pennon inscribed *X*. Sprays of thistles either side of the tower. In white-metal (Fig. 1135).

(2) Within a thistle-wreath, St. Andrew's Cross. Across the base of the cross a tablet inscribed *Tyneside Scottish*. Superimposed on the cross a tower, with on the base *XX*. Issuing from the tower a lion holding a forked pennon inscribed *X*. In white-metal (Fig. 1136).

(3) General design as (2) but the tower is now taller and rests on the title-tablet and the *XX* on the base of the tower in the previous pattern is removed. Also a complete lion is now issuing from the tower. In white-metal (Fig. 1137). Also for officers in hall-marked silver.

1134   1135   1136   1137

1138   1139   1140   1141

1142   1143   1144   1145

1146 ✓   1147   1148   1149

1150   1151   1152   1153

24th, 25th, 26th, 27th and 30th Battalions (Tyneside Irish)
The Harp and Crown resting on a scroll inscribed *Tyneside Irish*. In gilding-metal (Fig. 1138).

The Royal Warwickshire Regiment

14th, 15th and 16th Battalions (1st, 2nd and 3rd Birmingham)
('Birmingham Pals')
  (1) The Antelope with collar and chain in white-metal. Below a double-scroll in gilding-metal. The top-scroll inscribed *Royal Warwickshire* and the bottom *1st Birmingham Battalion* (Fig. 1139).
  (2) As above but lower scroll inscribed *2nd Birmingham Battalion* (Fig. 1140). Also in bronze.
  (3) As above but lower scroll inscribed *3rd Birmingham Battalion* (Fig. 1141).

The Royal Fusiliers (City of London Regiment)

25th Battalion (Frontiersmen)
  (1) A fused grenade with the numeral *25* on the ball. Below, a scroll inscribed *Royal Frontiersmen Fusiliers*. In gilding-metal (Fig. 1142). It is believed that this early badge was made from Grenadier Guards cap-badges with the scroll added in a local garage.
  (2) A fused grenade with the numerals *25* on the ball, and a crown on the neck of the grenade. A tri-part scroll, with the ends reaching the flames of the grenade, is inscribed *Royal Frontiersmen Fusiliers*. In gilding-metal (Fig. 1143).
  (3) A fused grenade with the numerals *25* on the ball and a crown on the neck of the grenade. On the flames a flat circular plate and on this, superimposed on a red cross, the Great Union in the centre of which is a smaller circle inscribed *God Guard Thee*. Below the grenade a scroll inscribed *Frontiersmen*. In gilt with red-, white- and blue-enamel (Fig. 1144).

38th, 39th, 40th and 42nd Battalions
A seven-branched candlestick resting on a scroll inscribed in Hebrew *Kadimah* (Eastward). In gilding-metal (Fig. 1145). Also in bronze.

The King's (Liverpool Regiment)

17th, 18th, 19th and 20th Battalions (1st, 2nd, 3rd and 4th City)

('Liverpool Pals')
The crest of Lord Derby.
With the approval of H.M. The King, Lord Derby presented to each man who joined before 16th October 1914 the badge in hall-marked silver (Fig. 1146).
Subsequent issues were in gilding-metal. Also in bronze.

The Prince of Wales's Own (West Yorkshire Regiment)

15th (Leeds) Battalion ('Leeds Pals')
The Arms of the City of Leeds in gilding-metal (Fig. 1147). Also in bronze.

The East Surrey Regiment

13th (Wandsworth) Battalion

An eight-pointed star, the topmost point displaced by an Imperial crown. In the centre of the star a shield bearing the Arms of Wandsworth resting on a scroll inscribed *We serve*. Below the star a scroll inscribed *East Surrey*. The star in white-metal, remainder in gilding-metal (Fig. 1148). Also in bronze.

The Border Regiment

11th Battalion (Lonsdale)

The crest of the Earl of Lonsdale resting on a double-scroll inscribed *Eleventh Battalion Border Regiment*. The first issue in hall-marked silver (Fig. 1149).
Later issues in gilding-metal. Also in bronze.

The Welsh Regiment

16th Battalion (Cardiff City) ('Cardiff Pals')

The Arms and supporters of the City of Cardiff resting on a scroll inscribed *Cardiff*. The two mottoes in Welsh on the badge are: (top) *Deffro mae'n Ddydd* (Awake! it is day), and (bottom) *Y ddraig goch ddyry gychwyn* (The Red Dragon shall lead). In bronze (Fig. 1150).
Officially worn as a collar-badge.

The Duke of Cambridge's Own (Middlesex Regiment)

18th Battalion (1st Public Works) (Pioneers)

A laurel-wreath. Within the wreath the Prince of Wales's plumes, coronet and motto. Below this the coronet and cypher of H.R.H. The Duke of Cambridge. On the lower bend of the wreath a scroll inscribed *Albuhera*. Below the wreath two scrolls: the top inscribed *Middlesex Regt* and the bottom *Public Works Pioneer Battalion*. The plumes, motto and top title-scroll in white-metal, remainder in gilding-metal (Fig. 1151).

The Royal Irish Rifles

14th Battalion (Young Citizens)

   (1) A shamrock-leaf surmounted by an Imperial crown. On the leaf the Red Hand of Ulster. Below the leaf a scroll inscribed *Young Citizens of Ireland Volunteers*. In silver for officers (Fig. 1152).
   (2) A veined shamrock-leaf surmounted by an Imperial crown. On the leaf the Red Hand of Ulster. Other-ranks' pattern in white-metal (Fig. 1153). Also in gilding-metal.

Machine Gun Corps

Crossed machine-guns surmounted by an Imperial crown. In gilding-metal (Fig. 1154). Also in bronze, and silver both plated and hall-marked. There are several varieties of the machine-guns due to different strikings.

Motor Machine Gun Corps

Crossed machine-guns surmounted by an Imperial crown. Between the base of the guns the letters *MMG*. The letters in white-metal, remainder in gilding-metal (Fig. 1155). Also in bronze with smaller letters, and in bronze with white-metal letters.

Tank Corps

A laurel-wreath surmounted by an Imperial crown. Across the top of the wreath a scroll inscribed *Tank* and across the bottom of the wreath a scroll inscribed *Corps*. Within the wreath an early-pattern tank. In gilding-metal (Fig. 1156). Also in bronze.

Labour Corps

A 'pile' of a pick, head-downwards, rifle with sling and shovel on which a laurel-wreath. Above the 'pile' an Imperial crown and below it a scroll inscribed *Labor omnia vincit*. In gilding-metal (Fig. 1157).

THE ROYAL NAVAL DIVISION

The Royal Naval Division was formed mainly from the Royal Naval Volunteer Reserve, Royal Naval Reserve and the Royal Fleet Reserve. It included the 1st and 2nd Naval Brigades and a brigade of the Royal Marine Light Infantry.

The composition of the Naval Brigades was:

1st Royal Naval Brigade: 1st (Drake) Battalion, 2nd (Hawke) Battalion, 3rd (Benbow) Battalion, 4th (Collingwood) Battalion.

2nd Royal Naval Brigade: 5th (Nelson) Battalion, 6th (Howe) Battalion, 7th (Hood) Battalion, 8th (Anson) Battalion.

The division was employed at Antwerp in 1914 and later was used in the Gallipoli operations. Khaki uniforms were issued in December 1914 and included khaki sailor-caps with tally-bands embroidered with the name of the battalion. Such severe losses were incurred in this campaign that the Benbow and Collingwood Battalions were disbanded.

The division afterwards served in France where service-dress caps and metal-badges were issued.

Officers' badges

The Royal Navy officers' pattern cap-badge in bronzed-brass (Fig. 1158). Other patterns bore a small tablet just below the anchor inscribed *RNR* or *RNV*.

Royal Naval Division

Petty Officers' cap-badge as Royal Navy in blackened-brass (Fig. 1159).

Royal Naval Air Service Armoured Car Section

An oval plaque surmounted by an Imperial crown. On this an armoured-car with the letters *RNAS* above and two sprays of laurel below. In bronzed-brass (Fig. 1160). It is believed that this badge was worn on collar only.

1158

1159

1160

1161

1162

1163

1164

1165

1166

1167

Drake Battalion

An oak-wreath joined at the head with a scroll inscribed *Drake* and surmounted by an Imperial crown. Within a voided centre a ship in full-sail resting on the top-half of the globe. Below the globe a scroll inscribed *Auxilio Divino*. The ship in white-metal, remainder in gilding-metal (Fig. 1161).

Hawke Battalion

A hawk with a fleur-de-lys on its breast standing on a scroll inscribed *Strike*. Below this a tablet inscribed *Hawke*. In gilding-metal (Fig. 1162).

Nelson Battalion

A representation of H.M.S. *Victory* resting on a tablet inscribed *Nelson*. In gilding-metal (Fig. 1163).

Howe Battalion

A Naval crown resting on a scroll inscribed *Howe*. In gilding-metal (Fig. 1164).

Hood Battalion

A Cornish chough and anchor from the crest of Admiral Hood (1724–1816) resting on a wreathed-scroll. Below this a scroll inscribed *Steady* and below this a tablet inscribed *Hood*. In gilding-metal (Fig. 1165).

Anson Battalion

Out of a coronet a spear-head, from the crest of the Earl of Lichfield. Below this a scroll inscribed *Nil desperandum*, and below this another scroll inscribed *Anson*. In gilding-metal (Fig. 1166).

Royal Naval Division Machine Gun Battalion

Crossed machine-guns surmounted by an Imperial crown and, below the guns, the letters *RND*. In gilding-metal (Fig. 1167).

This badge was made in the workshops of the Division by soldering the curved shoulder-title of the Division onto the badge of the Machine Gun Corps.

CHAPTER 23

The Militia

As the Militia wore similar head-dresses to the Regular army, changes in the pattern of their badges occurred as the various types were taken into use.

Unlike the Regular army where the Order of Precedence was governed by the date the regiment came on to the English establishment, that of the Militia was decided by lot. A ballot for precedence was taken annually from 1778 to 1782, then in 1793, 1803, 1833 and finally in 1855 after which year no further ballots were taken. At this last ballot there were no less than 29 regiments of Artillery Militia and 135 of Infantry Militia.

Because of the ballot regiments had different numbers at different times and, as some regiments included their precedence number in the design of their badge, it is possible to find badges of the same regiment bearing different numbers.

The badge of the mens' round forage-cap of 1858 for all Militia Regiments was a scroll inscribed with the title of the regiment. In the case of Light Infantry Regiments a bugle-horn was added above the scroll. (Authority: Circular Memorandum, Horse Guards, 7th October 1858.)

Besides the individual regimental badges there was a general-pattern worn on the shako by several regiments. It consisted of an eight-pointed star, the topmost point displaced by a Victorian crown: on the star was the Garter with the Royal Crest in the centre.

In 1881 Regular, Militia and Volunteer battalions all became component parts of a single regiment. The Militia battalions were numbered-on after the Regulars. This meant a change of designation for all Militia regiments and in the descriptions, which follow, the new title awarded in 1881 is also given.

ENGLISH, SCOTTISH AND WELSH MILITIA

2nd Royal Surrey Militia
(1881: 3rd Battalion, The Queen's (Royal West Surrey Regiment).)

Shako-plate: 1869–78
A laurel-wreath surmounted by a Victorian crown. Within this a circlet inscribed *Second Royal Surrey Militia*. In the centre the Royal Crest. In blackened-copper (Fig. 1168).

Glengarry: 1874–81
The Star of the Order of the Garter. In white-metal (Fig. 1169).

Helmet-plate: 1878–81
An eight-pointed star, the topmost point displaced by a Victorian crown. On this a laurel-wreath. Within the wreath the Garter. In the centre the Royal Crest. In silver or white-metal (Fig. 1170).

East Kent Militia
(1881: 3rd Battalion, The Buffs (East Kent Regiment).

Shako-plate: 1840
An eight-pointed star, the topmost point displaced by a Victorian crown. On this an oak-wreath with the White Horse of Kent in the centre. Above, a scroll inscribed *East Kent*. Below, a scroll inscribed *Invicta*. The star and crown in gilt, remainder in silver.

1st Royal Lancashire Militia (Duke of Lancaster's Own)
(1881: 3rd Battalion, The King's Own (Royal Lancaster Regiment).)

Officers' shako-plate: 1812-16
On the universal plate of shield-and-crown with the Royal Cypher. Below the cypher the red Rose of Lancaster with crossed palm-sprays below and an inscription above the Rose of Lancaster.

Officers' shako-plate: c. 1860
An eight-pointed star, the topmost point displaced by a Victorian crown. On this a complete wreath of palm with, in the centre, the red Rose of Lancaster.

Glengarry: 1874–81
Within a wreath of palm the Rose of Lancaster surmounted by the Royal Crest. Below the wreath a scroll inscribed *The Duke of Lancaster's Own*. In white-metal (Fig. 1171).

1st Warwickshire Militia
(1881: 3rd Battalion, The Royal Warwickshire Regiment.)

Helmet-plate: 1878–81
An eight-pointed star, the topmost point displaced by a Victorian crown. On this a laurel-wreath. Within the wreath a circlet inscribed *Warwick Militia*. In the centre the Bear and Ragged Staff.

2nd Warwickshire Militia
(1881: 4th Battalion, The Royal Warwickshire Regiment.)

Glengarry: 1874–81
A lion's face within a heart-shaped border inscribed *Second Warwick* and the motto *Souveigne vous de moy*. The whole surmounted by a bunch of ivy.

3rd or Royal Westminster Middlesex (Light Infantry) Militia
(1881: 3rd Battalion, The Royal Fusiliers (City of London Regiment).)

Shako-badge: c. 1860
An eight-pointed star, the topmost point displaced by a Victorian crown. On this a circlet inscribed *3rd or Royal Westminster Middlesex*. In the centre a shield bearing the Arms and Crest of Westminster together with the Arms of Middlesex and a bugle-horn below. In white-metal (Fig. 1172).

Helmet-plate: 1878–81
An eight-pointed star, the topmost point displaced by a Victorian crown. On this a laurel-wreath and within this a circlet inscribed *3rd or Royal Westminster Middlesex*. In the centre a shield bearing on the left side the portcullis from the Arms of Westminster and on the right

three seaxes from the Arms of Middlesex. The shield surmounted by a bugle with strings. Across the base of the wreath a scroll inscribed *Mediterranean*. In white-metal (Fig. 1173).

Forage-cap: 1902

A fused grenade. On the ball the Garter surmounted by an Imperial crown. In the centre the Rose. All in gilding metal except the Rose which is in white-metal (Fig. 1174).

The Royal London Militia

(1881: 4th Battalion, The Royal Fusiliers (City of London Regiment).)

Helmet-plate: 1878

An eight-pointed star, the topmost point displaced by a Victorian crown all in silver. On this in gilt an oak-wreath and within this a strap inscribed *Domine dirige nos*. In the centre a shield bearing the Arms of the City of London (Fig. 1175).

Glengarry: 1874–81

A strap inscribed *Domine dirige nos* surmounted by a Victorian crown. In the centre a shield bearing the Arms of the City of London. In white-metal (Fig. 1176).

1st or West Norfolk Militia

(1881: 3rd Battalion, The Norfolk Regiment.)

Shako-plate: 1844–56

An eight-pointed star, the topmost point displaced by a Victorian crown. On this a wreath of oak and within this a castle. Blue ground to the castle.

Glengarry: 1874–81

An eight-pointed star on which a strap inscribed *First Norfolk*. In the centre a castle. In white-metal (Fig. 1177).

2nd or East Norfolk Militia

(1881: 4th Battalion, The Norfolk Regiment.)

Shako-plate: 1855

An eight-pointed star, the topmost point displaced by a Victorian crown. On this a circlet inscribed *East Norfolk Militia*. In the centre the Royal Cypher *VR*. In white-metal (Fig. 1178).

Shako-plate: 1855–61

An eight-pointed star, the topmost point displaced by a Victorian crown. On the star an oak-wreath. Within the wreath a strap inscribed *East Norfolk Militia*. In the centre a lion surmounted by a castle (Fig. 1179).

1179

Glengarry: 1874–81

A strap inscribed *East Norfolk Militia* surmounted by a
Victorian crown. In the centre a lion surmounted by a
castle (Fig. 1180).

Royal North Lincolnshire Militia

(1881: 3rd Battalion, The Lincolnshire Regiment.)

Glengarry: 1874–81

A strap inscribed *Royal North Lincoln Militia.* Within this
a shield bearing the Arms of the Earls of Lindsey (three
battering rams). In white-metal (Fig. 1181).

Royal South Lincolnshire Militia

(1881: 4th Battalion, The Lincolnshire Regiment.)

1180

Shako-plate: 1829–44

On the universal gilt star-and-crown plate a silver star on which a gilt Garter with St. George's
cross in red-enamel in the centre. Below the Garter a gilt scroll inscribed *Royal South Lincoln.*

Glengarry: 1874–81

A strap inscribed *Royal South Lincoln Regt of Militia* surmounted by a Victorian crown. In a
voided centre the crest of Earl Brownlow (a lion's head with a plain collar). In white-metal
(Fig. 1182).

Helmet-plate: 1878–81

An eight-pointed star, the topmost point displaced by a Victorian crown. On this a laurel-
wreath. Within the wreath a circlet inscribed *South Lincolnshire Regiment.* In the centre a
lion's head on a wreathed scroll. Dark-blue ground to centre. In silver-plate (Fig. 1183).

1st or East Devon Militia

(1881: 4th Battalion, The Devonshire Regiment.)

Shako-plate: 1855–61

An eight-pointed star, the topmost point displaced by a Victorian crown. On this a circlet,
the top-half inscribed *Semper Fidelis* and the bottom half *Devon.* In the centre the castle of
Exeter and below this the numeral *1.*

Officers' glengarry-badge

A strap inscribed *Semper Fidelis* surmounted by the castle of Exeter. In a voided centre the
numeral *1.*

Glengarry: 1874–81

A strap inscribed *Semper Fidelis* surmounted by the castle of Exeter. In a voided centre the
numeral *1* above the letters *DM.* In gilding-metal (Fig. 1184). Also found with solid centre.

Glengarry: c. 1890

The Castle of Exeter with a scroll below inscribed *Semper Fidelis* and beneath this a scroll
inscribed *First Devon.* In gilding-metal (Fig. 1185).

1169

1172

1170

1177

1168

1173

1176

1184

1171

1182

1181

1175

1178

1183

2nd or South Devon Militia
(1881: 3rd Battalion, The Devonshire Regiment.)

Glengarry: 1874–81
A strap inscribed *South Devon 25th Regt of Militia* surmounted by a Victorian crown. In the centre a lion rampant (from the Arms of the Earls of Devon). In gilding-metal (Fig. 1186).

West Suffolk Militia
(1881: 3rd Battalion, The Suffolk Regiment.)

Helmet-plate: 1878–81
An eight-pointed star, the topmost point displaced by a Victorian crown. On this a laurel-wreath and within this the Garter. In the centre a castle. Below the Garter a three-part scroll inscribed *West Suffolk Militia.*

Officers' forage-cap: 1874–81
A castle embroidered in gold on a green ground with, on either side, a spray of laurels embroidered in silver. Above the castle a crown and across the base of the laurels a scroll inscribed *West Suffolk Militia* in gold letters on a blue ground.

Cambridgeshire Militia
(1881: 4th Battalion, The Suffolk Regiment.)

Shako-plate: 1829–44
(1) On the universal star-and-crown plate a silver cut star. On this in gilt a castle with, below, a scroll inscribed *Cambridge.* Below this the numerals *68* (Fig. 1187).
(2) As above but with the numerals *68* within a bugle-horn (Fig. 1188).

1187

1st Somersetshire Light Infantry Militia
(1881: 3rd Battalion, The Prince Albert's (Somersetshire Light Infantry).)

Shako-plate: 1844–55
On an eight-pointed gilt crowned-star a silver cut star. On this a strap inscribed *1st Somerset Regt* with the Royal Cypher *VR* in the centre. A scroll below inscribed *Defendemus.* All gilt with title and motto in silver letters.

Glengarry: 1874–81
A strap inscribed *First Somerset* surmounted by a Victorian crown. In the centre the Cap of Maintenance of the Duke of Monmouth. Below, a scroll inscribed *Defendemus.* In gilding-metal (Fig. 1189).

2nd Somersetshire Light Infantry Militia
(1881: 4th Battalion, The Prince Albert's (Somersetshire Light Infantry).)

Shako-plate: 1844–55
An eight-pointed star, the topmost point displaced by a Victorian crown. On this a silver star with an oak-wreath in the centre of which a strap inscribed *Second Somerset* with the Royal

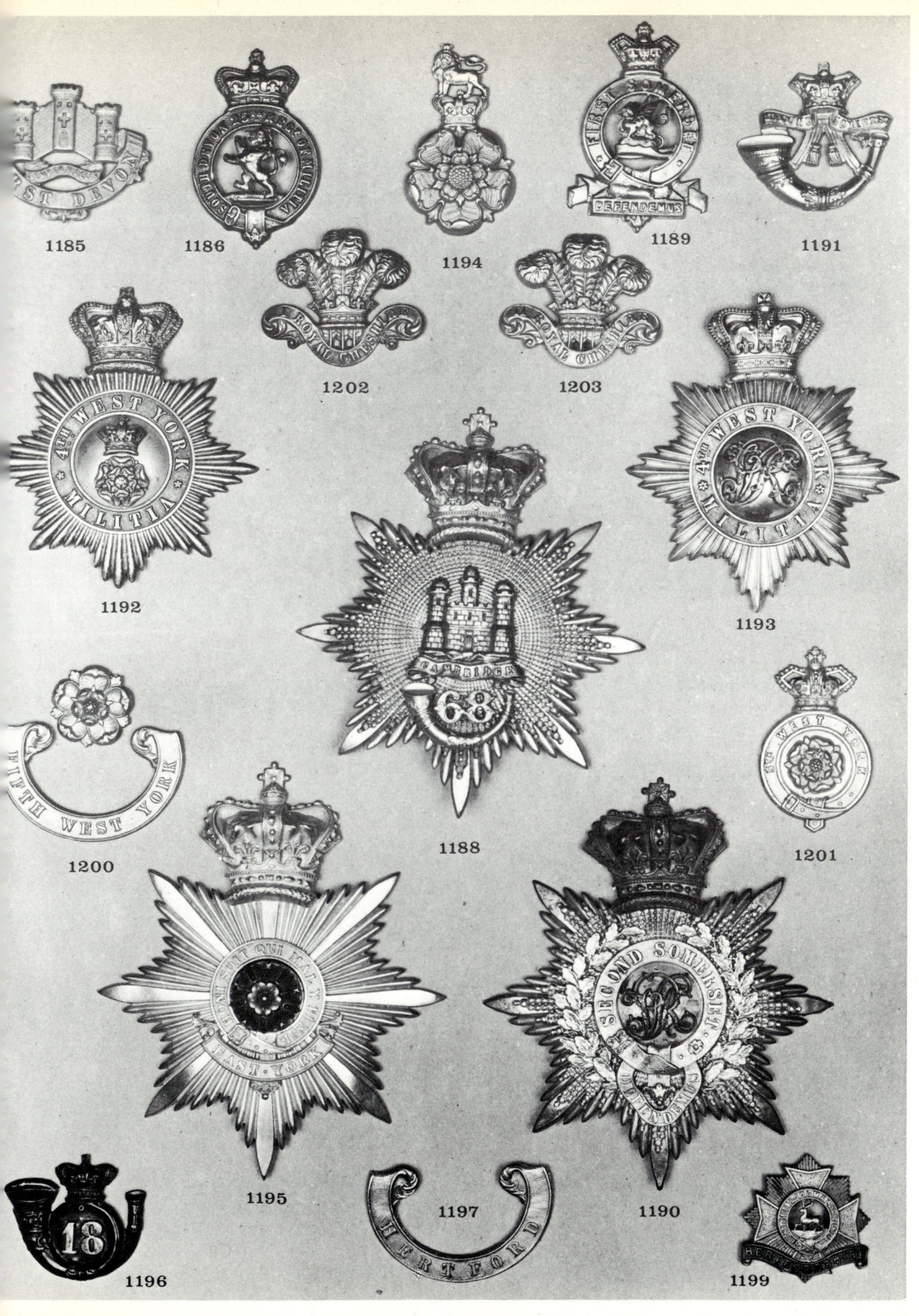

1185

1186

1194

1189

1191

1202

1203

1192

1188

1193

1200

1195

1201

1190

1196

1197

1199

Cypher *VR* in the centre. Below the strap a U-shaped scroll inscribed *Defendemus*. The Cypher in gilt, remainder in silver (Fig. 1190).

Glengarry: 1874–81

(1) A strap inscribed *Second Somerset* surmounted by a Saxon crown. In the centre a Cornish Celtic Cross.

(2) A bugle with strings surmounted by a Victorian crown. Below the crown a two-part scroll inscribed *Second Somerset*. In white-metal (Fig. 1191).

2nd West York Light Infantry

(1881: 3rd Battalion, The Prince of Wales's Own (West Yorkshire Regiment).)

Officers' shako-plate: 1812–16

On the universal plate of shield-and-crown with the Royal Cypher. The White Rose of York below the Royal Cypher and below this a scroll inscribed *2nd West York*. The Rose and Scroll in silver.

4th West York Militia

(1881: 4th Battalion, The Prince of Wales's Own (West Yorkshire Regiment).)

Shako-plate: 1855–61

An eight-pointed star, the topmost point displaced by a Victorian crown. On this a circlet inscribed *4th West York Militia*. In the centre a Rose surmounted by a crown. In silver-plate and also white-metal (Fig. 1192).

Shako-plate: 1861–69

As above but with the Royal Cypher *VR* in the centre. In white-metal (Fig. 1193).

Glengarry: 1874–81

The White Rose of York surmounted by the Royal Crest (Fig. 1194).

Officers' glengarry: 1874–81

Within a wreath of roses surmounted by a crown the numeral *4* above the letters *WY*.

The East Yorkshire Militia

(1881: 3rd Battalion, The East Yorkshire Regiment.)

Shako-plate: 1835–44

A gilt eight-pointed star, the topmost point displaced by a Victorian crown. On this the Garter with a silver rose in the centre. Below the Garter a gilt scroll inscribed *East York* (Fig. 1195).

Glengarry: 1874–81

A Rose surmounted by a crown. Below the rose a scroll inscribed *East York*.

Officers' glengarry: 1874–81

A white rose with the letters *EY* in the centre. All within a plain circle of gold wire.

Bedfordshire Light Infantry Militia

(1881: 3rd Battalion, The Bedfordshire Regiment.)

Glengarry: 1874–81

(1) A bugle-horn surmounted by a Victorian crown with the numerals *18* in the curl on a solid background. In blackened-brass with the numerals in white-metal (Fig. 1196).

(2) A bugle-horn with, in the curl, a circlet inscribed *Bedfordshire Militia* and in the centre an Eagle with a castle superimposed thereon.

Hertfordshire Militia
(1881: 4th Battalion, The Bedfordshire Regiment.)

Round forage-cap: 1858
A scroll inscribed *Hertford*. In white-metal (Fig. 1197).

1198

Glengarry: 1874–81
A strap inscribed *Harts Regt Militia* surmounted by a Victorian crown. In the centre a hart crossing a ford (Fig. 1198).

Helmet-plate: 1878–81
An eight-pointed star, the topmost point displaced by a Victorian crown. On this a laurel-wreath and within the wreath the Garter. In the centre a hart crossing a ford within a scroll inscribed *Hertfordshire*.

Forage-cap: 1898
On an eight-pointed star a Maltese cross on which the Garter. In a voided centre a hart crossing a ford. At the base a scroll inscribed *Hertfordshire*. Title-scroll in gilding-metal, remainder in white-metal (Fig. 1199).

Leicestershire Militia
(1881: 3rd Battalion, The Leicestershire Regiment.)

Shako-plate: 1869–78
A laurel-wreath surmounted by a Victorian crown. Within this a circlet inscribed *Leicestershire Militia* with, in the centre, the Royal Cypher *VR*. All in silver.

Glengarry: 1874–81
A strap inscribed *Vestigia nulla retrorsum* surmounted by a crown. In the centre the Irish Harp.

Helmet-plate: 1878–81
An eight-pointed star, the topmost-point displaced by a Victorian crown. On this a laurel-wreath and within this a circlet inscribed *Leicestershire Militia* and in the centre the Irish Harp. On the base of the wreath a scroll inscribed *Vestigia nulla retrorsvm*. In gilt for officers.

5th West York Militia
(1881: 3rd Battalion, The Princess of Wales's Own (Yorkshire Regiment).)

Round forage-cap: 1858
A scroll inscribed *Fifth West York*. Above this, and separate, the White Rose. In white-metal (Fig. 1200).

Glengarry: 1874–81
A strap inscribed *5th West York* surmounted by a crown. On a solid centre the White Rose of York. In white-metal (Fig. 1201).

7th Lancashire Rifle Militia
(1881: 3rd Battalion, The Lancashire Fusiliers.)

Glengarry: 1874–81
A shield displaying a lion with, below, the fleur-de-lys. Suspended from the shield a strung bugle with a rose between the strings. Above and around the shield a scroll inscribed *VII Royal Lancashire Militia*.

Dumfries, Roxburgh, Kirkcudbright, Selkirk (Scottish Borderers) Militia
(1881: 3rd Battalion, The Royal Scots Fusiliers.)

Glengarry: 1868–81
A wreath of thistles surmounted by a crown. Within this a strap inscribed *The Scottish Borderers*. In the centre St. Andrew and Cross. In white-metal.

Royal Ayrshire and Wigtown Rifles (The Prince Regent's)
(1881: 4th Battalion, The Royal Scots Fusiliers.)

Glengarry: 1868–81
A strap inscribed *Prince Regent's Royal Ayr and Wigtown* surmounted by the Prince of Wales's plumes, coronet and motto. In the centre a thistle. In white-metal.

1st Royal Cheshire Light Infantry Militia
(1881: 3rd Battalion, The Cheshire Regiment.)

Shako-plate: 1829–44
On the universal star-and-crown plate the star of the Order of the Garter in cut silver and scarlet-enamel. Across the base of the star Roman fasces in gilt inscribed *Cheshire*.

Shako-plate: 1869–78
A laurel-wreath surmounted by a Victorian crown. Within this a circlet inscribed *First Royal Cheshire Militia* with, in the centre, a bugle-horn.

Glengarry: 1874–81
The Prince of Wales's plumes and coronet above a scroll inscribed *I Royal Cheshire*. In white-metal (Fig. 1202).

Helmet-plate: 1878–81
On the standard plate a circlet inscribed with the regiment's title. In the centre the Prince of Wales's plumes, coronet and motto on a red-cloth ground.

2nd Royal Cheshire Militia
(1881: 4th Battalion, The Cheshire Regiment.)

Glengarry: 1874–81
The Prince of Wales's plumes and coronet above a scroll inscribed *II Royal Cheshire*. In white-metal (Fig. 1203).

Royal Denbigh Rifles
(1881: 3rd Battalion, The Royal Welsh Fusiliers.)

Glengarry: 1874–81
The Welsh Dragon within a strap inscribed *Y ddraig goch a ddyry gychwyn* in bronze.

Royal Merioneth Rifles
(1881: 4th Battalion, The Royal Welsh Fusiliers.)

Round forage-cap: 1858
A scroll inscribed *Merioneth*. Above, and separate, a bugle-horn with strings. In blackened-brass (Fig. 1204).

Royal Carnarvon Rifle Corps
(1881: 4th Battalion, The Royal Welsh Fusiliers.)

Shako-plate: c. 1868
A Maltese cross with lions between the limbs and surmounted by a Victorian crown. On the cross a circlet inscribed *Royal Carnarvon Rifle Militia*. In the centre a bugle-horn with the numerals *56* within the strings. In blackened white-metal with the high points polished. Green cloth-backing to the centre (Fig. 1205).

Helmet-plate: 1878–81
An eight-pointed star, the topmost point displaced by a Victorian crown. On this a laurel-wreath. Within the wreath a circlet inscribed *Royal Carnarvon Rifles*. In the centre the Prince of Wales's plumes, coronet and motto. In bronze.

Royal South Wales Borderers (Royal Radnor and Brecknock Rifles)
(1881: 3rd Battalion, The South Wales Borderers.)

Shako-plate: c. 1861
An eight-pointed star, the topmost point displaced by a Victorian crown. In the centre the Welsh Dragon in white-metal, remainder in brass (Fig. 1206).

Shako-plate: 1868
A laurel-wreath surmounted by a Victorian crown. Within the wreath a Maltese cross. On this a circlet inscribed *Royal Radnor Rifles*. In the centre the Prince of Wales's plumes, coronet and motto.

Glengarry: 1874–76
Within a laurel-wreath an oval inscribed *Royal Brecknock Rifles* surmounted by a Victorian crown. In the centre the Prince of Wales's plumes, coronet and motto with, below, a bugle with strings with the numerals *132* within the strings. In silver.

Glengarry: 1876–81
A wreath of palm surmounted by a Victorian crown. Within this an oval inscribed *Royal South Wales Borderers Militia*. In the centre the Prince of Wales's plumes, coronet and motto with a bugle with strings below. In gilding-metal with voided centre (Fig. 1207). Same design but with non-voided centre (Fig. 1208).

Royal Montgomery Rifles
(1881: 4th Battalion, The South Wales Borderers.)

Shako-plate: c. 1877
A Maltese cross with a voided centre in which the Welsh Dragon. In blackened white-metal (Fig. 1209).

1204

1205

1208

1206

1209

2nd Royal Lanark Militia
(1881: 3rd and 4th Battalions, The Cameronians (Scottish Rifles).)

Glengarry: 1868–81
Within a wreath of laurel an oval inscribed *Nemo me impune lacessit* and in the centre a double-headed eagle surmounted by a coronet. Below the oval a scroll inscribed *2 Royal Lanark Militia*. With solid background in white-metal.

Royal South Gloucestershire Militia
(1881: 3rd Battalion, The Gloucestershire Regiment.)

Glengarry: 1874–81
A strap inscribed *Royal South Gloucester Militia* surmounted by a crown. Within this a bugle-horn.

Royal North Gloucestershire Militia
(1881: 4th Battalion, The Gloucestershire Regiment.)

Glengarry: 1874–81
Within a crowned laurel-wreath the letters *RNGM*.

1211

1210

1212

1217

1219

1218

1207

1214

1213

1220

1221

1174

1216

1215

1222

The Worcestershire Militia
(1881: 3rd and 4th Battalions, The Worcestershire Regiment.)

Shako-plate: 1869–78
An eight-pointed star, the topmost point displaced by a Victorian crown. On this the Garter with, in the centre, the Tower of Worcester Castle. Below the Garter a scroll inscribed *Worcester*. In silver-plate (Fig. 1210).

Glengarry: 1874–81
A strap inscribed *Worcester Militia* surmounted by a Victorian crown. In the centre a shield bearing the Tower with three pears in the first canton.

Helmet-plate: 1878–81
An eight-pointed star, the topmost point displaced by a Victorian crown. On this a laurel-wreath. Within the wreath the Garter. In the centre the Tower of Worcester Castle. Below the Garter a scroll inscribed *Worcester*.

5th Royal Lancashire Militia
(1881: 3rd Battalion, The East Lancashire Regiment.)

Forage-cap: 1881–1902
Within a laurel-wreath surmounted by a Victorian crown the Sphinx superscribed *Egypt* with the white rose below. On the base of the wreath a scroll inscribed *East Lancashire*. The Rose in white-metal, remainder in gilding-metal (Fig. 1211).

Forage-cap: 1902–14
As above but with Imperial crown (Fig. 1212).

1st Royal Surrey Militia
(1881: 3rd Battalion, The East Surrey Regiment.)

Shako-plate: 1844–55
A gilt eight-pointed star, the topmost point displaced by a Victorian crown. On this an oak-wreath. Within the wreath the Garter. In the centre in silver the monogram *RSM* with the numeral *1* below (Fig. 1213).

Glengarry: 1874–81
A circlet inscribed *First Royal Surrey* surmounted by a Victorian crown. In a voided centre the Roman numerals *XX*. In white-metal (Fig. 1214).

3rd Royal Surrey Militia
(1881: 4th Battalion, The East Surrey Regiment.)

Shako-plate: 1855–61
An eight-pointed star, the topmost point displaced by a Victorian crown. On this a silver oak-wreath. Within the wreath a strap inscribed *3rd Royal Surrey Regt* in silver with blue-enamel ground. In the centre the Garter star in silver with St. George's cross in red-enamel (Fig. 1215).

Shako-plate: 1861
An eight-pointed star, in silver, the topmost point displaced by a Victorian crown. On this in gilt the Garter with St. George's cross in the centre (Fig. 1216).

Glengarry: 1874–81
A strap inscribed *Third Royal Surrey Militia*. Within this the Star of the Order of the Garter. In white-metal (Fig. 1217).

Officers' Glengarry: 1874–81
The Roman numerals *III* between the letters *RS* and reversed on either side. All within a crowned oak-wreath. In silver embroidery on a red-ground.

Royal Cornwall Rangers, Duke of Cornwall's Light Infantry
(1881: 3rd Battalion, The Duke of Cornwall's Light Infantry.)

Round forage-cap: 1858–73
A bugle-horn with a scroll under inscribed *Cornwall Rangers*. In bronze with red-cloth backing.

Shako-plate: 1861–69
An eight-pointed star, the topmost point displaced by the Prince of Wales's plumes, coronet and motto. On this a shield bearing fifteen bezants. Below, a scroll inscribed *One and All*. The shield and motto in white-metal, remainder in blackened-brass (Fig. 1218).

Glengarry: 1874–81
A strap inscribed *Royal Cornwall Rangers* surmounted by a coronet. Within this a shield bearing fifteen bezants and, below, a scroll inscribed *One and All*. In brass (Fig. 1219).

6th West York Militia
(1881: 3rd and 4th Battalions, The Duke of Wellington's (West Riding Regiment).)

Glengarry: 1874–81
A strap inscribed *West York Militia* surmounted by a crown. In a voided centre the numeral *6* surmounted by the white rose. In white-metal (Fig. 1220).

The Royal Cumberland Militia
(1881: 3rd Battalion, The Border Regiment.)

Shako-plate: 1861–69
An eight-pointed star, the topmost point displaced by a Victorian crown. On this a wreath of oak. Within the wreath a circlet inscribed *Royal Cumberland Militia*. In the centre the Royal Cypher *VR* with the county precedence number *9* below the Cypher. In silver-plate.

Glengarry: 1874–81
A strap inscribed *Royal Cumberland Militia* surmounted by a crown. Within the strap the Lion of England above a castle with a rose on either side.

Helmet-plate: 1884–1902
An eight-pointed star, the topmost point displaced by a Victorian crown. On this a laurel-wreath. Within the wreath a Maltese cross with a lion between each division of the cross. On the cross a circlet inscribed *Arroyo dos Molinos*. In the centre the China Dragon. Below the wreath a scroll inscribed *The Border Regt*. Plate in gilt with silver mounts and red- and white-enamel centre.

Forage-cap: 1902–
An eight-pointed star, the topmost point displaced by an Imperial crown. On this a laurel-

wreath on which is superimposed a Maltese cross with a lion between each division of the cross. In the centre of the cross a circlet inscribed *Arroyo dos Molinos* and within this on the lower half the China Dragon. At the base of the cross a scroll inscribed *The Border Regt.* In white-metal, the lower half of the centre pierced to show a red-cloth backing to the Dragon (Fig. 1221).

Royal Westmoreland Light Infantry Militia
(1881: 4th Battalion, The Border Regiment.)

Shako-plate: 1855–60
An eight-pointed star, the topmost point displaced by a Victorian crown. On the star a bugle with the Royal Cypher *VR* in the curl. Below the bugle a scroll inscribed *Royal Westmoreland*. In silver-plate (Fig. 1222).

Helmet-plate: 1878–81
An eight-pointed star, the topmost point displaced by a Victorian crown. On the star a laurel-wreath. Within the wreath a bugle with the Royal Cypher *VR* in the curl. On the lower ends of the wreath a scroll inscribed *Royal Westmoreland*. In silver-plate.

Royal Sussex Light Infantry Militia
(1881: 3rd Battalion, The Royal Sussex Regiment.)

Shako-plate: 1844–52
An eight-pointed star, the topmost point displaced by a Victorian crown. On this a bugle-horn and within the strings the Garter star in silver and enamel. Below the bugle a scroll inscribed *Royal Sussex*.

Shako-plate: 1861–69
A silver eight-pointed star, the topmost point displaced by a Victorian crown. On this a pierced strap inscribed *Royal Sussex Light Infantry* with the Garter Star in silver and enamel in the centre. Below the strap a bugle-horn.

Glengarry: 1874–81
The Garter star surmounted by a bugle-horn. Below, a scroll inscribed *Royal Sussex*.

Hampshire Militia
(1881: 3rd Battalion, The Hampshire Regiment.)

Shako-plate: 1844–55
An eight-pointed silver star, the topmost point displaced by a Victorian crown. On this a gilt Garter surmounted by the numerals *13* (the precedence number of the regiment in 1833) and a scroll inscribed *Hampshire* below the Garter. In the centre the Hampshire Rose in gilt and red- and green-enamel (Fig. 1223).

Shako-plate: 1855–61
As above but with the numerals *122* above the Garter (the precedence number of the regiment in 1855). (Fig. 1224.)

Shako-plate: 1861–69
As above but without a precedence number.

Shako-plate: 1861–69
As above but with rose in gilding-metal, remainder in white-metal and no precedence number (Fig. 1225).

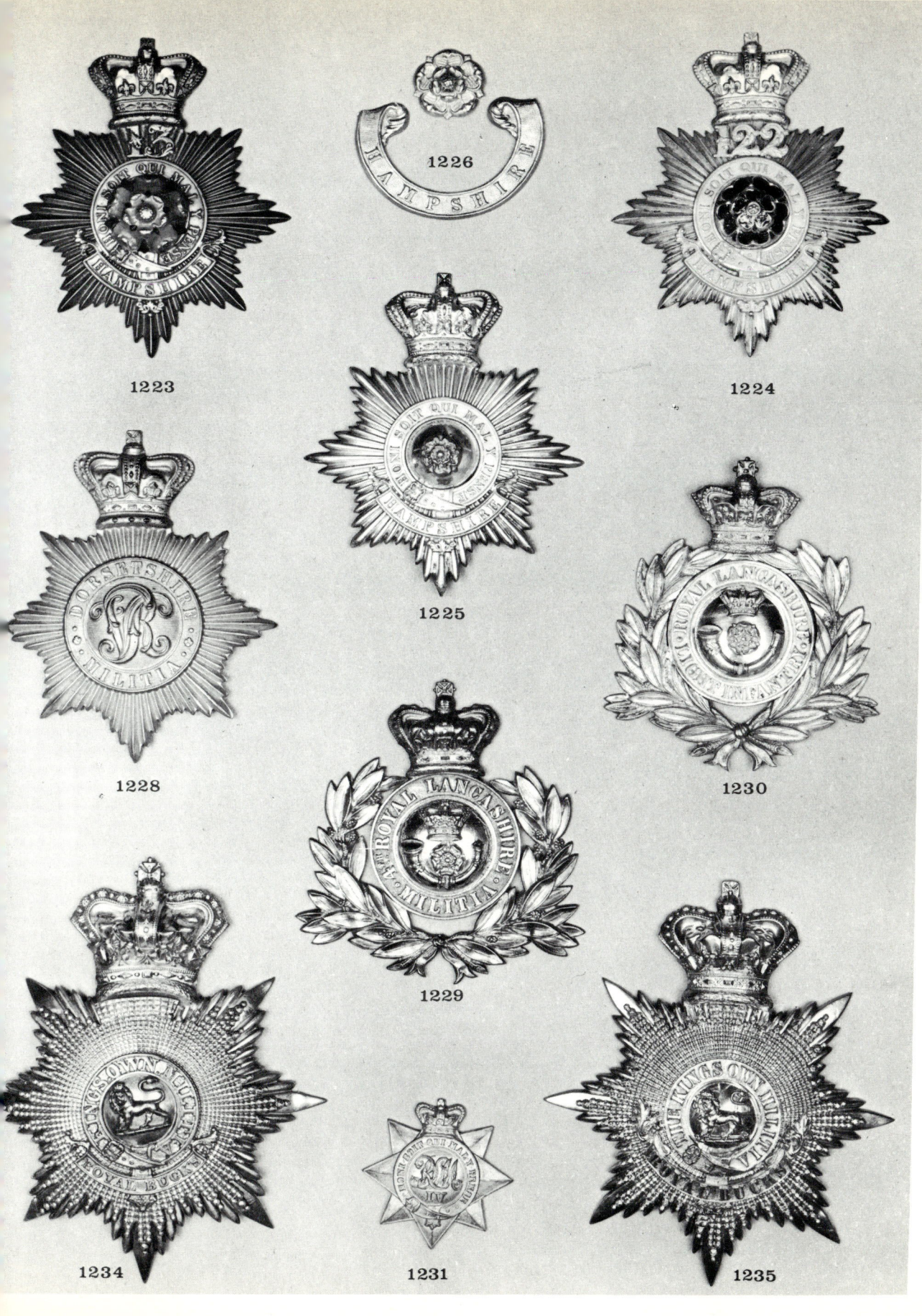

1226

1223

1224

1225

1228

1230

1229

1234

1231

1235

Round forage-cap: 1858
A scroll in white-metal inscribed *Hampshire* with a separate white-metal Hampshire Rose above (Fig. 1226).

Glengarry: 1874–81
The Hampshire Rose surmounted by a crown. Below the Rose a scroll inscribed *Hampshire*

**The (King's Own) 1st Stafford-
shire Militia**
(1881: 3rd Battalion, The South Staffordshire Regiment.)

Shako-plate: 1844–55
An eight-pointed star, the topmost point displaced by a Victorian crown. On this a circlet inscribed *Windsor 1798 to 1812* and within this a representation of Windsor Castle surmounted by a scroll inscribed *George III Regnante*. Below the circlet a scroll inscribed *King's Own Stafford Mila* and below this the Stafford Knot (Fig. 1227).

Glengarry: 1874–81
A laurel-wreath joined at the top by a scroll inscribed *First Stafford*. In the centre the Stafford Knot with a Victorian crown above.

Helmet-plate: 1878–81
An eight-pointed star, the topmost point displaced by a Victorian crown. On this a laurel-wreath. Within the wreath a circlet inscribed *King's Own 1st Staffordshire Militia*. In the centre a representation of Windsor Castle with a scroll below inscribed *Windsor Castle 1798–1812*. On the bottom-join of the laurel-wreath the Stafford Knot.

Dorsetshire Militia
(1881: 3rd Battalion, The Dorsetshire Regiment.)

Shako-plate: 1855–66
An eight-pointed star, the topmost point displaced by a Victorian crown. On this a circlet inscribed *Dorsetshire Militia* with the Royal Cypher in the centre. In white-metal (Fig. 1228).

4th Royal Lancashire (Duke of Lancaster's Own) Light Infantry Militia

(1881: 3rd Battalion, The Prince of Wales's Volunteers (South Lancashire Regiment).)

Shako-plate: 1869–78

(1) A laurel-wreath surmounted by a Victorian crown. Within the wreath a circlet inscribed *4th Royal Lancashire Militia*. In the centre a bugle with the White Rose of Lancaster in the curl and surmounted by a Victorian crown. The wreath, crown and Rose in silver-plate, remainder in gilt (Fig. 1229).

(2) A white-metal laurel-wreath surmounted by a gilt crown. In the centre a gilt circlet inscribed *Royal Lancashire Light Infantry*. On a gilt centre in bronze a bugle with a rose in the curl surmounted by a Victorian crown (Fig. 1230).

Helmet-plate: 1878–81

An eight-pointed star, the topmost point displaced by a Victorian crown. On this a laurel-wreath and within the wreath a circlet inscribed *Royal Lancashire Light Infantry*. In the centre a crowned bugle with strings with the Rose of Lancaster within the strings.

Glengarry: 1874–81

An eight-pointed star, the topmost point displaced by a Victorian crown. On this the Garter and within this the monogram *RLM* and below this the Roman numerals *IV*. In white-metal (Fig. 1231).

Royal Glamorgan Light Infantry

(1881: 3rd Battalion, The Welsh Regiment.)

Shako-plate: 1852–61

An eight-pointed star, the topmost point displaced by a Victorian crown. On the star a bugle-horn with the Prince of Wales's plumes, coronet and motto within the strings. Below, a scroll inscribed *Royal Glamorgan*. Star and crown in gilt, remainder in silver (Fig. 1232).

Shako-plate: 1861–77

An eight-pointed star, the topmost point displaced by a Victorian crown. On the star a pierced circlet inscribed *Royal Glamorgan Light Infy*. In the centre the Royal Cypher *VR*. Below the circlet a bugle-horn without strings. All in silver (Fig. 1233).

1232

1233

Royal Perth Rifles
(1881: 3rd Battalion, The Black Watch (Royal Highlanders).)

Glengarry: 1874–81
A Thistle surmounted by a crown. In black-metal.

Royal Bucks King's Own Militia
(1881: 3rd Battalion, The Oxfordshire Light Infantry.)

Shako-plate: 1829–44
On the universal star-and-crown plate in silver, a silver cut star. On this in gilt a strap inscribed *King's Own Militia* with, in the centre, a Lion on a wreathed scroll. Below the strap a scroll inscribed *Royal Bucks* (Fig. 1234).

Shako-plate: 1845–
As above but with smaller crown which is without pearls on the orb. Also the title now reads *The King's Own Militia* (Fig. 1235).

Oxfordshire Militia
(1881: 4th Battalion, The Oxfordshire Light Infantry.)

Shako-plate: 1855–61
An eight-pointed star, the topmost point displaced by a Victorian crown. On this a strap inscribed *Fortis est veritas* and in the centre an ox crossing a ford (Fig. 1236).

Shako-plate: 1855
Similar to above but the motto on a circlet instead of a strap (Fig. 1237).

Glengarry: 1874–81
An ox crossing a ford. Below, a scroll inscribed *Oxfordshire*.

Essex Rifles Militia
(1881: 3rd Battalion, The Essex Regiment.)

Glengarry: 1874–81
A strap inscribed *The Essex Rifles* surmounted by a Victorian crown. Within this a shield bearing the County Arms of Essex. Suspended from the strap a bugle-horn.

Forage-cap: 1908
Within a wreath of oak the Castle and Key of Gibraltar surmounted by the Sphinx superscribed *Egypt*. At the base of the wreath a scroll inscribed *The Essex Regt*. The title-scroll and Sphinx in gilding-metal, remainder in white-metal (Fig. 1238).
Note: Same badge as the Regulars but metals reversed.

West Essex Militia
(1881: 4th Battalion, The Essex Regiment.)

Glengarry: 1874–81
A strap inscribed *West Essex Militia* surmounted by a Victorian crown. Within this a shield bearing the County Arms of Essex. In white-metal (Fig. 1239).

2nd Derbyshire Militia (The Chatsworth Rifles)
(1881: 3rd Battalion, The Sherwood Foresters (Derbyshire Regiment).)

Shako-plate: 1864
A cross similar to that of the Order of the Bath surmounted by a Victorian crown. In the centre of the cross a circlet inscribed *Derby Militia* and within this a bugle with the numeral *2* in the strings. In blackened white-metal with the high points polished and red-cloth backing in the centre (Fig. 1240).

Shako-plate: 1878
A cross similar to that of the Order of the Bath surmounted by a Victorian crown. In the centre of the cross a circlet inscribed *2nd Derby Militia Chatsworth Rifles* and in a voided centre a bugle-horn with strings. In black-metal (Fig. 1241).

Royal Sherwood Foresters or Nottinghamshire Regiment of Militia
(1881: 4th Battalion, The Sherwood Foresters (Derbyshire Regiment).)

Round Forage-cap: 1858
A scroll inscribed *Royal Nottingham*. Above this a bugle with strings. In brass.

Shako-plate: 1855–61
An eight-pointed star, the topmost point displaced by a Victorian crown. On the star the Garter with St. George's Cross in the centre. Below the Garter a scroll inscribed *Nottingham* (Fig. 1242).

1238

1242

Shako-plate: 1861–69

An eight-pointed star, the topmost point displaced by a Victorian crown. On this an oak-wreath and within the wreath a pierced circlet inscribed *Royal Sherwood Foresters*. In the centre the Arms of the City of Nottingham. In silver, blue-enamel backing to circlet.

Glengarry: 1874–98

(1) Within an oak-wreath a strap inscribed *Royal Sherwood Foresters* surmounted by a Victorian crown. In the centre the Arms of the City of Nottingham. In white-metal (Fig. 1243).

(2) A strap inscribed *Royal Sherwood Foresters* surmounted by a Victorian crown. In the centre the Arms of the City of Nottingham. In white-metal (Fig. 1244).

(3) As (2) but with different shape of crown. In white-metal (Fig. 1245).

Northamptonshire and Rutlandshire Militia

(1881: 3rd Battalion, The Northamptonshire Regiment.)

Shako-plate: 1861–69

An eight-pointed star, the topmost point displaced by a Victorian crown. On this the Garter with St. George's Cross in the centre. Above the Garter a scroll inscribed *Northamptonshire* with the ends joined to palm-fronds meeting a scroll below inscribed *& Rutland Militia*. On the lowest point of the star a horseshoe.

Shako-plate: 1869–78

A laurel wreath surmounted by a Victorian crown. In the centre the Garter and within this St. George's Cross. Above the Garter a scroll inscribed *Northamptonshire* with the ends, joined to palm-fronds, meeting a scroll below the Garter inscribed *& Rutland Militia*. Below this a horseshoe. The cross in red-enamel, Garter and title-scrolls gilt, remainder in silver (Fig. 1246).

Royal Berkshire Militia

(1881: 3rd Battalion, Princess Charlotte of Wales's (Berkshire Regiment).

Shako-plate: 1852–73

An eight-pointed star, the topmost point displaced by a Victorian crown. On this a strap with the buckle at the top. The strap inscribed *Pro aris et focis*. In the centre a stag under an oak-tree. On the base of the star a scroll inscribed *Royal Berks*.

West Kent Light Infantry Militia
(1881: 3rd Battalion, The Queen's Own (Royal West Kent Regiment).)

Shako-plate: 1835
The universal gilt star-and-crown plate. On this a silver cut star with on this a gilt Garter with enamelled cross in the centre. The numerals *37* above and below a scroll inscribed *West Kent*.

Shako-plate: 1847
The standard star-and-crown plate in silver. On this an oak-wreath with, in the centre, the White Horse of Kent. A scroll across the top of the wreath inscribed *West Kent* and one across the base inscribed *Invicta*.

Light Company Shako-plate: 1847
As above but with large bugle-horn in centre, the ends of the horn protruding into the oak-wreath on either side. Below the motto scroll the numerals *37*.

Shako-plate: 1855–61
The standard star-and-crown plate in white-metal. On this a circlet inscribed *West Kent Light Infantry Militia*. In the centre a bugle with strings and within this the White Horse of Kent standing on a scroll inscribed *Invicta* (Fig. 1247).

Shako-plate: 1870–78
A laurel-wreath surmounted by a Victorian crown. Within the wreath a circlet inscribed *West Kent Light Infantry Militia*. In the centre a bugle with strings and within this the White Horse of Kent standing on a scroll inscribed *Invicta*. All in silver.

Helmet-plate: 1878–81
The standard star-and-crown plate and within the laurel-wreath a circlet inscribed *West Kent Light Infantry Militia*. In the centre a bugle with strings and within this the White Horse of Kent standing on a scroll inscribed *Invicta*. In silver.

Shropshire Militia
(1881: 3rd Battalion, The King's (Shropshire Light Infantry).)

Shako-plate: 1844–55
An eight-pointed star, the topmost point displaced by a Victorian crown. On this a strap inscribed *Shropshire Militia*. In the centre the Royal Cypher *VR*.

Shako-plate: 1855–61
An eight-pointed star, the topmost point displaced by a Victorian crown. On this a circlet inscribed *Shropshire Militia*. In the centre the Royal Cypher *VR*.

Glengarry: 1881–96
A circlet inscribed *Shropshire* in the top-half, and a sprig of laurel in the bottom-half, surmounted by a crown. In the centre a bugle with strings. In silver-plate.

Royal Herefordshire Militia
(1881: 4th Battalion, The King's (Shropshire Light Infantry).)

Helmet-plate: 1878–81
An eight-pointed star, the topmost point displaced by a Victorian crown. On this a laurel-wreath and within this a strap inscribed *Herefordshire Militia*. In the centre a shield bearing the Arms of Hereford with the crest above.

Helmet-plate: 1881–1902

An eight-pointed star, the topmost point displaced by a Victorian crown. In the centre the Royal Crest. Across the base of the wreath a scroll inscribed *Hereford*. In silver-plate with blue-velvet ground to centre (Fig. 1248).

Royal Elthorne or 5th Middlesex Light Infantry Militia

(1881: 3rd Battalion, The Duke of Cambridge's Own (Middlesex Regiment).)

Helmet-plate: 1878–81

A gilt eight-pointed star, the topmost point displaced by a Victorian crown. On this a circlet inscribed *5th Middlesex Militia*. In the centre the Royal Cypher *VR* above a bugle-horn (Fig. 1248A).

Royal East Middlesex Militia

(1881: 4th Battalion, The Duke of Cambridge's Own (Middlesex Regiment).)

Glengarry: 1874–81

A circlet inscribed *Royal East Middlesex Militia* surmounted by a Saxon crown of five points. In the centre the Arms of Middlesex. In white-metal (Fig. 1249).

Huntingdonshire Rifle Militia

(1881: 5th Battalion, The King's Royal Rifle Corps.)

Glengarry: 1874–81

An oblong bronze plaque. On this the Arms of Huntingdon (a hunting scene with a forester in the foreground). In relief.

Royal Flint Rifles

(1881: 6th Battalion, The King's Royal Rifle Corps.)

Glengarry: 1874–81

An oval inscribed *Royal Flint Militia*. Within this the Prince of Wales's plumes, coronet and motto. A double scroll at the base inscribed *Ffyddlawn a pharod*. In black-metal.

Royal Wiltshire Militia

(1881: 3rd Battalion, The Duke of Edinburgh's (Wiltshire Regiment).)

Shako-plate: 1861–69

An eight-pointed star, the topmost point displaced by a Victorian crown. On this an oak-wreath. Within the wreath a strap inscribed *Royal Wiltshire Militia*. In the centre St. George's Cross.

Glengarry: 1874–82

A Maltese cross on which a strap inscribed *Royal Wilts Militia*. In the centre St. George's Cross. On the top arm of the cross the honour *Mediterranean*.

6th Royal Lancashire Militia

(1881: 3rd Battalion, The Manchester Regiment.)

Shako-plate: 1861–69

An eight-pointed star, the topmost point displaced by a Victorian crown. On this a circlet inscribed *6th Royal Lancashire Militia* with, in the centre, the Royal Cypher *VR*.

The (King's Own) 2nd Staffordshire (Light Infantry) Militia
(1881: 3rd Battalion, The Prince of Wales's (North Staffordshire Regiment).)

Shako-plate: 1853–55
A gilt eight-pointed star, the topmost point displaced by a Victorian crown. On this a silver star with a gilt strap inscribed *King's Own 2nd Staffordshire Militia* with a representation of Windsor Castle in the centre. Below the strap a bugle-horn with the Stafford Knot within the strings (Fig. 1250).

Shako-plate: 1855–61
A silver eight-pointed star, the topmost point displaced by a Victorian crown. In the centre a circlet inscribed *The King's Own 2nd Staffordshire Militia*. In the centre Windsor Castle and below the circlet a bugle-horn with the Stafford Knot within the curl (Fig. 1251).

Glengarry: 1874–81
Within the strings of a bugle-horn the Stafford Knot.

Helmet-plate: 1878–81
An eight-pointed star, the topmost point displaced by a Victorian crown. On this a laurel-wreath. Within the wreath a circlet inscribed *King's Own 2nd Staffordshire Militia*. In the centre the Royal Cypher on a backing of dark-blue velvet. All in silver-plate except the Royal Cypher which is in gilt (Fig. 1252).

3rd King's Own Staffordshire Rifle Militia
(1881: 4th Battalion, The Prince of Wales's (North Staffordshire Regiment).)

Glengarry: 1874–81
The Stafford Knot within the curl of a French bugle-horn.

3rd West York Light Infantry Militia
(1881: 3rd Battalion, The York and Lancaster Regiment.)

Shako-plate: 1853–57
A gilt eight-pointed star, the topmost point displaced by a Victorian crown. On this a silver bugle with the White Rose within the strings. Below the bugle a gilt scroll inscribed *3rd West York*.

Shako-plate: 1857–75
An eight-pointed star, the topmost point displaced by a Victorian crown. On this a circlet inscribed *Third West York* with a spray of laurel in the bottom-half. In the centre a bugle with a rose within the strings. All in white-metal (Fig. 1253).

Helmet-plate: 1878–81
An eight-pointed star, the topmost point displaced by a Victorian crown. On this a laurel-wreath. Within the wreath a circlet inscribed *Third West York* with a spray of laurel in the bottom half. In the centre a bugle with a rose within the strings. All in bronze except the circlet which is gilt (Fig. 1254).

Forage-cap: 1853–73
A bugle surmounted by a Victorian crown with a rose within the strings. Other-ranks pattern in white-metal (Fig. 1255).

Glengarry: 1874–81
A strap inscribed *Third West York* surmounted by a Victorian crown. In the centre a bugle with a rose within the curl. In white-metal (Fig. 1256).

1st South Durham Militia (Unofficially Durham Fusilier Militia)
(1881: 3rd Battalion, The Durham Light Infantry.)

Glengarry: 1874–81
A strap inscribed *Durham Fusiliers* surmounted by a Victorian crown. In the centre a fused grenade with, on the ball, St. George's cross.

2nd North Durham Militia
(1881: 4th Battalion, The Durham Light Infantry.)

Shako-plate: 1844–55
A diamond-cut eight-pointed silver star, the topmost point displaced by a Victorian crown. On this a shield bearing the Cross from the Arms of the City of Durham in gold and red-enamel on dark-blue velvet. Below this in gilt a scroll inscribed *North Durham Militia* (Fig. 1257).

Glengarry: 1874–81
A strap inscribed *43rd North Durham Militia* surmounted by a Victorian crown. In the centre a shield bearing the cross with a lion rampant in each quarter (from the Arms of the City of Durham).

1st Royal Lanark Militia
(1881: 3rd Battalion, The Highland Light Infantry.)

Shako-plate: 1855
A star of eight points surmounted by a crown. On this a circlet inscribed *1st Royal Lanark Militia*. In the centre the Royal Cypher *VR*. In white-metal.

1240

1244

1239

1245

1241

1243

1237

1249

1247

1251

1248ᴬ

1248

1252

Glengarry: 1868–81

The Star of the Order of the Thistle surmounted by a crown. Below this a scroll inscribed *1st Royal Lanark Militia*.

Ross, Caithness, Sutherland, Cromarty (The Highland Rifle Militia)

(1881: 3rd Battalion, Seaforth Highlanders (Ross-shire Buffs, The Duke of Albany's).)

Glengarry: 1868–81

A chevron and bugle-horn within the outline of a heart surmounted by a crown. In white-metal (Fig. 1258).

Royal Aberdeenshire Highlanders

(1881: 3rd Battalion, The Gordon Highlanders.)

Glengarry: 1874–81

Within a wreath of ivy, St. Andrew and Cross. In white-metal (Fig. 1259).

Inverness, Banff, Moray and Nairn (Highland Light Infantry) Militia

(1881: 2nd Battalion, The Queen's Own Cameron Highlanders.)

Glengarry: 1868–81

A circlet inscribed *Inverness, Banff, Moray, Nairn Militia*. Within this St. Andrew and cross. Officers: silver. Other-ranks: white-metal.

Stirling, Dumbarton, Clackmannon, and Kinross (Highland Borderers) Light Infantry

(1881: 3rd Battalion, Princess Louise's (Argyll and Sutherland Highlanders).)

Glengarry: 1868–81

St. Andrew with Cross within a strap inscribed *Highland Borderers*. In white-metal.

The Prince of Wales's Royal Regiment of Renfrew Militia

(1881: 4th Battalion, Princess Louise's (Argyll and Sutherland Highlanders).)

Shako-plate: 1861–68

An eight-pointed star, the topmost point displaced by a Victorian crown. On this a wreath of oak. Within the wreath a circlet inscribed *Renfrew Militia*. In the centre the Prince of Wales's plumes, coronet and motto. All in silver.

Glengarry: 1874–81

A strap inscribed *Royal Renfrew Militia*. Within this in a voided centre the Prince of Wales's plumes, coronet and motto. In white-metal.

2nd Royal Tower Hamlets Militia (Queen's Own Light Infantry)

(1881: 5th Battalion, The Rifle Brigade (Prince Consort's Own).)

Shako-plate: 1855

A silver star of eight points, the topmost point displaced by a Victorian crown. On this in gilt a pierced circlet inscribed *The Queen's Own Light Infantry* with, in the centre, on a raised ribbed background, a crowned bugle-horn (Fig. 1260).

1255

1253

1256

1258

1259

1262

1260

1261

1254

1257

Glengarry: 1874–81

A strap inscribed *The Queen's Own Light Infantry* surmounted by the Royal Crest. In a voided centre the Tower of London surmounted by a bugle with strings. In white-metal (Fig. 1261). Also found with solid centre.

1st Royal Tower Hamlets Militia (King's Own Light Infantry)

(1881: 7th Battalion, The Rifle Brigade (Prince Consort's Own).)

Glengarry: 1874–81

Within a spray of oak-leaves a bugle-horn with the Tower of London in the curl and surmounted by a Victorian crown.

Royal Anglesey Light Infantry

(1877: Royal Anglesey Engineers Militia.)

Shako-plate: 1840–52

A gilt wreath, on a silver star of eight points surmounted by a Victorian crown. Within the wreath a strap inscribed *Royal Anglesey Light Infantry* with a purple-enamel ground. In the centre the Prince of Wales's plumes in silver and the coronet and motto in gilt on a purple-enamel ground. Above the strap a gilt crown with a crimson-velvet cushion. Beneath the wreath a gilt Light Infantry bugle-horn.

Glengarry: 1874–77

The head of St. David with a spray of oak on either side within the strings of a bugle-horn (Fig. 1262).

Royal Monmouth Light Infantry

(1877: Royal Monmouthshire Engineers Militia.)

Shako-plate: 1852–77

An eight-pointed beaded star, the topmost point displaced by a Victorian crown. On this a bugle with the Prince of Wales's plumes, coronet and motto in the curl. Below the bugle a scroll inscribed *Royal Monmouth*. Coronet and title-scroll in gilt, remainder in silver (Fig. 1263).

1263

IRISH MILITIA

Antrim Militia (Queen's Royal Rifles)
(1881: 4th Battalion, The Royal Irish Rifles.)

Glengarry
A cross similar to that of the Order of the Bath with a scroll above inscribed *Queen's* surmounted by a Victorian crown. On the top arm of the cross the word *Royal* with Gaelic characters on the other three arms. On the centre of the cross a circlet inscribed *Antrim Rifle Corps* and within this the Red Hand of Ulster. In gilding-metal, also in blackened-brass (Fig. 1264).

Shako-plate: c. 1865
A cross similar to that of the Order of the Bath with on the top arm the word *Queen's* with Gaelic characters on the other three arms. In the centre of the cross a circlet inscribed *Royal Antrim Rifles* and within this the Red Hand of Ulster. In blackened-brass (Fig. 1265).

Armagh Light Infantry
(1881: 3rd Battalion, Princess Victoria's (Royal Irish Fusiliers).)

Shako-plate: 1861–69
An eight-pointed star, the topmost point displaced by a Victorian crown. On the star a bugle with the numerals *75* within the strings. Below the bugle a scroll inscribed *Armagh Regiment* (Fig. 1266).

Glengarries
(1) A bugle with strings surmounted by a Victorian crown. In white-metal (Fig. 1267).
(2) A bugle with strings surmounted by a Victorian crown. Within the curve of the bugle the numerals *75*, the whole resting on a bed of shamrock.
(3) A strap inscribed *Armagh Light Infantry* surmounted by a Victorian crown. In a voided centre St. Patrick's Cross on which is superimposed an Irish harp above a bugle with strings. In white-metal (Fig. 1268).

Carlow Rifles
(1881: 8th Battalion, The King's Royal Rifle Corps.)

Glengarry

A strap inscribed: (top) *Erin go bragh*, (bottom) *Carlow Rifles*; surmounted by a Victorian crown. In the centre the Irish harp. Below the strap two sprays of shamrock. In blackened-brass (Fig. 1269).

Cavan Militia
(1881: 4th Battalion, Princess Victoria's (Royal Irish Fusiliers).)

Shako-plate: 1861

An eight-pointed star, the topmost point displaced by a Victorian crown. On this a circlet inscribed *Cavan Militia* and within this the Irish harp. In silver (Fig. 1270).

Glengarry

A strap inscribed *Cavan Militia* surmounted by a crown. Within this on a solid background a bugle with strings with, in the curve of the bugle, the Star of the Order of St. Patrick. In white-metal (Fig. 1271).

Clare Militia
(1881: 7th Clare Brigade, South Irish Division Artillery.)

Glengarry

An eight-pointed star, the topmost point displaced by a crown. On this a strap inscribed *Clare Militia* and, in a voided centre, the Irish harp. In silver (Fig. 1272).

North Cork Rifles
(1881: 9th Battalion, The King's Royal Rifle Corps.)

Round forage-cap: 1858

A scroll inscribed *North Cork* in gilding-metal (Fig. 1273).

Glengarry

A complete wreath of shamrock surmounted by a Victorian crown. In the centre a Maltese cross with a circlet in the centre of the cross inscribed *North Cork Rifles*. Above the cross a bugle with strings. In gilding-metal (Fig. 1274).

South Cork Light Infantry
(1881: 3rd Battalion, The Royal Munster Fusiliers.)

Glengarry

A shamrock-wreath surmounted by a crown. Within this a bugle with strings.

Prince of Wales's Own Donegal Militia
(1881: 3rd Brigade, North Irish Division Artillery.)

Glengarry

The Prince of Wales's plumes, coronet and motto within a scroll inscribed *Donegal Militia*. In white-metal (Fig. 1275).

1264

1265

1267

1268

1270

1269

1271

1272

1273

1274

1275

1276

Royal North Down Rifles
(1881: 3rd Battalion, The Royal Irish Rifles.)

Glengarry
A Union wreath of roses, thistles and shamrocks surmounted by a crown. Within this a cross similar to that of the Order of the Bath with a plain tablet above. In the centre of the cross a circlet inscribed with the motto of the Order of the Garter and within this an Irish harp. Below the wreath a scroll inscribed *Royal North Down Militia*. In black-metal (Fig. 1276). Also in white-metal.

Royal South Down Light Infantry
(1881: 5th Battalion, The Royal Irish Rifles.)

Glengarry
A bugle inscribed *South Down* with three shamrock-leaves either side joining it to a crown inscribed *Royal* at its base. Within the bugle an Irish harp surmounted by the bow of the bugle strings. In white-metal (Fig. 1277).

Queen's Own Royal Dublin City Militia
(1881: 4th Battalion, The Royal Dublin Fusiliers.)

Glengarry
A wreath of shamrock surmounted by a Victorian crown. Within this a strap inscribed *Queen's Own Royal Regiment* and in the centre on a solid background the Arms of the City of Dublin. In silver (Fig. 1278).

Dublin County Light Infantry
(1881: 5th Battalion, The Royal Dublin Fusiliers.)

Glengarry
A Union wreath of roses, thistles and shamrocks surmounted by a Victorian crown. In a voided centre the Irish harp above a bugle with strings. Below the wreath a scroll inscribed *Dublin County Light Infantry*. In white-metal (Fig. 1279).

Fermanagh Light Infantry
(1881: 3rd Battalion, The Royal Inniskilling Fusiliers.)

Glengarry
Within the curl of a bugle-horn a castle with flag flying. In silver (Fig. 1280).

Galway Militia
(1881: 4th Battalion, The Connaught Rangers.)

Glengarry
A strap inscribed *Galway* surmounted by a crown. Within the strap an Irish harp.

Kerry Militia
(1881: 4th Battalion, The Royal Munster Fusiliers.)

Glengarry
A strap inscribed *Kerry Regiment*. Within this the Irish harp. The whole resting on a bed of shamrock.

1277

1278

1279

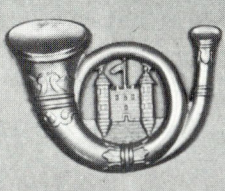

1280

1281

1282

1283

1284

1286

1287

1288

1285

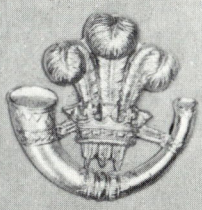

1289

Kildare Rifles
(1881: 3rd Battalion, The Royal Dublin Fusiliers.)

Glengarry
A strap inscribed *Kildare Rifles* surmounted by a crown. Within this on a solid background two serpents intertwined with heads facing and, between these, the inscription *Prudens et Serpens*. In blackened-brass (Fig. 1281).

Kilkenny Fusiliers
(1881: 5th Battalion, The Royal Irish Regiment.)

Glengarry
A strap inscribed *Kilkenny* surmounted by a Victorian crown. In the centre a fused grenade. In white-metal (Fig. 1282).

King's County Royal Rifles
(1881: 3rd Battalion, The Prince of Wales's Leinster Regiment (Royal Canadians).)

Round forage-cap: 1858
A scroll inscribed *King's County* in gilding-metal (Fig. 1283).

Glengarry
A bugle-horn with, in the curl, the numerals *98*.

Leitrim Rifles
(1881: 8th Battalion, Rifle Brigade (The Prince Consort's Own).)

Glengarry
A Celtic cross surmounted by a crown. On the top arm of the cross a bugle with strings and in the centre the Irish harp. Two sprays of shamrock at the base of the cross which rests on a tablet inscribed *Leitrim*. In black-metal (Fig. 1284).

Royal Limerick County Militia (Fusiliers)
(1881: 5th Battalion, The Royal Munster Fusiliers.)

Round forage-cap: 1858
A scroll inscribed *Royal Limerick*. In white-metal (Fig. 1285). This is of a different design to the universal pattern.

Glengarries
  (1) Within a Union wreath of roses, thistles and shamrocks a fused grenade with, on the ball, an Irish harp surmounted by a crown. Beneath the wreath a scroll inscribed *Royal Limerick County*. In white-metal (Fig. 1286).
  (2) As above but with a plain ball of the grenade. In gilding-metal, also in white-metal (Fig. 1287).

Londonderry Light Infantry
(1881: 9th Brigade, North Irish Division Artillery.)

Glengarry
A strap inscribed *Londonderry Regiment* surmounted by a castle. In a voided centre a bugle with strings. In white-metal (Fig. 1288).

1290

1292

1291

1293

1294

1295

1296

1297

1298

1299

1300

1302

The Prince of Wales's Royal Regiment of Longford Light Infantry
(1881: 6th Battalion, Rifle Brigade (The Prince Consort's Own).)

Glengarry
Within a bugle-horn the Prince of Wales's plumes and coronet. In silver (Fig. 1289). Also in blackened-brass.

Louth Rifles
(1881: 6th Battalion, The Royal Irish Rifles.)

Glengarry
Within a wreath of shamrock a Maltese cross surmounted by a crown.

North Mayo Fusiliers
(1881: 6th Battalion, The Connaught Rangers.)

Glengarry
(1) A phoenix arising from a mural crown. Below, a scroll inscribed *North Mayo*. In white-metal (Fig. 1290).
(2) Same design as above but in two separate pieces. In silver (Fig. 1291).

South Mayo Rifles
(1881: 3rd Battalion, The Connaught Rangers.)

Helmet-plate: 1878
A cross based on that of the Order of the Bath surmounted by a Victorian crown. On this a circlet inscribed *South Mayo Militia*. In the centre a bugle with strings. In blackened-brass (Fig. 1292).

Glengarry
A wreath of shamrock surmounted by a Victorian crown. Within this an oval inscribed *South Mayo Rifles 15* and in the centre the Arms of the Marquis of Sligo. In white-metal (Fig. 1293).

Royal Meath Militia
(1881: 5th Battalion, The Prince of Wales's Leinster Regiment (Royal Canadians).)

Glengarry
A Tara brooch surmounted by a Victorian crown. The top part of the brooch inscribed *Royal Meath*. In white-metal (Fig. 1294).

Monoghan Militia
(1881: 5th Battalion, Princess Victoria's (Royal Irish Fusiliers).)

Glengarry
A strap inscribed *Monoghan Regiment* surmounted by a Victorian crown. In the centre the Irish harp. In white-metal (Fig. 1295).

Royal Queen's County Rifles
(1881: 4th Battalion, The Prince of Wales's Leinster Regiment (Royal Canadians).)

Glengarry
A bugle with strings surmounted by a crown. Below the bugle a scroll inscribed *Queen's County Rifles*. In blackened-brass (Fig. 1296).

Roscommon Militia
(1881: 5th Battalion, The Connaught Rangers.)

Glengarry
Within a wreath of shamrock an Irish harp surmounted by a crown. Across the base of the wreath a scroll inscribed *Roscommon*. In white-metal (Fig. 1297).

Sligo Rifles
(1881: 8th Brigade, North Irish Division Artillery.)

Glengarry
A Celtic cross surmounted by a crown below which the numerals *124*. The left arm of the cross inscribed *Sligo* and on the right arm *Rifles*. In the centre of the cross an Irish harp above a scroll inscribed *Quis Separabit*. On the bottom arm of the cross a bugle with strings.

Royal Tyrone Fusiliers
(1881: 4th Battalion, The Royal Inniskilling Fusiliers.)

Glengarries
(1) A fused grenade with the numerals *80* on the ball. In white-metal (Fig. 1298).
(2) A strap inscribed *Royal Tyrone Fusiliers* surmounted by a Victorian crown. In a voided centre a fused grenade with a plain ball. In white-metal (Fig. 1299).

Westmeath Rifles
(1881: 9th Battalion, Rifle Brigade (The Prince Consort's Own).)

Glengarry
A bugle surmounted by a crown with, in the curl of the bugle, a shamrock. Below the bugle a scroll with a Gaelic inscription (Westmeath Rifles). In blackened-brass (Fig. 1300).

Wexford Militia
(1881: 3rd Battalion, The Royal Irish Regiment.)

Officers' shako-plate: 1829
An eight-pointed star, the topmost point displaced by a crown. On this the Irish harp with a scroll below inscribed *Wexford*. All in gilt (Fig. 1301).

Glengarry
Within a wreath of shamrock, surmounted by a crown, a strap inscribed *Wexford Militia*. In a voided centre the Irish harp. In white-metal (Fig. 1302).

1301

CHAPTER 24

The Imperial Yeomanry

The British Army suffered a series of reverses in the early period of the conflict in South Africa and, in December 1899, it was decided to ask for volunteers from Yeomanry regiments.

Sir Redvers Buller, then commanding the troops in Natal, asked for 8,000 men to serve as Irregular Mounted Infantry and to be organised into battalions each consisting of four companies.

At a conference held at the War Office on the 18th December it was decided to raise a force of 3,000 men, mainly from the Yeomanry, and this force to be known as *The Imperial Yeomanry*.

Early in 1901 it was decided to relieve the First Contingents. Second Contingents were raised immediately and Third Contingents, at the end of that year.

By virtue of an Army Order of April 1901, the entire Yeomanry was designated Imperial Yeomanry and this title was kept until the formation of the Territorial Force in 1908, when the word 'Imperial' was dropped.

The Yeomanry units which fought in the South African War normally retained their territorial title in addition to their company number and a list of these follows:

Ayrshire	17
Bedfordshire	28
Berkshire	39, 58
Buckinghamshire	37, 38, 56, 57
Cheshire	21, 22
Denbighshire	29
Derbyshire	8, 104
Devonshire	27
Dorset	26
Fife and Forfar Light Horse	20
Glamorgan	4
Gloucestershire	3
Hampshire	41, 50
Hertfordshire	42
Kent, East	33, 53
Kent, West	36
Lanarkshire	18, 107
Lancashire	23, 32

Leicestershire	7, 65
Lothians and Berwickshire	19
Middlesex	34, 35, 62, 112
Montgomeryshire	31, 49
North Irish Horse	60
Northumberland	14, 15, 55, 100, 101, 110
Nottinghamshire	
Sherwood Rangers	10
South Nottinghamshire	12
Oxfordshire	40, 59
Pembrokeshire	30
Queen's Own Royal Glasgow	108
Roughriders	72, 76, 78, 84, 85, 86, 87
Sharpshooters	67, 70, 71, 75, 80, 81, 82, 83, 90, 91, 92, 93, 115, 116, 117, 118
Shropshire	13
Somerset, West	25
Somerset, North	48
South Irish Horse	61
Staffordshire	6, 106
Suffolk	43, 44
Sussex	69
Warwickshire	5, 103
Westmorland and Cumberland	24
Wiltshire	1, 2, 63
Worcestershire	16, 102
Yorkshire	9, 11, 66
Yorkshire Dragoons	111
Yorkshire Hussars	108

In addition to those above, the following Companies also carried titles and, in some instances, wore special badges.

Belfast	46, 54
Dublin	45, 74
Fincastle's Horse	139, 140, 141, 142, 177
Highland Horse	163, 164, 165, 166
Irish	99
Irish Horse	131, 132, 133, 134, 175, 176
Lord Donoughmore's	47
Lovat Scouts	113, 114
Manchester	77, 105
Metropolitan Mounted Rifles	94, 95, 96, 97
Paget's Horse	51, 52, 68, 73

Badges of the Imperial Yeomanry as distinct from Yeomanry are:

Wiltshire
Officers' felt-hat badge: The Prince of Wales's plumes, coronet and motto in white-metal with a pin-brooch fastening. Approved 11th March 1903 (Fig. 1303).

1303   1304   1305   1307

Warwickshire

Officers' felt-hat badge: The Bear and Ragged Staff in white-metal. Large size, 3·8 cms. high. Approved 15th January 1903 (Fig. 1304).

Yorkshire Hussars

The White Rose of York in white-metal surmounted by the Prince of Wales's plumes, coronet and motto in gilding-metal. Approved 19th March 1907.

Staffordshire

(1) Officers' felt-hat badge: A Stafford Knot. In white-metal. Approved 30th March 1903 (Fig. 1305).
(2) The Stafford Knot with, below, the letter *S* and below this the letters *IY*. In white-metal (Fig. 1306).

Shropshire

(1) The letters *SIY* in brass 4·7 cms. wide and 1·5 cms. high. Approved 7th October 1902 (Fig. 1307).
(2) Three loggerheads (Leopards' faces) on a shield within a strap inscribed *Shropshire IY*, surmounted by an Imperial crown. In gilding-metal (Fig. 1308).
(3) As (2) but with a circlet containing the title instead of a strap. Approved 20th July 1906. In gilding-metal (Fig. 1309).

Ayrshire

A lion's head and neck winged. Approved 7th October, 1902. In silver-and-gilt for officers. Also in bronze and in gilding-metal (Fig. 1310).

Cheshire

(1) The Prince of Wales's plumes, coronet and motto. Below, a scroll inscribed *Earl of Chester's IY*. In white-metal (Fig. 1311).
(2) Same general design but with different arrangement of plumes; the coronet in gilding-metal and the remainder in white-metal. Approved 11th September 1902 (Fig. 1312).
(3) Same general design as (2) but all in white-metal (Fig. 1313).
(4) Same general design as (2) but all in bronze (Fig. 1314).

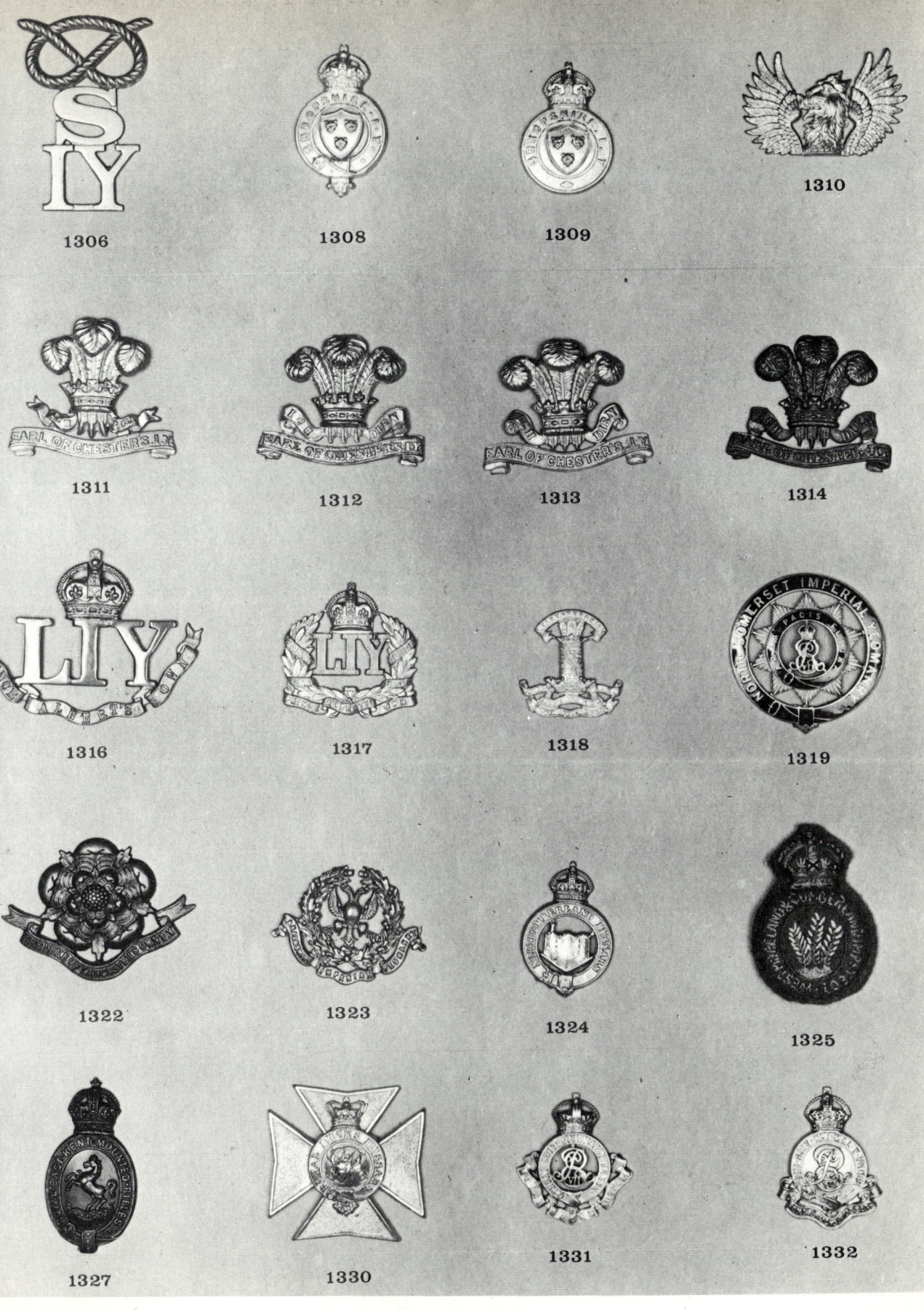

1306   1308   1309   1310

1311   1312   1313   1314

1316   1317   1318   1319

1322   1323   1324   1325

1327   1330   1331   1332

Yorkshire Dragoons
Officers' felt-hat badge: A rose in white-metal size 2·8 cms. set on a rosette of dark-blue corded-ribbon size 6·5 cms. overall. Worn with a plume of dark-fawn. Approved 9th September 1902 (Fig. 1315).

Leicestershire
  (1) The letters *LIY* surmounted by an Imperial crown. Below, a scroll inscribed *Prince Albert's Own*. In gilding-metal (Fig. 1316).
  (2) The letters *LIY* within a laurel-wreath on which are four scrolls inscribed *South, Africa, 1900, 1901–2* surmounted by an Imperial crown. Below, a scroll inscribed *Prince Albert's Own*. In white-metal (Fig. 1317).
  (3) The crest of the Prince Consort with a scroll below inscribed *Leicestershire* and a scroll below this inscribed *Prince Albert's Own IY*. Below this a third scroll inscribed *South Africa 1900–02*. In white-metal (Fig. 1318). Also found in silver, and bronze.
  (4) An embroidered Imperial crown above *LIY* in script characters on scarlet cloth.

North Somerset
  (1) A ten-pointed star on which a strap inscribed *Arma pacis fulcra* and in the centre the cypher of King Edward VII. The whole surrounded by a strap inscribed *North Somerset Imperial Yeomanry*. In silver with blue-enamel backing to the lettering (Fig. 1319).
  (2) An embroidered Imperial crown above *NSIY* in script characters. In silver on white cloth.
  (3) Officers' slouch-hat badge: The letters *NS* in brass. 4·2 cms. wide, 2·4 cms. high. Approved 7th October 1902 (Fig. 1320).

Duke of Lancaster's Own
  (1) Officers' slouch-hat badge: A small rose 2·8 cms. high in gilding-metal with two small loops as fasteners. Approved 30th March 1903 (Fig. 1321).
  (2) A rose with, beneath, a scroll inscribed *The Duke of Lancaster's Own IY*. In bronze (Fig. 1322).

Lanarkshire
Within a wreath of thistles a double-headed eagle grasping a bell in its right claw. Below, a scroll inscribed *Lanarkshire Imperial Yeomanry*. In gilding-metal. Approved 16th May 1902 (Fig. 1323). Also found in gilt, bronze, black, and hall-marked silver.

Northumberland Hussars
A strap inscribed *Northumberland Hussars* ensigned with the Imperial crown. In a voided centre a castle. In white-metal (Fig. 1324).

1320

1315

1321

South Nottinghamshire
A slip of oak with acorn. In white-metal. Approved 24th April, 1902.

Westmorland and Cumberland
(1) An embroidered badge on khaki cloth. A circlet surmounted by an Imperial crown inscribed *Westmorland & Cumberland Impl Yeo* within which three sprigs of heather (Fig. 1325).
(2) Officers' slouch-hat badge: A small rosette of white-silk ribbon 3·5 cms. wide with three sprigs of artificial white heather behind. Approved 16th March 1904 (Fig. 1326).

East Kent
(1) The White Horse of Kent on a scroll inscribed *Invicta* surrounded by the Garter and surmounted by an Imperial crown. In white-metal. Approved 7th October 1902. (Same design as shown in Chapter 25, Fig. 1438.)
(2) The White Horse of Kent on a scroll inscribed *Invicta* surrounded by a strap inscribed *Royal East Kent Mounted Rifles* and surmounted by an Imperial crown. In blackened-brass (Fig. 1327).

West Kent
Officers' slouch-hat badge: The White Horse of Kent standing on a tablet inscribed *Invicta*. Below this a scroll inscribed *West Kent IY*. 4·5 cms high in white-metal.
Approved as hat badge 8th November 1902 and as slouch-hat badge 26th November 1902 (Fig. 1328).

Hampshire
Felt-hat badge: The Hampshire Rose within an oval inscribed *Hampshire Yeomanry* supported by crossed carbines and surmounted by a Victorian crown. Below, a scroll inscribed *Carabiniers*. All in brass. Approved 4th February 1903 (Fig. 1329).

Buckinghamshire
(1) A Maltese cross with, in the centre, the cypher of King Edward VII surrounded by a strap inscribed *Royal Bucks Hussars* and surmounted by a Victorian crown. In white-metal (Fig. 1330).
(2) The cypher of King Edward VII within the Garter and surmounted by an Imperial crown. Below, a three-part scroll inscribed *Royal Bucks Hussars*. In white-metal (Fig. 1331).
(3) Same design as (2) but solid background behind the Royal Cypher and the title on a continuous scroll. In white-metal (Fig. 1332).

Derbyshire
(1) Officers' felt-hat badge: A large rose in khaki-bronze matt-finish paint 5 cms. in diameter. Worn with a stamen between two petals at top-centre. Approved 25th August 1902 (Fig. 1333).
(2) A rose within a laurel-wreath surmounted by an Imperial crown. On the wreath, scrolls inscribed *South, Africa, 1900, 1901*. Below, a scroll inscribed *Derbyshire Imperial Yeomanry*. Size 59mm. by 62mm. In bronze (Fig. 1334).

(3) Exactly as above but size 53mm. by 54mm. In gilding-metal (Fig. 1335). Also found in size 35mm. by 40mm. in bronze, and silver-gilt; in bronze in sizes 38mm. by 43mm., and 34mm. by 38mm.

Dorset
(1) The Garter ensigned with the Imperial crown. Within the Garter the wording *QO. Dorset IY.*, the whole within a laurel-wreath. Approved 11th March 1903. In bronze (Fig. 1336).
(2) The Garter ensigned with the Imperial crown. Within the Garter the wording *QO Dorset IY*, the word *Dorset* being inscribed on a diagonal scroll between *QO* and *IY*. The whole within a laurel-wreath. On the wreath, scrolls inscribed *South, Africa, 1900, 1901*. In white-metal (Fig. 1337). Also found in bronze.

Royal Gloucestershire Hussars
The crest of the Duke of Beaufort, *viz.* a portcullis with chains surmounted by a ducal coronet. The letters *I* on the left and *Y* on the right of the portcullis. The portcullis enclosed in a scroll inscribed *Royal Gloucestershire Hussars*. Approved 31st December 1902. In gilding-metal (Fig. 1338). Also found in gilt and in bronze, and another pattern with the portcullis non-voided.

Hertfordshire
A Hart on a scroll inscribed *Hertfordshire* and below this the letters *IY*. The whole enclosed in a large brass circle. Approved 7th October 1902 (Fig. 1339).
Worn on a large maroon rosette 6·5 cms. in diameter.

1329

1326

1328

1333

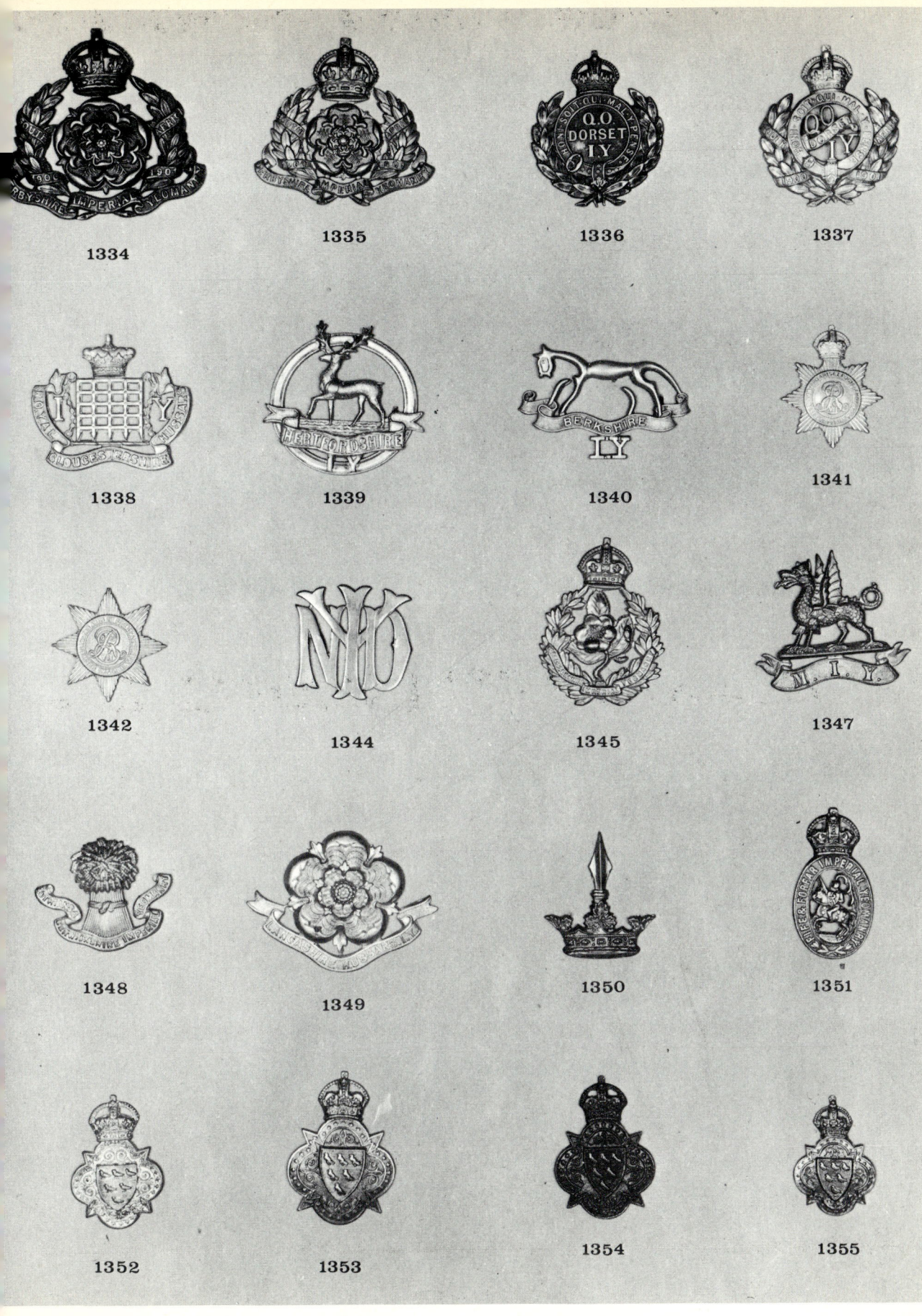

1334

1335

1336

1337

1338

1339

1340

1341

1342

1344

1345

1347

1348

1349

1350

1351

1352

1353

1354

1355

Berkshire

The White Horse of Berkshire with a scroll below inscribed *Berkshire* and below this the letters *IY*. In brass. Approved 23rd August 1902 (Fig. 1340). Also found in hall-marked silver, and in gilt, for officers: in gilding-metal and in white-metal for other-ranks.

Middlesex

(1) An eight-pointed star, the topmost point displaced by an Imperial crown. In the centre a circlet inscribed *Pro aris et focis* and *Middlesex Imperial Yeomanry*. Within the circlet the cypher of King Edward VII. In gilt (Fig. 1341).

(2) Same design as above but without the crown. In white-metal (Fig. 1342). Also found in gilding-metal.

Royal First Devon

Officers' slouch-hat badge: The Royal Crest in white metal 3cms. high. Worn on a rosette of black-felt 4·3 cms. wide over a red-felt. Overall size 7cms. Approved 29th October 1902 (Fig. 1343).

North Devon

The monogram *NDIY* in brass (Fig. 1344). Worn on a red circle 52mms. wide backed by a piece of stag's hide. Approved 19th January 1903.

Loyal Suffolk Hussars

A castle. Below this the date *1793* and a scroll inscribed *Loyal Suffolk Hussars*. The castle and date in gilding-metal and the scroll in white-metal. Approved 4th May 1904.

Worcestershire

(1) A laurel-wreath surmounted by an Imperial crown. On the lower part of the wreath a scroll inscribed *Worcestershire Imperial Yeomanry*. In the centre a spray of pear-blossom. In gilding-metal. Approved 18th August 1902 Fig. 1345).

(2) A spray of pear-blossom embroidered on silk.

West Somerset

Officers' slouch-hat badge: The letters *WSIY* in hand-cut brass. Size 5cms. wide by 1·85cms. high. Approved 7th October 1902 (Fig. 1346).

Montgomeryshire

The Welsh Dragon standing on a scroll inscribed *MIY*. In gilding-metal. Approved 14th October 1902 (Fig. 1347). Also found in white-metal.

1346

1343

1356   1357   1358   1359

1360   1361   1362   1363

1364   1365   1366   1367

1368   1369   1370   1371

1372   1373   1374   1375

Lothians and Berwickshire

A garb (the heraldic term for a sheaf of wheat) below which a scroll inscribed *Lothians & Berwickshire Imperial Yeomanry*. In gilding-metal (Fig. 1348). Also found in bronze.

Lancashire Hussars

A rose beneath which a scroll inscribed *Lancashire Hussars IY*. Worn on a red-cloth backing cut to the shape of the badge. Approved 14th January 1903 (Fig. 1349).
In bronze for officers, in gilding-metal for other-ranks.

Surrey

The crest of Lord Middleton (a spear-head issuing from a coronet). In gilding-metal (Fig. 1350).
Also found in silver, white-metal, and brass.
Note: The arm-badge was the same but with the addition of a scroll inscribed *Surrey, P'cess of Wales' IY*. In white-metal.

Fife and Forfar

The County badge, known as the Thane of Fife, within an oval inscribed *Fife & Forfar Imperial Yeomanry* and surmounted by an Imperial crown. Approved 7th October 1902. In white-metal (Fig. 1351).

Sussex

(1) On a shield, six martlets, the whole on an ornamental ground surmounted by an Imperial crown. In gilding-metal (Fig. 1352).
(2) Same design, but larger. In gilt for officers (Fig. 1353).
(3) Same design in bronze (Fig. 1354).
(4) Same design only smaller. In gilt for officers and gilding-metal for other-ranks (Fig. 1355).

Glamorgan

The Prince of Wales's plumes, coronet and motto. Below, a scroll inscribed *Glamorgan Imperial Yeomanry*. The coronet and scroll in gilding-metal, remainder in white-metal. Approved 29th May 1903 (Fig. 1356). Also found all in white-metal.

Lincolnshire

The Arms of the City of Lincoln (a shield bearing the Cross of St. George with a fleur-de-lys in the centre) surrounded by a laurel-wreath. On the wreath, a scroll inscribed *Lincolnshire Imperial Yeomanry*. The whole ensigned with an Imperial crown. Approved 7th October 1902. In silver (Fig. 1357).
Also found in white-metal, and bronze.

The City of London (Rough Riders)

(1) A white-metal spur bearing the letters *RR* in gilding-metal. Approved 9th January 1902 (Fig. 1358).
In silver-and-gilt for officers.
(2) The Arms of the City of London on a solid background within a circlet inscribed *The City of London Imperial Yeomanry*, surrounded by a laurel-wreath, and surmounted by an Imperial crown. Below the circlet a scroll inscribed *Rough Riders*. Approved 7th October 1902 (Fig. 1359). In gilding-metal, but officers in silver-and-gilt. Found with both loops and screw-studs as fasteners.

(3) As (2) but with white-metal Arms in centre and with an additional scroll at foot inscribed *South Africa 1900–02* (Fig. 1360). Also found in gilt-and-silver, and bronze with white-metal Arms. All with loops or screw-stud fasteners.

2nd County of London (Westminster Dragoons)

The Arms of the City of Westminster. Below, a scroll inscribed *Westminster Dragoons IY.* In gilt for officers and gilding-metal for other-ranks (Fig. 1361).

3rd County of London (Sharp Shooters)

(1) The letters *SS* on a solid background within a circlet inscribed *3rd County of London* surrounded by a laurel-wreath and surmounted by an Imperial crown. Approved 18th December 1901. In gilt with silver letters *SS* for officers. All in gilding-metal for other-ranks (Fig. 1362).

(2) Crossed rifles surmounted by an Imperial crown. Below, a scroll inscribed *Sharp-shooters*. For other-ranks. In gilding-metal (Fig. 1363).

Bedfordshire

(1) An eagle, on which is superimposed a castle, surmounted by a coronet. Approved 7th October 1902. In brass.

(2) An eagle of a narrower width, on which is superimposed a castle, surmounted by a coronet. 33mm. by 35mm. In white-metal (Fig. 1364).

Essex

(1) The Essex County Arms (three Seaxes) within a strap inscribed *Audacter et sincere* and surmounted by an Imperial crown. A red background in the centre. In gilding-metal (Fig. 1365). The motto is that of Lieutenant-Colonel R. B. Colvin c.b., who raised the regiment.

(2) The Essex County Arms within a circlet inscribed *Audacter et sincere* and surmounted by an Imperial crown. Below, a scroll inscribed *Essex Imperial Yeomanry*. Approved 18th April 1903. In gilt (Fig. 1366).

(3) The Essex County Arms surmounted by an Imperial crown embroidered in gilt-and-silver wire (Fig. 1367).

(4) The Essex County Arms surmounted by an Imperial crown. In gilt for officers, in gilding-metal for other-ranks (Fig. 1368).

(5) The Essex County Arms within a circlet inscribed *Audacter et sincere* and surmounted by an Imperial crown. In gilt, bronze, and gilding-metal (Fig. 1369).

The King's Colonials

The King's Colonials, created in 1901 from Colonials residing in and near London, was formed originally of four squadrons representing the senior members of the Empire. A fifth squadron, 'New Zealand', was formed in 1903 but was disbanded the following year.

The first head-dress was a tall felt hat, rather like an inverted flower-pot, with a broad brim turned up and fastened to the left side of the crown. It was unique in bearing three badges: at the top-front was the first regimental badge; on the hat-band was the squadron badge or, in the case of H.Q. staff, a secondary regimental badge; on the side, where the turned-up brim was attached to the crown was a small version of the secondary badge.

Regimental badges
(1) The complete Arms of H.R.H. The Prince of Wales beneath which is a scroll bearing his motto *Ich Dien* and, below that, a further scroll inscribed *The King's Colonials*. In gilt, and yellow-brass (Fig. 1370).
(2) The letters *KC*, in which is interwoven a scroll inscribed *Regi Adsumus Colon*, surmounted by the Prince of Wales's plumes, coronet and motto. In gilt, bronze, and gilding-metal (Fig. 1371) and in two sizes.
  This secondary badge ultimately superseded (1) to become the regimental badge and was worn alone on the second pattern of head-dress, a form of bush-hat, and on the peaked service-cap.

Squadron badges
(1) Africa: an ostrich with a background of mountains and a scroll at the base inscribed *British Africa*. In gilt, bronze and in brass-finish (Fig. 1372).
(2) Asia: an elephant with a palm-tree background and a scroll at the base inscribed *British Asian*, the two words divided by a star and crescent. In brass (Fig. 1373).
(3) North America: a beaver with a maple-leaf background and a scroll at the base inscribed *British American*. Officers' and Senior N.C.O.s' in gilt, other-ranks' in brass (Fig. 1374).
(4) Australasia: a kangaroo on a rising-sun with a fern-leaf in the foreground and a scroll at the base inscribed *Australasian*. In brass (Fig. 1376).
  Superseded by (5) when the separate 'New Zealand' squadron was formed.
(5) Australia: a kangaroo on a scroll inscribed *Australia*. In brass (Fig. 1375).
(6) New Zealand: a fern-leaf inscribed with the letters *NZ*. In brass (Fig. 1377).

Northamptonshire
The White Horse within an oval scroll inscribed *Northamptonshire Imperial Yeomanry*. Below the horse the rose, thistle and shamrock in a spray. Officers: gilt with silver horse. Other-ranks: gilding-metal with horse in white-metal (Fig. 1378).

East Riding of Yorks
A fox in full cry towards the left. In white-metal. Approved 9th May 1903.

Lovat Scouts
(1) A circlet inscribed *Lovat Scouts IY*. In the centre a stag's head with the antlers extending into the circlet. In gilt and silver-plate (Fig. 1379).
(2) Design as above but with antlers inside the circlet. In gilding-metal (Fig. 1380).

Scottish Horse
(1) A voided oval inscribed *Scottish Horse 1900* with St. Andrew's Cross superimposed. In hand-cut brass (Fig. 1381).
(2) As above, but in bronze and worn on yellow cloth with serrated edge (Fig. 1382). Both patterns also found without date.
(3) An oval inscribed *Scottish Horse* with St. Andrew's Cross superimposed. Solid background to oval and centre. In white-metal (Fig. 1383).
  The above three patterns were worn by the regiment raised in South Africa and not by the regiment formed in Scotland after the conclusion of the South African War.

1376

1377

1378

1379

1380

1381

1382

1383

1384

1385

1386

1387

1388

1389

1390

1391

1392

1393

1394

1395

(4) A circle inscribed *Scottish Horse* with St. Andrew's Cross in the centre. In bronze (Fig. 1384).
This pattern worn in South Africa by the regiment formed in Scotland.

(5) An oval inscribed *Scottish Horse 1900* with St. Andrew's Cross superimposed. A wreath of juniper (left-branch) and bay (right-branch) encloses the oval. In white-metal and gilding-metal. Approved 1903 (Fig. 1385).

(6) Same design as (5) but smaller and in white-metal (Fig. 1386).

(7) An oval inscribed *Scottish Horse 1900* surmounted by a Scottish crown and with St. Andrew's Cross superimposed. A wreath of juniper and bay encloses the oval. Below the oval two scrolls, the top one inscribed *South Africa* and the bottom one with three dates *1900, 1901, 1902*. Size 45mm. by 32mm. In white-metal, also in gilding-metal. Approved 1906 (Fig. 1387).

(8) Similar to (7) but size 50mm. by 32mm. In gilt, silver, bronze and white-metal (Fig. 1388).

South of Ireland

(1) A shamrock-leaf not veined. On this the letters *SIY*. In gilt, bronze, and gilding-metal (Fig. 1389).

(2) A small veined shamrock-leaf. On this the letters *SIY*. In gilding-metal (Fig. 1390).

North of Ireland

(1) The Irish Harp surmounted by an Imperial crown. Below, a scroll inscribed *North of Ireland IY*. In silver with strings of harp voided. In bronze, white-metal and gilding-metal with non-voided strings (Fig. 1391).

(2) As above but smaller. In bronze and gilding-metal (Fig. 1392).

(3) The Irish Harp within a circlet inscribed *North of Ireland Imperial Yeomanry* and with five shamrock-leaves in base of circlet. Surmounted by an Imperial crown. In white-metal (Fig. 1393). Officers: in silver, worn on a rosette of white-silk edged green. Overall measurement, 10cms. wide.

Imperial Yeomanry Hospital

The Prince of Wales's plumes, coronet and motto above a scroll inscribed *Imperial Yeomanry Hospital*. The plume and motto in white-metal, the coronet and scroll in gilding-metal (Fig. 1394).

Commander-in-Chief's Yeomanry Escort

On an egg-shell blue-enamel circle the cypher of Lord Roberts (a coronet above the letter *R*). A circlet surrounding this inscribed *Commander-in-Chief's Yeomanry Escort South African Field Force*. Extensions on both sides and the base of the circlet. The left inscribed *19*, the right *00* and the base *Virtute et valore*. All in gilt (Fig. 1395).

This was not an independent unit, but was in fact the 48th (North Somerset) Company, Imperial Yeomanry, whose Commander, Major W. M. Sherston, D.S.O., was Lord Roberts' nephew and A.D.C.

It was Major Sherston who, with Lord Roberts' consent, presented the badge, but it is doubtful if it was ever worn.

The Yeomen's period of duty as the escort lasted for only eight months from the time of their arrival in South Africa until Lord Roberts left for home.

Special badges worn by Imperial Yeomanry Companies during the South African War:

General Service
A rosette of scarlet and purple. On this in bronze or brass the Prince of Wales's plumes, coronet and motto with separate letters *I* and *Y* below (Fig. 1396).

Imperial Yeomanry Scouts
The letters *IY* cut out in sheet-brass with a scroll below inscribed *Scouts*.

7th Leicestershire
The numeral *7* in brass on the general-service rosette.

16th (Worcestershire) Company
A spray of pear blossom in embroidered silk.

5th Battalion
The numeral *5* in brass between the Prince of Wales's plumes and the letters *IY* on the general-service rosette.

21st (Cheshire) Company
The Roman numerals *XXI* in brass below the Prince of Wales's plumes on a maroon patch.

10th Battalion
The Roman numeral *X* in brass below the Prince of Wales's plumes on a red-and-blue rosette (Fig. 1397).

47th Company, 13th Battalion
The letters *DCO* in script and intertwined. Below these the numerals *13*. In gilding-metal (Fig. 1398).

61st Company, 17th Battalion
A shamrock-leaf inscribed: (left) *61*, (top) *IY*, (right) *XVII*. In brass (Fig. 1399).

65th (Leicestershire) Company
The numerals *65* in brass on the general-service rosette.

74th (Dublin) Company
A shamrock-leaf above a scroll inscribed *74 Dublin IY*. In silver. Solid manufacture. Maker's name 'Batton and Wyeth, Kimberley' on reverse (Fig. 1400).

18th Battalion (Sharpshooters)
The letters *SS* surmounted by a Victorian crown in brass on a red-and-blue rosette (Fig. 1401).

20th Battalion (Rough Riders)
  (1) A large brass spur with rowel to the right entwined with the letters *RR*. Part of spur behind the first stroke of the letter. In die-struck solid gilding-metal (Fig. 1402).
  (2) Similar to above but part of the spur in front of the first stroke of the letter. In hollow gilding-metal, lead filled, with three wire-fasteners (Fig. 1403).

25th Battalion
The Prince of Wales's plumes, coronet and motto. Below this the numerals *25* and below this a scroll inscribed *Imperial Yeomanry*. In white-metal (Fig. 1404). Also found in silver.

29th Battalion (Irish Horse)
A triple shamrock-spray above the letters *IH*. In brass, also in silver (Fig. 1405).

31st Battalion (Fincastle's Horse)
On a five-pointed star a circlet inscribed *Fincastle's Horse* and, in the centre, the numerals *31*. The star in white-metal, remainder in gilding-metal (Fig. 1406).

1396

1397

1398

1399

1402

1403

1401

1404

1400

1406

1405

CHAPTER 25

Yeomanry Forage-Cap Badges: 1908 to 1922

In the reorganisation of 1908, during which the Volunteer units became the Territorial Force, Yeomanry regiments dropped the title 'Imperial' and their badges were altered accordingly.

At the same time The King's Colonials, The North of Ireland, and The South of Ireland Yeomanry regiments were transferred to Special Reserve Cavalry: a title changed later to Cavalry Militia when the Special Reserve was abolished.

The King's Colonials became King Edward's Horse (The King's Oversea Dominions Regiment) on 12th July 1910 and was disbanded on 31st March 1924.

The South of Ireland became the South Irish Horse and was disbanded on 31st July 1922.

The North of Ireland became the North Irish Horse and, although not recruited after the close of the Great War, they were re-activated in 1939.

In the designations of the regiments we have indicated whether these were dressed as Hussars, Dragoons or Lancers as this does not always appear in the official title.

The Prince of Wales's Own Royal Wiltshire Yeomanry (Hussars)
The Prince of Wales's plumes, coronet and motto. The coronet in gilding-metal, remainder in white-metal (Fig. 1407). Also in bronze.

The Warwickshire Yeomanry (Hussars)
The Bear and Ragged Staff. In gilding-metal (Fig. 1408). Also in bronze.

The Alexandra, Princess of Wales's Own Yorkshire Yeomanry (Hussars)
The White Rose of York surmounted by the Prince of Wales's plumes, coronet and motto. The coronet in gilding-metal, remainder in white-metal (Fig. 1409).
There are several variants in the rose and also in the size of the badge.

The Sherwood Rangers Yeomanry (Hussars)
  (1) A bugle-horn strung. In brass (Fig. 1410).
  (2) A bugle-horn strung. For officers: in gilt (Fig. 1411). Also in bronze.

The Queen's Own Royal Staffordshire Yeomanry (Hussars)
  (1) The Stafford Knot surmounted by a Victorian crown in gilding-metal (Fig. 1412). Also in blackened-brass.
  (2) The Stafford Knot surmounted by an Imperial crown. In gilding-metal (Fig. 1413).

(3) The Garter surmounted by an Imperial crown. In the centre the Stafford Knot. Below, a scroll inscribed *Pro aris et focis*. In white-metal (Fig. 1414). Officers: same design in bronze.

The Shropshire Yeomanry (Dragoons)

A circlet inscribed *Shropshire Yeomanry* surmounted by an Imperial crown. In the centre a shield on which three loggerheads (leopards' faces). Solid background. In gilding-metal (Fig. 1415).

The Earl of Carrick's Own Ayrshire Yeomanry (Hussars)

A lion's head and neck winged on a wreath. Below, a scroll inscribed *Earl of/Ayrshire Yeomanry/ Carrick's*. In gilding-metal (Fig. 1416). Also in bronze.

The Earl of Chester's Cheshire Yeomanry (Hussars)

(1) The Prince of Wales's plumes, coronet and motto. Below, a scroll inscribed *Earl of Chester's Y*. Coronet and scroll in gilding-metal, remainder in white-metal (Fig. 1417).
(2) Same design as above but only the scroll in gilding-metal, remainder in white-metal (Fig. 1418).
(3) The Prince of Wales's plumes, coronet and motto. Below, a scroll inscribed *Cheshire (Earl of Chester's) Yeomanry*. All in gilding-metal (Fig. 1419). Also in bronze.

The Queen's Own Yorkshire (Yeomanry) Dragoons

(1) The Yorkshire Rose surmounted by an Imperial crown. In brass (Fig. 1420). Also in blackened-brass.
(2) A circlet inscribed *Yorkshire Dragoons (Queen's Own)* and surmounted by an Imperial crown with the Yorkshire Rose in the centre. Below, a scroll inscribed *South Africa 1900–02*. In bronze for officers (Fig. 1421).

The Prince Albert's Own Leicestershire Yeomanry (Hussars)

(1) Within a laurel-wreath the letters *LY* surmounted by an Imperial crown. On the wreath, scrolls inscribed *South Africa, 1900, 1901–2*. Below, a scroll inscribed *Prince Albert's Own*. In white-metal (Fig. 1422). Also in gilding-metal.
(2) The crest of the Prince Consort with a scroll above inscribed *Leicestershire* and a scroll below inscribed *Prince Albert's Own Yeomanry*. In gilding-metal (Fig. 1423).
(3) The crest of the Prince Consort with a scroll above inscribed *Leicestershire* and a scroll below inscribed *Prince Albert's Own Yeo* and below this another scroll inscribed *South Africa 1900–02*. In gilding-metal (Fig. 1424).

The North Somerset Yeomanry (Dragoons)

(1) A ten-pointed star, the topmost point displaced by an Imperial crown. In the centre a circlet inscribed *Arma pacis fulcra*. Within the circlet the cypher of King Edward VII. In white-metal (Fig. 1425).
(2) As above but with the cypher of King George V. In bronze (Fig. 1426). Also in white-metal.
(3) As (2) but larger and with solid background to the cypher and with a scroll under the star inscribed *North Somerset Yeomanry*. In bronze (Fig. 1427).

1407

1408

1409

1410

1411

1412

1413

1414

1415

1416

1417

1418

1419

1420

1421

1422

1423

1424

1425

1426

The Duke of Lancaster's Own Yeomanry (Dragoons)

(1) A rose within a wreath, laurel on left, oak on right. On the wreath, scrolls inscribed *Duke of Lancaster's Own*, the whole ensigned with the Duke's coronet. In gilding-metal (Fig. 1428).

(2) A strap inscribed *Duke of Lancaster's Own* surmounted by the Duke's coronet. In the centre a rose within a laurel-wreath. In gilding-metal (Fig. 1429).

The Lanarkshire Yeomanry (Lancers)

A double-headed eagle grasping a bell in its right claw, the whole surmounted by an Imperial crown. Below, a scroll inscribed *Lanarkshire Yeomanry*. In gilding-metal (Fig. 1430).

The Northumberland (Yeomanry) Hussars

A circlet inscribed *Northumberland Hussars* surmounted by an Imperial crown. In the centre the Norman castle from the Arms of Newcastle-on-Tyne. Below the circlet a scroll inscribed *South Africa 1900–02*. In gilding-metal (Fig. 1431).

The South Nottinghamshire (Yeomanry) Hussars

A slip of oak with acorn. In brass or gilding-metal (Fig. 1432).

The Denbighshire Yeomanry (Hussars)

(1) The Prince of Wales's plumes, coronet and motto. In bronze (Fig. 1433). Also a brass economy pattern worn *c.* 1917.

(2) As above but with a scroll under inscribed *Denbighshire Hussars*. In bronze (officers' pattern). (Fig. 1434.) Also with silver plumes and motto scrolls and gilt coronet and title scroll.

The Westmorland and Cumberland Yeomanry (Hussars)

(1) An oval within a laurel-wreath inscribed *Westmorland & Cumberland Y* surmounted by an Imperial crown. In the centre three sprigs of heather. In gilding-metal (Fig. 1435). Also in bronze.

(2) A circlet inscribed *Westmorland & Cumberland Yeo* surmounted by an Imperial crown. In the centre three sprigs of heather. In bronze (Fig. 1436). Also in gilding-metal with heather-sprigs in white-metal.

The Pembrokeshire (Castlemartin) Yeomanry (Hussars)

The Prince of Wales's plumes, coronet and motto. Below, a scroll inscribed *Fishguard*. The coronet in gilding-metal, remainder in white-metal (Fig. 1437). Also all in white-metal, all in gilding-metal, and in bronze.

The Duke of Connaught's Own Royal East Kent Yeomanry (Mounted Rifles)

(1) The Garter surmounted by the Imperial crown. Within this the White Horse of Kent on a scroll inscribed *Invicta*. In bronze with red-cloth backing (Fig. 1438). Also in black-finish.

(2) Officers' pattern: The Garter, crown and Horse in silver, *Invicta* scroll in gilt (Fig. 1439).

The Hampshire Yeomanry (Carabiniers)

The Hampshire Rose within an oval inscribed *Hampshire Yeomanry* supported by crossed carbines and surmounted by an Imperial crown. Below, a scroll inscribed *Carabiniers*. In gilding-metal (Fig. 1440).

1427   1428   1429   1430

1431   1432   1433   1434

1435   1436   1437   1438

1439   1440   1441   1442

1443   1444   1445   1446

The Royal Buckinghamshire (Yeomanry) Hussars

A circlet inscribed *Yeomen of Bucks strike home*. Within the circlet a swan with a coronet round its neck. The circlet surmounted by an Imperial crown. Below, a scroll inscribed *Royal Bucks Hussars*. In gilding-metal (Fig. 1441). Also in bronze.

The Derbyshire Yeomanry (Dragoons)

(1) A rose within a laurel-wreath surmounted by an Imperial crown. On the wreath, scrolls inscribed *South Africa 1900–02*. Below, a scroll inscribed *Derbyshire Yeomanry* with a spray of laurel in the centre replacing the former word *Imperial*. In gilding-metal (Fig. 1442).

(2) Similar to above but smaller and with a different pattern-rose and with blank centre to scroll. In gilding-metal (Fig. 1443).

The Queen's Own Dorsetshire Yeomanry (Hussars)

(1) The monogram *QODY* with a separate Imperial crown. In white-metal (Fig. 1444).

(2) The Garter surmounted by an Imperial crown. Within the Garter *Q O Dorset Y*, the word *Dorset* being borne on a scroll, the whole within a laurel-wreath. On the wreath, scrolls inscribed *South Africa 1900 1901*. In bronze (Fig. 1445). Also in white-metal and in gilding-metal.

(3) As (2) but with the addition of a scroll at the base of the wreath inscribed *The Great War*. In white-metal (Fig. 1446). Also in bronze.

The Royal Gloucestershire (Yeomanry) Hussars

A portcullis with chains surmounted by a ducal coronet (the insignia of the Duke of Beaufort). Below, a scroll inscribed *Royal Gloucestershire Hussars*. In gilding-metal (Fig. 1447).

The Hertfordshire Yeomanry (Dragoons)

A Hart trippant on a ford (the County crest of Hertfordshire). In gilding-metal (Fig. 1448). Also in white-metal.

The Royal Berkshire (Hungerford) Yeomanry (Dragoons)

The White Horse of Berkshire above a scroll inscribed *Berkshire*. The Horse in white-metal, the scroll in gilding-metal (Fig. 1449). Also in bronze, and all in gilding-metal.

The Duke of Cambridge's Middlesex Yeomanry (Hussars)

(1) An eight-pointed star. On this a circlet inscribed *Pro aris et focis Middlesex Yeomanry*. In the centre the cypher of King Edward VII. In white-metal (Fig. 1450).

(2) As above but with the cypher of King George V (Fig. 1451). In white-metal.

(3) An eight-pointed star, the topmost point displaced by a crown. On this a circlet inscribed *Pro aris et focis M D C H*. In the centre the cypher of King George V. In bronze (Fig. 1452). Also in gilding-metal.

The Royal First Devonshire Yeomanry (Hussars)

The Royal Crest in bronze (Fig. 1453). Also in white-metal.

The Royal Devon Yeomanry

The Royal First Devonshire Yeomanry and the Royal North Devonshire Yeomanry were

1447   1448   1449   1450

1451   1452   1453   1454

1455   1456   1457   1458

1459   1460   1461   1462

1463   1464   1465   1466

amalgamated after the Great War and, in 1920, became the 96th (Royal Devon Yeomanry) Field Brigade, Royal Field Artillery.

A circlet inscribed *Royal Devon Yeomanry R F A* surmounted by the Royal Crest. In the centre the crest of Lord Rolle. In gilding-metal (Fig. 1454).

The Duke of York's Own Loyal Suffolk (Yeomanry) Hussars

A castle below which the date *1793* and a scroll inscribed *Loyal Suffolk Hussars*. The castle and date in gilding-metal, the scroll in white-metal (Fig. 1455). Also in bronze, and all in gilding-metal.

The Royal North Devonshire Yeomanry (Hussars)

(1) The monogram *NDH* surmounted by a crown. In bronze (Fig. 1456). Also in white-metal.

(2) A circlet inscribed *Royal North Devon Hussars* surmounted by an Imperial crown. In the centre the crest of Lord Rolle. In bronze (Fig. 1457).

The Queen's Own Worcestershire (Yeomanry) Hussars

Within a laurel-wreath surmounted by an Imperial crown a sprig of pear-blossom. Superimposed on the wreath a scroll inscribed *Queen's Own Worcestershire Hussars*. The pear-blossom in white-metal, remainder in gilding-metal (Fig. 1458). Also in bronze.

The Queen's Own West Kent Yeomanry (Hussars)

The White Horse of Kent on a scroll inscribed *Invicta*. In white-metal (Fig. 1459).

The West Somersetshire Yeomanry (Hussars)

An oval inscribed *West Somerset Yeomanry*. In the centre a Wyvern. Below, a scroll inscribed *S. Africa 1900–01*. In gilding-metal (Fig. 1460). Also in white-metal.

The Queen's Own Oxfordshire (Yeomanry) Hussars

(1) The cypher *AR* of Queen Adelaide surmounted by her crown. Below, a scroll inscribed *Queen's Own Oxfordshire Hussars*. In bronze (Fig. 1461). Also in white-metal, and in brass.

(2) As above but with different shaped crown. In white-metal (Fig. 1462).

(3) As above but with Imperial crown. In white-metal (Fig. 1463). Also in bronze.

(4) As (3) but smaller and in brass (Fig. 1464).

The Montgomeryshire Yeomanry (Dragoons)

The Welsh Dragon. Below, a scroll inscribed *MY*. In white-metal (Fig. 1465). Also in bronze.

The Lothians and Border (Yeomanry) Horse

(1) A Garb. Below, a scroll inscribed *Lothians and Border Horse Yeomanry*. In gilding-metal (Fig. 1466).

(2) A Garb only. In gilding-metal (Fig. 1467).

The Queen's Own Royal Glasgow Yeomanry (Dragoons)

(1) The Crest of Scotland over a wreath of thistles. A small size. In gilding-metal (Fig. 1470).

1467

1468

1469

1470

1471

1472

1473

1474

1475

1476

1477

1478

1479

1480

1481

1482

1483

1484

1485

1486

(2) A strap inscribed *Queen's Own Royal Glasgow Yeomanry* surmounted by the Royal Crest. In the centre the Crest of Scotland. In gilding-metal (Fig. 1468).

(3) A strap inscribed *Queen's Own Royal Glasgow Yeomanry* surmounted by the Royal Crest. In the centre the Scottish Lion crowned. In gilding-metal (Fig. 1469).

The Lancashire (Yeomanry) Hussars

(1) The Red Rose of Lancaster. Below, a scroll inscribed *Lancashire Hussars*. Note the space on the right where *IY* has been removed. In gilding-metal (Fig. 1471).

(2) As above but the title evenly spaced in the scroll. In gilding-metal (Fig. 1472).

The Queen Mary's Surrey Yeomanry (Lancers)

(1) The crest of Lord Middleton (a spear head emerging from a coronet). In gilding-metal. Same pattern as Imperial Yeomanry badge, see Fig. 1350.

(2) Within the Garter surmounted by an Imperial crown the cypher of Queen Mary. Below, a scroll inscribed *Queen Mary's Regiment of Surrey Yeomanry*. In gilding-metal (Fig. 1473).

The Fifeshire and Forfarshire Yeomanry (Dragoons)

(1) The County badge known as the Thane of Fife. In white-metal (Fig. 1474). Also in gilding-metal.

(2) A circular disc on which the Thane of Fife surrounded by a circlet inscribed *Fife & Forfar Yeomanry*. In gilding-metal (Fig. 1475).

The King's Own Royal Norfolk Yeomanry (Dragoons)

(1) The cypher of King Edward VII in gilding-metal (Fig. 1476). Also in white-metal.

(2) The cypher of King George V in gilding-metal (Fig. 1477).

The Sussex Yeomanry (Dragoons)

(1) On a shield six martlets, the whole on an ornamental ground surmounted by an Imperial crown. In gilding-metal (Fig. 1478).

(2) As above but with the addition of a scroll at the base of the design inscribed *Sussex Yeomanry*. In gilding-metal (Fig. 1479).

(3) As (2) but larger. In gilding-metal (Fig. 1480).

The Glamorganshire Yeomanry (Dragoons)

(1) The Prince of Wales's plumes and coronet, but the scrolls normally carrying the motto are left blank. Below, a scroll inscribed *Glamorgan Yeomanry* with a space between, where the former word *Imperial* was engraved. Coronet and scroll in gilding-metal, remainder in white-metal (Fig. 1481).

(2) As above but with the blank centre of the scroll now engraved with two circles and a diamond. Same metals as above.

The Welsh (Yeomanry) Horse (Lancers)

A leek with the letters *W* on the left and *H* on the right. In bronze (Fig. 1482). Also in brass.

The Lincolnshire Yeomanry (Lancers)

Within a laurel-wreath the Arms of the City of Lincoln surmounted by an Imperial crown. On the wreath a scroll inscribed *Lincolnshire Yeomanry*. In gilding-metal (Fig. 1483). Also in bronze.

1487

1488

1489

1490

1491

1492

1493

1494

1495

1496

1497

1498

1499

1500

1501

1502

1503

1504

1505

The City of London Yeomanry (The Roughriders) (Lancers)
Within a laurel-wreath a circlet inscribed *The City of London Yeomanry* and surmounted by an Imperial crown. In the centre the Arms of the City of London. Below the circlet, two scrolls: the top inscribed *Rough Riders* and the bottom, *South Africa 1900–02.* The Arms in white-metal, remainder in gilding-metal (Fig. 1484).

The Westminster (Yeomanry) Dragoons
The Arms of the City of Westminster. Below, a scroll inscribed *Westminster Dragoons TY.* In gilding-metal (Fig. 1485).

The 3rd County of London Yeomanry (The Sharpshooters) (Hussars)
(1) A circlet inscribed *County of London Yeomanry* and surmounted by an Imperial crown. In the centre the numeral *3*, the whole superimposed on crossed rifles. Below, a scroll inscribed *South Africa 1900–02.* In gilding-metal (Fig. 1486).
(2) A circlet inscribed *London Armoured Car Company* and surmounted by an Imperial crown. In the centre the Roman numerals *XXIII*, the whole superimposed on crossed rifles. Below, a scroll inscribed *Sharpshooters.* The numerals in white-metal, remainder in gilding-metal (Fig. 1487).

The Bedfordshire Yeomanry (Lancers)
(1) An eagle, on which is superimposed a castle, surmounted by a coronet. In gilding-metal (Fig. 1488).
(2) As above but with the castle in white-metal and the eagle in gilding-metal (Fig. 1489).

The Essex Yeomanry (Dragoons)
(1) A circlet inscribed *Audacter et sincere* surmounted by an Imperial crown. In the centre a shield bearing the Essex County Arms. Worn from 1905 to 1909. In gilding-metal (Fig. 1490). Also in bronze.
(2) As above but the motto changed to *Decus et tutamen.* Worn from 1909 to 1916. In gilding-metal (Fig. 1491). Also in bronze.
(3) A circlet inscribed *Essex Yeomanry* surmounted by a flat-topped crown. In the centre the Essex County Arms. Below, a scroll inscribed *Decus et tutamen.* In gilding-metal (Fig. 1492).
(4) As (3) but with Imperial crown. Approved 18th April 1916. In gilding-metal (Fig. 1493).

The Northamptonshire Yeomanry (Dragoons)
The White Horse of Hanover. In silver-plate for officers (Fig. 1494). In white-metal for other-ranks.

The East Riding Yeomanry (Lancers)
(1) A fox in full cry. In gilding-metal (Fig. 1495). Also in white-metal.
(2) A fox in full cry. Below, a scroll inscribed *Forrard.* The fox in gilding-metal, the scroll in white-metal (Fig. 1496). Also in bronze, and all in gilding-metal.

The Lovat (Yeomanry) Scouts
(1) A circlet inscribed *Lovat Scouts Y.* In the centre a stag's head, the antlers extending into the circlet. In gilding-metal (Fig. 1497).
(2) As above but with the antlers inside the circlet. In gilding-metal (Fig. 1498).

(3) As (1) but larger. In gilding-metal (Fig. 1499).

(4) A circlet inscribed *Lovat's Scouts*. In the centre a stag's head. In white-metal (Fig. 1500).

The Scottish (Yeomanry) Horse

(1) An oval inscribed *Scottish Horse 1900* with scrolls below inscribed *South Africa 1900, 1901, 1902*. A wreath of juniper and bay encloses the oval. St. Andrew's Cross is superimposed on the oval which is ensigned with a Scottish crown. In gilding-metal (Fig. 1501). Also in white-metal.

(2) As above but with Imperial crown. In white-metal (Fig. 1502). Also in gilding-metal.

SPECIAL RESERVE (CAVALRY) (LATER CAVALRY MILITIA)

North Irish Horse

(1) The Irish Harp surmounted by an Imperial crown. Below, a scroll inscribed *North Irish Horse*. In gilding-metal (Fig. 1503). Also with the harp-strings voided.

(2) A circlet inscribed *North Irish Horse*, with a wreath of shamrocks at the base, surmounted by an Imperial crown. In the centre the Irish Harp. In white-metal (Fig. 1504).

South Irish Horse

A veined shamrock-leaf. On this the letters *SIH*. In gilding-metal (Fig. 1505).

King Edward's Horse (The King's Overseas Dominions Regiment)

(1) Within a wreath of laurel (left) and oak (right), a shield bearing the Royal Arms of England. Above this a three-part scroll inscribed *King Edward's Horse* surmounted by the Royal Crest. On the wreath, two scrolls each side: (left) *Canada, N. Zealand*; (right) *Australia, S. Africa*. Below the shield a scroll inscribed *India* and, below this, a further scroll inscribed *KODR*. At the base, below the wreath, a tri-part scroll inscribed *Regi adsumas coloni*. In yellow-brass (Fig. 1506).

(2) As above but with the Imperial crown in the Royal Crest. In gilding-metal (Fig. 1507).

(3) As (2) but with incorrect spelling of the motto *Regi ausumas coloni*. In gilding-metal (Fig. 1508).

(4) Officers' service-dress: A circlet inscribed *Regi adsumas coloni* surmounted by an Imperial crown. In the centre, the monogram *KEH*. In bronze (Fig. 1509).

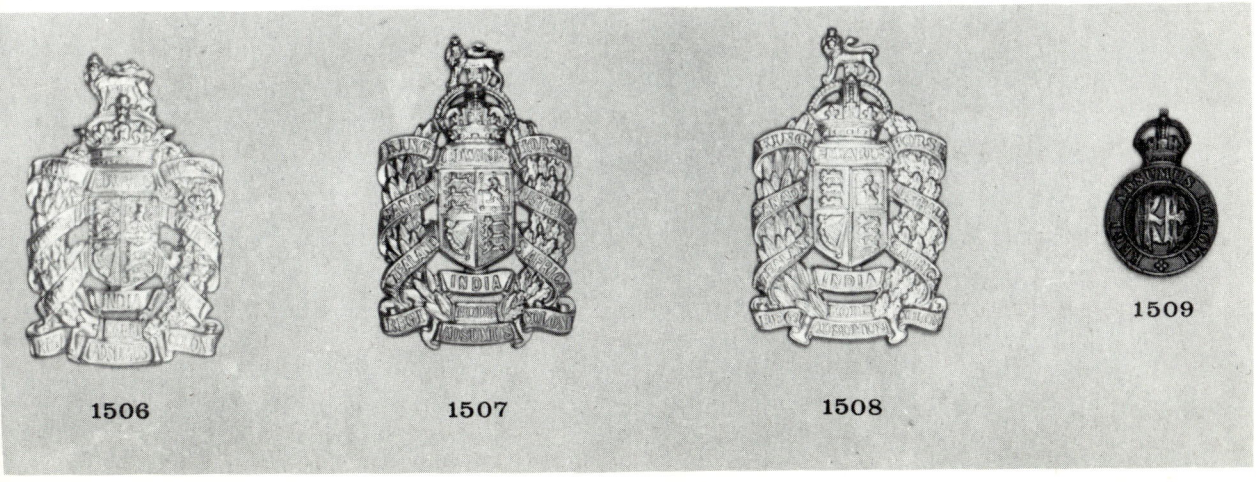

1506   1507   1508   1509

1510   1513   1515

YEOMANRY FULL-DRESS HEAD-DRESSES

In general, regiments classified as Dragoons wore a helmet similar to the regular pattern of the period; and Lancer regiments, the lance-cap. Regiments which became Hussars before they adopted the busby mostly wore the shako with the Maltese cross pattern badge similar to that of the Light Dragoons.

There were exceptions, of course, and possibly the most remarkable was the Lanarkshire Yeomanry who from 1884 to 1903 wore an infantry-pattern cloth helmet with spike, although dressed as Lancers.

Some of the badges worn in full-dress at different periods are described below:

The Royal Wiltshire Yeomanry

Officers' shako: c. 1848

A Maltese cross surmounted by a Victorian crown. On this a circlet inscribed *Prince of Wales's Own Royal Regiment.* In the centre the Prince of Wales's plumes and coronet. In silver-plate (Fig. 1510).

The Warwickshire Yeomanry

Officers' shako: 1857 to 1869

An eight-pointed star on which a strap inscribed *Warwickshire* with, in the centre, the Royal Cypher *VR.* Above the star, and separate, a Victorian crown.

1st West York Yeomanry Cavalry (later The Yorkshire Dragoons)

Helmet: 1876 to 1898

Within a laurel-wreath, surmounted by a Victorian crown, a star on which a strap inscribed *1st West Yorkshire* with, in the centre, the white Rose of York. On the left of the strap a scroll inscribed *Yeomanry* and, on the right, a similar scroll inscribed *Cavalry.*

1516

1514

1512

1511

1519

The Yorkshire Dragoons

Helmet: 1900

Within a laurel-wreath surmounted by a Victorian crown, a star on which the Garter with, in the centre, the White Rose of York. On the left of the strap a scroll inscribed *Yorkshire* and on the right, a similar scroll inscribed *Dragoons*. In white-metal (Fig. 1511).

The Staffordshire Yeomanry (Queen's Own Royal Regiment)

Helmet: 1850 to 1893

Within a wreath of laurel (left) and oak (right) an ornamental shield surmounted by a Victorian crown. On the shield a beaded star and on this a pierced strap inscribed *The Queen's Own Royal Yeomanry* with the Stafford Knot in the centre. The star and background to the Knot in silver, remainder in gilt (Fig. 1512).

The North Somerset Yeomanry

Helmet: 1847 to 1871

Within a wreath of laurel (left) and oak (right) an ornamental shield surmounted by a Victorian crown. On the shield a star and on this a strap inscribed *The North Somerset* with, in the centre, the Royal Cypher *VR*.

The helmet worn in 1902 was similar but with the Imperial crown and the cypher of King Edward VII in the centre.

The Duke of Lancaster's Own Yeomanry

Helmet: 1865 to 1870

Within a wreath of laurel (left) and oak (right) an ornamental shield surmounted by a Victorian crown. On the shield the Arms of the County Palatine of Lancaster (three lions in pale).

The Lanarkshire Yeomanry

Helmet: 1884 to 1903

An eight-pointed star. On this a strap inscribed *Lanark Yoemanry* with, in the centre, a double-headed eagle grasping a bell in its right claw and surmounted by a crown. (From the Seal of the Royal Burgh of Lanark.)

The Hampshire Yeomanry

Helmet: 1895

On an eight-pointed star a strap inscribed *Hampshire Yeomanry* and surmounted by a Victorian crown. In the centre the Hampshire Rose.

The Hertfordshire Yeomanry

Helmet: 1894

On an ornamental shield surmounted by a Victorian crown a hart trippant. In gilt or gilding-metal (Fig. 1513).

The Royal Berkshire Yeomanry

Helmet: 1897
On an eight-pointed star a strap inscribed *Royal Berks Yeomanry Cavalry*. In the centre the star and crescent from the Seal of the Borough of Hungerford in Berkshire.
Hungerford Troop, c. 1836. On an ornamental shield surmounted by a crown, a star. On this a strap inscribed *Hungerford Troop R.B.Y.C.* In the centre the star and crescent (Fig. 1513A).

The Royal First Devon Yeomanry

Helmet: 1852
Within a wreath of laurel (left) and oak (right) the Garter enclosing the Royal Cypher *VR*. Below the Garter, among palm-sprays, three scrolls inscribed *Royal 1st Devon, Yeomanry Cavalry*. Silver background to the cypher, remainder in gilt (Fig. 1514).

The East Devon Yeomanry (disbanded 1838)
A plate with two bands of ornamental scrolls at the base and a continuous band on the edge of the plate inscribed *East Devon Volunteer Cavalry*. In the centre a Victorian crown.

The Suffolk Yeomanry

Helmet: 1883
Within a wreath of laurel (left) and oak (right) an ornamental shield surmounted by a Victorian crown. On the shield an eight-pointed star and on this a strap inscribed *Suffolk Yeomanry Cavalry* with the Royal Cypher *VR* in the centre.

The Montgomeryshire Yeomanry

1513A

Helmet: 1860
The Welsh Dragon within a strap inscribed *Anorchfygol* and surrounded by a three-part scroll inscribed *Montgomeryshire Yeomanry Cavalry*. All on a rayed-plate in white-metal.

Helmet: 1882
On an eight-pointed star a strap inscribed *Montgomeryshire Yeomanry Cavalry* and within this the Welsh Dragon. In white-metal (Fig. 1515).

The East Lothian Yeomanry (1908: The Lothians and Border Horse)

Helmet: 1860
The Garter, enclosing the Order of the Thistle, surmounted by a Victorian crown and within a thistle-wreath. Below the Garter, among thistle-sprays, four scrolls inscribed *East, Lothian, Yeomanry, Cavalry*. In gilding-metal (Fig. 1516).

The Lothians and Berwickshire Yeomanry

Helmet: 1897 to 1900

Within a wreath of thistles the Garter surmounted by a Victorian crown. Within the Garter, the Star of the Order of the Thistle with the Royal Cypher *VR* in the centre. Below the wreath, among sprays of thistles, four scrolls inscribed *Lothians and*, *Berwickshire*, *Yeomanry*, *Cavalry* (Fig. 1517). All in brass.

Fife Mounted Rifles (1908: The Fife and Forfar Yeomanry)

Helmet: 1864 to 1895

A star of four points with the Roman numerals *IX* on the lowest point. On this a cross with, superimposed, the Thane of Fife. Below the star a scroll inscribed *Pro aris et focis* broken in the centre by the monogram *FMR*.

The Royal Glasgow Yeomanry

Helmet: 1860

Within a wreath of thistles an ornamental shield surmounted by a Victorian crown. On the shield the Star of the Order of the Thistle with, in the centre, a lion rampant.

The Surrey Yeomanry

Shako: 1831

A beaded cross with plain edges. In the centre a laurel wreath surrounding the letter *S* in old English characters.

The Royal Norfolk Yeomanry

Officers' helmet: 1911 to 1914

Within a laurel wreath an eight-pointed star. On this the cypher of King George v surmounted by an Imperial crown. On the base of the wreath a scroll inscribed *King's Own Norfolk Impl. Yeomy*. Star and wreath in gilt, remainder in silver (Fig. 1518).

1517

1518

Fife Light Horse (1908: The Fife and Forfar Yeomanry)

Helmet: 1896 to 1900

A four-pointed beaded star surmounted by a Victorian crown. On the star a cross with, superimposed, the Thane of Fife. Below the star a scroll inscribed *Pro aris et focis* broken in the centre by the letters *FLH*.

The Sussex Yeomanry

Helmet: 1914

An eight-pointed star. On this a circlet inscribed *Sussex Yeomanry*. In the centre, on an ornamental background, a shield bearing six martlets. The shield surmounted by an Imperial crown.

The City of London Yeomanry (Rough Riders)

Lance-cap: 1907

On the standard pattern rayed-plate a wreath of oak with a scroll on the left inscribed *South Africa* and one on the right inscribed *1900–02*. Within this the Arms, crest, supporters and motto of the City of London with a scroll above inscribed *Rough Riders* surmounted by an Imperial crown. On the base of the plate a scroll inscribed *The City of London Imperial Yeomanry*. Officers: Crown, wreath and Arms silver-plated, remainder gilt. Other-ranks: all gilding-metal.

The Westminster Dragoons

Helmet: 1902

An eight-pointed star. On this the Garter surmounted by an Imperial crown with, in the centre, the numeral *2*. On the left of the Garter a scroll inscribed *2nd County*, on the right, *of London* and below, the letters *IY*. The star, numeral and letters *IY* in gilt, remainder in white metal (Fig. 1519).

The West Essex Yeomanry (disbanded 1877)

Helmet: 1854

Within a laurel-wreath an ornamental shield surmounted by a Victorian crown. On the shield a strap inscribed *Essex Cavalry* with, in the centre, three seaxes. Across the base of the wreath a scroll inscribed *Decus et tutamen*.

The Northamptonshire Yeomanry

Helmet: 1907

On an eight-pointed star a strap inscribed *Northamptonshire Imperial Yeomanry*. In the centre the White Horse of Hanover with, below, a spray of rose, thistle and shamrock.

The East Riding of Yorkshire Yeomanry

Lance-cap: 1907

On the standard-pattern rayed-plate a fox in full cry surmounted by the cypher of King Edward VII and above this an Imperial crown. A wreath of laurel (left) and palm (right) and on the base of the wreath a scroll inscribed *East Riding of Yorkshire Imperial Yeomanry* with, below *Yorkshire*, the White Rose of York.

CHAPTER 26

The Volunteers

The attempt on the life of Napoleon III by Orsini was followed by articles in the French press denouncing England as the shelterer of assassins and the general attitude was so hostile that fears were entertained of a possible outbreak of war. The nation awoke to the gravity of the situation and numerous Volunteer Corps were formed under the jurisdiction of the Lords-Lieutenant of Counties pending official sanction.

This came on May 12th 1859 by the issue of a War Office Circular, addressed by General Peel to the Lords-Lieutenant, authorising the raising of Volunteer Corps under the Act passed in 1804. The chief, essential, condition laid down by the circular was that the Volunteer Corps should bear the entire expense of their equipment and maintenance, except in the event of assembly for active service.

A supplementary circular was issued on May 25th which gave more detailed instructions as regards the organisation of companies and the institution of a system of drill and training. A third letter followed on the 13th July.

With official authority to provide their own uniforms a large variety of dress came into being. Head-dress varied from low-crowned peaked-caps to shakos with plumes or tufts, as well as glengarries, and helmets with plumes or spikes.

As Rifle Corps, pouch-belts were widely worn and, in some instances, the badge was worn on the pouch-belt and not on the head-dress. This explains why some units do not appear to have a cap-badge.

Badges, too, often incorporated the bugle-horn which is associated with all Rifle Corps and the simplest form of badge was just the bugle-horn, with or without the crown, and with a number in the curl.

The number can be confusing for sometimes it was the precedence number of the County and, sometimes, the precedence number alloted by the County to the Corps. Gloucestershire is an interesting example. The County precedence number was 20 and that appears on the badges of several of the Gloucestershire Rifle Volunteer Corps, but the Corps numbered only sixteen in all.

The badges can be grouped into periods: the early individual Corps badges followed by those when the Corps were grouped into Administrative Battalions; the introduction of the Cardwell system in 1881, when the various Rifle Corps became Volunteer battalions of the Regular infantry; and, finally, the period following the death of Queen Victoria when the Victorian crown gave way to the Imperial crown until 1908, when the Territorial Force was formed. As a guide to dating badges which incorporate the unit's title, it should be noted that Rifle Volunteer Corps were redesignated Volunteer Rifle Corps in December 1891.

Changes in designation due to reorganisation are reflected in the titles displayed on many badges but it would not be possible within the scope of this work to give a comprehensive list of all Volunteer Corps which existed in the Country. To aid collectors who wish to place Volunteer badges with their parent unit, we have, in those badges illustrated and described, given the designation of the regiment of which they subsequently became Volunteer battalions. Incidentally the movement was confined to England, Scotland and Wales: it did not include Ireland.

When the Territorial Force was formed in 1908, four regiments were not affiliated to Regular army units and these have been dealt with in a separate chapter, where we show their lineage from 1859 to 1922.

The examples illustrated and the descriptions which follow are but a few of the enormous number in existence and have been selected chiefly to show the variety in design. Officers', as well as other-ranks', are depicted as the former were often far more elaborate in concept.

Only Rifle Volunteer Corps are dealt with here: those of the Royal Artillery, Royal Engineers and the Departmental Corps are shown in their respective chapters.

Besides the Volunteer Rifle Corps there were also raised at this time several Light Horse and Mounted Rifle Volunteer Corps. Most of these were short-lived, only the Fife Light Horse surviving to become the Fife and Forfar Imperial Yeomanry in 1901. Details of the uniform of many of these units are unknown but some were dressed as Hussars and did not wear head-dress badges. Of the few badges that are in existence, it is uncertain whether these were worn on the head-dress, on the pouch, or on the pouch-belt. Details of some known to have been worn in the head-dress are recorded at the end of this chapter.

36th West Yorkshire Rifle Volunteer Corps (Rotherham)
1883: 2nd Volunteer Battalion, The York and Lancaster Regiment.

Shako-badge: 1860
A bugle-horn surmounted by a Victorian crown with the numerals *36* in the curl. In black-metal (Fig. 1520).

1st Middlesex (Victoria) Rifle Volunteer Corps
1908: 9th (County of London) Battalion, The London Regiment (Queen Victoria's).

Officers' shako-plate: 1859
A bronze eight-pointed star. On this in silver St. George killing the Dragon within a laurel-wreath surmounted by a Victorian crown (Fig. 1521).

29th Middlesex (North Middlesex) Rifle Volunteer Corps
1891: 17th Middlesex (North Middlesex) Volunteer Rifle Corps. 1908: 19th (County of London) Battalion, The London Regiment (St. Pancras).

Shako-badge: 1860
A bugle-horn with a solid centre and the numerals *29* in the curl. In bronze (Fig. 1522).

37th Middlesex (St. Giles and St. Georges, Bloomsbury) Rifle Volunteer Corps
1880: 19th Middlesex Rifle Volunteer Corps.
1908: Amalgamated with 1st Middlesex Volunteer Rifle Corps.

Officers' shako-plate: 1860
A strap inscribed *Middlesex Bloomsbury Rifle Volunteers* surmounted by a Victorian crown. In the centre the numerals *37*. In silver (Fig. 1523).

20th Middlesex (Euston Square) Rifle Volunteer Corps
1890: 3rd Volunteer Battalion, The Royal Fusiliers.
1908: 3rd (City of London) Battalion (The Royal Fusiliers), The London Regiment.

Shako-plate: 1860
A plain strap surmounted by a Victorian crown. In the centre the numerals *20*. In silver (Fig. 1524).

7th Lanarkshire Rifle Volunteer Corps
1873: Amalgamated with 31st Lanarkshire Rifle Volunteer Corps.
1887: 3rd (The Blythewood) Volunteer Battalion, The Highland Light Infantry.

Shako-badge: 1863 to 1873
Below a bugle with strings the numeral *7* and a large capital *L* and a small capital *K*. In white-metal (Fig. 1525).

41st Middlesex (Enfield Lock) Rifle Volunteer Corps
Part of 6th Administrative Battalion. Amalgamated 1862 with 2nd Administrative Battalion.
1891: 3rd Middlesex Rifle Volunteer Corps.
1908: 7th Battalion, The Middlesex Regiment.

Shako-badge: 1860
A strap inscribed *Bello parati pacem volentis* surmounted by a Victorian crown. In the centre a shield bearing the monogram *RSAF* (Royal Small Arms Factory); beneath this three rifles with, below, three bayonets. Beneath the strap a scroll inscribed *41st Middlesex*. In white-metal (Fig. 1526).

6th Carmarthenshire Rifle Volunteer Corps
1908: 4th Volunteer Battalion, The Welsh Regiment.

Shako-badge: c. 1865
The numeral *6* surmounted by the Prince of Wales's plumes, coronet and motto. Below the numeral a scroll inscribed *Carmarthenshire*. In bronze (Fig. 1527).

1st Wiltshire Rifle Volunteer Corps
1891: 1st Wiltshire Volunteer Rifle Corps.
1908: 4th Volunteer Battalion, The Wiltshire Regiment.

Shako-badge: 1860
A bugle-horn surmounted by a Victorian crown. The numeral *1* within the strings. In blackened-brass (Fig. 1528).

2nd Lancashire Rifle Volunteer Corps (Blackburn)
1889: 1st Volunteer Battalion, The East Lancashire Regiment.

Shako-badge: 1860
A bugle-horn with strings. The numeral *2* within the strings. In white-metal (Fig. 1529).

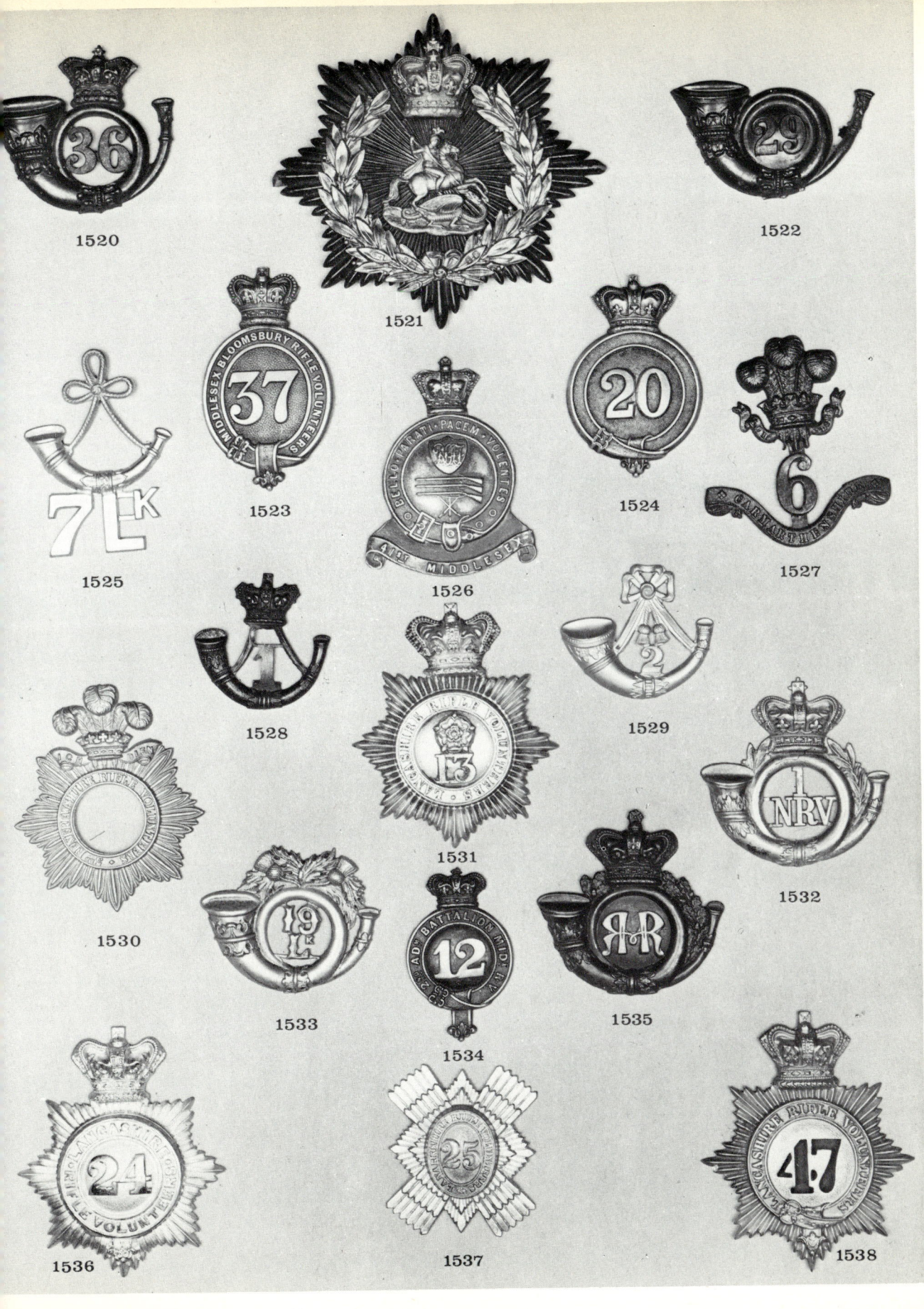

1520

1521

1522

1525

1523

1526

1524

1527

1528

1531

1529

1530

1532

1533

1534

1535

1536

1537

1538

3rd Renfrewshire Rifle Volunteers (Paisley)
1887: 2nd (Renfrewshire) Volunteer Battalion, The Argyll and Sutherland Highlanders.

Shako-badge: 1862 to 1880
An eight-pointed star, the topmost point displaced by the Prince of Wales's plumes, coronet and motto. On the star a circlet inscribed *3rd Renfrewshire Rifle Volunteers*. In the voided centre was worn a piece of tartan cloth in the form of a St. Andrew's Cross. In white-metal (Fig. 1530).

13th Lancashire Rifle Volunteer Corps. (Southport)
1888: 3rd Volunteer Battalion, The King's (Liverpool Regiment). Disbanded in 1908.

Officers' shako-plate: 1878
An eight-pointed star, the topmost point displaced by a Victorian crown. On this a circlet inscribed *Lancashire Rifle Volunteers* with, in the centre, the numerals *13* surmounted by a Rose. In silver (Fig. 1531).

1st Northamptonshire Rifle Volunteer Corps
1887: 1st Volunteer Battalion, The Northamptonshire Regiment.

Shako-badge: c. 1860
A bugle-horn surmounted by a Victorian crown with sprays of laurel joining the bugle to the crown. In the curl of the bugle the numeral *1* with the letters *NRV* below. In white-metal (Fig. 1532).

19th Lanarkshire (Glasgow, 2nd Northern) Rifle Volunteer Corps
1887: 1st Volunteer Battalion, The Highland Light Infantry.

Shako-badge: 1860
A bugle-horn surmounted by a thistle spray. In the curl of the bugle the numerals *19* above a large capital *L* and a small capital *K*. In white-metal (Fig. 1533).

12th Middlesex (Barnet) Rifle Volunteer Corps
Part of 6th Administrative Battalion which was amalgamated with the 2nd Administrative Battalion in 1862.
1891: 3rd Middlesex Volunteer Rifle Corps.
1908: 7th Battalion, The Middlesex Regiment.

Shako-badge: 1863
A strap inscribed *2nd Adm Battalion Midx R.V.* surmounted by a Victorian crown. In the centre the numerals *12*. In blackened brass with the numerals in white-metal (Fig. 1534).

1st Nottinghamshire (Robin Hood) Rifle Volunteer Corps
1909: 7th (Robin Hood) Battalion, The Sherwood Foresters.

Shako-badge: c. 1860
A bugle-horn surmounted by a Victorian crown with sprays of oak joining the bugle to the crown. In the curl of the bugle the monogram *RH* entwined and reversed. In blackened-brass with the monogram in white-metal (Fig. 1535).

24th Lancashire (Rochdale) Rifle Volunteer Corps
Re-numbered 12th in 1880.
1883: 2nd Volunteer Battalion, The Lancashire Fusiliers.

Officers' shako-plate: 1864

An eight-pointed star, the topmost point displaced by a Victorian crown. On this a circlet inscribed *Lancashire Rifle Volunteers* with, in the centre, the numerals *24*. In silver (Fig. 1536).

25th Lanarkshire (Glasgow) Rifle Volunteer Corps
1887: 2nd Volunteer Battalion, The Highland Light Infantry.

Shako-badge: 1873

The Star of the Order of the Thistle. On this an oval inscribed *Lanarkshire Rifle Volunteers* with, in the centre, the numerals *25*. In silver (Fig. 1537).

47th Lancashire (St. Helens) Rifle Volunteer Corps
1886: 2nd Volunteer Battalion, The Prince of Wales's Volunteers (South Lancashire Regiment).

Other-ranks' shako-plate: 1864

An eight-pointed star, the topmost point displaced by a Victorian crown. On this a strap inscribed *Lancashire Rifle Volunteers* In the centre in cut-out form the numerals *47* with a red-cloth backing. In white-metal (Fig. 1538).

2nd Company, 21st (Aboyne) Aberdeen Highland Rifle Volunteers
1884: 4th Volunteer Battalion, The Gordon Highlanders.

Glengarry: 1872 to 1884

A strap with rope edging inscribed *Defence not Defiance* with a thistle and leaves either side of the buckle. In the centre a demi-lion holding a sword in its right paw and on a wreathed scroll. Below this is inscribed *2nd 21st AHRV*. In brass (Fig. 1539).

12th Gloucestershire (Forest of Dean) Rifle Volunteer Corps
1883: 2nd Volunteer Battalion, The Gloucestershire Regiment.

Shako-plate: c. 1870

An eight-pointed star, the topmost point displaced by a Victorian crown. On this a laurel wreath and within this a bugle with strings. Below the bugle the numerals *20*. In bronze (Fig. 1540).

1st Administrative Battalion (14th Birnam) Perthshire Rifle Volunteer Corps
1887: 4th (Perthshire) Volunteer Battalion, The Black Watch.

Glengarry: 1860

A strap inscribed *Birnam Rifle Volunteers* surmounted by a Victorian crown. In the centre an oak-tree on a wreathed scroll. In pewter (Fig. 1541).
This is one of the very few pewter badges ever worn.

40th Lancashire (3rd Manchester) Rifle Volunteer Corps
1888: 4th Volunteer Battalion, The Manchester Regiment.

Shako-plate: 1861
An eight-pointed star, the topmost point displaced by a Victorian crown. On this a circlet inscribed *3rd Manchester RV. Defence not Defiance*. In the centre a bugle with strings. In blackened-brass (Fig. 1542).

78th Lancashire (Manchester) Rifle Volunteer Corps
Absorbed in 1862 by 33rd Lancashire (2nd Manchester) Rifle Volunteer Corps.
1888: 5th (Ardwick) Volunteer Battalion, The Manchester Regiment.

Plume-holder: 1865
An eight-pointed star, the topmost point displaced by a thistle with two leaves. The centre raised to resemble the ball of a grenade and on this the Arms, Crest, Supporters and Motto of the City of Manchester with a scroll above inscribed *Nemo me impune lacessit*. On the lowest point of the star the numerals *78*. In white-metal (Fig. 1543).

22nd Lancashire (Liverpool) Rifle Volunteer Corps
Absorbed by 1st Lancashire Rifle Volunteer Corps in 1863.
1880: 1st Volunteer Battalion, The King's (Liverpool Regiment).
1908: 5th Battalion, The King's (Liverpool Regiment).

Shako-plate: 1861
An eight-pointed star, the topmost point displaced by a Victorian crown. On this a strap inscribed *Lancashire Volunteer Rifles* with the numerals *22* in the centre. In bronze (Fig. 1544).

5th Northumberland (Alnwick) Rifle Volunteer Corps
1883: 1st Volunteer Battalion, The Northumberland Fusiliers.

Shako-plate: c. 1865
Within a laurel-wreath a circlet inscribed *5th Northumberland Rifle Volunteers* surmounted by a Victorian crown. In the centre a bugle with strings. In bronze (Fig. 1545).

1st Administrative Battalion, East Yorkshire (Beverley) Rifle Volunteer Corps
1883: 2nd Volunteer Battalion, The East Yorkshire Regiment.

Officers' shako-plate: c. 1865
An eight-pointed star, the topmost point displaced by a Victorian crown. On this a strap inscribed *1st Ad Batt. E. York R.V.* In the centre a Rose. In gilt with the ground to the centre burnished (Fig. 1546).

1st Battalion, Glamorgan Rifle Volunteers
1908: 7th (Cyclist) Battalion, The Welsh Regiment.

Shako-plate: 1880
A laurel-wreath surmounted by the Prince of Wales's plumes, coronet and motto. Within the wreath a strap inscribed *1st Battn Glamorgan Rifle Volunteers*. In the centre the numeral *7*. In bronze (Fig. 1547).

1539

1540

1541

1542

1543

1544

1545

1546

1547

1548

1549

1550

15th Lancashire (Liverpool) Rifle Volunteer Corps
1888: 4th Volunteer Battalion, The King's (Liverpool Regiment).

Other-ranks' shako-plate: 1869 to 1878
A laurel-wreath surmounted by a Victorian crown. Within the wreath a strap inscribed *Lancashire Rifle Volunteers* with the numerals *15* in the centre. In white-metal (Fig. 1548).

27th Lancashire (Bolton) Rifle Volunteer Corps
1883: 2nd Volunteer Battalion, The Loyal North Lancashire Regiment.

Other-ranks' shako-plate: 1869 to 1878
A laurel-wreath surmounted by a Victorian crown. Within the wreath a strap inscribed *27th Lancashire* with, in the centre, three lions in pale. In white-metal (Fig. 1549).

21st Durham (Barnards Castle) Rifle Volunteer Corps
1887: 2nd Volunteer Battalion, The Durham Light Infantry.

Shako-plate: c. 1865 to 1878
A laurel-wreath surmounted by a Victorian crown. Within the wreath a strap inscribed *4th AB Durham RVC*. In the centre a bugle with strings with the numerals *21* within the strings. On the bottom-join of the wreath a scroll inscribed *North York*. In white-metal (Fig. 1550).

48th Lancashire (Prescott) Rifle Volunteer Corps
Renumbered 21st in 1880.
1886: 2nd Volunteer Battalion, The Prince of Wales's Volunteers (South Lancashire Regiment).

Officers' helmet-plate: 1878 to 1880
A Maltese cross with a lion between each division of the cross surmounted by a Victorian crown. On this a circlet inscribed *Lancashire Rifle Volunteers* with, in the centre, a strung bugle with the numerals *48* within the strings. In blackened gilding-metal with the high-points polished (Fig. 1551).

5th Lancashire Rifle Volunteer Corps (Liverpool Rifle Volunt ⁓ Brigade)
1888: 2nd Volunteer Battalion, The King's (Liverpool Regiment).

Officers' helmet-plate: 1870 to 1902
A Maltese cross with a lion between each division of the cross. On this a circlet inscribed *Liverpool Rifle Volunteer Brigade*. In the centre on a red-cloth ground the Liver bird standing on a wreathed scroll. Above the cross a scroll inscribed *Fifth* which is surmounted by a Victorian crown. Below the cross a scroll inscribed *Lancashire*. In blackened white-metal with the high-points polished (Fig. 1552).

1st Gloucestershire (City of Bristol) Rifle Volunteer Corps
1883: 1st (City of Bristol) Volunteer Battalion, The Gloucestershire Regiment.

Officers' helmet-plate: 1880 to 1902
A Maltese cross, with a lion between each division of the cross, surmounted by a Victorian crown. On this a circlet inscribed *1 Glos. City of Bristol RV* at the top of the circlet, and a scroll inscribed *In danger ready* on the bottom part of the circlet. In the centre the Arms of the

1551

1552

1553

1554

1555

1556

1557

1558

1559

1560

1561

City of Bristol surmounted by crossed rifles. In blackened white-metal with the high-points polished (Fig. 1553).

1st North Riding of Yorkshire Rifle Volunteer Corps
1883: 2nd Volunteer Battalion, The Princess of Wales's Own (Yorkshire Regiment).

Other-ranks' glengarry: c. 1870
A Maltese cross with a ball on each corner and a lion between each division. On this a strap inscribed *1st North Riding Rifle Volunteers* and in the centre a Rose. Above the cross a tablet inscribed *Yorkshire* surmounted by a Victorian crown. In white-metal (Fig. 1554).

6th Lancashire (1st Manchester) Rifle Volunteer Corps
1888: 2nd Volunteer Battalion, The Manchester Regiment.

Officers' helmet-plate: 1880 to 1902
An eight-pointed star, the topmost point displaced by a Victorian crown. On this a wreath of oak and within the wreath a strap inscribed *Sixth Lancashire First Manchester Rifles* and in the centre the numeral *6*. In silver with black-leather backing to the centre (Fig. 1555).

The Border Rifle Volunteers
1887: 1st Volunteer Battalion, The King's Own Borderers.

Other-ranks' glengarry: 1880 to 1902
A circlet inscribed *Border Rifle Volunteers* surmounted by a Victorian crown. In the centre a crowned heart with a scroll above inscribed *Doe or Die*. In blackened-brass (Fig. 1556).

23rd Middlesex Rifle Volunteer Corps
1883: 2nd Volunteer Battalion, The Royal Fusiliers.

Officers' helmet-plate: 1880 to 1883
An eight-pointed star, the topmost point displaced by a Victorian crown. On this a laurel-wreath. Within the wreath a strap inscribed *23rd Middlesex Rifle Volunteer Corps*. In the centre on a green ground a portcullis with chains. In silver (Fig. 1557).

2nd Cheshire Rifle Volunteer Corps
1887: 2nd (Earl of Chester's) Volunteer Battalion, The Cheshire Regiment.

Other-ranks' helmet-plate: 1880 to 1887
An eight-pointed star, the topmost point displaced by a Victorian crown. On this a laurel-wreath. Within the wreath a strap inscribed *2nd Cheshire Rifle Volunteers*. In the centre a garb of wheat. In white-metal (Fig. 1558).

Isle of Man Rifle Volunteers
1888: 7th (Isle of Man) Volunteer Battalion, The King's (Liverpool Regiment).

Other-ranks' glengarry: c. 1870
A strap inscribed *Quocunque jeceris stabit* surmounted by a Victorian crown. In the centre the Arms of the Isle of Man. A hunting-horn is suspended from the bottom of the strap. In white-metal (Fig. 1559).

1st Newcastle-on-Tyne Rifle Volunteer Corps
1883: 3rd Volunteer Battalion, The Northumberland Fusiliers.

Officers' helmet-plate: 1880 to 1902
A star of eight points, the topmost point displaced by a Victorian crown. On this a laurel-wreath. Within the wreath a strap inscribed *1st Newcastle on Tyne Rifle Volunteers*. In the centre on a blue-velvet ground the crest of Newcastle-upon-Tyne within the strings of a bugle-horn. In silver (Fig. 1560).

15th Lancashire Rifle Volunteer Corps
1888: 4th Volunteer Battalion, The King's (Liverpool Regiment).

Other-ranks' glengarry: 1880 to 1888
A circlet inscribed *15th Lancashire RV Corps* surmounted by a Victorian crown. In the centre the White Horse of Hanover. In white-metal (Fig. 1561).

6th Volunteer Battalion, The Gordon Highlanders

Officers' glengarry: 1891 to 1908
Within a wreath of ivy the crest of the Marquis of Huntley: a stag's head within a coronet. Below, a scroll inscribed *Bydand* and below this a scroll inscribed *6th VBGH*. The whole design raised, the stag's head modelled and standing out from the centre. In silver (Fig. 1562).

Other-ranks' glengarry: 1891 to 1908
Same general design as for officers but flat and with shorter antlers to the stag. In white-metal (Fig. 1563).

2nd Volunteer Battalion, The Royal Sussex Regiment

Other-ranks' helmet-plate: 1883 to 1908
An eight-pointed star, the topmost point displaced by a Victorian crown. On this a laurel-wreath. Within the wreath a circlet inscribed *2nd Volr Battn Royal Sussex*. In the centre the badge of the Royal Sussex Regiment, *viz.*: a Maltese cross on which a laurel-wreath. Within the wreath the Garter with St. George's Cross in the centre. All superimposed on the Roussillon plume. In white-metal (Fig. 1564).

3rd Volunteer Battalion, The Prince of Wales's Own (West Yorkshire Regiment)

Busby-badge: 1883 to 1898
Within a laurel-wreath a Maltese cross with a lion between each division of the cross. On the cross a circlet inscribed *Leeds Rifles* with, in the centre, a bugle with strings surmounted by a crown. Above the cross a blank tablet surmounted by a crown. Across the base of the wreath a scroll inscribed *3 VBPWO. West Yorkshire Regt.* In white-metal (Fig. 1565).

5th Middlesex ((West Middlesex) Volunteer Rifle Corps (Harrow Rifles))
1908: 9th Battalion, The Middlesex Regiment.

Field-service cap: 1898 to 1908
Superimposed on crossed arrows, points downwards and tied with a bow of ribbon in the

centre, a complete laurel-wreath with a scroll at the top inscribed *5th West* and one at the bottom inscribed *Middlesex*. In white-metal (Fig. 1566).

1st Volunteer Battalion, The Black Watch (Royal Highlanders)

Officers' glengarry: 1887 to 1902

The Star of the Order of the Thistle. On this a wreath of thistles. Within the wreath an oval inscribed *Nemo me impune lacessit* surmounted by a Victorian crown. In the centre St. Andrew and Cross. A half-scroll to the left of the crown inscribed *The Royal* and a half-scroll to the right of the crown inscribed *Highlanders*. Below the wreath the Sphinx on a blank tablet. To the left of the Sphinx a half-scroll inscribed *Black* and to the right a similar scroll inscribed *Watch*. Across the bottom points of the star a scroll inscribed *1st Volunteer Battalion*. Star and title-scrolls in silver, remainder in gilt (Fig. 1567).

3rd City of London Rifle Volunteers

1908: 7th (City of London) Battalion, The London Regiment.

Officers' helmet-plate: 1883 to 1902

An eight-pointed star, the topmost point displaced by a Victorian crown. On this a laure wreath. Superimposed on the wreath crossed mace and sword. On these a strap inscribed *Domine dirige nos*. In the centre, on a ground of black velvet, a fused grenade with the numeral *3* on the ball. Below the strap a scroll inscribed *London* and below this a shield bearing the Arms of the City of London. The mace and sword, grenade, and edges and lettering of bottom scroll in gilt; remainder in silver (Fig. 1568).

3rd Volunteer Battalion, The Black Watch (Royal Highlanders)

Other-ranks' glengarry: 1887 to 1902

The Star of the Order of the Thistle. On this a wreath of thistles. Within the wreath an oval inscribed *Nemo me impune lacessit* surmounted by a Victorian crown. In the centre St. Andrew and Cross. A half-scroll to the left of the crown inscribed *The* and a half-scroll to the right of the crown inscribed *Dundee*. Below the wreath a scroll inscribed *Highlanders*. In white-metal (Fig. 1569).

4th Volunteer Battalion, The Cameronians (Scottish Rifles)

Other-ranks' helmet-plate: 1887 to 1904

A wreath of thistles surmounted by a crown. On the left spray the Sphinx on a blank tablet. On the right spray the China Dragon on a blank tablet. In the centre a bugle-horn with strings surmounted by a mullet. Below the bugle a scroll inscribed *4th Volr Battn* and below this a scroll inscribed *The Scottish Rifles*. In gilding-metal (Fig. 1570).

19th Middlesex (St. Giles and St. Georges, Bloomsbury) Volunteer Rifle Corps

Amalgamated in 1908 with 1st Middlesex Volunteer Rifle Corps to form 9th (County of London) Battalion, The London Regiment (Queen Victoria's).

Officers' helmet-plate: 1880 to 1895

Within a laurel-wreath a Maltese cross with a lion between each division of the cross. On the cross a circlet inscribed *Rifle Brigade* with, in the centre, a bugle with strings surmounted by a crown. Above the cross a scroll inscribed *Bloomsbury Rifles* surmounted by a Guelphic

1562

1564

1563

1565

1566

1567

1569

1570

1568

1571

1572

1573

1574

1575

1576

crown. On the wreath two blank scrolls either side. Across the base of the wreath a scroll inscribed *The Prince Consort's Own*. In blackened-silver with the high-points polished (Fig. 1571).

Cyclist Company, 1st Volunteer Battalion, The Loyal North Lancashire Regiment

Glengarry: 1882 to 1898

A circlet inscribed *1st Volr Batn Loyal North Lancashire* surmounted by a Victorian crown. In the centre a cycle-wheel. In white-metal (Fig. 1572).

3rd Volunteer Battalion, The Royal Fusiliers

Officers' glengarry: 1883 to 1898

A fused grenade. On the ball, the Garter surmounted by a Victorian crown with a rose in the centre. Below the Garter the White Horse of Hanover. Below the grenade a scroll inscribed *3rd Volunteer Battln*. Garter and scroll in gilt with a blue-enamel ground. Crown in gilt with red-enamel ground. Remainder in silver (Fig. 1573).

1st Volunteer Battalion, The Lancashire Fusiliers

Other-ranks' fur-cap: 1884 to 1908

A fused grenade. On the ball, a circlet inscribed *Ist VB Lancashire Fusiliers*. Within this the Sphinx superscribed *Egypt*, surrounded by a laurel-wreath. In white-metal (Fig. 1574).

1st Volunteer Battalion, The Royal Fusiliers

Other-ranks' glengarry: 1885 to 1898

A fused grenade. On the ball the Garter surmounted by a crown. Within this a rose. Below the grenade a scroll inscribed *1st Volunteer Battalion*. In white-metal (Fig. 1575).

2nd Volunteer Battalion, The East Kent Regiment

Officers' glengarry: 1883 to 1898

A circlet inscribed *2nd Volr Battn East Kent Regt* surmounted by a Victorian crown. In the centre the White Horse of Kent on a scroll inscribed *Invicta*. Silver-plated (Fig. 1576).

1st Volunteer Battalion, The Essex Regiment

Forage-cap: 1905 to 1908

A wreath of oak joined at the top by the Sphinx on a tablet inscribed *1st VB* and across the foot with a scroll inscribed *The Essex Regt*. In the centre the Castle and Key of Gibraltar. Below the title-scroll, a scroll inscribed *South Africa, 1900–02*. In white-metal (Fig. 1577).

1st Brecknockshire Rifle Volunteers

1908: The Brecknockshire Battalion, The South Wales Borderers.

Other-ranks' helmet-plate: 1902 to 1908

An eight-pointed star, the topmost point displaced by an Imperial crown. On this a laurel-wreath. Within the wreath a circlet inscribed *1st Brecknockshire RV*. In the centre the Prince of Wales's plumes, coronet and motto above a scroll isncribed *Gwell angau na chwilydd*. In white-metal (Fig. 1578).

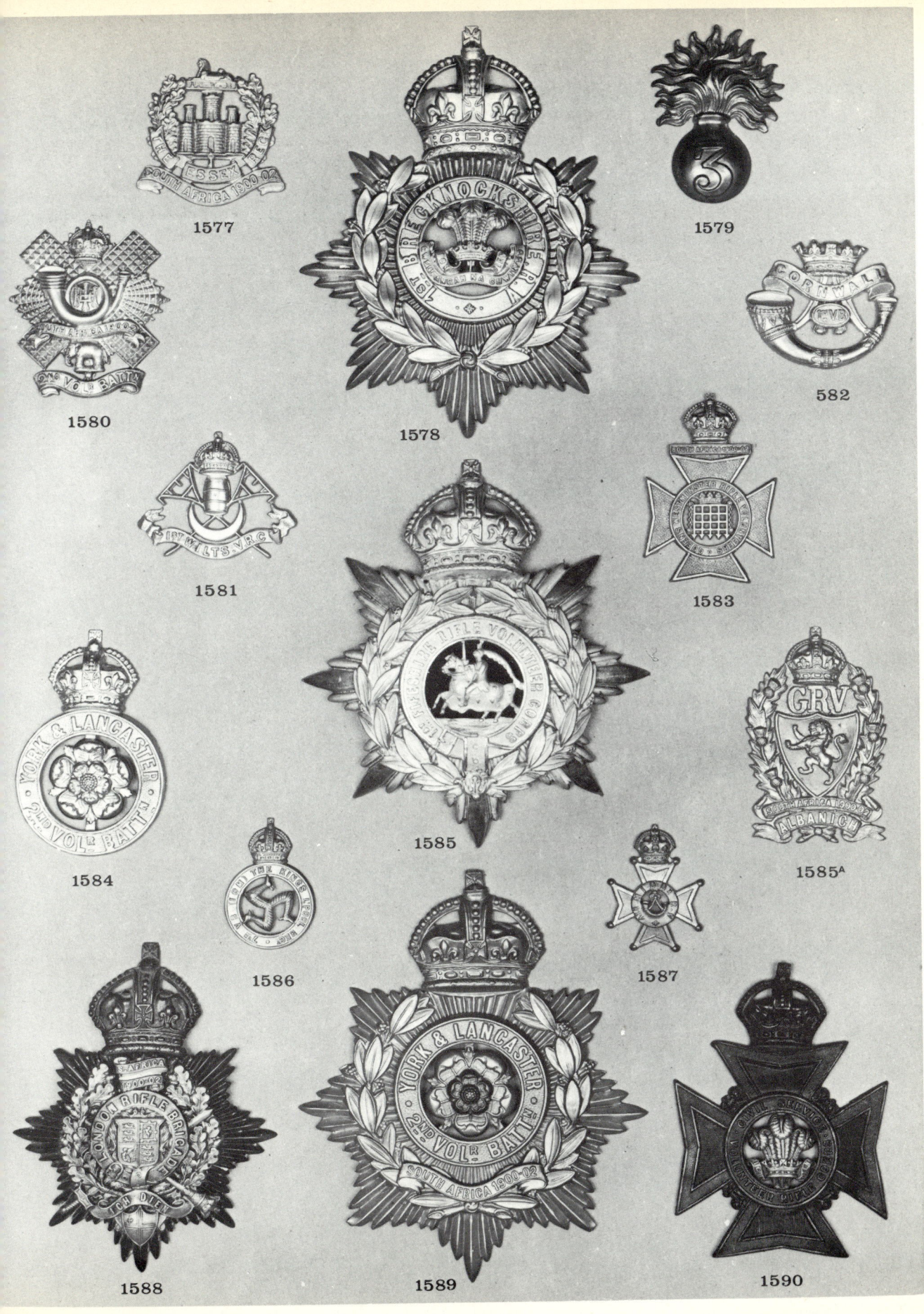

1577

1578

1579

1580

582

1581

1583

1584

1585

1585ᴬ

1586

1587

1588

1589

1590

3rd City of London Rifle Volunteers
1908: 7th (City of London) Battalion, The London Regiment.

Forage-cap: 1898 to 1908
A fused grenade with the numeral *3* on the ball. In gilding-metal (Fig. 1579).

2nd Volunteer Battalion, The Highland Light Infantry

Other-ranks' glengarry: 1905 to 1908
On the Star of the Order of the Thistle a bugle-horn with the monogram *HLI* in the curl and surmounted by an Imperial crown. Below the bugle a scroll inscribed *South Africa 1900–2* and below this the Elephant. Beneath the Star a scroll inscribed *2nd Volr Battn*. In white-metal (Fig. 1580).

1st Wiltshire Volunteer Rifle Corps
1908: 4th Volunteer Battalion, The Wiltshire Regiment.

Forage-cap: 1902 to 1908
On crossed rakes a barrel with, above, an Imperial crown and, below, a crescent-moon. Below, a scroll inscribed *1st Wilts V.R.C.* In white-metal (Fig. 1581).

1st Volunteer Battalion, The Duke of Cornwall's Light Infantry

Other-ranks' forage-cap: 1899 to 1908
A bugle-horn with the strings taken up into a coronet. Below the coronet a scroll inscribed *Cornwall* and below this an oval inscribed *1st VB*. In white-metal (Fig. 1582).

13th Middlesex (Queen's) Volunteer Rifle Corps (Westminster)
1908: 16th (County of London) Battalion, The London Regiment (Queen's Westminster Rifles).

Other-ranks' forage-cap: 1905 to 1908
A Maltese cross with a tablet above inscribed *South Africa 1900–02* and surmounted by an Imperial crown. On the cross a circlet inscribed *Queen's Westminster Rifle Volunteers*. In the centre a portcullis with chains surmounted by a coronet. In white-metal (Fig. 1583).

2nd Volunteer Battalion, The York and Lancaster Regiment

Glengarry: 1902 to 1908
A circlet inscribed *2nd Volr Battn York & Lancaster* surmounted by an Imperial crown. In the centre the Union Rose. All in white-metal except the Rose which is in gilding-metal with a white-metal centre (Fig. 1584).

1st Fifeshire Rifle Volunteer Corps
1887: 6th (Fifeshire) Battalion, The Black Watch (Royal Highlanders).

Officers' helmet-plate: 1902 to 1908
An eight-pointed star, the topmost point displaced by an Imperial crown. On this a laurel-wreath. Within the wreath a strap inscribed *1st Fifeshire Rifle Volunteer Corps*. In the centre on a black-velvet ground the Thane of Fife. In silver (Fig. 1585).

Galloway (Kirkcudbright and Wigtown) Volunteer Rifle Corps
1908: Part of 5th (Dumfries and Galloway) Battalion, The King's Own Scottish Borderers.

Glengarry: 1905 to 1908
A wreath of thistles surmounted by an Imperial crown. Within the wreath a shield bearing the Scottish Lion and surmounted by the letters *GRV*. On the base of the wreath a scroll inscribed *South Africa 1900–02* and below this a further scroll inscribed *Albanich*. In white-metal (Fig. 1585A).

7th Volunteer Battalion (Isle of Man) The King's (Liverpool Regiment)

Forage-cap: 1902 to 1908
A circlet inscribed *7th VB (IOM) The King's L'pool Regt* surmounted by an Imperial crown. In the centre the Arms of the Isle of Man. In white-metal (Fig. 1586).

4th Middlesex (West London) Volunteer Rifle Corps
1908: 13th (Princess Louise's Kensington) County of London Battalion, The London Regiment.

Forage-cap: 1902 to 1908
A Maltese cross surmounted by an Imperial crown. On the cross a circlet inscribed *4th Middx RV*. In the centre a bugle with strings. In gilding-metal (Fig. 1587).

1st London Volunteer Rifle Corps (City of London Volunteer Rifle Brigade)
1908: 5th (City of London) Battalion, The London Regiment (London Rifle Brigade).

Shako-plate: 1905
An eight-pointed star, the topmost point displaced by an Imperial crown. On this a wreath of oak on which is superimposed a sword and mace. At the top junction of the wreath a double scroll inscribed *S. Africa 1900-02*. Within the wreath a strap inscribed *London Rifle Brigade* with, in the centre, a shield bearing the Royal Arms. Beneath the strap a scroll inscribed *Ich Dien* and below this a shield bearing the Arms of the City of London. The star in blackened-brass, the crown in brass, remainder in white-metal (Fig. 1588).

2nd Volunteer Battalion, The York and Lancaster Regiment

Other-ranks' helmet-plate: 1905 to 1908
An eight-pointed star, the topmost point displaced by an Imperial crown. On this a laurel-wreath. Within the wreath a circlet inscribed *2nd Volr Battn York & Lancaster*. In the centre the Union Rose. On the bottom-join of the wreath a scroll inscribed *South Africa 1900–02*. All in white-metal except the Rose which has a gilding-metal centre (Fig. 1589).

The Prince of Wales's Own 12th Middlesex (Civil Service) Volunteer Rifle Corps
1908: 15th (County of London) Battalion, The London Regiment (Prince of Wales's Own Civil Service Rifles).

Other-ranks' helmet-plate: 1905 to 1908
A Maltese cross, with a lion between each division of the cross, surmounted by an Imperial crown. On the cross a circlet inscribed *Civil Service Volunteer Rifle Corps* with, in the centre, the Prince of Wales's plumes, coronet and motto. The Prince of Wales's plumes, coronet and motto in white-metal, remainder in black-metal (Fig. 1590).

MOUNTED RIFLES AND LIGHT HORSE VOLUNTEERS

1st Devonshire Mounted Rifles

Shako-badge: 1860

An eight-pointed star, the topmost point displaced by a Victorian crown, in bronze. On this, in white-metal, a circlet inscribed *Clyst Rifle Volunteers* and in the centre the numeral *1* with the words *Devon* above and *Mounted* below (Fig. 1591).

1st Huntingdonshire Mounted Rifles

Helmet-plate: 1860

The monogram *MV* surmounted by a ducal coronet. Below the cypher a scroll inscribed *1st or Duke of Manchester's*. In white-metal (Fig. 1592).

Lancashire Mounted Rifle Volunteers

Officers' helmet-plate: 1860

On a background of laurels surmounted by a Victorian crown an eight-pointed star. On this a strap inscribed *Mounted Rifle Volunteers* and within this a shield bearing three lions in pale, the topmost one bearing a label of three points, being the Arms of the County Palatine of Lancaster. All in silver.

1st Oxfordshire Light Horse

Helmet-badge: 1864 to 1870

The monogram *OLH* surmounted by a Victorian crown. Below the monogram a scroll inscribed *Fortis est veritas*. All in white-metal.

Border Mounted Rifles

Other-ranks' helmet: 1880 to 1892

An eight-pointed star. On this a strap inscribed *Whau daur meddle wi' me* with, in the centre, the monogram *BMR*. In white-metal.

1591

1592

CHAPTER 27

The Volunteer Force of 1914 to 1919

On the outbreak of war in August 1914, Volunteer Units were formed all over the country and, although some wore uniform of a military pattern, they mostly wore button-hole badges in their civilian dress. (These are not shown here as this work is confined to badges worn on the head-dress.)

The units were recognised by a War Office letter dated 19th November 1914 and control was vested in the Central Association of Volunteer Training Corps. This did not include Scotland which, however, had a similar controlling body.

Uniforms were now worn of a green-grey colour, but rank-markings were different to the Regular forces. Badges were worn on the head-dress; most units having the normal pattern forage-cap, others a slouch-hat, and some the side-cap. Scottish units wore either a glengarry or a tam o'shanter.

All units were to wear a red armlet with the letters *GR* in black, and a standard-pattern badge was designed for those units without special badges.

On the 19th April 1916, the Volunteer Training Corps became the Volunteer Force and the Central Association of Volunteer Training Corps became the Central Association of Volunteer Regiments. In October of that year the badges of rank were altered to conform with those of the army and regimental cap-badges were to be replaced by the Royal Arms: officers' in bronze, other-ranks' in gilding-metal.

Finally in July 1918, with the exception of the City and County of London Regiments, all County Volunteer Regiments were made Volunteer Battalions of Line Regiments. They were authorised to wear the same badges, but no battle-honours were to appear thereon.

The war came to an end before this scheme was fully implemented. In Scotland only those affiliated to the Royal Scots, The King's Own Scottish Borderers and the Black Watch were completed, and in England, Huntingdonshire, Rutlandshire and the Isle of Wight Regiments were left untouched.

At the time of disbandment a variety of badges were being worn. A few had the badge of the line regiment of which they now formed a part, some the Royal Arms and others the original Volunteer Regiment badge.

The selection of badges chosen to illustrate this chapter fall into two categories: those based on the standard-pattern with the addition of a title-scroll at the base, and those based on the arms of the city or borough of origin. Where these are too small to show the detail clearly the heraldic description of the arms is also given. One regiment which did adopt the regular regiment's badge was the Hampshire Volunteer Regiment—but in white-metal as distinct from the gilding-metal used by all other elements of the regiment whether regular, territorial or service battalions.

Athletes' Volunteer Force

This organisation had several hundred branches throughout the country and was subsequently amalgamated with the Central Association of Volunteer Training Corps. An oval inscribed *Athletes' Volunteer Force 1914*. In the centre crossed rifles. In brass with blue-enamel backing to the oval (Fig. 1593).

Athletes' Volunteer Force (City of Exeter)

The above was one of the branches which adopted a distinctive badge after the organisation was administered by the Central Association of Volunteer Training Corps.

The Arms of the City of Exeter within a wreath, laurel on left and oak on right. Above this a scroll inscribed *Athletes Volunteer* with the word *Force* below the scroll. The scroll surmounted by an Imperial crown. Below the Arms a scroll inscribed *City of Exeter*. In bronze (Fig. 1594). The Arms of the City of Exeter are: Parted palewise gules and sable a three-turreted tri-angular castle or. The crest: On a wreath or and sable a demi-lion rampant gules wearing a gold crown and carrying a golden orb with an azure band. The supporters are two silver winged horses, their wings charged with three bars wavy azure. The motto: *Semper fidelis* (ever faithful).

Volunteer Training Corps (General pattern)

(Worn by units without special badges)
    (1) On a laurel-wreath, surmounted by an Imperial crown, crossed rifles with the letters *VTC* superimposed and the date *1914* below. In gilding-metal (Fig. 1595).
    (2) As above but with the date *1915*. In gilding-metal (Fig. 1596).

Argyllshire Volunteer Regiment

Argyllshire National Guard Volunteer Corps

A strap inscribed *Argyllshire NGVC*. In the centre a boar's head. In white-metal (Fig. 1597).

Berkshire Volunteer Regiment

(Later 1st Volunteer Battalion, The Royal Berkshire Regiment.)

Newbury Volunteer Training Corps

On a shield a castle of three turrets with flags flying from each turret and below a scroll inscribed *Burgus de Newburie*. The whole enclosed by a laurel-wreath. At the base a scroll inscribed *Newbury VTC*. In bronze (Fig. 1598).

City of Bristol Volunteer Regiment

(Later 2nd, 4th and 6th Volunteer Battalions, The Gloucestershire Regiment.)

Bristol Volunteer Training Corps

On a laurel-wreath, surmounted by an Imperial crown, crossed rifles with the letters *VTC* superimposed and the date *1915* below. Beneath the wreath a scroll inscribed *Bristol*. In gilding-metal (Fig. 1599).

Buckinghamshire Volunteer Regiment

(Later 3rd, 4th and 5th Volunteer Battalions, The Oxfordshire and Buckinghamshire Light Infantry.)

1593

1594

1595

1596

1597

1598

1599

1600

1601

1602

1603

1604

1605

1606

1607

1608

1609

1610

1611

1612

1613

1614

1615

1616

1617

1618

Buckinghamshire Volunteer Defence Corps

A swan, with a coronet round its neck and affixed thereto a chain turned over the back, standing on ground. Below this a tablet inscribed *Bucks VDC 1914*. In bronze (Fig. 1600). The swan was the ancient badge of the de Bohun family from whence it passed to the Stafford Dukes of Buckingham.

Cambridgeshire Volunteer Regiment

(Later 1st Volunteer Battalion, The Cambridgeshire Regiment.)

Cambridge Volunteers

The Arms of Cambridge City Council resting on a scroll inscribed *Cambridge Volunteers*. In bronze (Fig. 1601).

The Arms of Cambridge are: A gold arched-bridge with three towers. Above it a fleur-de-lys or, between two roses argent, and in base barry wavy silver and azure, and thereon three ships sable, each with one mast and the sail furled. The crest: On a wreath, or and gules, a grassy mound, and thereon a silver castle. The supporters are two sea-horses.

Caernarvonshire Volunteer Regiment

(Later 3rd Volunteer Battalion, The Royal Welsh Fusiliers.)

A pear-shaped scroll inscribed *Carnarvonshire Volunteer Regiment VTC* and surmounted by an Imperial crown. Within this the Arms of Caernarvon Borough Council, i.e. a shield bearing the Arms of England with a label of five points, and above the shield an eagle—a combination of the insignia of the English Princes of Wales and Owain Gwynedd, native Prince of North Wales. In bronze (Fig. 1602).

Cheshire Volunteer Regiment

(Later 1st–10th Volunteer Battalions, The Cheshire Regiment.)

(1) A shield bearing three garbs (wheat sheaves) within a circlet inscribed *Cheshire Volunteer Regiment*. In bronze (Fig. 1603).

(2) A shield bearing three Garbs surmounted by an Imperial crown. Two scrolls at base. The top one inscribed *Vol Regt* bisected by the shield. The bottom one superimposed on the base of the shield and inscribed *Cheshire*. Officers' pattern in bronze (Fig. 1604).

(3) As (2) but with the addition of a wreath of laurel (left) and oak (right). Other-ranks pattern in bronze (Fig. 1605). The three Garbs are from the Arms of the ancient Earldom of Chester.

Birkenhead and District Volunteer Training Corps

(Later the 2nd Volunteer Battalion, The Cheshire Regiment.)

Two shields, that on the left bearing the Arms of Birkenhead; between these a stalk bearing a rose and two leaves, all within a circlet inscribed *Birkenhead & Dist Volunteer*. Surrounded by a laurel-wreath and surmounted by a Victorian crown. Across the base a scroll inscribed *Training Corps*. In bronze (Fig. 1606).

Cornwall Volunteer Regiment

(Later 1st and 2nd Volunteer Battalions, The Duke of Cornwall's Light Infantry.)

Cornwall Volunteer Training Corps

On an ornamental shield a scroll at the head inscribed *Cornwall* and the letters *VTC* in the base. On this a small shield bearing fifteen bezants (from the Arms of the Duchy of Cornwall). In bronze (Fig. 1607).

Cumberland and Westmorland Volunteer Regiment
(Later 1st and 2nd Volunteer Battalions, The Border Regiment.)

Cumberland Volunteer Regiment
A circlet inscribed *Cumberland Volunteer Regiment* and surmounted by an Imperial crown. In the circlet a shield bearing the Arms of Carlisle, *viz*: a cross patée with four roses in each quarter and a further rose in the centre of the cross. In bronze (Fig. 1608).

Derbyshire Volunteer Regiment
(Later 1st–8th Volunteer Battalions, The Sherwood Foresters.)

Derbyshire Volunteer Regiment of Home Guards
(1) On a Maltese cross a circlet inscribed *Derbyshire Volunteer Regiment of Home Guards*. In the centre a stag within palings. In bronze (Fig. 1609).
(2) A Tudor Rose surmounted by a crown within an oval inscribed *Derbyshire Volunteer Regiment of Home Guards*. In bronze (Fig. 1610).

Devonshire Volunteer Regiment
(Later 1st, 2nd and 3rd Volunteer Battalions, The Devonshire Regiment.)

Exeter Volunteer Regiment
Crossed cartridges on a scroll inscribed *Pro aris et focis*. In white-metal (Fig. 1611).
(Exeter Volunteer Regiment was later the 1st Volunteer Battalion, The Devonshire Regiment.)

Plymouth Volunteer Training Corps
On a laurel-wreath, surmounted by an Imperial crown, crossed rifles with the letters *VTC* superimposed and the date *1915* below. Beneath the wreath a scroll inscribed *Plymouth*. In gilding-metal (Fig. 1612).
(Plymouth Volunteer Training Corps was later the 2nd Volunteer Battalion, The Devonshire Regiment.)

Dorsetshire Volunteer Regiment
(Later 1st Volunteer Battalion, The Dorsetshire Regiment.)
A circlet inscribed *Volunteer Regiment 1915* surmounted by an Imperial crown and within a laurel-wreath. In the centre three lions passant guardant in pale from the Arms of Dorset County Council. At the base of the wreath a scroll inscribed *Dorset*. In bronze (Fig. 1613).

Dumfries-shire Volunteer Regiment
(Later 3rd Volunteer Battalion, The King's Own Scottish Borderers.)
Within an oak-wreath the winged figure of Victory bearing a sword in the right hand and a shield on the left and standing on a dragon. Below this scrolls inscribed *Praesidium Burgi de Dumfries Aloreburn*. In bronze (Fig. 1614).

Stewartry Volunteer Training Corps
A lion rampant crowned. Below, a scroll inscribed *Stewartry VTC*. In white-metal (Fig. 1615).

Durham Volunteer Regiment
(Later 1st–7th and 9th–12th Volunteer Battalions, The Durham Light Infantry.)

3rd Battalion, Durham Volunteer Training Corps
On a laurel-wreath, surmounted by an Imperial crown, crossed rifles with the letters *VTC* superimposed and the numeral *3* below. Beneath the wreath a scroll inscribed *Durham*. In bronze (Fig. 1616). The 3rd Battalion was Auckland.

Essex Volunteer Regiment
(Later 1st–7th Volunteer Battalions, The Essex Regiment.)
  (1) A shield bearing the Arms of Essex surmounted by an Imperial crown. Below, a scroll inscribed *Essex Volunteer Regt.* In gilding-metal (Fig. 1617).
  (2) On a laurel-wreath, surmounted by an Imperial crown, crossed rifles with the letters *VTC* superimposed and the date *1915* below. Beneath the wreath a scroll inscribed *Essex*. In gilding-metal (Fig. 1618).

Rayleigh and District Volunteer Training Corps
A heart-shaped plate with a continuous scroll around the edge inscribed *Rayleigh & District Volunteer Training Corps*. In the centre a shield bearing the Arms of Rayleigh: a seax above which a rising sun and, below, a mount surmounted by a castle. In bronze (Fig. 1619).

East Ham Volunteer Defence Corps
A shield bearing the Arms of Essex surmounted by a crown which bisects a scroll inscribed *East Ham*. Below the shield a scroll inscribed *Volunteer Defence Corps*. In bronze (Fig. 1620).

Fifeshire Volunteer Regiment
(Later 7th, 8th and 9th Volunteer Battalions, The Black Watch.)

St. Andrew's Volunteer Training Corps
An oval inscribed *St. Andrew's Volunteer Training Corps*. In the centre St. Andrew with Cross. In bronze (Fig. 1621).
(St. Andrew's became the 9th Volunteer Battalion, The Black Watch.)

Flintshire and Denbighshire Volunteer Regiment
(Later 2nd Volunteer Battalion, The Royal Welsh Fusiliers.)

Denbighshire Volunteer Regiment
An eight-pointed star, the topmost point displaced by an Imperial crown. On this an oval inscribed *Denbighshire Volunteer Regiment 1915*. Within the oval a shield bearing a lion rampant (part of the Arms of Denbigh Borough Council). In bronze (Fig. 1622).

Glamorgan Volunteer Regiment
(Later 2nd–6th Volunteer Battalions, The Welsh Regiment.)

Glamorgan Volunteer Training Corps
A circlet inscribed *Glamorgan VTC*. In the centre a shield bearing three chevrons. In bronze (Fig. 1623).

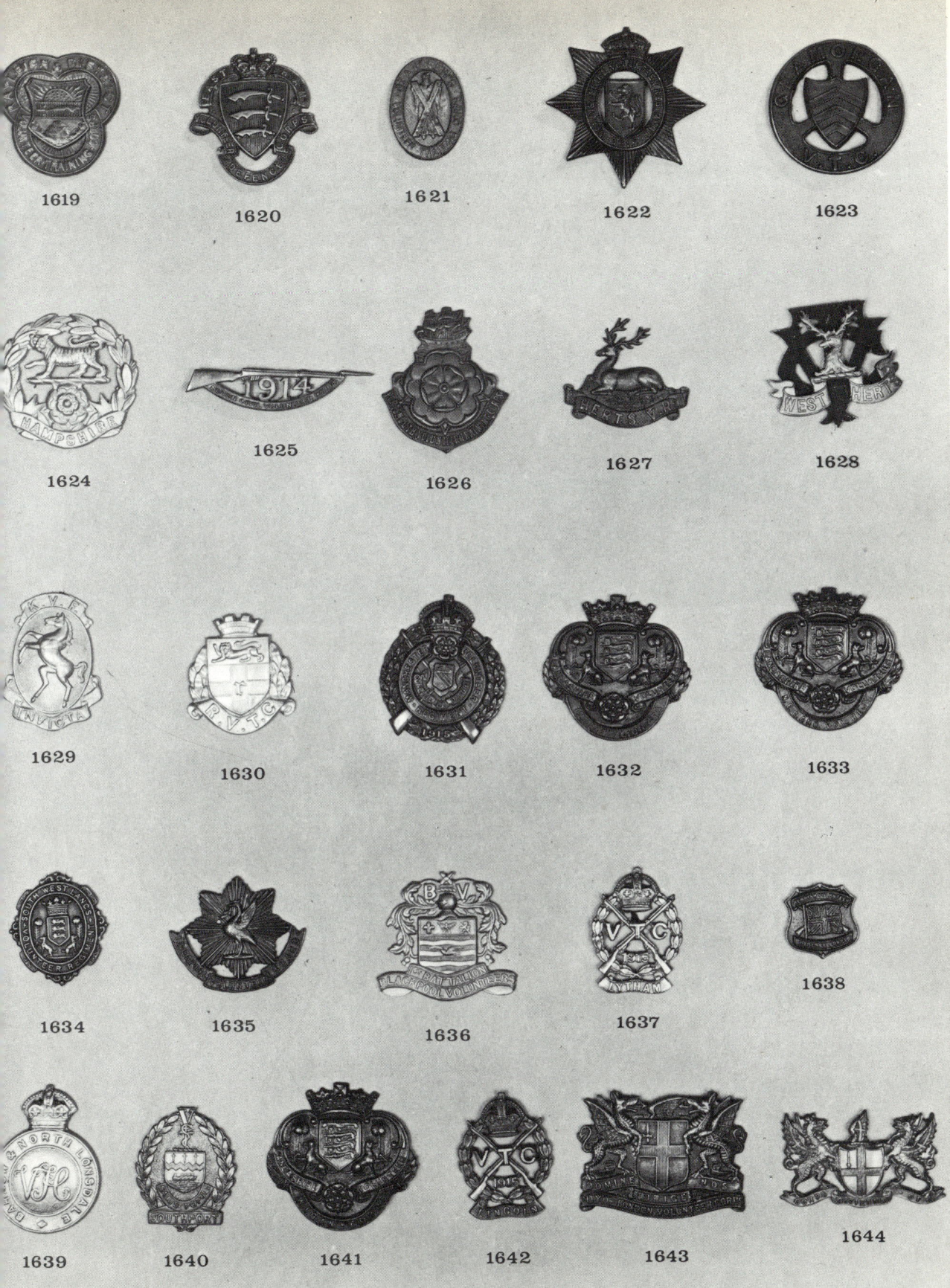

1619   1620   1621   1622   1623

1624   1625   1626   1627   1628

1629   1630   1631   1632   1633

1634   1635   1636   1637   1638

1639   1640   1641   1642   1643   1644

Hampshire Volunteer Regiment
(Later 1st–4th Volunteer Battalions, The Hampshire Regiment.)
Within a laurel-wreath a Tiger above the Hampshire Rose. Across the base of the wreath a scroll inscribed *Hampshire,* In white-metal (Fig. 1624).

Southampton Civil Volunteer Corps
(Southampton became the 2nd Volunteer Battalion, The Hampshire Regiment.)
A rifle with bayonet fixed with a sling on which is inscribed *Soton Civil Volunteer Corps.* Between the sling and the rifle the date *1914.* In gilding-metal (Fig. 1625).

Portsmouth Volunteer Training Corps
(Portsmouth became the 3rd Volunteer Battalion, The Hampshire Regiment.)
The Hampshire Rose surmounted by a representation of H.M.S. *Victory.* Below the Rose a scroll inscribed *Portsmouth Volunteer Training Corps.* In bronze (Fig. 1626).

Hertfordshire Volunteer Regiment
(Later 1st, 2nd and 3rd Volunteer Battalions, The Hertfordshire Regiment.)
A Hart lodged. Below a scroll inscribed *Herts VR.* In bronze (Fig. 1627).

West Hertfordshire Volunteer Training Corps
A monogram of the letters *VTC,* a stag's head and neck on a wreath superimposed and below this a scroll inscribed *West Herts.* The monogram in black-metal, remainder in gilding-metal (Fig. 1628).

Kent Volunteer Regiment
(Later 1st–4th Volunteer Battalions, The Buffs and 1st–4th Volunteer Battalions, The Queen's Own Royal West Kent Regiment.)

Kent Volunteer Fencibles
The White Horse of Kent on an oval. Above this a scroll inscribed *KVF.* Below the oval a scroll inscribed *Invicta.* In white-metal (Fig. 1629).

Rochester Volunteer Training Corps
(Rochester was incorporated into the Kent Volunteer Fencibles.)
Within a laurel-wreath the Arms of the City of Rochester (the letter *R* on a cross surmounted by a lion). Above this a mural crown. Below the shield a scroll inscribed *RVTC.* In white-metal (Fig. 1630).

Lancashire Volunteer Regiment
The regiment was divided into four Groups as follows:
Manchester Group: 1st, 2nd, 3rd and 4th Volunteer Battalions, The Manchester Regiment; 1st, 2nd, 3rd and 4th Volunteer Battalions The Lancashire Fusiliers; and 2nd Volunteer Battalion, The Loyal North Lancashire Regiment.
Liverpool Group: 1st, 2nd and 3rd Volunteer Battalions, The King's Liverpool Regiment and 1st Volunteer Battalion, The Prince of Wales's Volunteers.
North East Group: 1st, 2nd, 3rd and 4th Volunteer Battalions, The East Lancashire Regiment.
North West Group: 1st Volunteer Battalion, The Loyal North Lancashire Regiment and 1st and 2nd Volunteer Battalions, The King's Own Royal Lancaster Regiment.

Manchester Volunteer Regiment

A laurel-wreath surmounted by an Imperial crown with the date *1915* on the base of the wreath. Superimposed crossed rifles and on these a circular scroll inscribed *Manchester Volunteer Regiment* with the Red Rose of Lancaster at the top of the scroll. In the centre the Arms and motto of the City of Manchester (Three bendlets with, on the chief, a ship in full sail on the sea: the motto is *Concilio et labore*). In bronze (Fig. 1631).

1st Battalion, Lancashire Volunteers

A heart-shaped plate surmounted by a coronet. Below this a shield bearing the Arms of England with a label of three points. On either side a talbot holding an ostrich feather. Below the shield the Red Rose of Lancaster. Scrolls either side of the Rose inscribed *Lancashire Volunteers*. A further scroll at the base of the design inscribed *1st Battalion 47A*. Sprigs of laurel at both ends of the scroll. In bronze (Fig. 1632).

North East Lancashire Volunteer Regiment

Exactly the same design as above but the bottom scroll inscribed *N. E. Lanc Vol Regt*. In bronze (Fig. 1633).

South West Lancashire Volunteer Regiment

An oval inscribed *South West Lancs Volunteer Regiment*. The oval has ornamental edges. In the top centre a shield bearing the Arms of England surmounted by a coronet. At the base and on either side of the shield a talbot holding an ostrich feather. In bronze (Fig. 1634).

Liverpool Volunteer Guard

On an eight-pointed star a liver bird. Below a scroll inscribed *Liverpool Volunteer Guard*. In bronze (Fig. 1635).

1st Battalion, Blackpool Volunteers

The Arms of Blackpool surmounted by a helmet with mantling and with the letters *B* and *V* either side of the crest. Below the Arms two scrolls, the top inscribed *1st Battalion* and the bottom, *Blackpool Volunteers*. In gilding-metal (Fig. 1636).
The Arms of Blackpool are: Barry wavy of eight pieces sable and gold, thereon a flying seagull proper; on a chief argent a thunderbolt proper between a fleur-de-lys and a lion rampant both gules. The Crest: On a wreath or and sable the battlements of a tower gold, and thereon the sails of a windmill proper, with a Red Rose of Lancaster at the centre.

Lytham Volunteer Training Corps

On a laurel-wreath surmounted by an Imperial crown crossed rifles with the letters *VTC* superimposed and the date *1915* below. Beneath the wreath a scroll inscribed *Lytham*. In gilding-metal (Fig. 1637).

Reddish Volunteer Defence Corps

On a shield crossed rifles on which is superimposed the Great Union. Above this a scroll inscribed *Reddish Volunteer* and, below, a similar scroll inscribed *Defence Corps*. In bronze (Fig. 1638).

Barrow and North Lonsdale Volunteer Training Corps

A circlet inscribed *Barrow & North Lonsdale* surmounted by an Imperial crown. In the centre in interwoven script the letters *VTC*. In white-metal (Fig. 1639).

Southport Volunteers

A laurel-wreath surmounted by the letter *V*. Within this the Arms and crest of Southport with below the Arms the motto *Salus populi*. At the base a scroll inscribed *Southport*. In bronze (Fig. 1640).

Wigan Corps, Lancashire Volunteers

A heart-shaped plate surmounted by a coronet. Below this a shield bearing the Arms of England with a label of three points. Either side a talbot holding an ostrich feather. Below, the shield the Red Rose of Lancaster. Scrolls at either side of the Rose inscribed *Lancashire Volunteers*. A further scroll at the base of the design inscribed *Wigan Corps*. Sprigs of laurel at both ends of the scroll. In bronze (Fig. 1641).

Lincolnshire Volunteer Regiment

(Later 1st–4th Volunteer Battalions, The Lincolnshire Regiment.)

Lincoln Volunteer Training Corps

On a laurel-wreath surmounted by an Imperial crown crossed rifles with the letters *VTC* superimposed and the date *1915* below. Beneath the wreath a scroll inscribed *Lincoln*. In gilding-metal (Fig. 1642).

City of London Volunteer Regiment

The London Volunteers were not affiliated to the existing London Regiments of the Territorial Force and kept their separate identity.

The City Regiments were organised in two Groups.

Group 'A': 1/1st, 2/1st and 2nd Battalions.

Group 'B': 4th, 5th and 6th National Guard Battalions.

(1) The Arms of the City of London. Below, a scroll inscribed *Domine dirige nos* and below this a further scroll inscribed *City of London Volunteer Corps*. In bronze (Fig. 1643).

(2) The Arms of the City of London. Below, a scroll inscribed *Corps/Citizens/of*. In gilding-metal (Fig. 1644).

(3) The Arms and motto of the City of London but with the crest resting on a knight's helm. In gilding-metal (Fig. 1645).

(4) Scottish Company: The Star of the Order of the Thistle in white-metal. Superimposed the Arms and motto of the City of London in gilding-metal (Fig. 1646).

County of London Volunteer Regiments

The County of London Regiments covered the whole of the London County Council area and, for administrative purposes, were divided into six Groups as under:

Central Group	1st Battalion (Kensington and United Arts)
	2nd Battalion (Inns of Court Reserve Corps)
	3rd Battalion (Old Boys Corps)
	4th Battalion (London Volunteer Rifles)
Eastern Group	5th Battalion (Bethnal Green)
	1/6th Battalion (Poplar and Holborn)
	2/6th Battalion (Finsbury)
	3/6th Battalion (Stepney)
Northern Group	7th Battalion (Hampstead)
	8th Battalion (St. Pancras)
	9th Battalion (Stoke Newington and Hackney)

South East Group	1/11th Battalion (Southwark)
	2/11th Battalion (Bermondsey)
	16th Battalion (Deptford)
	17th Battalion (Lewisham)
South West Group	10th Battalion (Lambeth)
	1/12th Battalion (Dulwich)
	2/12th Battalion (Camberwell)
	13th Battalion (Southfields and Putney)
	14th Battalion (Wandsworth)
	15th Battalion (Streatham)
	18th Battalion (Westminster)
Western Group	19th Battalion (Kensington and Paddington)
	20th Battalion (Hammersmith)
	21st Battalion (St. Marylebone)

United Arts Volunteer Rifles (later 1st Battalion)
An oval inscribed *United Arts Volunteer Rifles,* surmounted by a small Maltese cross, with in the centre an eagle grasping a sword in its beak. In bronze with red-enamel background to the centre (Fig. 1647).

Inns of Court Reserve Corps (later 2nd Battalion)
Within a laurel-wreath four shields placed in the form of a cross with the bottom points touching in the centre, each shield bearing the Arms of one of the following Inns, *viz*: Lincoln's Inn at the top, Inner Temple on the right, Gray's Inn at the bottom, and Middle Temple on the left. On the base of the wreath a scroll inscribed *Inns of Court RC.* In gilding-metal (Fig. 1648).

Old Boys Corps (later 3rd Battalion)
A monogram of the letters *OBC* surmounted by an Imperial crown. Below, a scroll inscribed *Pro patria.* In bronze (Fig. 1649).

Old Boys Corps
A circular boss with, on the edge, a complete laurel-wreath. Within this a circlet inscribed *Pro patria* and in the centre in old English characters the letters *OBC.* In bronze (Fig. 1650).

Optimists National Corps (afterwards London Volunteer Rifles)
A large letter *V* supporting on its head the letters *ONC.* In brass (Fig. 1651).

London Volunteer Rifles (later 4th Battalion)
A bugle with strings, the strings tied in three knots. On the bugle the word *Volunteers* is inscribed. Within the strings a lion carrying a banner on which is inscribed the letters *LVR.* In black-metal (Fig. 1652).

Poplar Volunteer Training Corps (later 1/6th Battalion)
A pear-shaped oval inscribed *Poplar Battalion VTC* surmounted by an Imperial crown. In the centre three shields representing the three parishes from the Borough Council's Seal. Below, a scroll inscribed *East London Regt.* In gilding-metal (Fig. 1653).

Hampstead Volunteer Training Corps (later 7th Battalion)

A circlet inscribed *Central Assocn VTC* surmounted by an Imperial crown and with oak sprays either side. In the centre a shield bearing the Arms of Hampstead (a Cross charged with a mitre and four fleurs-de-lys; a chief fretted). Below the shield a scroll inscribed with Hampstead's motto *Non sibi sed toti*. In bronze (Fig. 1654).

Southwark Volunteer Battalion (later 1/11th Battalion)

A circlet inscribed *Southwark Volunteer Battalion* surmounted by a crown. In the centre the Arms of Southwark (a cross quartered: in the first quarter a rose; in the second a lily; in the third the Southwark Cross; and in the fourth a stag's head and antlers). Below the shield the Borough's motto *United we serve*. In bronze (Fig. 1655).

South London Volunteer Training Corps

(For units in this area without special badges)
On a laurel-wreath, surmounted by an Imperial crown, crossed rifles with the letters *VTC* superimposed and the date *1915* below. Beneath the wreath a scroll inscribed *South London*. In gilding-metal (Fig. 1656).

Dulwich and District Defence League (later 1/12th Battalion)

On a shield crossed rifles with bayonets fixed. On these a laurel-wreath surmounted by a scroll inscribed *Volunteer*. Within the wreath a circlet inscribed *Defence League Dulwich & District* with, in the centre, a small shield inscribed with the letter *A*. Below the wreath a scroll inscribed *Defend our liberty*. In bronze (Fig. 1657).

Fulham (later 13th Battalion)

A shield bearing the Arms of Fulham. Below, a scroll inscribed *Fulham*. In bronze (Fig. 1658).

Wandsworth Volunteer Training Corps (later 14th Battalion)

A ten-pointed star. On this a shield bearing the Arms of Wandsworth with a scroll below inscribed *We serve*. In gilding-metal (Fig. 1659).

Wandsworth

A six-pointed star. On this a shield bearing the Arms of Wandsworth. The letters *VTC* inscribed below the shield. Above the star a scroll inscribed *1st VB Wandsworth*. Below the star a scroll inscribed *We serve*. In gilding-metal (Fig. 1660).

City of Westminster Volunteers (later 18th Battalion)

A shield bearing the Arms of the City of Westminster. Below the shield a scroll inscribed *City of Westminster Volunteers*. In bronze (Fig. 1661).

Kensington (later 19th Battalion)

Within a laurel-wreath surmounted by an Imperial crown a shield bearing the Arms of Kensington. Below the wreath a scroll inscribed *Quid nobis ardu*. In bronze (Fig. 1662).

St. Marylebone Volunteer Training Corps (later 21st Battalion)

A circlet inscribed *Volunteer Training Corps* surmounted by an Imperial crown. Within this crossed rifles on which is superimposed a scroll inscribed *St. Marylebone*. In bronze (Fig. 1663).

1645

1646

1647

1648

1649

1650

1651

1652

1653

1654

1655

1656

1657

1658

1659

1660

1661

1662

1663

1664

1665

1666

1667

1668

1669

1670

Northern London Polytechnic Volunteer Training Corps

On a laurel-wreath, surmounted by an Imperial crown, crossed rifles with the letters *VTC* superimposed and the date *1914* below. Beneath the wreath a scroll inscribed *Northern London Polytechnic*. In bronze (Fig. 1664).

Metropolitan Water Board Volunteer Training Corps

A circlet inscribed *Metropolitan Water Board 1914* surrounded by a scalloped border. A scroll above the circlet inscribed *Volunteer* and a two-part scroll below the circlet inscribed *Training Corps*. In the centre a female figure with a pitcher in her right hand and a watering pot in her left hand. Water gushes from a rock on the right and flows before the female figure. Top left, the Houses of Parliament and, top right, St. Paul's Cathedral. In bronze.

Post Office Engineers' Volunteer Training Corps

On a laurel-wreath, surmounted by an Imperial crown, crossed rifles with the letters *VTC* superimposed and the date *1915* below. Beneath the wreath a scroll inscribed *PO Engineers*. In gilding-metal (Fig. 1665).

Middlesex Volunteer Regiment

(Later 1st–7th Volunteer Battalions, The Middlesex Regiment.)
An eight-pointed star, the topmost point displaced by a crown. On this an oval inscribed *Middlesex Volunteer Regiment*. In the centre a shield bearing three seaxes surmounted by a Saxon crown. In bronze (Fig. 1666).

Friern Barnet Volunteer Training Corps

An oval inscribed *Friern Barnet VTC Esse quam videre* surmounted by an Imperial crown with the letter *B* in the centre. Gold on blue-enamel oval, gold-and-red crown, intitial in white-edged gold on gilt background (Fig. 1667).

Norfolk Volunteer Regiment

(Later 1st–4th Volunteer Battalions, The Norfolk Regiment.)
(1) Above crossed rifles with slings the letters *NVR* and above these a coronet. In black-metal (Fig. 1668).
(2) A castle with three turrets and flags flying from each turret. Below this a lion. To either side and below the lion a scroll inscribed *The Norfolk Volunteers*. The lion in gilding-metal, remainder in white-metal (Fig. 1669).

Northamptonshire Volunteer Regiment

(Later 1st and 2nd Volunteer Battalions, The Northamptonshire Regiment.)

Northampton Citizen Corps

An oval inscribed *Northampton Citizen Corps* surmounted by an Imperial crown. In the centre the Arms and motto of Northampton (a tower supported by two lions; the motto *Castello fortior concordia*). In bronze (Fig. 1670).

Kettering Volunteer Corps

An oval inscribed *Kettering Volunteer Corps* surmounted by an Imperial crown. In the centre crossed keys. In bronze (Fig. 1671).

Nottinghamshire Volunteer Regiment
(Later 9th–12th Volunteer Battalions, The Sherwood Foresters.)
A wreath of oak surmounted by a crown and on this crossed rifles. Superimposed, a band inscribed *Nottinghamshire Volunteer Regiment* and in the centre the Arms, crest, supporters and motto of the City of Nottingham. In bronze (Fig. 1672).

Oxfordshire Volunteer Regiment
(Later 1st and 2nd Volunteer Battalions, The Oxfordshire and Buckinghamshire Light Infantry.)
A circular scroll inscribed *Oxfordshire Volunteer Regiment* surmounted by a crown. In the centre an ox fording water. At the base a scroll inscribed *Fortis est veritas*. In bronze (Fig. 1673).

Pembrokeshire and Carmarthenshire Volunteer Regiment
(Later 1st Volunteer Battalion, The Welsh Regiment.)

Carmarthenshire Volunteer Training Corps
On a laurel-wreath, surmounted by an Imperial crown, crossed rifles with the letters *VTC* superimposed and the date *1915* below. Beneath the wreath a scroll inscribed *Carmarthenshire*. In gilding-metal (Fig. 1674).

Perthshire Volunteer Regiment
(Later 5th and 6th Volunteer Battalions, The Black Watch.)
A circlet inscribed *Perthshire Volunteers 1916*. In the centre a mullet. In white-metal (Fig. 1675).

Shropshire Volunteer Regiment
(Later 1st and 2nd Volunteer Battalions, The King's Shropshire Light Infantry.)
Within a wreath of laurel on left and oak on right, a circlet inscribed *Shropshire Volunteers* and surmounted by an Imperial crown. In the centre a shield bearing three loggerheads (leopards' faces) from the Arms of Shrewsbury. Below the shield a scroll inscribed *Regiment* and below this a further scroll inscribed *VTC*. In bronze (Fig. 1676).

Somerset Volunteer Regiment
(Later 1st, 2nd and 3rd Volunteer Battalions, The Somerset Light Infantry.)
A circlet inscribed *Somerset County* surmounted by an Imperial crown. In the centre a shield bearing the Wessex Wyvern. Below the circlet a scroll inscribed *Volunteer Regiment*. In bronze (Fig. 1677).

Staffordshire Volunteer Regiment
(Later 1st and 2nd Volunteer Battalions, The North Staffordshire Regiment and 1st and 2nd Volunteer Battalions, The South Staffordshire Regiment.)

Wolverhampton Volunteer Defence Force
An eight-pointed star, the topmost point displaced by an Imperial crown. On the star a shield bearing the Arms of Wolverhampton, *viz*: a cross formy between a pillar, a woolpack, an open book and a padlock. Below the shield a scroll inscribed *WVDF*. In bronze.
(Wolverhampton became the 2nd Volunteer Battalion, The South Staffordshire Regiment.)

Suffolk Volunteer Regiment
(Later 1st–6th Volunteer Battalions, The Suffolk Regiment.)

Suffolk Volunteer Training Corps
On a laurel-wreath, surmounted by an Imperial crown, crossed rifles with the letters *VTC* superimposed and the date *1915* below. Beneath the wreath a scroll inscribed *Suffolk*. In gilding-metal (Fig. 1678).

Surrey Volunteer Regiment
(Later 1st, 2nd and 3rd Volunteer Battalions, The Queen's Royal West Surrey Regiment and the 1st, 2nd and 3rd Volunteer Battalions, The East Surrey Regiment.)

Surrey Volunteer Training Corps
On a laurel-wreath, surmounted by an Imperial crown, crossed rifles with the letters *VTC* superimposed and the date *1915* below. Beneath the wreath a scroll inscribed *Surrey*. In gilding-metal (Fig. 1679).

6th (Guildford) Battalion, Surrey Volunteer Training Corps
A strap inscribed *6th (Guildford) Battalion* surmounted by a crown. In the centre the Arms of Guildford with the letters *S* at top, *V* left, *T* right and *C* bottom, surrounding it. In bronze (Fig. 1680).

Sussex Volunteer Regiment
(Later 1st-6th Volunteer Battalions, The Royal Sussex Regiment.)

Sussex Volunteer Training Corps
On a shield six martlets. Below the shield a scroll inscribed *Sussex VTC*. In bronze (Fig. 1681).

Warwickshire Volunteer Regiment
(Later 1st–5th Volunteer Battalions, The Royal Warwickshire Regiment.)
The Bear and Ragged Staff on a wreath. Below this a scroll inscribed *1st Batt Warwickshire Voltr Regt*. In bronze (Fig. 1682).

Isle of Wight Volunteer Regiment
Within a laurel-wreath Carisbrooke Castle. Below, a scroll inscribed *Isle of Wight VTC*. In gilding-metal (Fig. 1683).

Wiltshire Volunteer Regiment
(Later 1st Volunteer Battalion, The Wiltshire Regiment.)

Swindon and District Volunteer Training Corps
Within a laurel-wreath a shield bearing the Arms of Swindon and surmounted by the crest. Below the shield a scroll inscribed *Swindon & Dist. VTC*. In bronze (Fig. 1684).

Malmesbury Volunteer Training Corps
Upon crossed rakes, surmounted by an Imperial crown, a barrel with a crescent moon below. At the base a scroll inscribed *Malmesbury VTC*. In bronze (Fig. 1685).

1671

1672

1673

1674

1675

1676

1677

1678

1679

1680

1681

1682

1683

1684

1685

1686

1687

1688

1689

1690

1691

1692

1693

1694

1695

1696

Worcestershire Volunteer Regiment
(Later 1st, 2nd and 3rd Volunteer Battalions, The Worcestershire Regiment.)
   (1) On an ornamental shield a diamond on which a pear-tree bearing fruit. In bronze
       (Fig. 1686).
   (2) Superimposed on the letter *V* an eight-pointed star. On this the Garter with the Lion
       of England in the centre and a scroll inscribed *Firm* on the bottom-ray. A scroll below
       the star inscribed *Worcestershire Volunteer Regt.* In bronze (Fig. 1687).

West Riding Volunteer Regiment
The regiment later consisted of the following battalions:
1st–4th Volunteer Battalions, The York and Lancaster Regiment; 1st–5th Volunteer
Battalions, The Duke of Wellington's Regiment; 1st–8th Volunteer Battalions, The West
Yorkshire Regiment; 1st–3rd Volunteer Battalions, The King's Own Yorkshire Light
Infantry.

West Riding Volunteers
The Rose of York resting on a scroll inscribed *West Riding Volunteers.* In gilding-metal
(Fig. 1688).

Huddersfield District Volunteer Corps
(Later 2nd Volunteer Battalion, The Duke of Wellington's Regiment.)
A circlet inscribed *Huddersfield Dist Volunteer Corps.* Within this a shield bearing the Arms of
Huddersfield (a chevron between three rams passant and on the chevron three towers).
In bronze (Fig. 1689).

Leeds Volunteer Training Corps
(Later 5th and 6th Volunteer Battalions, The West Yorkshire Regiment.)
A circlet inscribed *Leeds Volr Training Corps* surmounted by a crown. Within the circlet a
shield bearing the Arms of Leeds (a golden fleece; on a chief three stars: the crest an owl,
and the supporters crowned owls). Below the circlet a scroll with the City motto *Pro Rege et
Lege.* In bronze (Fig. 1690).

Wakefield
(Later 1st Volunteer Battalion, The King's Own Yorkshire Light Infantry.)
A fleur-de-lys. Below this a scroll inscribed *Wakefield.* In bronze (Fig. 1691).

Todmorden Volunteer Training Corps
Within a laurel-wreath a strap inscribed *Volunteer Training Corps* surmounted by an Imperial
crown. In the centre the Arms of Todmorden. At the base a scroll inscribed *Todmorden.* In
white-metal (Fig. 1692).

Besides the Infantry there were Volunteer units of other Arms.
These were: Royal Garrison Artillery (Volunteers)
           Royal Engineers (Volunteers)
           Army Service Corps (Volunteers)
           Army Service Corps (Motor Transport) (Volunteers)
           Royal Army Medical Corps (Volunteers)

These formations later wore the same badges as the Regular forces, but while they were administered by the Central Association some wore special badges. Two of these are described below:

Corps of Volunteers Artillery Regiment
Within a laurel-wreath a shield. On this in chief a label inscribed *Corps of Volunteers*. On the shield a wheel with the letter *V* in the centre and inscribed *Protect the populace*. In the top left-hand corner a small shield inscribed with the letter *A*, and in the top right a similar shield inscribed with the letter *R*. In the bottom left- and right-hand corners guns with the barrels raised. In gilding-metal (Fig. 1693).

National Motor Volunteers
A wheel inscribed *National Motor Volunteers*. On this the figure of Mercury holding a caduceus in his left-hand, his right-hand held aloft. Below the wheel a scroll inscribed *Pro patria*. The figure of Mercury in gilding-metal, remainder in white-metal (Fig. 1694).
(This unit was later part of the Army Service Corps (Volunteers).)

Irish Association of Volunteer Training Corps
A number of units were formed in Ireland. Some of these in Dublin and Belfast were:

Dublin
The Volunteer Training Corps in Dublin city consisted of a number of individual Corps organised into the 1st Battalion. These were:
The Irish Rugby Football Union Volunteer Training Corps
The Dublin Veterans' Corps
The Glasnevin Volunteer Training Corps (This Unit formed 'C' Company)
The City Volunteer Training Corps
The Railway Volunteer Training Corps

Also in the Dublin Area were:
The Greystones Volunteer Training Corps
The Bray Volunteer Training Corps
The Kingstown and District Volunteer Training Corps
(Note: Of the above, the Irish Rugby Football Union V.T.C., The Railway V.T.C. and The Kingstown and District V.T.C. had special badges, as did St. Andrews V.T.C. (O.T.C.).)

Dublin Veterans' Corps
On an eight-pointed star, the topmost point displaced by an Imperial crown, a shield bearing the Arms of the City of Dublin surrounded by a circlet inscribed *Dublin Veterans' Corps*.

Belfast
The Belfast Volunteer Defence Corps was affiliated to the Irish Association of Volunteer Training Corps on the 8th June, 1915. It was disbanded in 1917.
Badge: An eight-pointed star, the topmost point displaced by an Imperial crown. On this a circlet inscribed *Belfast Volunteers* with, in the centre, a shamrock. In bronze.

Queen's University Belfast Veterans' Corps
Within a laurel wreath surmounted by an Imperial crown a shield bearing the Arms of the University. Below, two scrolls, the upper one inscribed *Queen's* and the lower one *Veterans' Corps 1914*. In bronze (Fig. 1695).

————————

The Channel Islands also raised Volunteer Forces, but we have been able to trace details of the Guernsey contingent only.

Guernsey Volunteer Corps
A circlet inscribed *Diex Aie Guernsey Volunteer Corps* surmounted by an Imperial crown. In the centre a shield bearing the Arms of Guernsey. In bronze (Fig. 1696).

CHAPTER 28

The Territorial Force of 1908 to 1921

The Volunteers were formed into the Territorial Force in 1908 in implementation of Lord Haldane's reorganisation of the Reserve Forces of the Crown.

The infantry battalions took their place as integral units of the Line Regiments, being numbered-on from the Militia.

They were authorised to wear the same badges as the Regular component with one exception, that battle-honours awarded to parent regiments and borne on their badges were not to be displayed on those of the Territorial element.

This resulted in badges being struck with blank scrolls or tablets. In some instances, where a Volunteer unit had been awarded the South African War honour this took the place of the honour on the Regulars' badge.

Some Volunteers who had been classified previously as Rifles wore a similar badge to the Line regiment of which they now formed a part, but with a black finish, and a small number of units wore a badge with very little change from the one they had worn previously.

This chapter deals only with the Territorial Force infantry units affiliated to the Regular Infantry of the Line. The Honourable Artillery Company, The London Regiment, cyclist battalions and the four regiments which formed their own Corps (Monmouthshire, Cambridgeshire, Hertfordshire and Herefordshire) are dealt with in other sections of this book.

The Royal Scots (Lothian Regiment)

4th and 5th Battalions (Queen's Edinburgh Rifles)
The Star of the Order of the Thistle with an Imperial crown above the motto and a bugle-horn below. In white-metal (Fig. 1697). Officers: in silver-plate with gilt crown and bugle, and gilt centre with green-enamel backing.

The Queen's (Royal West Surrey Regiment)

5th Battalion
The Paschal Lamb on a scroll inscribed *The Queen's*. In blackened-brass (Fig. 1698).

The Buffs (East Kent Regiment)

4th Battalion
The Dragon on a scroll inscribed *4th Bn The Buffs*. In bronze (Fig. 1699).

The Northumberland Fusiliers

4th, 5th and 6th Battalions

A fused grenade with, on the ball, a circlet inscribed *Northumberland Fusiliers* with, in the centre, St. George and the Dragon. Below the grenade a scroll inscribed *South Africa 1900–02*. Circlet and St. George in silver-plate, remainder in gilt (Fig. 1700). Also in bronze.

The King's (Liverpool Regiment)

5th Battalion

The White Horse of Hanover on a scroll inscribed *The King's*. In blackened-brass (Fig. 1701).

6th (Rifle) Battalion

A bugle-horn surmounted by the Rose of Lancaster. In blackened-brass (Fig. 1702). Officers wore a blackened-silver bugle-horn on a black-cord boss.

7th Battalion

The White Horse of Hanover on ground above a scroll inscribed *The King's*. All in white-metal (Fig. 1703).

8th (Irish) Battalion

(1) The Irish Harp surmounted by an Imperial crown and resting on a wreath of shamrocks. Below, a scroll inscribed *8th (Irish) Bn King's Liverpool Regt.* In gilding-metal (Fig. 1704).

(2) The Irish Harp surmounted by an Imperial crown resting on a scroll inscribed *Erin go brach* within a wreath of shamrocks from which a bugle-horn is suspended. Below the wreath a scroll inscribed *8th Irish Batt King's L'pool Regt* with a straight scroll below inscribed *South Africa 1900–02*. In silver-plate for officers (Fig. 1705).

10th (Scottish) Battalion

(1) Superimposed on St. Andrew's Cross the White Horse of Hanover standing on ground and below this a scroll inscribed *The King's* and below this two thistle-sprays, joining the tops of which a scroll inscribed *Liverpool Scottish*. In white-metal (Fig. 1706). Also in silver.
A variant is with the Cross, wreath and top-scroll in gilt and the White Horse and scroll in silver. The top-scroll is inscribed *Scottish Liverpool*.

(2) Superimposed on St. Andrew's Cross a wreath of thistles surmounted by an Imperial crown. In the centre the White Horse of Hanover on a scroll inscribed in Old English lettering *King's*. In white-metal (Fig. 1707). Worn by pipers.

The Lincolnshire Regiment

4th and 5th Battalions

The Sphinx resting on a blank tablet above a scroll inscribed *Lincolnshire*. The scroll in gilding-metal, remainder in white-metal (Fig. 1708).

The Devonshire Regiment

4th Battalion

An eight-pointed star, the topmost point displaced by an Imperial crown. On this a circlet inscribed *The Devonshire Regiment*. In the centre the castle of Exeter. In blackened-brass.

1697

1698

1699

1700

1701 ✓

1702 ✓

1703 ✓

1704 ✓

1705 ✓

1706

1707

1708

1709

1710

1711

1712

1713

1714

1715

1716

1717

1718

1719

1720

1721

5th Battalion
As 4th Battalion but all in white-metal (Fig. 1709).

The Suffolk Regiment

4th, 5th and 6th Battalions
Within a wreath of oak a plain circlet surmounted by an Imperial crown. In the centre a castle and, below, a scroll inscribed *The Suffolk Regt.* The scroll in gilding-metal, remainder in white-metal (Fig. 1710).
Also found in bronze and in all-brass.

Prince Albert's (Somerset Light Infantry)

4th and 5th Battalions
A bugle with strings surmounted by a mural crown. Above this a scroll inscribed *South Africa 1900–01.* The letters *PA* within the strings of the bugle. In white-metal (Fig. 1711). Officers: in hall-marked silver, also in bronze.

The Prince of Wales's Own (West Yorkshire Regiment)

7th and 8th Battalions (Leeds Rifles)
(1) A cross based on that of the Order of the Bath surmounted by an Imperial crown. In the centre of the cross a circlet inscribed *Leeds Rifles* and within this a bugle with strings surmounted by a crown. The whole surrounded by a laurel-wreath. Across the base of the wreath a scroll inscribed *7 (or 8) Bn PWO West Yorkshire Regt.* In blackened-metal (Fig. 1712). Also in white-metal.
(2) A cross based on that of the Order of the Bath with, on the top arm, *South Africa 1900–02.* In the centre of the cross a circlet inscribed *Leeds Rifles* and within this a bugle surmounted by a crown (Fig. 1713).
For officers: in silver-plate, also in bronze and in black.

The Leicestershire Regiment

4th, 5th and 6th Battalions
The Tiger on ground. Below this a scroll inscribed *Leicestershire.* The scroll in white-metal, remainder in gilding-metal (Fig. 1714). Also an all-brass economy issue.

Alexandra, Princess of Wales's Own (Yorkshire Regiment)

4th and 5th Battalions
The letter *A*, cypher of the late Queen Alexandra, thereon the Danebrog surmounted by a coronet and on these the date *1875* and *Alexandra*, all resting on a tablet inscribed *Yorkshire.* Below, a scroll inscribed *The Princess of Wales's Own Regt.* Below this a scroll inscribed *South Africa 1900–02* (Fig. 1715). In bronze.

The Lancashire Fusiliers

5th, 6th, 7th and 8th Battalions
A fused grenade with, on the ball within a laurel-wreath, the Sphinx resting on a blank tablet. Below, a scroll inscribed *The Lancashire Fusiliers.* The scroll in white-metal, remainder in gilding-metal (Fig. 1716). Officers: in gilt-and-silver, also in bronze.

1722

1723

1724

1725

1726

1727

1728

1729

1730

1731

1732

1733

1734

1735

1736

1737

1738

1739

1740

1741

1742

1743

1744

1745

1746

The South Wales Borderers

The Brecknockshire Battalion
(1) The Welsh Dragon on a scroll inscribed *Brecknockshire*. In gilding-metal (Fig. 1717). Also in silver, white-metal and bronze.
(2) As above but with longer scroll (Fig. 1718). In same metals as above.

The Cameronians (Scottish Rifles)

5th Battalion
Within a complete wreath of thistles a bugle with strings surmounted by a mullet. The numeral *5* within the strings of the bugle. In white-metal (Fig. 1719).

The Gloucestershire Regiment

5th and 6th Battalions
The Sphinx resting on a blank tablet above two sprigs of laurel. Below, a scroll inscribed *Gloucestershire* (Fig. 1720). In white-metal, also an all-brass economy issue and in bronze.

4th Battalion
The above badge in blackened-brass.

The East Lancashire Regiment

4th and 5th Battalions
(1) Within a laurel-wreath surmounted by an Imperial crown the Sphinx resting on a blank tablet and beneath this a rose. At the base of the wreath a scroll inscribed *East Lancashire* and below this a smaller scroll inscribed *South Africa 1900–02*. In white-metal (Fig. 1721).
(2) As above but without the honour-scroll. All in white-metal except the rose which is in gilding-metal (Fig. 1722).

The East Surrey Regiment

6th Battalion
(1) A Maltese cross, the edge of the top arm inscribed *South Africa* and the edge of the bottom arm, *1900–1902*. In the centre a circlet inscribed *The East Surrey Regt 6th Battalion*. In the centre an eight-pointed star with, in its centre, the Arms of Guildford. In blackened-brass (Fig. 1723). Officers': in blackened-silver with raised parts polished.
(2) An eight-pointed star, the topmost point displaced by an Imperial crown. In the centre a shield bearing the Arms of Guildford. Below, a scroll inscribed *East Surrey*. In blackened-brass (Fig. 1724).

The Border Regiment

4th Battalion
On an eight-pointed star, the topmost point displaced by an Imperial crown, a Maltese cross. On this a circlet inscribed *South Africa 1900–02* with, in the centre, *4th*. At the base a scroll inscribed *Border Cumberland & Westmorland Regiment* (Fig. 1725). In white-metal, also in bronze.

5th Battalion

Same design as above but honour is *South Africa 1901–02*, in the centre *5th* and the scroll at the base reads *Border Cumberland Regiment* (Fig. 1726). In white-metal, also in bronze.

The Royal Sussex Regiment

5th (Cinque Ports) Battalion

(1) A Maltese cross behind which the Roussillon plume. In the centre, on a circular background, a shield bearing the Arms of the Cinque Ports. Below the cross a scroll inscribed *Cinque Ports*. In silver with red (left) and blue (right) enamel in the Arms (Fig. 1727).

(2) Same design as above but all in gilding-metal (Fig. 1728). Also in bronze.

The Hampshire Regiment

6th (Duke of Connaught's Own) Battalion

(1) Within a laurel-wreath a strap inscribed *Duke of Connaught's Own* surmounted by a ducal coronet. In the centre the Hampshire Rose (Fig. 1729). Officers' pattern in silver with blue-enamel behind lettering and the rose in red- and white-enamel. Also in bronze.

(2) Same design as above but with the addition of a scroll inscribed *Hampshire* at the base (Fig. 1730).
Other-ranks' pattern: the Rose and bottom scroll in gilding-metal, remainder in white-metal. Also in all-brass.

7th Battalion

(1) Within a laurel-wreath surmounted by an Imperial crown, a dog gauge. Below, a scroll inscribed *7th Bn Hampshire Regt* (Fig. 1731). Officers' pattern in bronze, also in gilt.

(2) As above but without the crown (Fig. 1732). Other-ranks' pattern in gilding-metal and in white-metal. Also in bronze, worn by officers until 1918 when the above pattern (1) was taken into use.

8th (Isle of Wight Rifles, Princess Beatrice's) Battalion

Within a laurel-wreath a circlet inscribed *Isle of Wight Rifles* and in the centre the Tower of Carisbrooke Castle. Above the circlet a scroll inscribed *South Africa 1900–01* and above this the Imperial crown. Below the circlet a scroll inscribed *Princess Beatrice's* (Fig. 1733). In black-, white-metal and silver.

The Dorsetshire Regiment

4th Battalion

The Castle and Key of Gibraltar with, above, the Sphinx resting on a blank tablet. Below the Castle a scroll inscribed *Primus in Indis*. A laurel-wreath encloses the castle and motto and is continued below the motto by a scroll inscribed *Dorsetshire*. The wreath and title-scroll in gilding-metal, remainder in white-metal (Fig. 1734).

The Prince of Wales's Volunteers (South Lancashire Regiment)

4th Battalion

The Prince of Wales's plumes, coronet and motto. Below, a Sphinx resting on a blank tablet. Above the plumes a scroll inscribed *South Lancashire* and below the Sphinx a scroll inscribed *Prince of Wales's Vols*. Branches of laurel connect the ends of the scrolls. The plumes, motto and Sphinx in white-metal, remainder in gilding-metal (Fig. 1735).

5th Battalion

As above but in blackened-brass.

The Black Watch (Royal Highlanders)

4th, 5th, 6th and 7th Battalions

The Star of the Order of the Thistle. On the Star a thistle-wreath enclosing an oval inscribed *Nemo me impune lacessit* and surmounted by an Imperial crown. Within the oval St. Andrew and Cross. Across the top of the wreath a scroll inscribed *Royal Highlanders* and, across the bottom, a two-part scroll inscribed *Black Watch*. In white-metal (Fig. 1736). The badge is found with the spellings *lacessit* and *lacesset*.

The Oxfordshire and Buckinghamshire Light Infantry

Buckinghamshire Battalion

A Maltese cross surmounted by an Imperial crown. On this a circlet inscribed *Buckinghamshire Battalion*. In the centre a swan with a coronet round its neck. In white-metal (Fig. 1737). Also in silver, bronze, and black.

The Essex Regiment

4th, 5th, 6th and 7th Battalions

The Castle and Key of Gibraltar. Above the Castle the Sphinx resting on a blank tablet. The whole, except the Sphinx, enclosed in a wreath of oak. On the base of the wreath a scroll inscribed *The Essex Regt* and below this a further scroll inscribed *South Africa 1900–02*. The title-scroll and Sphinx in white-metal, remainder in gilding-metal (Fig. 1738).

8th Battalion

The same design as above but without the bottom scroll (Fig. 1739). In same metals as above, also all in brass.

The Sherwood Foresters (Nottinghamshire and Derbyshire Regiment)

7th (Robin Hood) Battalion

A laurel-wreath surmounted by an Imperial crown. Within this a cross based on that of the Order of the Bath. On the arms of the cross: (left) *South*, (right) *Africa*, (bottom) *1900–02*. In the centre of the cross a circlet inscribed *The Robin Hoods* and in its centre a bugle with strings surmounted by a crown (Fig. 1740). In white-metal, also in black.
Officers': in silver, also in blackened white-metal with high points polished to show white.

The Northamptonshire Regiment

4th Battalion

(1) The Castle and Key of Gibraltar within a laurel-wreath. Above the castle a scroll

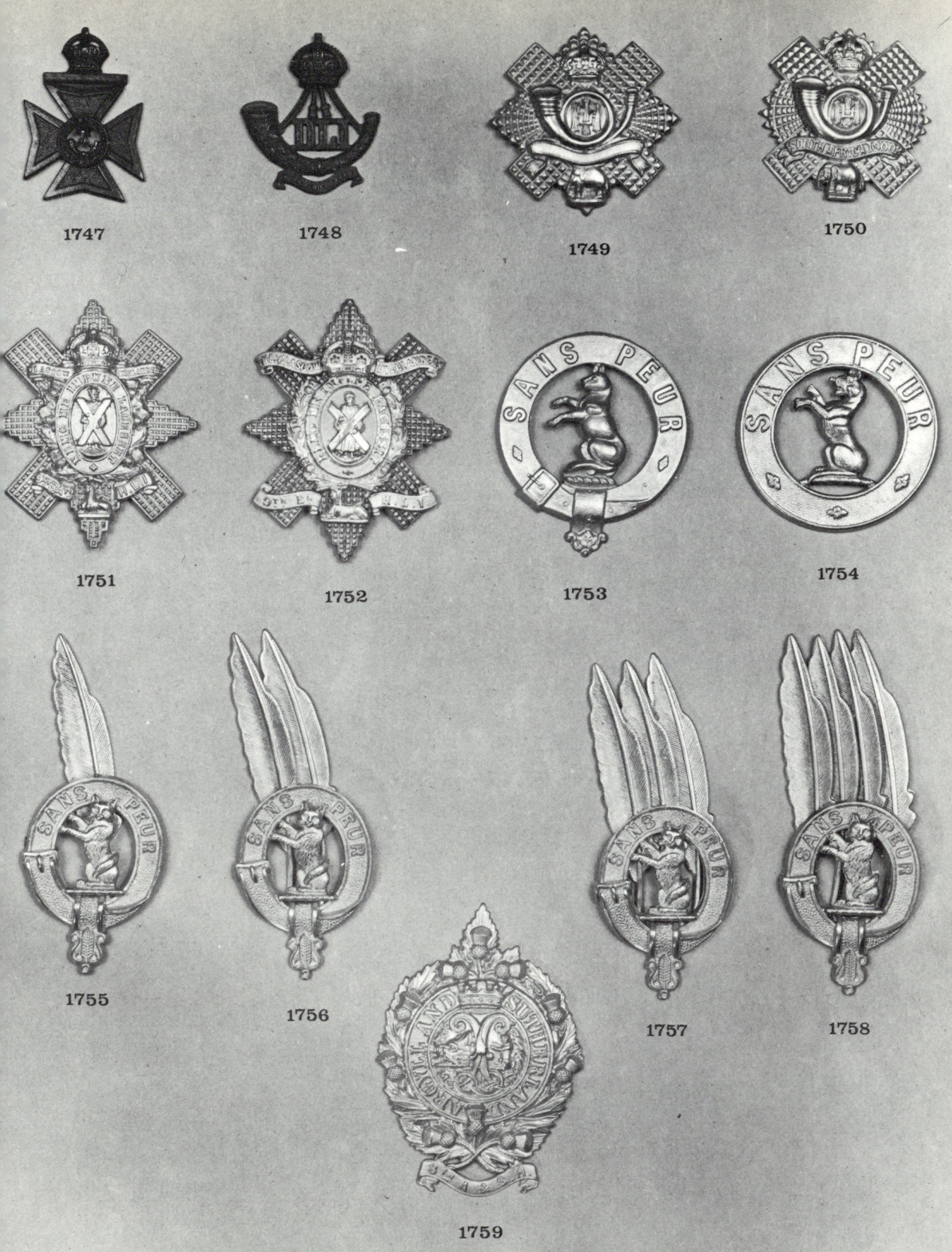

1747

1748

1749

1750

1751

1752

1753

1754

1755

1756

1757

1758

1759

inscribed *4th Battalion* and below the castle a scroll inscribed *South Africa 1900–02*. On the base of the wreath a scroll inscribed *Northamptonshire* (Fig. 1741). The title-scroll in gilding-metal, remainder in white-metal. Also in bronze.

(2) As above but with blank scrolls above and below the castle (Fig. 1742). Title-scroll in gilding-metal, remainder in white-metal. Also in all-brass.

The Duke of Cambridge's Own (Middlesex Regiment)

7th, 8th and 9th Battalions

The Prince of Wales's plumes, coronet and motto. Below the coronet the cypher *G* of the Duke of Cambridge interlaced and reversed, all within a laurel-wreath. Across the base of the wreath a scroll inscribed *South Africa 1900–02*. Below the wreath a scroll inscribed *Middlesex Regt.* The plumes, motto and title scroll in white-metal, remainder in gilding-metal (Fig. 1743).

Also in silver and in bronze for officers.

10th Battalion

As above but with the honour-scroll left blank (Fig. 1744).

In same metals as above.

The Duke of Edinburgh's (Wiltshire Regiment)

4th Battalion

A cross patée lined with burnished edges. On the cross a circular convex plate and thereon the cypher of the Duke of Edinburgh. Above the cross a coronet. Below, a scroll inscribed *The Wiltshire Regiment*. All in black-metal (Fig. 1745).

The Manchester Regiment

7th (Ardwick) Battalion

A floriated fleur-de-lys (Fig. 1746). In bronze.

The Durham Light Infantry

6th Battalion

A Maltese cross with a blank bar above the cross and on this an Imperial crown. In the centre a circlet inscribed *6th Battn The Durham Light Infantry* with, in the centre, a bugle with strings (Fig. 1747). In blackened-brass for officers. Other-ranks wore the bugle surmounted by the Imperial crown with the letters *DLI* within the strings in blackened-brass.

5th, 7th, 8th and 9th Battalions

A bugle with the strings surmounted by an Imperial crown and the letters *DLI* within the strings. Underneath the bugle a scroll inscribed *South Africa 1900–02*. For officers: in bronze, also in silver (Fig. 1748).

The Highland Light Infantry

5th, 7th and 8th Battalions

(1) The Star of the Order of the Thistle and thereon a bugle-horn. In the twist of the horn the monogram *HLI*. Above the horn an Imperial crown and below it a blank scroll and beneath this the Elephant. In white-metal (Fig. 1749). Also found with a shorter blank scroll.

(2) As above but with the scroll inscribed *South Africa 1900–02*. In white-metal (Fig. 1750).

9th (Glasgow Highland) Battalion

(1) The Star of the Order of the Thistle. On the Star a thistle-wreath enclosing an oval inscribed *Nemo me impune lacessit* and surmounted by an Imperial crown. Within the oval St. Andrew and Cross. Across the top of the wreath a two-part scroll inscribed *Glasgow Highlanders* and a similar scroll at the base inscribed *9th Batt H.L.I.* with, between the two parts, the Sphinx on a blank tablet (Fig. 1751). In white-metal; also in silver-plate. Both types are found with the alternative spelling of *lacessit* and *lacesset*.

(2) Similar to above but with longer scrolls, the top one inscribed *The Glasgow Highlanders* and the bottom *9th Bn H.L.I.* (Fig. 1752). For officers: St. Andrew and Cross and the title-scrolls in silver, remainder in gilt.

Seaforth Highlanders (Ross-shire Buffs, The Duke of Albany's)

5th (The Sutherland and Caithness Highland) Battalion

(1) Within a strap inscribed *Sans peur* a cat-a-mountain. In white-metal (Fig. 1753).
(2) Within a circlet inscribed *Sans peur* a cat-a-mountain. In white-metal (Fig. 1754).

Officers' badges

Subaltern:　Within a strap inscribed *Sans peur* a cat-a-mountain, with one silver feather behind the strap (Fig. 1755).
Captain:　As above but with two silver feathers (Fig. 1756).
Field officer: As above but with three silver feathers (Fig. 1757).
Full colonel: As above but with four silver feathers (Fig. 1758).

Princess Louise's (Argyll and Sutherland Highlanders)

8th (Argyllshire) Battalion

A circlet inscribed *Argyll and Sutherland*. Within the circlet the letter *L*, the cypher of the late Princess Louise, interlaced and reversed. Within the circlet and on the left of the cypher the Boar's Head and on the right of the Cypher the Cat. Above the cypher the Princess's coronet, the whole within a wreath of thistles. At the base, a scroll inscribed *8th A & SH*. In white-metal (Fig. 1759).

CHAPTER 29

The Territorial Regiments

When the Territorial Force was formed in 1908 the majority of the Volunteer battalions or Rifle Volunteers became Territorial Force battalions of the regiments to which they were already affiliated, but four units were constituted regiments in their own right, *viz.*: the Monmouthshire, Herefordshire, Hertfordshire, and Cambridgeshire Regiments.

In April 1882, the three Monmouthshire Rifle Volunteer Corps had become Volunteer battalions of the South Wales Borderers. These now became the 1st, 2nd and 3rd Battalions, The Monmouthshire Regiment.

Although in 1888 the 1st and 2nd Shropshire Rifle Volunteers became the 1st and 2nd Volunteer battalions of the King's (Shropshire Light Infantry), the Herefordshire Rifle Volunteers did not take the title of the 3rd Battalion although it formed part of that Corps and continued under its old title. In the reorganisation of 1908 it was designated at first the Herefordshire Battalion of the King's (Shropshire Light Infantry) but in March 1909 it received the title of 1st Battalion, The Herefordshire Regiment.

The two Hertfordshire Rifle Volunteer Corps had become the 1st and 2nd (Hertfordshire) Battalions of the Bedfordshire Regiment in 1887, but the new organisation provided for only one infantry battalion in Hertfordshire. Accordingly, the two battalions were amalgamated and became the 1st Battalion, The Hertfordshire Regiment.

In 1887 too, the 1st Cambridgeshire Rifle Volunteers had become the 3rd (Cambridgeshire) Volunteer Battalion, The Suffolk Regiment. In March 1909, the battalion was detached from the Suffolk Regiment and became the 1st Battalion, The Cambridgeshire Regiment.

When the London Regiment was formed it was intended that it should consist of twenty-eight battalions, the 26th being the Honourable Artillery Company and the 27th, the Inns of Court Rifle Volunteers. These two units, however, did not become part of the regiment: the Inns of Court was converted into an Officers Training Corps and the Honourable Artillery Company retained its independent existence.

The five regiments mentioned above are dealt with in this chapter.

THE HONOURABLE ARTILLERY COMPANY

By order of King William IV the Company was to wear a uniform similar to that of the Grenadier Guards but substituting silver lace for gold. Their badges, therefore, closely resemble those of the Grenadier Guards.

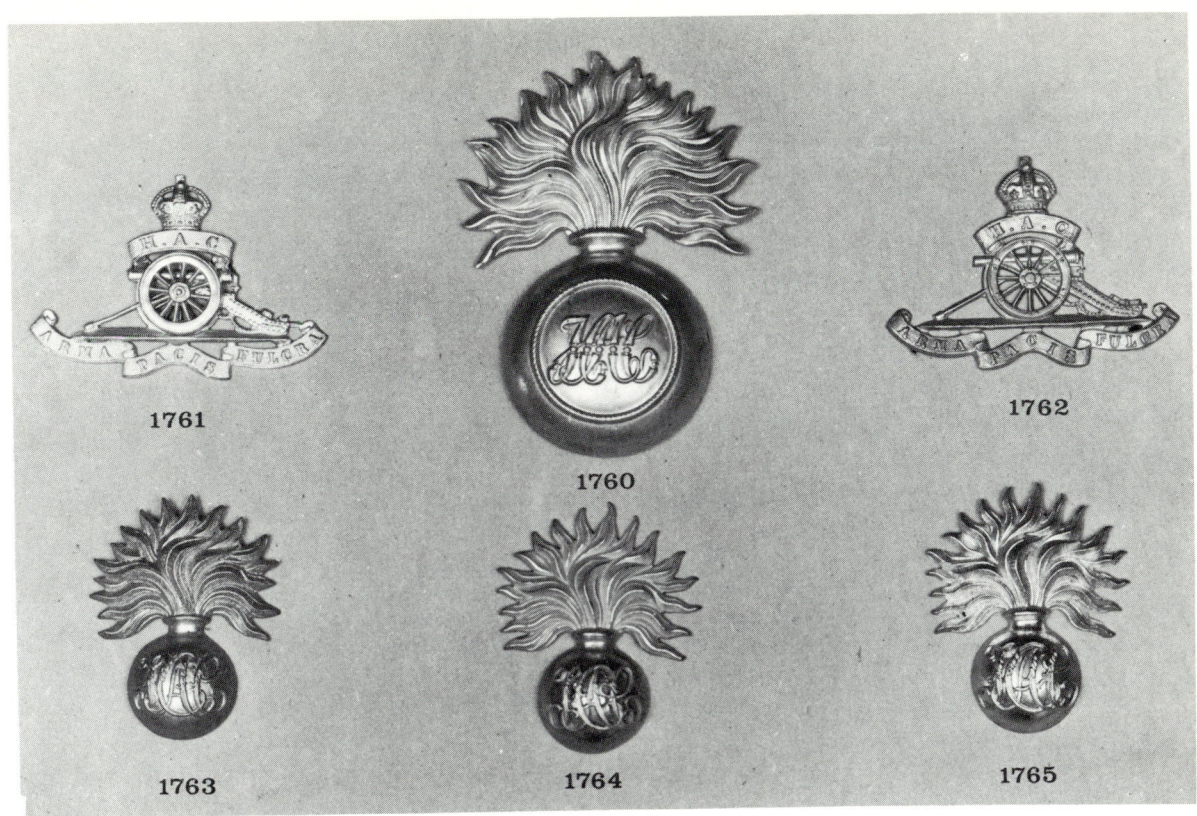

1761   1760   1762

1763   1764   1765

Artillery

Busby-grenade: c. 1879
A fused grenade. On the ball a rope circle and within this the letters *HAC*. In gilding-metal (Fig. 1760).

Forage-cap: 1902–
Officers': A gun with a scroll above inscribed *HAC* surmounted by an Imperial crown. Below the gun a scroll inscribed *Arma pacis fulcra*. In gilt with an extra wheel on the gun (Fig. 1761). Also in bronze.
Other-ranks': Same design as for officers but all in gilding-metal (Fig. 1762).

Infantry

Forage cap: 1902–
Officers': A fused grenade. On the ball the letters *HAC*. All in gilt (Fig. 1763).
Warrant-Officers and Sergeants: Same design as above but with the grenade in gilding-metal and the letters in white-metal (Fig. 1764).
Other-ranks': Same design as above but all in gilding-metal (Fig. 1765).

THE MONMOUTHSHIRE REGIMENT

Ten Corps of Monmouthshire Rifle Volunteers were raised in 1859 and 1860. They were:

     1st (Chepstow V.R.C.)
     2nd (Pontymoel (Pontypool) V.R.C.)
     3rd (Newport Town V.R.C.)
     4th (Blaenavon V.R.C.)
     5th (Hanbury (Pontypool) V.R.C.)
     6th (Monmouth V.R.C.)
     7th (Newport Borough V.R.C.)
     8th (Usk and Raglan V.R.C.)
     9th (Abergavenny V.R.C.)
     10th (Risca V.R.C.)

1st Chepstow V.R.C.

Superimposed on a laurel wreath a crossed sword and rifle with, in the centre, a strap inscribed *1st Monmouthshire Rifles* and surmounted by a Victorian crown. In the centre of the strap an eight-pointed star. Across the base of the wreath a scroll inscribed *Pro aris et focis* (Fig. 1766).

3rd Newport V.R.C.

Design exactly the same as above except that the title on the strap reads *No. 3. Monmouthshire Rifles* (Fig. 1767).

In December 1860 the Corps were consolidated into three main units as follows:
The 1st, 3rd and 10th Corps were formed into the 1st Administrative Battalion, Monmouthshire Rifle Volunteers. The 10th Corps was, however, disbanded in 1875 and its place taken by the 11th (Tredegar V.R.C.) in 1877.
The 4th, 5th, 6th, 7th, 8th and 9th Corps were formed into the 2nd Administrative Battalion, Monmouthshire Rifle Volunteers. The 2nd (Pontymoel) Pontypool Corps was a very strong unit, with several sub-units in its immediate vicinity, and it was designated the 2nd (Consolidated) Battalion, Monmouthshire Rifle Volunteers.

The next change of title came in April 1882, when the three units became Volunteer Battalions of the South Wales Borderers and eventually the 1st Administrative Battalion was titled the 2nd Volunteer Battalion, the 2nd Consolidated Battalion the 3rd Volunteer Battalion, and the 2nd Administrative Battalion the 4th Volunteer Battalion.

When the Territorial Force was formed in April 1908 the Monmouthshire Battalions became a Territorial Regiment; the 2nd Volunteer Battalion, the South Wales Borderers becoming the 1st Battalion, The Monmouthshire Regiment, the 3rd Battalion the 2nd Battalion, and the 4th Battalion the 3rd Battalion.

1st Battalion

Helmet-plate: 1878 to 1882

A Maltese cross, with a lion between each division, surmounted by a Victorian crown. On this a circlet inscribed *1st Monmouthshire Rifle Volunteers* with, in the centre, a Stag's head on a wreathed scroll. In blackened-brass. White-metal for sergeants and in blackened white-metal, with the outlines of the cross and the title polished in contrasting white-metal, for officers (Fig. 1768).

Forage-cap: 1908 to 1922

The Welsh Dragon standing on ground. In white-metal (Fig. 1769).

1766

1767

1768

1769

1770

1771

1772

1773

1774

1775

1778

Forage-cap: 1922–
A laurel-wreath surmounted by an Imperial crown. On the wreath are battle-honour scrolls inscribed as follows: (left) *South Africa, 1900–02, Ypres, 1915, '17, '18., Somme, 1916, Scarpe, 1917, Cambrai, 1917, '18*; (right) *St. Julien, Arras, 1917, Langemarck, 1917, Hindenburg Line, Aden.* Across the base of the wreath a scroll inscribed *France & Flanders, 1914–18.* In the centre, the Welsh Dragon standing on ground. In white-metal. Officers': in silver, also in bronze (Fig. 1770).

2nd Battalion

Shako-badge: 1859
A rampant leopard within a wreath of oak surmounted by a Victorian crown.

Shako-badge: 1861
Superimposed on crossed rifles, a bugle-horn with the numerals *32* in the curl, the strings and tassels brought over to the right outside the bugle. Above the bugle-horn a Victorian crown within a laurel-wreath. Below the bugle, joining the butts of the rifles, a scroll inscribed *Gwell angau na gwarth* (Fig. 1771).
   This badge was worn from 1861 to 1864 in brass on a grey kepi; from 1864 to 1866 in blackened-brass on a black shako and on the undress-cap. It continued to be worn on the busby from 1867 to 1878 and in white-metal by other-ranks on the undress-cap from 1866 to 1882. Officers wore it in silver-plate with gilt numerals from 1861 to 1878 on various patterns of head-dress. It was also worn by other Corps of the 1st and 2nd Administrative Battalions after the early individual Corps badges ceased to be worn.

Shako-plate: 1866
A laurel-wreath surmounted by a Victorian crown. Within the wreath the Garter proper and in the centre the voided stencilled numerals *36*. In white-metal (Fig. 1772).
Worn for a short time only.

Helmet-plate: 1878 to 1882
Same design as the shako-plate of 1861 (see above) but larger. In blackened-brass. White-metal for sergeants and in blackened white-metal, with the outlines of the cross and the title polished in contrasting white-metal, for officers (Fig. 1773).

Officers' undress-cap
The Welsh Dragon in silver. Beneath a black-cord boss bearing a Victorian crown in silver.

Officers' Helmet-plate: 1882 to 1902
An eight-pointed star, the topmost point displaced by a Victorian crown. On this a laurel-wreath and within this the Garter. In the centre the Welsh Dragon within a laurel-wreath. Across the base of the wreath a scroll inscribed *The South Wales Borderers* and below this a second scroll inscribed *3rd Volunteer Battalion.* The Dragon, wreath and the two title scrolls are in gilt, remainder in silver-plate (Fig. 1774).

Other-ranks' Helmet-plate: 1882 to 1902
An eight-pointed star, the topmost point displaced by a Victorian crown. On this a laurel-wreath in the centre of which a circlet inscribed *South Wales Borderers 3rd Volr. Battn.* In the centre a laurel-wreath enclosing the Welsh Dragon (Fig. 1775).

1776

1777

1779

1780

1781

1782

1783

Officers' Undress-cap

Within a laurel-wreath surmounted by a Victorian crown the Welsh Dragon. In silver with a blue-velvet ground to the Dragon (Fig. 1776).

Officers' Forage-cap: 1908

The Welsh Dragon on ground. Below a scroll inscribed *2nd Bn. Monmouthshire Regt.* In silver-plate, also in bronze (Fig. 1777).

Officers' Helmet-plate: 1908

An eight-pointed star, the topmost point displaced by an Imperial crown. On this a laurel-wreath and within this the Garter. In the centre the Welsh Dragon within a laurel-wreath. Across the base of the wreath a scroll inscribed *2nd Batn. The Monmouthshire Regiment.* The Dragon, wreath and title-scroll in silver, remainder in gilt (Fig. 1778).

3rd Battalion

Helmet-plate: 1878 to 1882

A Maltese cross with a lion between each division surmounted by a Victorian crown. On this a circlet inscribed *3rd Monmouthshire Rifle Volunteer Corps* with, in the centre, a bugle with strings. In blackened-brass. White metal for sergeants and in blackened white-metal, with the outlines of the cross and the title polished in contrasting white-metal, for officers (Fig. 1779).

Officers' Helmet-plate: 1882 to 1902

An eight-pointed star, the topmost point displaced by a Victorian crown. On this a laurel-wreath and within this the Garter. In the centre the Welsh Dragon within a laurel-wreath. Across the base of the wreath a scroll inscribed *The South Wales Borderers* and below this a second scroll inscribed *4th Volunteer Battalion.* The Dragon and wreath in gilt, remainder in silver-plate (Fig. 1780).

Glengarry-badge: 1882

A circlet inscribed *4th VB South Wales Borderers* surmounted by a Victorian crown. In the centre the Welsh Dragon within a laurel-wreath. In white-metal (Fig. 1781).

Other-ranks' helmet-plate: 1902 to 1908

An eight-pointed star, the topmost point displaced by an Imperial crown. On this a laurel-wreath in the centre of which a circlet inscribed *4th VB South Wales Borderers.* In the centre the Welsh Dragon within a laurel-wreath. In white-metal (Fig. 1782).

Officers' forage-cap badge, 1908

The Welsh Dragon rampant above a scroll inscribed *3rd Bn. Monmouthshire Regt.* In silver, also in bronze. (Fig. 1783).

THE HEREFORDSHIRE REGIMENT

In 1860, eight Corps of Rifle Volunteers were raised in Herefordshire and three in Radnorshire. These were:

> 1st (Hereford City V.R.C.)
> 2nd (Ross V.R.C.)
> 3rd (Ledbury V.R.C.)
> 4th (Bromyard V.R.C.)

1784

1786

1789

1785

1788

1792

1787

1793

1794

1790

1791

5th (South Archenfield V.R.C.)
6th (Leominster V.R.C.)
7th (Kingston V.R.C.)
8th (Hereford (Oddfellows) V.R.C.)
1st (Presteigne V.R.C.)
2nd (Knighton V.R.C.)
3rd (New Radnor V.R.C.)

Kepi and Forage-cap: 1860 to 1874

A lion passant guardant holding in its right paw a sword (from the Arms of Hereford) (Fig. 1784).
With this was combined the number of the various Corps and a bugle-horn (these are not shown).

In February 1861, these Corps were consolidated as the 1st Administrative Battalion, Herefordshire Rifle Volunteers with which were united the Radnorshire Rifle Volunteers.

Shako-plate: 1875 to 1879

A laurel-wreath surmounted by a Victorian crown. Within this a strap inscribed *1st AB Herefordshire Rifle Volunteers*. In the centre a bugle with strings. In white-metal. Officer's: in silver-plate (Fig. 1785).

Forage-cap: 1875 to 1880

A bugle-horn surmounted by a Victorian crown with the numerals *69* in the curl. In blackened white-metal (Fig. 1786).

In 1880, the unit was designated the 1st Herefordshire Rifle Volunteer Corps (Hereford and Radnor).

Helmet-plate: 1880 to 1908

Officers: An eight-pointed star, the topmost point displaced by a Victorian crown. On this a laurel-wreath and within this a strap inscribed *1st Herefordshire Rifle Volunteer Corps*. In the centre on black-velvet ground the Arms of the City of Hereford. In silver-plate (Fig. 1787).
Other-ranks': Same design as for officers. In white-metal (Fig. 1788).

Forage-cap: 1880 to 1908

Same design as previous badge but in silver-plate (Fig. 1789).

On the formation of the Territorial Force the title of the regiment became: 1st Battalion, The Herefordshire Regiment (T.F.).

Helmet-plate: 1908 to 1914

Officers': An eight-pointed star, the topmost point displaced by an Imperial crown. On this a laurel-wreath and within this the Garter, all in gilt. In the centre on a black-velvet ground the Arms with crest, supporters and motto of the City of Hereford in silver. On the base of the laurel-wreath a silver scroll inscribed *The Herefordshire Regt* (Fig. 1790).
Other-ranks': Same design as for officers but without the title-scroll. In gilding-metal with white-metal centre (Fig. 1791).

Forage-cap: 1908 to 1914

(1) The Arms with crest, supporters and motto of the City of Hereford in silver with a gilt scroll below inscribed *Herefordshire*. Worn by officers, also in bronze (Fig. 1792).
(2) The lion from the crest of the City of Hereford. Below, a scroll inscribed *Herefordshire*. Worn by officers in 1916. In bronze (Fig. 1793).

(3) As (2). Worn by other-ranks in all-brass from 1915 to 1918 (Fig. 1794).

(4) As (2). Worn by other-ranks. White-metal lion, gilding-metal scroll. Worn from 1908. In 1915, officers wore the lion in silver without the title-scroll.

THE HERTFORDSHIRE REGIMENT

The first Corps of Rifle Volunteers in Hertfordshire was raised in 1859 and by the following year there were twelve Corps in existence. These were:

1st Hertford	raised 22nd November 1859
2nd Watford	raised 5th January 1860
3rd St. Albans	raised 5th March 1860
4th Ashridge	raised March 1860
5th Hemel Hempstead	raised 10th March 1860
6th Bishops Stortford	raised 20th March 1860
7th Berkhamstead	raised 13th March 1860
8th Tring	raised 20th April 1860
(amalgamated with the 7th on the 1st May 1866)	
9th Ware	raised 13th June 1860
10th Royston and Baldock	raised 25th June 1860
11th Cheshunt	raised July 1860
(disbanded 22nd November 1870)	
12th Hitchin	raised 15th September 1860

A 13th Corps was raised in Watton at Stone on 8th September 1864 but was disbanded 28th July 1868, and a 14th Corps at Welwyn and Hitchin on 13th September 1876.

The 22nd Essex Volunteer Rifle Corps (Waltham Abbey) was incorporated into the 2nd Administrative Battalion in 1863 and partially absorbed the 11th Corps when they were disbanded.

In October 1860 two Administrative Battalions were formed: the 1st incorporating the six Corps in the Western half of the County (2nd, 3rd, 4th, 5th, 7th and 8th) and the 2nd, those in the Eastern half (1st, 6th, 9th, 10th, 11th and 12th). The Corps raised subsequently were incorporated into the latter battalion.

Judging from photographs, the early Corps do not appear to have worn a badge in the shako and the first badge of which we have record is:

1st Hertfordshire Rifle Volunteers (Hertford)
A circlet inscribed *2nd Battn. Herts Rifles* surmounted by a hart trippant. In the centre the numeral *1*. In blackened white-metal.

1st Administrative Battalion

Glengarry
A strap inscribed *1st Battalion Herts RV* surmounted by a Victorian crown. In the centre a hart trippant. In blackened white-metal with the high-points polished (Fig. 1795).

2nd Administrative Battalion

Glengarry

A strap inscribed *2nd Battalion Herts RV* surmounted by a Victorian crown. In the centre a hart trippant. In blackened white-metal with high-points polished (Fig. 1796).

Officers' helmet-plate

An eight-pointed star on which a hart trippant. In silver (Fig. 1797).
The same plate was worn when the 1st Hertfordshire Rifle Volunteers were formed in 1880. It was also worn by other-ranks in black-metal with a white-metal hart.

In March 1880, the 1st Administrative Battalion became the 2nd Hertfordshire Rifle Volunteer Corps and the 2nd Administrative Battalion, the 1st Hertfordshire Rifle Volunteer Corps, the precedence of the battalions being reversed so that the senior Corps was included in the 1st.

Hertfordshire Rifle Volunteer Corps

Helmet-plate, other-ranks': 1880

An eight-pointed star, the topmost point displaced by a Victorian crown. On this a laurel-wreath and within this a strap inscribed *Hertfordshire Rifle Volunteers* with, in the centre, a hart trippant. In blackened-brass with the hart in white-metal (Fig. 1798).

Helmet-plate, officers': 1880

An eight-pointed star, the topmost point displaced by a Victorian crown. On this a laurel-wreath and within this a strap inscribed *Hertfordshire Rifle Volunteers* with, in the centre, a hart trippant. All in white-metal with blue-velvet backing to the centre (Fig. 1799).

Glengarry: 1880

A circlet inscribed *Hertfordshire Rifle Volunteers* surmounted by a Victorian crown. In the centre a hart trippant (Fig. 1800). Officers: in silver or white-metal. Other-ranks': in black-metal.

In December 1887, the 1st Hertfordshire Rifle Volunteer Corps became the 1st (Hertfordshire) Volunteer Battalion, The Bedfordshire Regiment.

Glengarry: 1887 to 1898

A circlet inscribed *1st Hertfordshire Volr. Battn.* surmounted by a Victorian crown. In the centre a hart trippant. Below the circlet a scroll inscribed *The Bedfordshire Regt.* In gilding-metal (Fig. 1801).

Forage-cap: 1898 to 1908

A Maltese cross superimposed on an eight-pointed star. On this the Garter and within the Garter a hart trippant. Above the Garter a scroll inscribed *1st Herts. V Bn.* and below the Garter a scroll inscribed *Bedfordshire.* In white-metal (Fig. 1802).

In December 1887, the 2nd Hertfordshire Rifle Volunteer Corps became the 2nd (Hertfordshire) Volunteer Battalion, The Bedfordshire Regiment.

Forage-cap: 1898 to 1908

A Maltese cross superimposed on an eight-pointed star. On this the Garter and within the Garter a hart trippant. Above the Garter a scroll inscribed *2nd Volunteer. Battn* and below the Garter a scroll inscribed *Bedfordshire.* In white-metal (Fig. 1803).

1795

1797

1796

1800

1801

1802

1798

1803

1805   1806

1799   1804

In 1908 the two volunteer battalions were amalgamated to form the 1st Battalion, The Hertfordshire Regiment.

Officers' helmet-plate: 1908
An eight-pointed star, the topmost point displaced by an Imperial crown. On this a laurel-wreath and within the wreath a circlet inscribed *The Hertfordshire Regiment* and in the centre a hart lodged. In gilt with black-velvet backing to the centre (Fig. 1804).

Forage-cap: 1908
   (1) A circlet inscribed *The Hertfordshire Regiment* surmounted by an Imperial crown. In the centre a hart lodged (Fig. 1805).
     In gilding-metal. Officers': in gilt or bronze.
   (2) As above but with wider antlers on the hart (Fig. 1806). In same metals.

THE CAMBRIDGESHIRE REGIMENT

During 1860–1861, nine Corps of Rifle Volunteers were formed in Cambridgeshire. These were:

1st (Cambridge)	raised 16th January 1860
2nd (Wisbech)	raised 2nd January 1860
3rd (Cambridge University)	raised 10th January 1860
4th (Whittlesey)	raised 17th January 1860
5th (March)	raised 13th June 1860
6th (Ely)	raised 11th July 1860
7th (Upwell)	raised 7th September 1860
8th (Cambridge)	raised 6th November 1860
9th (Newmarket)	raised 15th January 1861

In June 1862, the 9th Corps became part of the 1st Administrative Battalion, Suffolk Rifle Volunteers and later was designated the 20th Suffolk Rifle Volunteer Corps.

The 1st Administrative Battalion was formed on the 7th December 1860 comprising the 2nd, 4th, 5th, 6th and 7th Corps and the 2nd Administrative Battalion, on 17th October 1862, of the 1st and 8th Corps.

The Cambridge University Corps was redesignated 2nd Cambridgeshire (Cambridge University) Rifle Volunteer Corps on 15th June 1880; 4th (Cambridge University) Volunteer Battalion, The Suffolk Regiment on 1st December 1887 and, by 1903, it was The Cambridge University Volunteer Rifle Corps. In 1908 it became the Cambridge University Contingent, Senior Division, Officers' Training Corps.

On the 15th January 1873 the 1st and 2nd Administrative Battalions were amalgamated and the battalion then consisted of the 1st, 2nd, 4th, 5th, 6th and 7th Cambridgeshire Rifle Volunteer Corps and the 17th Essex Rifle Volunteer Corps. The 7th Corps was disbanded between July 1872 and March 1873 but, during this period, the 1st Huntingdon Rifle Volunteer Corps was added to the battalion.

On the 16th March 1880, the 1st Administrative Battalion became the 1st Cambridgeshire Rifle Volunteers and, in 1887, the 3rd (Cambridgeshire) Volunteer Battalion, The Suffolk Regiment.

When the Territorial Force was formed in 1908 the battalion was first designated The Cambridgeshire Battalion, The Suffolk Regiment but, in March 1909, it was detached from The Suffolk Regiment and became the 1st Battalion, The Cambridgeshire Regiment.

1807

1812

1813

1809

1808

1810

1811

1814

1816

1817

1815

17th Essex Rifle Volunteer Corps

This Corps formed part of the 2nd Administrative Battalion, Cambridgeshire Rifle Volunteer Corps after October 1863.

An oval strap inscribed *Essex Rifle Volunteers* with the numerals *17* in the turn of the buckle of the strap. The strap surmounted by a Victorian crown. In the centre the Arms of Essex. In blackened white-metal with the high-points polished (Fig. 1807). This was the Corps' first shako-badge and was, therefore, worn when the Corps became part of the 2nd Administrative Battalion.

Cambridge University Volunteer Rifle Corps

Shako-badge: c. 1860

A strap inscribed *Cambridge University Rifles* surmounted by a Victorian crown. In the centre the Arms of Cambridge University (Fig. 1808). In white-metal, also blackened-brass. Silver-plated for officers.

Forage-cap badge

A shield bearing the Arms of Cambridge University. In white-metal (Fig. 1809).

Shako-badge: pre-1878

A shield bearing the Arms of Cambridge University surmounted by the monogram *CUR*. Below the Arms a scroll inscribed *Universitas Cantabregiensis* (Fig. 1810). In white-metal. Also in blackened-brass.

Helmet-plate: 1878

An eight-pointed star, the topmost point displaced by a Victorian crown. On the star a shield bearing the Arms of Cambridge University surmounted by the monogram *CUR*. Below the Arms a scroll inscribed *Universitas Cantabregiensis*. In white-metal (Fig. 1811).

1st Cambridgeshire Rifle Volunteer Corps

Shako-badge: c. 1860

The monogram *CRVC* surmounted by the numeral *1*. In white-metal (Fig. 1812).

Forage-cap, 1880

An eight-pointed star. On this a circlet inscribed *Cambridgeshire Essex Huntingdonshire*. In the centre the Arms, Crest, Supporters and Motto of Cambridge City Council. In white-metal (Fig. 1813).

In June 1880, the three counties merged to form one unit designated 1st Cambridgeshire (Cambridgeshire, Essex and Huntingdonshire) Rifle Volunteers, but were re-designated 3rd (Cambridgeshire) Volunteer Battalion, The Suffolk Regiment in December 1887.

Helmet-plate: 1878

An eight-pointed star, the topmost point displaced by a Victorian crown. On the star a laurel-wreath. Within the wreath a strap inscribed *1st Cambridgeshire Rifle Volr. Corps*. In the centre a castle with three turrets with a pennant flying to the right on all three turrets. In white-metal (Fig. 1814).

Helmet-plate: 1902

Same design as above but with Imperial crown. In white-metal (Fig. 1815).

The Cambridgeshire Regiment

Forage-cap: 1908

Officers': A bridge (the crest of Cambridge City Council) on which is superimposed a shield bearing the Arms of Ely. Beneath this a scroll inscribed *The Cambridgeshire Regt* and beneath this a further scroll inscribed *South Africa 1900–01* (Fig. 1816). In silver-plate, also in bronze.

Other-ranks': Same design as for officers but without the honour-scroll. The title in gilding-metal, remainder in white-metal (Fig. 1817).

There was also an all-brass economy issue and this design is also found in bronze.

A pattern of this badge exists with the spelling *Cambridgshire*.

CHAPTER 30

The London Regiment: 1908 to 1922

When the Territorial Force was formed in 1908, existing volunteer regiments became battalions of the Infantry of the Line but those in the London area were excluded from this scheme and formed into a new regiment which was designated *The London Regiment*.

Originally, the regiment was to consist of twenty-eight battalions with the Honourable Artillery Company infantry being the 26th Battalion and the Inns of Court Rifle Volunteers, the 27th. However, these numbers were never taken up: the Honourable Artillery Company remained as it was and the Inns of Court became an Officers Training Corps.

1st-4th City of London Battalions (The Royal Fusiliers)

A fused grenade with, on the ball, the Garter ensigned with an Imperial crown and within the Garter a rose. In gilding-metal. Officers': in bronze (Fig. 1818).

5th City of London Battalion (London Rifle Brigade)

(1) Within an oak-wreath a circlet inscribed *London Rifle Brigade South Africa 1900–02* and surmounted by an Imperial crown. In the centre a shield bearing the Royal Arms. Behind the circlet are crossed the City Mace and Sword. At the base of the wreath a scroll inscribed *Primus in Urbe* and, below this, a small shield bearing the Arms of the City of London, with the centre voided. In white-metal. Officers': silver-plated. (Fig. 1819.)

(2) As above but with non-voided centre (Fig. 1820).

(3) As (1) but with the Great War honours added as follows: below the crown *France & Flanders 1914–18*; between the circlet and motto *Ypres, 1915, '17*; on the left-hand wreath *Somme, 1916, '18, Albert, 1918, Arras, 1917, '18, Scarpe, 1917, '18*; on the right-hand wreath *Bullecourt, Menin Road, Cambrai, 1917, Canal du Nord*. In white-metal (Fig. 1821). Also in bronze.

(4) Full dress shako-badge: a star of eight points, the topmost point displaced by an Imperial crown. On this an oak-wreath with two scrolls at the top of the wreath inscribed *S. Africa 1900–02* and superimposed on the wreath crossed Mace and Sword of State. Within the wreath a strap inscribed *London Rifle Brigade* with, in the centre, a shield bearing the Royal Arms. Below the strap a scroll inscribed *Ich Dien* and below this, on the lowest point of the star, a shield bearing the Arms of the City of London. In blackened-brass (Fig. 1822).

1818

1819

1820

1821

1824

1826

1827

1828

1829

1830

1832

1833

1825

1823

1822

1831

6th City of London Battalion (City of London Rifles)

(1) Officers' full-dress busby: a Maltese cross with a tablet on the top arm inscribed *Domine dirige nos* and on the top arm the wording *South Africa 1900–02*. In the centre of the cross a circlet inscribed *6th City of London Rifles* and in the centre of this a bugle with strings. In blackened white-metal with high-points polished (Fig. 1823).

(2) A Maltese cross with the top arm inscribed *South Africa 1900–02* and, above this, a tablet inscribed *Domine dirige nos* surmounted by an Imperial crown. In the centre a circlet inscribed *6th Battn. City of London Regt.* and within this a bugle with strings. In black-metal (Fig. 1824).

7th City of London Battalion

(1) Officers' full-dress helmet-plate: A star of eight points, the topmost point displaced by an Imperial crown. On this an oak-wreath with crossed Mace and Sword of State superimposed. Within the wreath a circlet inscribed *Domine dirige nos* with, in the centre, a fused grenade with the numeral *7* on the ball. Across the base of the wreath a scroll inscribed *City of London* and below this a shield bearing the Arms of the City of London. In gilt except for the numeral *7*, on the ball of the grenade, which is in silver-plate.

(2) Other-ranks' full-dress helmet-plate: A star of eight points, the topmost point displaced by an Imperial crown. On this an oak-wreath with crossed Mace and Sword of State superimposed. Within the wreath a circlet inscribed *Domine dirige nos* with the numeral *7* in the centre. Across the base of the wreath a scroll inscribed *City of London* and below this a shield bearing the Arms of the City of London. In gilding-metal (Fig. 1825).

(3) A fused grenade with the numeral *7* on the ball. The grenade in gilding-metal and the numeral in white-metal (Fig. 1826).

8th City of London Battalion (Post Office Rifles)

A laurel-wreath on which are four scrolls inscribed: (left) *Egypt 1882* and (right) *S. Africa 1899–02*. Within this, a Maltese cross surmounted by a tablet inscribed *8th Battalion* above which is the Imperial crown. In the centre of the cross a circlet inscribed *The Post Office Rifles* and in the centre a stringed bugle surmounted by an Imperial crown. In white-metal (Fig. 1827). Also in bronze.

9th County of London Battalion (Queen Victoria's)

A Maltese cross. Above this a tablet inscribed *South Africa 1900–02* surmounted by an Imperial crown. In the centre of the cross a circlet inscribed *Queen Victoria's* with, in the centre, St. George and the Dragon (Fig. 1828). In blackened-brass and in white-metal. In different sizes and some with the centre voided. Officers wore a rifle-boss with a small replica of the badge in silver-plate; also in blackened-brass.

10th County of London Battalion (Paddington Rifles)

(1) A laurel-wreath on which are four scrolls inscribed: (left) *South, 1900* and (right) *Africa, 1902* and, across the base of the wreath, a further scroll inscribed *Paddington Rifles*. Within the wreath a circlet inscribed *10th Bn. County of London Regt* surmounted by an Imperial crown and in the centre two swords in saltire, enfiled by a mural crown, from the Arms of the Borough of Paddington. With voided centre (Fig. 1829). In black-metal, also in white-metal and in gilding-metal.

(2) As above but with non-voided centre and in same metals (Fig. 1830).
This battalion was disbanded in 1912.

1834

1835

1836

1839

1840

1842

1841

1843

1844

1845

1846

1847

1837

1842ᴬ

1838

10th County of London Battalion (Hackney)

(1) Officers' full-dress helmet-plate: an eight-pointed star, the topmost point displaced by an Imperial crown. On this a laurel-wreath and within this the Garter with, in the centre within a laurel-wreath, an eight-pointed star, the topmost point displaced by a crown. On the star a circlet inscribed *Justitia turris nostra* and within this a tower on ground from the Seal of the Borough of Hackney. Below the Garter a three-part scroll inscribed *Tenth London Hackney*. The device in the centre and the title-scroll in silver-plate, remainder in gilt with black-velvet backing to the centre (Fig. 1831).

(2) Within a laurel-wreath an eight-pointed star, the topmost point displaced by a crown. On the star a circlet inscribed *Justitia turris nostra* and within this a tower on ground. Below the star a three-part scroll inscribed *Tenth London Hackney* (Fig. 1832). In brass, also in bronze. Officers': silver star and scroll, gilt circlet, centre and crown.

(3) Similar to (2) but with more ground behind the tower and without the gap between the star and the wreath (Fig. 1833).

This unit was raised in October 1912 to replace the Paddington Rifles.

11th County of London Battalion (Finsbury Rifles)

A Maltese cross above which a tablet inscribed *South Africa 1900–02* and surmounted by an Imperial crown. On the four arms of the cross the motto *Pro aris et focis*. On the cross a circlet inscribed *Finsbury Rifles* with, in the centre, a strung bugle (Fig. 1834). In blackened-brass and in gilding-metal. Both types with and without voided centres.

12th County of London Battalion (The Rangers)

(1) A Maltese cross with, on the top arm, *South Africa 1900–02* and above this a tablet inscribed *Excel* surmounted by an Imperial crown. On the cross a circlet inscribed *12th County of London* with, in the centre, a bugle with strings. Below the cross a scroll inscribed *The Rangers* (Fig. 1835). In blackened-brass, also small replica in blackened-brass on a rifle-boss.

(2) As above but with battle honours on the cross as follows: (top) *South Africa 1900–02, St Julien*; (left) *Albert, 1916, '18, Cambrai, 1917, Epehy*; (right) *Somme, 1916 '18 Scarpe, 1917, Cinchy*; (bottom) *Frezenberg, Ypres, 1915, '17*. Also the circlet is now inscribed *12th London Regiment* and the scroll at the base inscribed *Rangers* only (Fig. 1836). In blackened-brass.

13th County of London Battalion (Kensington)

(1) Officers' full-dress helmet-plate: a star of eight points, the topmost point displaced by an Imperial crown. On this a wreath of laurel and within this a circlet inscribed *Kensington—13th County of London*. In the centre a shield bearing the Arms of Kensington with a scroll below inscribed *Quid nobis ardui*. On the base of the wreath a scroll inscribed *South Africa 1900–02*. In gilt with red-velvet backing to the centre (Fig. 1837).

(2) Other-ranks' full-dress helmet-plate: A star of eight-points, the topmost point displaced by an Imperial crown. On this a wreath of laurel and within this a circlet inscribed *Kensington—13th County of London*. In the centre a shield bearing the Arms of Kensington with a scroll below inscribed *Quid nobis ardui*. On either side of the shield the wording *South Africa 1900–02*. In gilding-metal; also found in white-metal (Fig. 1838).

(3) On an eight-pointed star the Arms of the Royal Borough of Kensington, *viz.*: A shield with red and gold quarters within a border quartered gold and black. In the first quarter a celestial crown above a gold fleur-de-lys and in the dexter chief point a five-pointed silver star. In the second a black cross flory and four black martlets. In the third a red cross bottony and four red roses with stems and leaves in natural colours and in the fourth a gold mitre (Fig. 1839). In gilding-metal; also in white-metal. Officers': in silver-plate, and in bronze.

14th County of London Battalion (London Scottish)

(1) St. Andrew's Cross on which is superimposed the Lion of Scotland, the whole upon a circlet inscribed *Strike sure,* with on the lower part of the circlet *S. Africa 1900–02.* Across the top of the cross a scroll inscribed *London* and on the bottom a scroll inscribed *Scottish.* The whole surrounded by a wreath of thistles. In white-metal (Fig. 1840). There was also a war emergency issue in 1916 in all-brass.

(2) Same design as above but of superior construction in separate parts and mounted. For officers, in silver-plate (Fig. 1841).

(3) Same design as above but very small size. Bronze painted (Fig. 1842). This was the puggaree-badge worn by the 2nd Battalion in 1917–18.

15th County of London Battalion (Prince of Wales's Own Civil Service Rifles)

(1) Officers' full-dress helmet-plate: An eight-pointed star, the topmost point displaced by an Imperial crown. On this a laurel-wreath and within this the Garter with, in the centre, the Prince of Wales's plumes, coronet and motto. All gilt except the Prince of Wales's plumes and motto. A black-velvet background to the centre (Fig. 1842A).

(2) The Prince of Wales's plumes, coronet and motto. In blackened-brass (Fig. 1843).

(3) As (2) but in white-metal (Fig. 1844). Silver-plated for officers.

16th County of London Battalion (Queen's Westminster Rifles)

A Maltese cross above which a tablet inscribed *South Africa, 1900–02* and surmounted by an Imperial crown. On the cross a circlet inscribed *16th County of London Queens Westminsters.* In the centre a portcullis surmounted by a ducal coronet (Fig. 1845). In blackened-brass, also in white-metal. Officer's: in blackened white-metal with high points polished. Worn with a red-cloth backing.

16th London Regiment (Queen's Westminster and Civil Service Rifles)

(The 15th and 16th Battalions were amalgamated in 1922.)
A Maltese cross surmounted by an Imperial crown. On the arms of the cross the following battle honours are inscribed: (top) *South Africa 1900–02, Hooge, 1915*; (left) *Somme, 1916, '18, Flers-Courelette, Arras, 1917, '18*; (right) *Messines, 1917, Ypres, 1917, '18, Cambrai, 1917*; (bottom) *France and Flanders 1914–18, Jerusalem, Jericho.* In the centre of the cross two oval escutcheons, the left bearing the portcullis and ducal coronet (from the Queen's West-minsters) and the right the Prince of Wales's plumes, coronet and motto (from the Civil Service Rifles). In blackened-brass (Fig. 1846). Also in white-metal. Officers': in silver, and in bronze.

17th County of London Battalion (Poplar and Stepney Rifles)

Within a laurel wreath a Maltese cross. On the arms of the cross the following: (top) *South*, (bottom) *Africa*, (left) *1899*, (right) *1902*. Above the cross a blank tablet surmounted by an Imperial crown. On the cross a circlet inscribed *Rifle Brigade* and in the centre a bugle with strings surmounted by a crown (Fig. 1847). In blackened-brass, white-metal and gilding-metal. Officers': in silver, and in bronze.

18th County of London Battalion (London Irish Rifles)
The Irish Harp surmounted by an Imperial crown (Fig. 1848). In blackened-brass, also in white-metal and gilding-metal. Officers: silver-plated.

19th County of London Battalion (St. Pancras)
(1) Officers' full-dress helmet-plate: an eight-pointed star, the topmost point displaced by an Imperial crown. On this a laurel-wreath and within this a circlet inscribed *XIX County of London St. Pancras*. In the centre the Arms, crest and motto of the Borough of St. Pancras. Below the circlet a scroll inscribed *South Africa 1900–02*. The central design and the honour-scroll in silver-plate, remainder in gilt. A black-velvet backing to the centre (Fig. 1849).

(2) Other-ranks' full-dress helmet-plate: a star of eight points, the topmost point displaced by an Imperial crown. On this a laurel-wreath and within this a circlet inscribed *XIX County of London St. Pancras*. On a solid centre the Arms, crest and motto of the Borough of St. Pancras. All in gilding-metal (Fig. 1850).

(3) Within a laurel-wreath a cross as in the Order of the Bath surmounted by an Imperial crown. On the top arm of the cross *South Africa* and on the bottom, *1900–02*. On the cross a circlet inscribed *County of London St. Pancras*, with, in the centre, the Roman numerals *XIX* (Fig. 1851). In blackened-brass, white-metal and gilding-metal. Officers': in silver-plate, and in bronze. All types are found with the incorrect date of *1899*.

20th County of London Battalion (Blackheath and Woolwich)
The White Horse of Kent standing on a scroll inscribed in old-English lettering *Invicta*. Below this another scroll inscribed *20th Batt. The London Regt.* (Fig. 1852). In white-metal, also in bronze. Officers': Horse and motto in silver-plate, title-scroll in gilt.

21st County of London Battalion (First Surrey Rifles)
A cross as in the Order of the Bath, on the top arm of which is inscribed *South Africa 1900–02* and on the bottom arm the date *1803* (this being the date of the formation of the first Surrey Volunteers). Above the cross a scroll inscribed *Concordia victrix* surmounted by an Imperial crown. On the cross a circlet inscribed *First Surrey* Rifles with, in the centre, a strung bugle. Below the cross a scroll inscribed *21st County of London* (Fig. 1853). In blackened-brass. Officers': in silver-plate or blackened white-metal with the high-points polished.

22nd County of London Battalion (The Queen's)
The Paschal Lamb with swallow-tail flag on a scroll inscribed *The Queen's*. In gilding-metal (Fig. 1854). The full-dress helmet-plates were, except for the change of title, similar to those of the 24th Battalion described below.

23rd County of London Battalion
An eight-pointed star, the topmost point displaced by an Imperial crown. On this a circlet inscribed *South Africa 1900–2* with, in the centre, a shield bearing the Arms of Guildford. Below the star, a scroll inscribed *23rd Bn. The London Regt* (Fig. 1855). The ground of

1848

1851

1852

1853

1854

1855

1857

1858

1859

1849

1856

1850

the shield, the crown and the scroll in gilding-metal, remainder in white-metal. Officers': in gilt-and-silver, also in bronze. There was also an all-brass economy issue.
All versions are found with the date *1900–02* instead of *1900–2*.

24th County of London Battalion (The Queen's)
(1) Officers' full-dress helmet-plate: an eight-pointed star, the topmost point displaced by an Imperial crown. On this a laurel-wreath and within this the Garter. In the centre the Paschal Lamb. Below the Garter a scroll inscribed *24th Battn. The London Regiment*. The centre and title-scroll in silver-plate, remainder in gilt. A red-velvet backing is worn behind the centre.
(2) Other-ranks' full-dress helmet-plate: an eight-pointed star, the topmost point displaced by an Imperial crown. On this a laurel-wreath and within this a circlet inscribed *24 County (T) of London—The Queen's* with sprigs of laurel between the two parts of the title. In the centre the Paschal Lamb. All in gilding-metal (Fig. 1856).
The field-service cap-badge was the same as for the 22nd Battalion (see above).

25th County of London (Cyclist) Battalion
Within a laurel-wreath surmounted by an Imperial crown a circlet inscribed *County of London Cyclists* with, in the centre, a cycle-wheel on which the numerals *25*. Below the wreath a tablet inscribed *Tenax et audax* (Fig. 1857). In brass, blackened-brass and in white-metal. Officers': in silver-plate, and in bronze.

28th County of London Battalion (Artists Rifles)
(1) The heads of Mars and Minerva with a scroll below inscribed *Artists*. This was the first pattern worn in the early period following 1908 and is found in both blackened-brass and white-metal.
(2) The heads of Mars and Minerva with a scroll below inscribed *Artists Rifles* (Fig. 1858). In blackened-brass, gilding-metal and white-metal. Officers': in silver-plate, and in bronze.

The Inns of Court Officers Training Corps
Within a laurel-wreath surmounted by an Imperial crown four shields placed in the form of a cross with the bottom points touching in the centre, each shield bearing the Arms of one of the following Inns, *viz*: Lincoln's Inn (a number of mill rinds) top; Inner Temple (a Pegasus) right; Gray's Inn (a Griffin) bottom; Middle Temple (St. George's Cross with the Paschal Lamb in the centre) left. On the bottom of the wreath a scroll inscribed *Inns of Court O.T.C.* (Fig. 1859). In gilding-metal. Officers': silver, also in bronze.

CHAPTER 31

The Cyclist Battalions: 1908 to 1920

The first regiment to be composed entirely of cyclists was the 26th Middlesex Cyclist Volunteers who, on the formation of the Territorial Force in 1908, became the 25th County of London Battalion, The London Regiment. At the same time nine other cyclist battalions were formed and every Territorial infantry battalion was authorised to form a cyclist section. The nine battalions were formed as follows:

  (1) 10th (Linlithgowshire) (Cyclist) Battalion, from the 8th (Volunteer) Battalion, The Royal Scots.
  (2) 5th (Cyclist) Battalion, from the 2nd Volunteer Battalion, The East Yorkshire Regiment.
  (3) The Highland Cyclist Battalion, from the 5th Volunteer Battalion, The Black Watch.

New Formations

  (1) The 6th Battalion, The Norfolk Regiment.
  (2) The 7th Battalion, The Devonshire Regiment.
  (3) The 7th Battalion, The Welsh Regiment.
  (4) The Northern Cyclist Battalion.
  (5) The Kent Cyclist Battalion.
  (6) The Essex and Suffolk Cyclist Battalion.

In 1911, the last-named was divided to form the 6th Battalion, The Suffolk Regiment and the 8th Battalion, The Essex Regiment, and two more battalions were raised: the 6th Battalion, The Royal Sussex Regiment, and the 9th Battalion, The Hampshire Regiment.

Finally, early in 1914, the Huntingdonshire Cyclist Battalion was raised so that on the outbreak of war in August 1914 there were fourteen Territorial cyclist battalions.

The Army Cyclist Corps was formed under Royal Warrant of 7th November 1914 and Divisional Cyclist Companies were transferred to it.

A large number of Yeomanry and Territorial second-line units were converted to cyclists during the war, but they continued to wear their own badges.

After the war, the Army Cyclist Corps and all other cyclist units were disbanded and by 1922 had disappeared from the Army List.

25th County of London (Cyclist) Battalion, The London Regiment

Within a laurel-wreath surmounted by an Imperial crown a circlet inscribed *County of London Cyclists*, with, in the centre, a cycle-wheel on which the numerals *25*. Below the wreath a tablet inscribed *Tenax et audax* (Fig. 1860). In white-metal, brass and blackened-brass. Officers': in silver, and bronze.

5th (Cyclist) Battalion, The East Yorkshire Regiment
An eight-pointed star. On this a laurel-wreath and within it a rose. Below the star a scroll inscribed *East Yorkshire* (Fig. 1861). In blackened-brass.

The Highland Cyclist Battalion
(1) The Star of the Order of the Thistle. On the star a thistle-wreath and within this an oval inscribed *Nemo me impune lacessit* and surmounted by an Imperial crown. Within the oval St Andrew and Cross. Across the top of the star two scrolls inscribed *Highland Cyclist* and two scrolls across the base of the star inscribed *Battalion TF* (Fig. 1862). Officers' service-dress: in very small size in bronze with single slider at back.

(2) Same design as above but large size. Officers': star, scrolls and St. Andrew with Cross in silver, remainder in gilt (Fig. 1863). Sergeants': in white-metal and gilding-metal. Rank-and-file: in white-metal (Fig. 1864). All types have alternative spellings of *Lacessit* and *Lacesset*.

7th Battalion, The Welsh Regiment
The Prince of Wales's plumes, coronet and motto resting on a scroll inscribed *The Welsh* (Fig. 1865). In blackened-brass.

The Northern Cyclist Battalion
A cycle-wheel superimposed on crossed rifles and surmounted by an Imperial crown (Fig. 1866). In gilding-metal, and bronze.

The Kent Cyclist Battalion
The White Horse of Kent standing on a scroll inscribed *Invicta* (Fig. 1867). In white-metal, also in bronze.

The Essex and Suffolk Cyclist Battalion
Within a wreath of oak a castle surmounted by a shield bearing the Arms of Essex and above this an Imperial crown. Across the base of the wreath a scroll inscribed *Essex & Suffolk Cyclist Battn.* (Fig. 1868). The scroll in white-metal, remainder in gilding-metal, also in bronze.

9th (Cyclist) Battalion, The Hampshire Regiment
A cycle-wheel surmounted by an Imperial crown. In the centre of the wheel the Hampshire Rose. Below the wheel a scroll inscribed *Hampshire Cyclist Battalion* (Fig. 1869). In gilding-metal, also in bronze.

The Huntingdonshire Cyclist Battalion
A stag springing on ground, below which a scroll inscribed *Huntingdonshire* (Fig. 1870). In gilding-metal, also in bronze.

The Army Cyclist Corps
(1) A cycle-wheel with sixteen spokes surmounted by an Imperial crown superimposed on crossed rifles with slings. Below the wheel a scroll inscribed *Army Cyclist Corps* (Fig. 1871). In gilding-metal, also in bronze.

(2) As above but with only twelve spokes in the wheel (Fig. 1872).

1st/1st London Divisional Cyclist Company

(Formed in February 1916 for the 58th (London) Division and transferred to 56th (London) Division. In May 1916, with 5th and 14th Cyclist companies, formed the 6th Corps Cyclist Battalion which was later the 6th Cyclist Battalion and a unit of the Army Cyclist Corps.) Within a laurel-wreath a cycle-wheel surmounted by an Imperial crown. In the centre of the wheel the Arms and crest of the City of London, the whole superimposed on crossed rifles. Beneath the wreath a scroll inscribed *City of London Cyclists* (Fig. 1873). In gilding-metal and in bronze.

1860

1862

1866

1867

1864

1868

1870

1869

1861

1863

1865

1873

1871

1872

CHAPTER 32

Insignia on Regular Army Badges

When the wearing of badges on the head-dress was introduced, regiments of the line were known by their regimental number and this forms the main feature of all early badges. As time progressed these badges, and particularly those of the officers, took on further embellishments. Most regiments received many battle-honours in the Peninsular War and these were added: they were confined to the officers' shako-plates, the men having only the regimental number on theirs.

Apart from these there were many other additions, some being connected with the county whose name the regiment bore in addition to its precedence number, some associated with the Colonel of the Regiment, and others related to those theatres of operations in which the regiment had served.

Probably the best known of all additions is the Sphinx superscribed *Egypt* which was granted by Horse Guards Circular Letter No. 170 dated 6th July 1802. It was awarded to all regiments that took part in the Egyptian campaign of 1801.

Those entitled to this distinction are: 8th, 11th Hussars, 12th Lancers, Coldstream Guards, Scots Guards, 1st, 2nd, 8th, 10th, 13th, 18th, 20th, 23rd, 24th, 25th, 26th, 27th, 28th, 30th, 40th, 42nd, 44th, 50th, 54th, 58th, 79th, 80th, 89th, 90th, 92nd and 96th Foot, and of them the majority have incorporated the Sphinx into their badges. The badge of the 54th Foot (later 2nd Battalion, The Dorsetshire Regiment) bears the Sphinx superscribed *Marabout* instead of *Egypt*, as the 54th captured Fort Marabout in this campaign.

There are four regiments whose badges carry the Castle and Key of Gibraltar with the motto *Montis insignia calpe*: the 12th (later Suffolk), 39th (later Dorsetshire), 56th (later Essex) and 58th (later Northamptonshire). These were granted the honour of *Gibraltar* by Horse Guards letter in 1784 and, at various subsequent dates, authority was granted to add the Castle, Key and motto. Finally, by Army Order 73 of 1908 the honour was extended to the Highland Light Infantry—though they have not incorporated it into their head-dress badges.

The capture of French 'Eagles' has resulted in the incorporation of the 'Eagle' in the badges of the four regiments concerned. The Royal Dragoons captured the 105th French Infantry Regiment's 'Eagle' at Waterloo and were authorised to bear it as a badge on 30th April 1838. The Royal Scots Greys, who captured that of the 45th French Infantry Regiment on the same occasion, received their authorisation on 13th March 1838.

The 1st Battalion of the Essex Regiment, the 44th Foot (incidentally the 2nd/44th), captured that of the 62nd French Regiment at Salamanca in 1812; and finally there is the Eagle with a wreath of laurel worn by the Royal Irish Fusiliers to commemorate the capture by the 87th of the 'Eagle' of the French 8th Regiment at Barrosa, authorised on the 11th April 1811.

Two more eagles appear on badges. The double-headed Eagle of Austria was adopted by the 1st King's Dragoon Guards in 1896 when H.I.M. The Emperor Francis Joseph was gazetted Colonel-in-Chief of the Regiment. This badge was discontinued in 1915, as the British were then in a state of war with Austria, but it was resumed in 1938. The Prussian Eagle worn by the 14th Hussars was adopted in 1798 when the 14th Light Dragoons received the title of *Duchess of York's Own*. The Duchess, who married the Duke of York in 1791, was Frederica Charlotte Ulrica Catherina, Princess Royal of Prussia. This badge also was discontinued in 1915, but restored in 1931.

Emblems connected with Royalty frequently appear on badges and probably that most in use is the Prince of Wales's plumes with coronet and motto. It is carried by regiments which include *Prince of Wales's* in their title as well as by Welsh regiments.

The 11th Hussars carry the crest and motto, *Treu und Fest*, of the Prince Consort and is the only regiment to have a German motto. Prince Albert was appointed Colonel of the Regiment on 30th April 1840 but authority to wear the crest was not granted until 17th November 1876.

Besides the Royal Cypher of the reigning monarch, borne by many Royal Regiments, the cypher or coronet of other members of the Royal family is borne by a number of regiments. The 89th Foot (later Royal Irish Fusiliers) was granted the cypher and coronet of Princess Victoria (later Queen Victoria) when the regiment received the title *Princess Victoria's* in 1866.

As one of the titles of the Prince of Wales is Duke of Cornwall the coronet of the Duke and the Arms of the Duchy are to be found on the badges of the Duke of Cornwall's Light Infantry.

The coronet of the 7th Dragoon Guards is that of H.M. The Empress of Germany as Princess Royal of Great Britain and was approved in 1899. The 77th (later 2nd Battalion, The Middlesex Regiment) added *Duke of Cambridge's Own* to their title in 1876 and were authorised to wear the Duke's coronet and cypher. The 99th (later 2nd Battalion, The Wiltshire Regiment) similarly added *The Duke of Edinburgh's* to their title on the 22nd April 1874 and were authorised to wear the coronet and cypher.

The double cypher *AR* of Queen Adelaide, the consort of King William IV, was given to the 9th Lancers with the title *Queen's Royal* on the 22nd July 1830.

Queen Alexandra was the eldest daughter of King Christian IX of Denmark and her cypher *A* and the Dannebrog is associated with two regiments, one cavalry and one infantry. The 19th Hussars became *Princess of Wales's Own* in 1885 and the 19th Foot, when the same title was conferred on them on the 11th October 1875.

The Danish Cross (The Dannebrog—The Strength of Denmark) has an interesting origin. During the battle of Lydanisse in Estonia in 1219, Archbishop Anders, who was then of great age, knelt praying for victory. While his hands were raised the Danes advanced but as soon as he tired, and lowered his hands, the Estonians appeared to have the advantage. As this was noticed, two monks stepped forward and held up the Archbishop's arms for him. Shortly afterwards the sky opened and the Dannebrog fell: at the same time a voice roared out *In hoc signo vinces* (In this sign conquer). From that time onwards the white cross on a red ground has been the blazon of the national flag of Denmark.

Finally there is the cypher and coronet of Princess Louise which was authorised when the 91st became the 91st (Princess Louise's Argyllshire) Highlanders in 1872.

The White Horse of Hanover features on the badges of the 3rd Hussars, 7th (Royal Fusiliers), 8th (King's Regiment) and 14th (West Yorkshire Regiment). This, and the motto

Nec aspera terrent, were directed to be worn on the flap of the grenadiers' cap in the 'Regulations for Colours and Clothing' of 1747 and, in the Royal Warrants of 1751 and 1768, it is shown as being borne on the housings and holster-caps of the 3rd (King's Own) Dragoons. At one time all regiments wore this device, but only the above still retain it as a badge, although it continues to be carried on the Guidons of cavalry regiments.

The Red Rose is associated naturally with Lancastrian regiments and the White Rose with those of Yorkshire, but the United Red-and-White Rose is directed for the Royal Fusiliers in the Regulations for Clothing and Colours of 1747, and the Union Rose was authorised as a badge for the 84th Foot on the 18th November 1820. They had received the title *York and Lancaster* in 1809. The Hampshire Rose adopted by that regiment in 1881 is a red rose: a badge of Henry v who, according to tradition, conferred it upon the City of Winchester in 1415 when he passed through on his way to Agincourt. It is incorporated in the County Arms.

A number of family crests and devices also appear on badges. One of the best-known is the Stafford Knot. This was a badge of the de Stafford family and is incorporated in the Arms of Staffordshire and Stafford. All regiments with Staffordshire in their title have added it to their badges.

The eighth Horse was commanded by Earl Ligonier for twenty-nine years. This regiment, which later became the 7th Dragoon Guards, was sanctioned in 1898 to bear his crest and motto.

The 26th (Cameronians) include a mullet (spur-rowel) from the coat of arms of James, Earl of Angus, who raised the regiment in April 1689. He was a member of the Douglas (Dukes of Hamilton) family.

The 33rd Foot was the first regiment to be commanded by the Duke of Wellington and was given the title *The Duke of Wellington's* on the 18th June 1853, and his crest and motto were authorised as a badge for the regiment.

Highland regiments have always had close family connections. The Seaforth have the stag's head and motto *Cuidich'n Righ* (Help to the King). The motto is that of the Clan MacKenzie and it is said to have been given, together with the badge of the stag's head, to the founder of the Clan in recognition of his saving King Alexander II of Scotland from the attack of a wounded stag. For many years the second word of the motto was spelt *Rhi* but it was amended to the correct spelling in 1869.

The 92nd (Gordon Highlanders) were raised in 1794 by George, Marquess of Huntley, later Duke of Gordon. His crest was the head of a stag with antlers of ten tines issuing from a crest coronet. The ivy is the badge of the Gordon family and forms the wreath around the regimental badge.

The Boar's Head is the crest of the Duke of Argyll, chief of Clan Campbell of Lochnell. This, together with his motto *Ne obliviscaris* (Forget not) and his badge of myrtle, were authorised to the 91st Highlanders on 14th March 1872.

The Wild Cat is the crest of the Sutherland Clan, butcher's broom their badge and *Sans peur* their motto. These are borne by the 93rd Sutherland Highlanders.

Most regiments with an Irish connection have the Harp and Crown as part of their badge, but it is remarkable to find this device on the badges of the Leicestershire Regiment. The reason is that the Leicestershire Militia assisted in quelling the rebellion in Ireland in 1798 and were granted the badge of the Irish Harp for their services. In the reorganisation of 1881 the Leicestershire Militia became the 3rd Battalion of the regiment and the whole regiment adopted the badge.

It is also strange to find the Arms of the City of Lincoln on the badge of the Loyal North

Lancashire Regiment. This came about because the 81st was raised in the City of Lincoln in 1793 and given the title *Loyal Lincoln Volunteers* as they were raised almost entirely from the Lincoln Militia, whose badge was the Arms of the City. The 81st became the 2nd Battalion of the Loyal North Lancashire Regiment in 1881.

At the same time the East Surrey Regiment adopted the Arms of Guildford and the Northamptonshire Regiment added to its badge the horseshoe: the old badge of the Rutland Militia which had become part of the regiment. It was derived from the Arms of Oakham which is a black horseshoe with silver nails on a gold ground. The origin of this is said to be that when Queen Elizabeth I was riding through the town her horse cast a shoe. From this incident the town acquired the right to claim a horseshoe from any Royal personage entering it.

In March 1883, the Devonshire Regiment adopted the Castle of Exeter as a badge and the motto *Semper fidelis*. The Castle had been previously the badge of the Devon Militia.

In 1881, the Royal Munster Fusiliers adopted the Arms of the Province of Munster: three golden crowns on a field of azure, the ancient Arms of Ireland. The Royal Dublin Fusiliers similarly took the Arms of the City of Dublin: three silver castles on an azure field that had been the badge of the Royal Dublin City Militia, which became the 4th Battalion of the regiment in 1881.

The Castle of Inniskilling with St. George's flag flying is mentioned in the Royal Warrant of 1751 for both the 6th (Inniskilling) Dragoons and the 27th (Enniskillen) Regiment of Foot.

Service in India is commemorated in the badges of several regiments. The 39th Foot was the first regiment of the line to serve in India, hence their motto *Primus in Indis*.

The 17th Foot was in India from 1804 to 1823 and, for their distinguished services, were awarded the Royal Tiger superscribed *Hindoostan*. The badge and honour were authorised on the 18th May 1825.

The 65th Foot was another regiment with long service in India (1796 to 1819) and the Royal Tiger was awarded to them. The 67th Foot was also awarded the Royal Tiger and *India* on the 20th December 1826. Their service was from 1805 to 1826.

The Royal Tiger is also borne by the Royal Munster Fusiliers which, as the 101st, was the original Honourable East India Company Bengal (European) Regiment formed in 1756.

Both regiments which formed the Royal Dublin Fusiliers in 1881 were entitled to the Royal Tiger as a badge. The 102nd had long and distinguished service in India and the award was made especially for their part in the capture of Nundy Droog in 1791. The badge was conferred on the 103rd on 6th November 1844.

The other badge connected with service in India is the Elephant which features on the badges of the 19th Hussars and the 74th, 76th, 78th, 88th and 103rd Regiments. The Elephant superscribed *Assaye* was granted to the old 19th Light Dragoons on 15th April 1803, and authorised to its successor regiment in 1874.

The award to the 74th and 78th was for the same battle. The 74th was presented with a third or honorary Colour, which had in its centre an Elephant within a wreath of laurel, on 15th April 1817. The award of the Elephant with *Assaye* was approved for the 78th on the 16th April 1807.

The Elephant with howdah was conferred on the 76th Regiment on 17th January 1807, to commemorate its service in India from 1788 to 1806, and the Elephant for the 103rd was granted on the 6th November 1844 to commemorate its Indian service, especially the campaigns in the Carnatic and Mysore.

A variation in design is the Elephant 'caparisoned'. This was originally authorised in

1807 with the honour *Seringapatam* to the old Scotch Brigade which was designated the 94th from 1802 to 1818. It was granted to the later 94th on the 18th March 1874.

Apart from the recording of battle-honours on badges there are a number of instances where, owing to the importance attached to a particular engagement, a special device in commemoration thereof is added.

The 13th (First Somersetshire) Light Infantry achieved great fame during the First Afghan War of 1839 to 1842 by its magnificent defence of Jellalabad. In the London Gazette of 30th August 1842 the War Office announced that Her Majesty The Queen had been graciously pleased to confer certain honours on the regiment in recognition of its distinguished gallantry displayed during the campaigns in Burma and Afghanistan. These honours included the granting of a Royal title *Prince Albert's* and the grant of a mural crown superscribed *Jellalabad* as a badge: 'as a memorial of the fortitude, perseverance and enterprise evinced by that regiment, and the several corps which served during the blockade of Jellalabad'.

The badge of the Roussillon Plume commemorates the services of the 35th (Royal Sussex) at the battle of Quebec on the 13th September 1759. They are said to have taken the white plumes from the head-dress of the French Regiment, Royal Roussillon Grenadiers, which they defeated on that occasion. Although worn for many years previously it was not authorised officially until 30th June 1880.

The 34th Foot distinguished itself at the action of Arroyo dos Molinos on 28th October 1811, capturing the 34th French Regiment of the Line, and subsequently wore red-and-white feathers (later, tufts) in their head-dress in memory of this occasion. When red-and-white tufts became general for all regiments of Foot, except Light Infantry and Rifles, this distinction was lost and in compensation the regiment was allowed to carry the honour *Arroyo dos Molinos* on their Colours. It is the only regiment authorised to bear this honour. Later it was allowed to wear a tuft of half-red and half-white, white uppermost, whereas the regulation tuft was two-thirds white and one-third red, white uppermost. On the introduction of the helmet this distinction was perpetuated by a red-and-white background to the plate and, later, to the cap and collar-badges.

Probably the earliest award is that of the Arms of Nassau with the motto *Virtutis Namurcensis Praemium* conferred on the 18th Royal Irish by King William III as a reward for their gallantry in the siege and assault of Namur in 1695.

Both the 49th and 55th were awarded the device of the China Dragon for their services in the war of 1840 to 1842. The date of the award was 12th August 1843.

On the later badges of the 24th (2nd Warwickshire)–after the 1881 reorganisation, the South Wales Borderers–is a wreath of immortelles. Queen Victoria directed that a silver wreath should be borne on the staff of the Queen's Colour to commemorate the devoted gallantry of Lieutenants Melville and Coghill in saving that Colour after the battle of Isandhwana and in memory of the defence of Rorke's Drift. Authorised 15th December 1880.

Two other battle honours of particular significance are those of Albuera and Talavera.

Talavera was granted as a battle-honour to the 48th by London Gazette of 12th November 1816. Both battalions of the 48th were present at the action which took place on 27th/28th July 1809. According to Napier, the Peninsular War historian, the 48th saved the day and were commended by Wellesley in his despatch.

Albuera is particularly associated with the 57th Middlesex Regiment. The battle was fought on the 16th May 1811. When Colonel Inglis was wounded, he laid on the ground and shouted: 'Die hard, my men, die hard.' Since that time, the regiment has been known invariably as *The Die Hards*.

The 17th Lancers refer to their badge as 'the Regimental motto'. Colonel John Hall, who raised the regiment, brought back the despatches relating to the capture of Quebec and the death of General Wolfe. It is believed traditionally that the design was in commemoration of the general's death: the interpretation of the badge being *Death or Glory*.

The feathers on the badge of the 46th are a reminder that their Light company, which formed part of a Light battalion during the American War of Independence, so harassed the enemy that the latter said they would give 'no quarter' to the 'Light Bobs'. Thereupon, the Light battalion dyed their feathers red so as to be unmistakeable.

To meet the demand for troops at the time of the Indian Mutiny a regiment was raised in Canada in 1858, as the 100th Prince of Wales's Royal Canadians (in 1881 it became the Leinster Regiment). The maple-leaves in the badge perpetuate the regiment's origin.

Practically all rifle and light infantry regiments use a bugle-horn as part of their badge. As these troops were designed for quick movement in the field, the drum normally used for conveying orders was substituted by the bugle. This practice has been indicated on their badges ever since.

In the Royal Warrant of 1751 certain regiments have their insignia described as 'ancient badge', indicating that it had been in use well before the date of the Warrant. The origin of these is uncertain and can only be surmised.

The Paschal Lamb of the 2nd Queen's is thought to have some connection with Catherine of Braganza, the consort of Charles II. The Dragon was one of the supporters of the Arms of Queen Elizabeth I and during her reign some independent companies were sent to the Netherlands and, afterwards, they formed the nucleus of the 3rd Buffs. It is thought that their badge of the Dragon stems from this incident.

The Lion of England of the 4th King's Own is believed to have been granted by King William III, but the origins of St. George and the Dragon of the 5th (Northumberland) and the Antelope of the 6th (1st Warwickshire) appear to have been lost in antiquity.

Only the regular army is dealt with here. Yeomanry, Volunteers and Territorials mostly used insignia connected with either the area in which they were raised or the person responsible for their raising. When these are of special significance a note is given with the description of the badge concerned.

CHAPTER 33

Hints on Collecting Badges

Let us start with a word of warning! Once you decide to join the ranks of enthusiastic badge-collectors, you are immediately in danger of contracting a 'disease' which, although not fatal, may well become obsessional. So guard against this and approach the subject with care and method.

Before you commence collecting, learn as much as you can about the hobby: it will help you to avoid making mistakes which could prove expensive.

Although this book gives a great deal of information on cap-badges worn up to the end of the Great War it covers by no means all of them. To do this would be almost an impossible task. Besides the Regular forces, there are the numerous regiments of Militia whilst the Volunteer revival of 1859 brought forth a unit in practically every town of any size, and most of them with their own individual badges. The Volunteer movement, at the commencement of the Great War, resulted in yet another large crop of badges.

One of the first considerations must therefore be a decision on what you intend to collect. Will your collection be of cap-badges only or will it extend to include shako- and helmet-plates? If cap-badges only, do you intend to confine it to other-ranks' patterns or will you include those of officers?

Again, besides badges worn on the head-dress, there are those on shoulder-belt plates, pouch-belts, collars and buttons, as well as shoulder-titles. All of these form part of the insignia of a regiment and should be included if the collection is intended to be specialised in just one regiment or group of regiments.

Having decided what you want to collect, the next consideration is the period at which you will start. The Imperial crown first made its appearance on badges when King Edward VII came to the throne in 1902 and remained in use up to the accession of Queen Elizabeth II: the badges issued in this period would give you ample scope to form a collection. Or you might go back a few years earlier to the time when cap-badges first made their general appearance on the field-service cap or, earlier still, to the time when glengarries were worn as undress-caps by all British infantry—most of these would be carrying the Victorian crown.

Assuming you wish to collect head-dress badges from the whole of the British Army, then probably it would be best to start with the regular infantry of the line, followed by the cavalry, then the various corps and departments, finally progressing to the Territorials and other units in their chronological order as raised.

If this appears too vast an undertaking, then an alternative is to devote the collection to a specific section of the army or a particular group of regiments. For example, all those raised in, say, Lancashire or some other county, or all Scottish, or Irish, or Welsh regiments, or even the regiment associated with the area in which you live.

At first, although you have determined your main sphere of activity, it is best to collect anything you can find at a reasonable price, or that you can obtain from friends, as those you do not need for your own collection can be exchanged with other collectors.

It is well therefore, at an early stage, to find out if there are others in your area who enjoy the same hobby. Make their acquaintance as they will be only too happy to talk about badges and show the gems of their own collections. In addition, they can give the beginner many useful tips.

There are a number of societies which cater specially for badge enthusiasts and you would be well advised to join one of these. Probably the best known is the Military Historical Society although its membership is not confined to badge-collectors alone. Its main head-quarters is at the Duke of York's Headquarters, Chelsea, London, S.W.3 where informal meetings are held every month. It publishes a list of members and their interests and this would enable you to correspond with others who are interested in your hobby.

It has a number of branches in the country, one of which may be near enough for you to attend, if London is too far away. Remember that, when corresponding with other members, you should give as much detail as possible and enclose rubbings of badges. This will often save answering queries and writing unnecessary letters. If you are writing initially it is only courteous to enclose a stamped and addressed envelope for a reply.

Badges are to be found in the most unexpected places. Friends may have hoarded a souvenir in a small tin-box or in the loft with other unwanted items. 'Junk' merchants have them, some antique- and jewellery-shops sell them and there are a number of dealers who cater specially for the hobby.

Considerable knowledge can be gained by attending auction sale-rooms, especially those run by the better-known firms. One such that has frequent sales of badges is Wallis and Wallis of Lewes, Sussex.

With the growth of interest in badge-collecting, the demand for specimens has increased, especially for the less common ones, and consequently a number of reproductions have appeared. The most clumsy of these emanate from overseas and are cast in either crude brass or white-metal and usually have rather thin copper-shanks or -prongs. They can be identified very easily as castings by the rough surface on the reverse of the badge.

Badges of the old Indian Army, before partition in 1947, were made by this process, and it would be very difficult to detect an original from a reproduction. However, very few British Army badges were made in this form as generally they were die-struck. To be on the safe side it would be as well to exclude any cast badges from your collection.

In recent years, some British badges – apparently struck from the original dies – have appeared and these are far more difficult to detect, but the reverse-side will often aid identification. Frequently, different prongs have been used: the most obvious being a rather broad slider which tapers from the shoulder. Badges have been struck also in a metal never worn by the unit concerned.

The production of copies from original dies seems to have started at the beginning of the century when a Southsea firm, Fox and Company, obtained the original dies of some of the glengarry badges and, to make these appear more authentic, they 'weathered' them before sale.

Some badges have been re-struck by the original makers and it is quite impossible to detect these as they are made from the original dies in the correct manner. If you are in any doubt as to the authenticity of any badge in your collection then possibly the best solution is to seek the advice of a more experienced collector, particularly if he has a long and accurate memory, and a comparison with a genuine specimen should solve the problem.

It is not possible to give any ruling regarding prices, which tend to fluctuate to a certain extent, but with the growth of interest in badge-collecting values have steadily risen in recent years.

A collector may be prepared to pay a price well above the normal for a specimen he particularly wants in order to fill a gap in his collection, whereas the same badge may be of little consequence to another collector.

One of the best guides to present-day values is the price offered for lots in the auction sale-rooms.

CHAPTER 34

Mounting and Framing a Collection

It is advisable not to frame your badges until you have sufficient to make a reasonable display, otherwise you will create extra work, dismantling and rearranging, thus wasting the time and trouble already spent on it.

When you start collecting, mount your badges on white card or any other colour which shows off the badges to your own satisfaction. Make certain that the card is stout enough to bear the weight of the specimens it will contain eventually, and leave gaps for those that you fully expect to obtain.

The cards can then be placed in drawers, but pieces of similar material or corrugated-cardboard cut to a slightly smaller size should be placed between them to protect the badges underneath from the shanks of those on the card above. Do not have too much weight on them and, therefore, do not stack too many cards in one drawer. If the holes made in the card are not too large the badges will be held firmly in place but, to make certain, use the split-wire pins or a strip of transparent adhesive-tape to hold prongs. This is not usually considered necessary until the actual framing is carried out.

Under no circumstances should the original shanks or slider be removed. It has been known for these to be removed laboriously and short screw-lugs soldered in their place: also small holes drilled and the badges held in place by thin wire. It is quite unnecessary to adopt either of these methods for not only does it spoil the badge but it renders it valueless.

Framing is a matter of personal choice governed by many factors—not the least being cost. Suitable frames can be obtained cheaply and adapted to your own requirements. Search your box-room and visit shops and sale-rooms as necessary.

Before you do this, decide on the type of frame required in relation to the place where you intend to keep your display. Pay attention to the colour-scheme so that, when hung, the frames harmonise with the general decor of the room.

It is an advantage to have a 'dummy run' by laying-out the specimens you intend to frame. You may wish to arrange these in order of precedence or as a balanced display which is more attractive.

Depending on the size of the frame, cardboard of sufficient thickness to carry the weight of metal, or thin plywood, covered with an attractive material ranging from velvet to hessian can be used. Ensure that the covering does not wrinkle by affixing the material evenly to the back and make the holes large enough for the shanks to penetrate without damage.

Make certain that all the badges are positioned flat against the surface. This can be done by using the split-wire pins and packing the space between them and the back of the board with small pieces of card or cork. Prongs can be held by strips of adhesive-tape and packing where needed.

It is essential that sufficient room is allowed between the board and the glass to take the deepest of the badges and, when fixed to the card, there is equally sufficient room at the back to cover the shanks with another piece of card. When completed, seal with adhesive-tape to render the display dust-proof.

Ensure that the brackets, both on the wall and on the frame, are strong enough to carry the weight, which will be surprisingly great, and that the cord or wire is also safe.

Colour-schemes for the backing-material are a matter of personal choice. White or light khaki will reflect the light and show off the badges well, but red is very popular. For Scottish badges a tartan background is very suitable and the Royal Stewart is much preferred for enhancing the appearance of the specimens.

Consider the colour-scheme carefully, particularly of the room in which you intend to mount your display, and avoid making it dark or dingy. A visit to other collectors or to military museums and a study of how their displays are mounted, and how the appearance strikes you, will help you to make the most of your own collection.

CLEANING AND PRESERVING BADGES

Be very careful indeed in your approach to cleaning badges. Many specimens have been ruined irretrievably by enthusiastic collectors who have removed the original finish of bronze or black. The main criterion is to obtain a specimen in, as near as possible, its original condition when issued. When you obtain a new item for your collection, first of all examine it carefully and determine what the original finish was, remembering that a very high polish is not what you require.

The reverse side of the badge will help a great deal in deciding on its original format. Should repairs to the shanks be necessary remember that any heat-treatment will weaken these so try to avoid this if possible.

In cleaning the various metals and finishes the following hints may be of assistance.

Gilt

If very dirty use a small amount of a mixture of liquid detergent and strong ammonia. Apply this with a small silver-brush and wash it off carefully with a gentle brushing in warm water. Dry and polish with a clean cloth.

Silver

Use a silver-brush and apply plate-powder dissolved in a small amount of methylated spirit, or rub with pure lemon-juice on cotton-wool. For stubborn corners splay out the end of a match-stick and use to apply mixture.

Brass or Gilding-metal

Prepare a weak solution of one-part sulphuric acid (H_2SO_4) to twenty-parts of water. **Add the acid to the water to avoid unpleasant results**. Soak the item in this solution for thirty minutes or up to one hour. Then scrub in warm water using a brass wire-brush (suede-cleaning brush) to remove the deposit which will have formed. Always wear rubber gloves whilst handling the object to protect your hands against the effect of the acid solution. Finish with a soft brush using liquid detergent and warm water. Dry well.

White-metal

The same instructions as for gilding-metal but do not use solution that you have already used for gilding-metal or brass for it may cause deposits of copper to stain the white-metal. When faced with the problem of a badge which consists of both white- and gilding-metal treat it with the solution which has been used for whichever metal forms the major part of the specimen.

Blackened-brass

If much of the original finish is removed use skill in replacing it. On a badge where the finish has been completely removed, spray carefully with a matt-finish black paint. Black-stove or boot polish can be used to refurbish such badges. Remember that some officers' badges of rifle regiments have had the high-points polished purposely to bring into relief the design or battle-honours. This should be preserved, so any cleaning will require great care and skill.

Bronze finish

When much of the finish has been removed it is very difficult to replace it unless you have the correct powder. A semi-matt brown paint of the right shade would be hard to find. Where much of the original finish has been retained a dark-brown boot polish may add some colour.

Enamel

Using tweezers or long-nosed pliers hold the badge in the steam of a gently-boiling kettle. Then, with great care, clean with a mild soap or detergent in warm water. Any vigorous action is to be avoided. Make sure when doing this that the small discs or rings which carry the enamel backing are not distorted to ensure that the enamel is not cracked or loosened.

Preservation

Old copal-varnishes are apt to turn yellow-brown and are most difficult to remove. It is preferable to leave the specimens without a coating of any kind and to frame them behind glass. Sealing the frames as much as possible is the best preservative. They should be kept in a warm and smoke-free atmosphere and will then last for many years. If you wish to have a more permanent finish, clean, then dry with a soft cloth and finally spray with a colourless acetate from an aerosol container. Leave to dry for at least an hour before handling and, afterwards, handle as little as possible. Alcohol will remove the coating if desired.

CHAPTER 35

Glossary of Terms Used

We have tried to be consistent in the description of badges given in this work and the following terms have been employed:

Circlet	The circular band, with unbroken edges, containing the title or motto.
Strap	Where the circle carrying the inscription has a buckle.
Garter	Only used when carrying the Garter motto of *Honi soit qui mal y pense*.

All the illustrations of badges have been numbered consecutively. Collectors may find it an advantage when writing to other collectors to use these numbers as a code and thereby avoid long written descriptions. For example: reference 'KK725' would avoid the necessity of describing in detail this particular lance-cap plate of the 21st Lancers.

Some terms commonly used by collectors are:

Crowns

Q.V.C.	The crown used during Queen Victoria's reign, 1837 to 1901. It varies slightly, usually rounded but sometimes square-ended.
K.C.	The crown used on badges struck between 1902 and 1954. Referred to sometimes as 'King's' or 'Tudor' crown and in this work as the 'Imperial' crown.
Q.C-EIIR	The St. Edward's crown of H.M. Queen Elizabeth II used from 1954 to date.
Flat-topped	A crown with a slightly-sloping curved-shape from the cross and orb. As an example see 9th Lancers: 1898 to 1901 (Fig. 763).
Looped	The Indian crown in which loops of pearls are a feature. As an example see 7th Hussars: 1898 to 1901 (Fig. 759).
Scottish	The crown as used on the badge of the Scottish Horse (Fig. 1387).

Description of Badges

Die-struck	Struck with considerable force using a steel die to effect the design. Fully die-struck badges are recognisable by the fact that the design can be seen clearly in reverse on the back of the badge.
H/P	Helmet-plate.
H.P.C.	Helmet-plate centre.
O.S.D.	Badges, invariably of bronze finish, used on officers' service-dress.
P/T	Pre-Territorial. Badges worn prior to 1881 when all Infantry of the Line were known by their regimental numbers.

Prong	Sometimes called a slider. A single tongue on the reverse of the badge. Used to a greater degree after 1914 to serve the same purpose as shanks. Puggaree-badges often had stouter, and longer, prongs.
Semi-solid	When manufactured, only part of the design can be seen on the reverse of the badge, other parts being solid usually to strengthen the design. Mostly found on officers' badges.
Shanks	The copper loops used to fasten the badge to the head-dress and through which is passed the split-wire pin to hold it firmly in position.
Solid	When referred to the frontal design of a badge it means non-'voided,' that is, the outline of the badge only being cut out.
	When referred to manufacture it implies that the reverse of the badge is made from heavy-gauge metal and appears smooth and devoid of features.
Voided	Describes the process whereby the format of the badge is enhanced by the removal of metal to give depth or to emphasise a design.

Metals

Anod	Anodised aluminium. Used in the manufacture of recent badges.
Bi/M.	When two metals are used on a single badge, i.e. white-metal and gilding-metal. Where bronzed-brass is used the abbreviation would be Bze and W/M.
Blk.	Blackened-brass. Usually found on rifle regiments' badges.
Brass	Yellow-brass: used for badge-making chiefly before 1883 although there are a few instances since that date. Not to be confused with gilding-metal.
Bze.	Bronze. Usually copper or gilding-metal finished in a dull service-dress brown. More often found on officers' service-dress badges but occasionally on other-ranks' badges.
Enam.	Enamelling. Either as part of the badge, and mounted thereon, or the badge itself.
Gilt	A plating of gold. (Requires gentle treatment for preservation).
G/M.	Gilding-metal. A brass-metal containing a higher content of copper than the yellow-brass mentioned above.
G/S/Enam.	A badge composed of gilt, silver and enamelling.
H.M. Sil.	Hall-marked silver. The marks give the identity of the Assay Office and the date of manufacture.
Sil.	Silver-plated.
W/M.	White-metal.

CHAPTER 36

The Marching Regiments of Foot and Their Titles in 1914

1st (Royal Scots)	The Royal Scots (Lothian Regiment).
2nd (Queen's Royal)	The Queen's (Royal West Surrey Regiment).
3rd (East Kent) (The Buffs)	The Buffs (East Kent Regiment).
4th (The King's Own)	The King's Own (Royal Lancaster Regiment).
5th (Northumberland Fusiliers)	The Northumberland Fusiliers.
6th (Royal 1st Warwickshire)	The Royal Warwickshire Regiment.
7th (or Royal Fusiliers)	The Royal Fusiliers (City of London Regiment).
8th (The King's)	The King's (Liverpool Regiment).
9th (East Norfolk)	The Norfolk Regiment.
10th (North Lincoln)	The Lincolnshire Regiment.
11th (North Devon)	The Devonshire Regiment.
12th (East Suffolk)	The Suffolk Regiment.
13th (1st Somersetshire)	Prince Albert's (Somerset Light Infantry).
14th (Buckinghamshire)	The Prince of Wales's Own (West Yorkshire Regiment).
15th (York East Riding)	The East Yorkshire Regiment.
16th (Bedfordshire)	The Bedfordshire Regiment.
17th (Leicestershire)	The Leicestershire Regiment.
18th (The Royal Irish)	The Royal Irish Regiment.
19th (1st York, North Riding)	Alexandra, Princess of Wales's Own (Yorkshire Regiment).
20th (East Devonshire)	The Lancashire Fusiliers.
21st (Royal North British Fusiliers)	The Royal Scots Fusiliers.
22nd (Cheshire)	The Cheshire Regiment.
23rd (Royal Welsh Fusiliers)	The Royal Welsh Fusiliers.
24th (2nd Warwickshire)	The South Wales Borderers.
25th (The King's Own Borderers)	The King's Own Scottish Borderers.
26th (Cameronians)	1st Bn. The Cameronians (Scottish Rifles).
27th (Inniskilling)	1st Bn. The Royal Inniskilling Fusiliers.
28th (North Gloucestershire)	1st Bn. The Gloucestershire Regiment.
29th (Worcestershire)	1st Bn. The Worcestershire Regiment.
30th (Cambridgeshire)	1st Bn. The East Lancashire Regiment.

31st (Huntingdonshire)	1st Bn. The East Surrey Regiment.
32nd (Cornwall Light Infantry)	1st Bn. The Duke of Cornwall's Light Infantry.
33rd (1st Yorkshire West Riding)	1st Bn. The Duke of Wellington's (West Riding Regiment).
34th (Cumberland)	1st Bn. The Border Regiment.
35th (Royal Sussex)	1st Bn. The Royal Sussex Regiment.
36th (Herefordshire)	2nd Bn. The Worcestershire Regiment.
37th (North Hampshire)	1st Bn. The Hampshire Regiment.
38th (1st Staffordshire)	1st Bn. The South Staffordshire Regiment.
39th (Dorsetshire)	1st Bn. The Dorsetshire Regiment.
40th (2nd Somersetshire)	1st Bn. The Prince of Wales's Volunteers (South Lancashire Regiment).
41st (Welsh)	1st Bn. The Welsh Regiment.
42nd (Royal Highland)	1st Bn. The Black Watch (Royal Highlanders).
43rd (Monmouthshire Light Infantry)	1st Bn. The Oxfordshire and Buckinghamshire Light Infantry.
44th (East Essex)	1st Bn. The Essex Regiment.
45th (Nottinghamshire)	1st Bn. The Sherwood Foresters (Nottinghamshire and Derbyshire Regiment).
46th (South Devonshire)	2nd Bn. The Duke of Cornwall's Light Infantry.
47th (The Lancashire)	1st Bn. The Loyal North Lancashire Regiment.
48th (Northamptonshire)	1st Bn. The Northamptonshire Regiment.
49th (Hertfordshire)	1st Bn. Princess Charlotte of Wales's (Royal Berkshire Regiment).
50th (or The Queen's Own)	1st Bn. The Queen's Own (Royal West Kent Regiment).
51st (2nd Yorkshire, West Riding Light Infantry)	1st Bn. The King's Own (Yorkshire Light Infantry).
52nd (Oxfordshire Light Infantry)	2nd Bn. The Oxfordshire and Buckinghamshire Light Infantry.
53rd (Shropshire)	1st Bn. The King's (Shropshire Light Infantry).
54th (West Norfolk)	2nd Bn. The Dorsetshire Regiment.
55th (Westmorland)	2nd Bn. The Border Regiment.
56th (West Essex)	2nd Bn. The Essex Regiment.
57th (West Middlesex)	1st Bn. The Duke of Cambridge's Own (Middlesex Regiment).
58th (Rutlandshire)	2nd Bn. The Northamptonshire Regiment.
59th (2nd Nottinghamshire)	2nd Bn. The East Lancashire Regiment.
60th King's Royal Rifle Corps	The King's Royal Rifle Corps.
61st (South Gloucestershire)	2nd Bn. The Gloucestershire Regiment.
62nd (Wiltshire)	1st Bn. The Duke of Edinburgh's (Wiltshire Regiment).
63rd (West Suffolk)	1st Bn. The Manchester Regiment.
64th (2nd Staffordshire)	1st Bn. The Prince of Wales's (North Staffordshire Regiment).
65th (2nd Yorkshire North Riding)	1st Bn. The York and Lancaster Regiment.
66th (Berkshire)	2nd Bn. Princess Charlotte of Wales's (Royal Berkshire Regiment).

67th (South Hampshire)	2nd Bn. The Hampshire Regiment.
68th (Durham Light Infantry)	1st Bn. The Durham Light Infantry.
69th (South Lincolnshire)	2nd Bn. The Welsh Regiment.
70th (The Surrey)	2nd Bn. The East Surrey Regiment.
71st (Highland Light Infantry)	1st Bn. The Highland Light Infantry.
72nd (Duke of Albany's Own Highlanders)	1st Bn. Seaforth Highlanders (Ross-shire Buffs, The Duke of Albany's).
73rd (Perthshire)	2nd Bn. The Black Watch (Royal Highlanders).
74th (Highlanders)	2nd Bn. The Highland Light Infantry.
75th (Stirlingshire)	1st Bn. The Gordon Highlanders.
76th	2nd Bn. The Duke of Wellington's (West Riding Regiment).
77th (East Middlesex)	2nd Bn. The Duke of Cambridge's Own (Middlesex Regiment).
78th (Highland or Ross-shire Buffs)	2nd Bn. Seaforth Highlanders (Ross-shire Buffs, The Duke of Albany's).
79th (Cameron Highlanders)	The Queen's Own Cameron Highlanders.
80th (Staffordshire Volunteers)	2nd Bn. The South Staffordshire Regiment.
81st (Loyal Lincoln Volunteers)	2nd Bn. The Loyal North Lancashire Regiment.
82nd (The Prince of Wales's Volunteers)	2nd Bn. The Prince of Wales's Volunteers (South Lancashire Regiment).
83rd (County of Dublin)	1st Bn. The Royal Irish Rifles.
84th (York and Lancaster)	2nd Bn. The York and Lancaster Regiment.
85th (The King's Light Infantry)	2nd Bn. The King's (Shropshire Light Infantry).
86th (Royal County Down)	2nd Bn. The Royal Irish Rifles.
87th (The Prince of Wales's Own Irish Fusiliers)	1st Bn. Princess Victoria's (Royal Irish Fusiliers).
88th (Connaught Rangers)	1st Bn. The Connaught Rangers.
89th (The Princess Victoria's)	2nd Bn. Princess Victoria's (Royal Irish Fusiliers).
90th (Perthshire Volunteers Light Infantry)	2nd Bn. The Cameronians (Scottish Rifles).
91st (Argyllshire Highlanders)	1st Bn. Princess Louise's (Argyll and Sutherland Highlanders).
92nd (Gordon Highlanders)	2nd Bn. The Gordon Highlanders.
93rd (Sutherland Highlanders)	2nd Bn. Princess Louise's (Argyll and Sutherland Highlanders).
94th	2nd Bn. The Connaught Rangers.
95th (The Derbyshire)	2nd Bn. The Sherwood Foresters (Nottinghamshire and Derbyshire Regiment).
96th	2nd Bn. The Manchester Regiment.
97th (Earl of Ulster's)	2nd Bn. The Queen's Own (Royal West Kent Regiment).
98th (The Prince of Wales's)	2nd Bn. The Prince of Wales's (North Staffordshire Regiment).
99th (Lanarkshire)	2nd Bn. The Duke of Edinburgh's (Wiltshire Regiment).
100th (Prince of Wales's Royal Canadian)	1st Bn. The Prince of Wales's Leinster Regiment (Royal Canadians).

101st (Royal Bengal Fusiliers)	1st Bn. The Royal Munster Fusiliers.
102nd (Royal Madras Fusiliers)	1st Bn. The Royal Dublin Fusiliers.
103rd (Royal Bombay Fusiliers)	2nd Bn. The Royal Dublin Fusiliers.
104th (Bengal Fusiliers)	2nd Bn. The Royal Munster Fusiliers.
105th (Madras Light Infantry)	2nd Bn. The King's Own (Yorkshire Light Infantry).
106th (Bombay Light Infantry)	2nd Bn. The Durham Light Infantry.
107th (Bengal Infantry)	2nd Bn. The Royal Sussex Regiment.
108th (Madras Infantry)	2nd Bn. The Royal Inniskilling Fusiliers.
109th (Bombay Infantry)	2nd Bn. The Prince of Wales's Leinster Regiment (Royal Canadians).
The Rifle Brigade	The Rifle Brigade (The Prince Consort's Own).

Index

Text references in roman type.
Figure references in bold face type.
Abbreviated titles are used in the Index.

Volunteers
General patterns: 224, 228, **824, 825, 826, 829A, 838, 839, 844, 845**
Ayrshire and Galloway Arty. Vols, 1st: 226, **832**
East Riding of Yorks. R.G.A. (Vols) 2nd: 226, **834**
Edinburgh City Arty. Vols, 1st: 224, 228, **827, 840, 841**
Fifeshire Arty. Vols: 226, **836, 837**
Glamorgan Arty. Vols, 1st Bde.: 224, **828**
Hampshire R.G.A. (Vols) 1st: 228, **846**
Kent Arty. Vols: 224, **828A**
Lancashire Vol. Arty.: 226, **829**
Lancashire Vol. Arty. 5th: 226, **833**
Lincolnshire Arty. Vols, 2nd: 226, **835**
Middlesex R.G.A. (Vols) 3rd: 228, **847**
Norfolk Arty. Vols, 1st: 226, **830**
North Riding of Yorks. Arty. Vols, 3rd: 228, **843**
Northumberland Arty. Vols, 1st: 226, **831**
Sussex Arty. Vols, 3rd: 228, **842**

ROYAL ENGINEERS
Regular
General patterns: 229, **848, 849, 850, 851, 852, 853**
Militia
General patterns: 230, **854, 855, 856, 857, 858, 859**
Territorial Force
General patterns: 230, **860**
Tyne Electrical Engineers: 230, **861**
Volunteers
General patterns: 230, 232, 234, **863, 866, 869, 870, 871, 872, 873, 880, 881, 882**
Bedfordshire R.E. Vols, 1st: 234, **879**
Cheshire Engineer Vols, 1st: 234, **875**
Cheshire Engineer Vols, 2nd: 236, **887**
City of Edinburgh Engineer Vols, 1st: 234, **885**
City of London Engineer Vols, 1st: 236, **886**
Gloucestershire Engineer Vols: 234, **878**
Gloucestershire Engineer Vols, 2nd: 234, **877**
Gloucestershire Vol. Engineers, 1st: 234, **876**
Middlesex Engineer Vols, 1st: 234, **868, 883**
R.E. Submarine Miners: 232, **874**
Sheffield Engineer Vols.: 234, **884**
Tower Hamlets Engineer Vols: 232, **864, 865, 867**
Cadets
Manchester Engineer Cadet Corps: 230, **862**

ROYAL CORPS OF SIGNALS: 236, **888**

FOOT GUARDS
Grenadier Guards: 12, 14, 237, **16, 889, 890, 891, 892, 893, 894, 895, 896**
Coldstream Guards: 10, 12, 33, 238, 450, **897, 898, 899, 900, 901, 902, 903, 904**
Scots Guards: 12, 17, 32, 238, 450, **905, 906, 907, 908, 909, 910, 911**
Irish Guards: 240, **912, 913, 914, 915, 916, 917, 918, 919**
Welsh Guards: 240, **920, 921**
Guards Machine Gun Regiment: 242, **922, 923**
Household Brigade Officer Cadet Battalion: 242, **924**
Royal Guards Reserve Regt.: 288

INFANTRY OF THE LINE *pre-1881*
General patterns: 8, 10, 16, **7A, 7B, 8, 9, 21**
1st Foot: 6, 10, 12, 37, 62, 85, 89, 97, 106, 109, 158, 450, **12, 48, 78, 111, 129, 150, 179, 184, 420**
2nd Foot: 6, 12, 17, 22, 37, 62, 97, 158, 450, **25A, 49, 50, 151, 421**
3rd Foot: 6, 8, 12, 18, 39, 62, 85, 97, 158, **6, 7, 79, 112, 113, 422, 423**
4th Foot: 6, 12, 14, 18, 39, 62, 97, 110, 160, **80, 424**
5th Foot: 6, 12, 14, 23, 39, 85, 160, **17, 50A, 114, 425**
6th Foot: 6, 12, 40, 66, 97, 110, 160, **81, 185, 426**
7th Foot: 6, 12, 40, 66, 160, **81A, 427, 428, 429**
8th Foot: 6, 12, 14, 18, 23, 40, 61, 66, 85, 90, 97, 110, 160, 450, **26, 50A, 81B, 115, 129A, 186, 430**
9th Foot: 12, 18, 40, 67, 90, 97, 160, **22, 51, 82, 130, 152, 431**
10th Foot: 40, 67, 97, 110, 160, 450, **51A, 187, 432, 433**
11th Foot: 23, 40, 110, 160, **434, 435, 436**
12th Foot: 23, 40, 67, 97, 110, 162, 450, **35, 52, 53, 83, 84, 85, 153, 188, 437**
13th Foot: 23, 42, 68, 90, 97, 106, 110, 117, 162, 450, 454, **54, 131, 132, 154, 204, 438**
14th Foot: 23, 42, 61, 68, 86, 90, 97, 110, 162, **27, 116, 133, 155, 189, 439, 440**
15th Foot: 23, 42, 61, 162, **28, 36, 55, 441, 442, 443**
16th Foot: 42, 162, **444, 445**
17th Foot: 23, 42, 68, 99, 110, 162, 453, **37, 38, 56, 86, 156, 157, 446, 447, 448, 449**
18th Foot: 6, 86, 99, 162, 450, 454, **116A, 158, 450**

THE VOLUNTEER FORCE pre-1908

SCHOOLS AND MISCELLANEOUS

WOMEN'S SERVICES